Carnegie Commission on Higher Education
Sponsored Research Reports

THE MULTICAMPUS UNIVERSITY:
A STUDY OF ACADEMIC GOVERNANCE
Eugene C. Lee and Frank M. Bowen

INSTITUTIONS IN TRANSITION:
A PROFILE OF CHANGE IN HIGHER
EDUCATION
(INCORPORATING THE 1970 STATISTICAL
REPORT)
Harold L. Hodgkinson

EFFICIENCY IN LIBERAL EDUCATION:
A STUDY OF COMPARATIVE INSTRUCTIONAL
COSTS FOR DIFFERENT WAYS OF ORGANIZ-
ING TEACHING-LEARNING IN A LIBERAL ARTS
COLLEGE
Howard R. Bowen and Gordon K. Douglass

CREDIT FOR COLLEGE:
PUBLIC POLICY FOR STUDENT LOANS
Robert W. Hartman

MODELS AND MAVERICKS:
A PROFILE OF PRIVATE LIBERAL ARTS
COLLEGES
Morris T. Keeton

BETWEEN TWO WORLDS:
A PROFILE OF NEGRO HIGHER EDUCATION
Frank Bowles and Frank A. DeCosta

BREAKING THE ACCESS BARRIERS:
A PROFILE OF TWO-YEAR COLLEGES
Leland L. Medkser and Dale Tillery

ANY PERSON, ANY STUDY:
AN ESSAY ON HIGHER EDUCATION IN THE
UNITED STATES
Eric Ashby

THE NEW DEPRESSION IN HIGHER
EDUCATION:
A STUDY OF FINANCIAL CONDITIONS AT 41
COLLEGES AND UNIVERSITIES
Earl F. Cheit

FINANCING MEDICAL EDUCATION:
AN ANALYSIS OF ALTERNATIVE POLICIES
AND MECHANISMS
Rashi Fein and Gerald I. Weber

HIGHER EDUCATION IN NINE COUNTRIES:
A COMPARATIVE STUDY OF COLLEGES AND
UNIVERSITIES ABROAD
*Barbara B. Burn, Philip G. Altbach, Clark Kerr,
and James A. Perkins*

BRIDGES TO UNDERSTANDING:
INTERNATIONAL PROGRAMS OF AMERICAN
COLLEGES AND UNIVERSITIES
Irwin T. Sanders and Jennifer C. Ward

GRADUATE AND PROFESSIONAL EDUCATION,
1980:
A SURVEY OF INSTITUTIONAL PLANS
Lewis B. Mayhew

THE AMERICAN COLLEGE AND AMERICAN
CULTURE:
SOCIALIZATION AS A FUNCTION OF HIGHER
EDUCATION
Oscar and Mary F. Handlin

RECENT ALUMNI AND HIGHER EDUCATION:
A SURVEY OF COLLEGE GRADUATES
Joe L. Spaeth and Andrew M. Greeley

CHANGE IN EDUCATIONAL POLICY:
SELF-STUDIES IN SELECTED COLLEGES AND
UNIVERSITIES
Dwight R. Ladd

STATE OFFICIALS AND HIGHER EDUCATION:
A SURVEY OF THE OPINIONS AND
EXPECTATIONS OF POLICY MAKERS IN NINE
STATES
Heinz Eulau and Harold Quinley

ACADEMIC DEGREE STRUCTURES:
INNOVATIVE APPROACHES
PRINCIPLES OF REFORM IN DEGREE
STRUCTURES IN THE UNITED STATES
Stephen H. Spurr

COLLEGES OF THE FORGOTTEN AMERICANS:
A PROFILE OF STATE COLLEGES AND
REGIONAL UNIVERSITIES
E. Alden Dunham

FROM BACKWATER TO MAINSTREAM:
A PROFILE OF CATHOLIC HIGHER
EDUCATION
Andrew M. Greeley

THE ECONOMICS OF THE MAJOR PRIVATE
UNIVERSITIES
William G. Bowen
(Out of print, but available from University Microfilms.)

THE FINANCE OF HIGHER EDUCATION
Howard R. Bowen
(Out of print, but available from University Microfilms.)

ALTERNATIVE METHODS OF FEDERAL
FUNDING FOR HIGHER EDUCATION
Ron Wolk

INVENTORY OF CURRENT RESEARCH ON
HIGHER EDUCATION 1968
Dale M. Heckman and Warren Bryan Martin

The following reprints and technical reports are available from the Carnegie Commission on Higher Education, 1947 Center Street, Berkeley, California 94704.

TRENDS AND PROJECTIONS OF PHYSICIANS IN THE UNITED STATES, 1967–2002, by Mark S. Blumberg, published by Carnegie Commission, Berkeley, 1971 ($4.75).

RESOURCE USE IN HIGHER EDUCATION: TRENDS IN OUTPUT AND INPUTS, 1930–1967, by June O'Neill, published by Carnegie Commission, Berkeley, 1971 ($5.75).

ACCELERATED PROGRAM OF MEDICAL EDUCATION, by Mark S. Blumberg, reprinted from JOURNAL OF MEDICAL EDUCATION, vol. 46, no. 8, August 1971.

SCIENTIFIC MANPOWER FOR 1970–1985, by Allan M. Cartter, reprinted from SCIENCE, vol. 172, no. 3979, pp. 132–140, April 9, 1971.

A NEW METHOD OF MEASURING STATES' HIGHER EDUCATION BURDEN, by Neil Timm, reprinted from THE JOURNAL OF HIGHER EDUCATION, vol. 42, no. 1, pp. 27–33, January 1971.

REGENT WATCHING, by Earl F. Cheit, reprinted from AGB REPORTS, vol. 13, no. 6, pp. 4–13, March 1971.

WHAT HAPPENS TO COLLEGE GENERATIONS POLITICALLY?, by Seymour M. Lipset and Everett C. Ladd, Jr., reprinted from THE PUBLIC INTEREST, no. 24, Summer 1971.

AMERICAN SOCIAL SCIENTISTS AND THE GROWTH OF CAMPUS POLITICAL ACTIVISM IN THE 1960s, by Everett C. Ladd, Jr., and Seymour M. Lipset, reprinted from SOCIAL SCIENCES INFORMATION, vol. 10, no. 2, April 1971.

THE POLITICS OF AMERICAN POLITICAL SCIENTISTS, by Everett C. Ladd, Jr., and Seymour M. Lipset, reprinted from PS, vol. 4, no. 2, Spring 1971.

THE DIVIDED PROFESSORIATE, by Seymour M. Lipset and Everett C. Ladd, Jr., reprinted from CHANGE, vol. 3, no. 3, pp. 54–60, May 1971.

JEWISH AND GENTILE ACADEMICS IN THE UNITED STATES: ACHIEVEMENTS, CULTURES AND POLITICS, *by Seymour M. Lipset and Everett C. Ladd, Jr., reprinted from* AMERICAN JEWISH YEAR BOOK, *1971.*

THE UNHOLY ALLIANCE AGAINST THE CAMPUS, *by Kenneth Keniston and Michael Lerner, reprinted from* NEW YORK TIMES MAGAZINE, *November 8, 1970 .*

PRECARIOUS PROFESSORS: NEW PATTERNS OF REPRESENTATION, *by Joseph W. Garbarino, reprinted from* INDUSTRIAL RELATIONS, *vol. 10, no. 1, February 1971.*

. . . AND WHAT PROFESSORS THINK: ABOUT STUDENT PROTEST AND MANNERS, MORALS, POLITICS, AND CHAOS ON THE CAMPUS, *by Seymour Martin Lipset and Everett Carll Ladd, Jr., reprinted from* PSYCHOLOGY TODAY, *November 1970. (Out of print.)**

DEMAND AND SUPPLY IN U.S. HIGHER EDUCATION: A PROGRESS REPORT, *by Roy Radner and Leonard S. Miller, reprinted from* AMERICAN ECONOMIC REVIEW, *May 1970. (Out of print.)**

RESOURCES FOR HIGHER EDUCATION: AN ECONOMIST'S VIEW, *by Theodore W. Schultz, reprinted from* JOURNAL OF POLITICAL ECONOMY, *vol. 76, no. 3, University of Chicago, May/ June 1968. (Out of print.)**

INDUSTRIAL RELATIONS AND UNIVERSITY RELATIONS, *by Clark Kerr, reprinted from* PROCEEDINGS OF THE 21ST ANNUAL WINTER MEETING OF THE INDUSTRIAL RELATIONS RESEARCH ASSOCIATION, *pp. 15–25. (Out of print.)**

NEW CHALLENGES TO THE COLLEGE AND UNIVERSITY, *by Clark Kerr, reprinted from Kermit Gordon (ed.),* AGENDA FOR THE NATION, *The Brookings Institution, Washington, D.C., 1968. (Out of print.)**

PRESIDENTIAL DISCONTENT, *by Clark Kerr, reprinted from David C. Nichols (ed.),* PERSPECTIVES ON CAMPUS TENSIONS: PAPERS PREPARED FOR THE SPECIAL COMMITTEE ON CAMPUS TENSIONS, *American Council on Education, Washington, D.C., September 1970. (Out of print.)**

STUDENT PROTEST—AN INSTITUTIONAL AND NATIONAL PROFILE, *by Harold Hodgkinson, reprinted from* THE RECORD, *vol. 71, no. 4, May 1970. (Out of print.)**

WHAT'S BUGGING THE STUDENTS?, *by Kenneth Keniston, reprinted from* EDUCATIONAL RECORD, *American Council on Education, Washington, D.C., Spring 1970. (Out of print.)**

THE POLITICS OF ACADEMIA, *by Seymour Martin Lipset, reprinted from David C. Nichols (ed.),* PERSPECTIVES ON CAMPUS TENSIONS: PAPERS PREPARED FOR THE SPECIAL COMMITTEE ON CAMPUS TENSIONS, *American Council on Education, Washington, D.C., September 1970. (Out of print.)**

**The Commission's stock of this reprint has been exhausted.*

The Multicampus University

The Multicampus University

A STUDY OF ACADEMIC GOVERNANCE

by *Eugene C. Lee*

Director, Institute of Governmental Studies,
University of California, Berkeley

and *Frank M. Bowen*

Consultant, State of California
Department of Finance

with a commentary by *William Friday*

A Report Prepared for
The Carnegie Commission on Higher Education

MCGRAW-HILL BOOK COMPANY

New York   St. Louis   San Francisco   Düsseldorf
London   Sydney   Toronto   Mexico   Panama
Johannesburg   Kuala Lumpur   Montreal
New Delhi   Rio de Janeiro   Singapore

*The Carnegie Commission on Higher Education,
1947 Center Street, Berkeley, California 94704,
has sponsored preparation of this report as
part of a continuing effort to present significant
information and issues for public discussion.
The views expressed are those of the authors.*

THE MULTICAMPUS UNIVERSITY
A Study of Academic Governance

Library of Congress catalog card number 74-163849

123456789MAMM7987654321
07-010032-2

Contents

Foreword

The multicampus system has become a significant feature of higher education in the United States since World War II. Forty percent of all students now attend schools which are parts of multicampus institutions, and more than one-fifth of all campuses are constituent elements of these new higher education conglomerates (see Table I). Particularly a phenomenon that marks public higher education, it is, however, not unknown in the private sector as well. Whether the multicampus system will become the dominant method of organization in the future remains to been seen but past trends, if continued, would make this seem likely. Already three-fourths of the students in public universities are enrolled within such systems.

Three organizational changes of great importance have affected higher education over the past quarter of a century: (1) the introduction of students into governing mechanisms, (2) the creation of statewide coordinating councils, and (3) the rise of the multicampus system. The first of these developments has been the subject of nationwide attention; the second, of a number of studies; and the third, of almost complete neglect—yet it is at least as important in actual governance as either of the other two.

Two of these developments (coordinating councils and multicampus systems) have been part of the fundamental process of shifting power in recent times from the campus to instrumentalities outside the campus to a greater extent than ever before in American history. While most eyes have been directed to the struggle over power within the campus (students versus faculty versus administration), the really important phenomenon has been that there is constantly less power on campus; the more meaningful but largely hidden battle has been over how much less campus authority there would be.

The freestanding campus with its own board, its one and only president, its identifiable alumni, its faculty and student body, all in a single location and with no coordinating council above it, is now the exception whereas in 1945 it was the rule. A whole series of new complexities, as a consequence, enter into what was already a highly complex system of governance even at its simplest. Two more layers of government have been added into many situations, and these new layers are also highly competitive with each other for authority—sometimes they are locked in mortal combat.

The superstructure of higher education has been gaining great weight in recent years just at the same time that the infrastructure on the campus has been undergoing substantial turmoil; and it has been the quiet revolution from above that has had the greater impact rather than the noisy revolt from below. Between the two developments, the governance of the campus has become a great issue.

Systems are the order of the day. National systems dominate in France, England, Russia, Sweden, and many other countries. The American counterpart has been the coordinating council and the multicampus institution, separately or in conjunction. So that here, as in much of the rest of the world, more is now done centrally and less is done by the campus itself. Several forces are working almost universally in this direction:

- The heightened interest in enrollment opportunities for more youth, skilled manpower for society, and the burden of mounting costs places more of higher education policy within the public domain and centralized control.

- The new dynamics of the growth of enrollments and of the enlargement of functions require more advance planning for new campuses, new admission policies, and new endeavors than did the older status quo of slow growth and change.

- The vastly improved techniques of centralized direction in industry and government are also applicable to higher education, and the new technology aids and abets these techniques.

So systems, in one form or another, proliferate.

The multicampus form is not entirely unique to the United States. The mammoth universities of India, such as Calcutta, are really systems of many largely independent colleges and institutes, running sometimes to more than 100, but, contrary to the United States, the central function of the "university" itself is examining — on the model of the older University of London with its external degrees. In Japan, groups of campuses comprise informal systems with all or nearly all the faculty drawn from the same "flagship" campus — thus a number of colleges recruit only from Tokyo, others only from Kyoto, and so forth; an American equivalent would be the "farm system" for baseball teams. The multicampus system in the United States, however, goes far beyond the examining of students and the farming out of faculty members.

The American multicampus system, as I have seen it and lived within it, and as this study notes, has some great advantages:

- It concentrates certain external relations, particularly with state and federal authorities, in a single office where they can usually be better performed.

- It facilitates long-range and overall planning of the creation of new places for students, of the provision of new services to new areas of the state, of the assignment of new endeavors among campuses, and of the continuing differentiation of functions between and among campuses.

- It makes possible (although by no means certain) the determination of diversity among campuses, as compared with the standardization that results from their competitive imitation of each other in the absence of central policy. Diversity is more likely to flow from central authority than from local autonomy.

- It facilitates greatly the creation of new campuses, and some of the most innovative have come from within multicampus systems, as in California, New York, Illinois, and Wisconsin.

- It encourages better management with the aid of specialists in the central administration and the exchange of experiences among campuses.

But the multicampus system inherently has some major liabilities as well:

- With its extra layer of management, it is almost inevitably more bureaucratic, more slow to move; it is less collegial in management and less personal in approach.

- Faculty senates and student governments have less influence. Both operate best on immediate, local, individual problems. It is the central expert who sees better and often analyzes better the more general and long-run problems. As a consequence, faculty unionization and student confrontation against the distant experts may be encouraged in lieu of more informal participation in decision making.

- The very process of centralized planning results in denying many expectations to many people at the same moment through the plan, as compared with case by case action where "gifts" are made to many over a period of time and denials take the form of individual postponements for later consideration. The case by case approach may be less rigorously thoughtful, but it is more adaptably politic.

- The lay board of the system is farther removed from the local atmosphere of the campus and the current practicalities of relationships. It is, as a consequence, more likely to react ideologically to problems, to respond to the personal whims of influential members and to current headlines, and to be concerned with external considerations. It is harder for even the best of boards to perform as well as it could if it were concerned only with a single campus with which its members are closely identified and intimately knowledgeable.

- There are more points of possible friction over who does what and how, and more places for personality clashes—especially between the campus executive and the system executive.

- The political impact of an untoward event on a single campus can affect the whole system rather than being isolated on the one campus; but, conversely, the whole system may protect the single campus from political retaliation—it is harder to get at and punish the particular campus.

- The multicampus system is more open to control by external authority, particularly by governors, than would be a series of separate campuses. Among other reasons, a governor can be effective on one board in a way he could not be on 10 or 20 or 50 campus boards.

- The roles of both the campus executive and the system executive are made more difficult. They must share authority and symbols of authority. The influence of each is diluted. Both must relate to more potential veto groups in trying to get anything done—the President of the University of California has had to take any matter of basic importance before at least a dozen separate instrumentalities each with the assigned or, at least, the assumed power to confirm or deny the action.

Thus, a multicampus system is strong on the possible positive results—diversity, specialization, cooperation, effective use of resources, advance planning, and so forth—and weak on the negative aspects of process—bureaucratization, disenfranchisement of faculty and student informal influence, complexities in administrative relationships, political interference, and so forth. The possible positive results are more likely to be seen in advance but the negative aspects of process only as history unfolds. The central question about any multicampus system is whether it improves results — particularly the adequacy of advance planning, the enhancement of diversity and quality, the effective use of resources, and the successful representation to external authorities — more than it impedes the processes of governance. Is the value worth the cost? Any answer to this question must be given system by system and not for all systems at once.

It is not necessary to have multicampus systems. They may be highly likely, nevertheless, with block grants from public authorities. If reliance, however, were to be placed on financing higher education through the students, then the market might supplant the central planning. Since that has not happened and may not happen, it is important to see to it that multicampus systems work as well as possible. Based on personal experience and the results of this study, I suggest the following:

- Decentralize to the maximum extent possible. The burden of proof should be on the centralizers. In particular, it is important to decentralize personal relations among people, while it is easier to centralize the handling of things — like purchasing, accounting, etc.

- Work with broad formulas for financing and broad policies to guide actions, rather than with line-item control and specific rules.

- Rely more on postaudit than preaudit.

- Create local boards with final authority in the maximum number of areas like grounds and buildings, faculty appointments and promotions, student disciplinary actions, and so forth. The central board, of necessity, will handle total operating and construction budgets; admissions requirements; policies on size, rate of growth, and functions of each campus; creation of new campuses; and major personnel appointments. I favor the selection of the members of such local boards from persons outside the campus itself but personally interested in it, with some chosen by the faculty, some by students, some by alumni of the campus, some by the local community, and some by the central board — perhaps two or three by each group. The nature of the assignments to the local board calls for identification with the campus and specific knowledge of it.

- Provide adequate administrative assistance of high quality so that delays will be minimized and the civil service of the system can be fully effective.

There will be more formal documents to handle and they will be more important in the life of the institution; they should be carefully prepared and thoughtfully reviewed.

▪ Select chief executives, in part, on their ability and willingness to be cooperative members of the system.

The multicampus system may be viewed, overall, as one facet of bureaucratic centralism in American society—in its government, its industry, its trade unions, its education at all levels. Particularly in higher education, the tidal wave of students, the mounting financial costs, the increased interest of all elements of the public, the new methods of management, and the new technology have encouraged bureaucratic centralism.

The multicampus system, combined with the related rise of coordinating councils, has turned higher education increasingly into a quasi-public utility with its prices (tuition and budget) controlled outside the campus, its services (functions) specified, and its customers (through admissions policies) determined; and with outside agencies also prepared to hear complaints about prices, services, and the acceptance and rejection of customers. The campus is less part of free enterprise and more part of the controlled public domain.

But the future is not likely to be simply a mirror of the past. Bureaucratic centralism is under attack in many places from many sources. The new theme is local control, voluntarism, and spontaneity. From right and from left comes the challenge to simplify and to personalize. It is unlikely that the multicampus systems of higher education in the United States will escape entirely from the impact of these new demands. This is a great unknown.

This present study is the first to examine the phenomenon of the multicampus system in detail. Eugene Lee, the senior author, is particularly suited to the task since he assisted in the massive reorganization and decentralization of one of these systems—the University of California—and thus knows from the inside the intricacies of such an institution. The Carnegie Commission takes pride in publishing this pioneer investigation of nine multicampus systems. This volume describes them and analyzes them in detail. It emphasizes that there are no easy answers and no single solutions that equally fit all systems with their differing histories and regional contexts. It also makes clear that there are still many problems to be solved in these evolving systems in the midst of both substantial confusion and almost infinite complexity. If greater understanding can help with solutions, then this study with its depth of understanding will have made a substantial contribution.

Clark Kerr

Chairman
The Carnegie Commission
on Higher Education

September 1971

TABLE 1
*Number and
enrollment of
multicampus
colleges and
universities,
1968*

Type of institution	Number of institutions	
	All institutions	*Multicampus institutions**
Public		
Universities	90	54
Other four-year colleges	235	20
Two-year colleges	530	29
TOTAL	855	103
Private		
Universities	65	9
Other four-year colleges	1,132	16
Two-year colleges	271	4
TOTAL	1,468	29
Total colleges and universities	2,323	132

* A multicampus institution is defined as one that reported in the U.S. Office of Education *Opening Fall Enrollment, 1968* questionnaire that it had two or more campuses (except that institutions that reported a main campus and one theological seminary branch campus, or one medical school branch campus, or one extension branch campus at a military installation are excluded); or the institution did not report enrollment data for branch campuses but further study revealed it did have at least two campuses (e.g., the Junior College District of St. Louis); or campuses were listed as separate institutions in *Opening Fall Enrollment, 1968* reports but further study revealed they were part of a unitary system (e.g., University of Nevada). The level of a multicampus system is determined by the level of its most senior institution.

SOURCE: Estimates developed by Carnegie Commission staff from U.S. Office of Education data.

	Number of campuses			*Enrollment*	
All institutions	*Multicampus institutions*	*Percent of campuses in multicampus institutions*	*All institutions (in thousands)*	*Multicampus institutions (in thousands)*	*Percent of enrollment in multicampus institutions*
389	344	88.4	2,342	1,808	77.2
332	117	35.2	1,636	680	41.6
590	89	15.1	1,492	374	25.1
1,311	550	42.0	5,470	2,862	52.3
86	28	32.6	704	127	18.0
1,176	45	3.8	1,249	71	5.7
277	10	3.6	149	7	4.6
1,539	83	5.4	2,102	205	9.7
2,850	633	22.2	7,572	3,067	40.5

The Multicampus University

1. *Introduction*

In American higher education, the decade of the 1960s was — among more obvious features — the decade of the *multiversity,* the complex, multipurpose campus. It was also, although less recognized, the decade of *multicampus systems,* the grouping of individual campuses under a common framework of governance. This grouping continues to be the fastest growing pattern of university organization in the United States.

Now, in the 1970s, both the multiversity and the multicampus system are under severe challenge. The criticism hurled at the multiversity stems from diverse and often conflicting viewpoints. Charges of "institutional overload" at the expense of undergraduate education are countered by demands that the university engage in yet more "relevant" social service programs, to suggest but one example.

The forces working upon multicampus systems of higher education are equally contradictory. Many persons claim that large state university systems are — like the metropolis — "ungovernable," that they should be disassembled into smaller groupings or even into the separate campuses of which they are composed. In contrast, still others demand more effective statewide "coordination" of higher education, with pressures upon multicampus systems to assume an even larger role.

The multiversity was full-grown long before it was identified as such eight years ago (Kerr, 1963). Its life and development have been closely scrutinized and extensively chronicled. Multicampus systems have had an even longer history, but almost no historians. Campuses have been organized under various forms of governing structures for decades. Only in recent years, however, have these alternative organizational patterns begun to be examined. This book describes one such alternative — the *multicampus university —* one of the most extensive and significant developments in university organization in the past quarter century. Specifically, this is a study of the governance of the Universities of California, Illinois, Missouri, North Carolina, Texas, and Wisconsin, the State and City Universities of New York, and the California State Colleges.

WHAT IS A MULTICAMPUS UNIVERSITY? The distinction between the multicampus university and the multiversity must be made clear at the outset. "The multiversity is not one community but several," the communities of the graduate students and the undergraduates, of the scientists and of the humanists, of the professional schools and many others. "Its edges are fuzzy—it reaches out to alumni, legislators, farmers, businessmen, who are all related to one or more of these internal communities." If a community should have a soul, "the multiversity has several— some of them quite good, although there is much debate on which souls really deserve salvation" (Kerr, 1963, pp. 18–19). A legion of academic goals, missions, and interests, often inconsistent and sometimes conflicting, are part of the multiversity.

If this more or less peaceful coexistence of a number of *academically* distinct communities is the defining characteristic of a multiversity, similar coexistence of *geographically* distinct communities defines the multicampus university. Not all multiversities are part of multicampus systems: Harvard and California are both multiversities, although the former has but one campus and the latter nine. But virtually all multicampus universities are multiversities, containing both large, complex single campuses and a number of highly differentiated and dissimilar smaller campuses.

Our definition of a multicampus university has as its starting point the work of Martorana and Hollis in their 1960 report, *State Boards Responsible for Higher Education.* Their comprehensive survey showed that all public campuses in the United States were allocated among two types of state boards:

Governing board—A board which is legally charged with the direct control and operation of only a single institutional unit.

Governing-coordinating board—A board having legal responsibility for functioning both as a coordinating board and a governing board for two or more institutional units which offer programs that have common elements.[1]

---

[1] Martorana and Hollis (1960, p. 6) distinguished two other types of boards: (1) "Coordinating boards" have statewide responsibility for "bringing together the overall policies or functions" of higher education, but do "*not* have authority to govern institutions." (2) "Other boards" supervise or accredit, but likewise lack direct governing authority. As noted in the following chapter, coordinating agencies are the subject of extensive current studies. "Other boards" appear to be unique to their states and are not subsequently cited in this study.

In this study, we have replaced their term *governing-coordinating board* with the more inclusive term, *multicampus systems,* because we are interested in the totality of the institution—the faculty, students, and administrators—as well as the board itself. Table 1 indicates the increase in the number of single-campus institutions and multicampus systems in the decade following Martorana and Hollis's survey.

By far the major portion of the growth in the number of institutions of higher education in recent years has taken place in a multi-campus context. Multicampus sytems which were in existence at an earlier date have added new campuses; formerly single-campus universities have branched out to new locations. Our attention is focused on nine of the multicampus systems—a special subset of this growth—which were selected for specific reasons.

Major and minor organizational differences among the 84 multi-campus systems allow almost endless schemes for classification. Some comprise all the senior public campuses in the state (e.g., Iowa and Florida); others have jurisdiction over community colleges as well (e.g., Georgia and Alaska). In Table 2, we distinguish the "single-board" systems from the systems comprising only a portion of higher education in a state. With respect to the latter category, some multicampus systems comprise one major campus with clearly subsidiary branches throughout the state (e.g., the Universities of Kentucky and South Carolina). In some, the chief executives of each campus are directly responsible to the governing board, while in others—including the nine subject to exploration in this study—a prestigious systemwide chief executive stands between the campus administration and the governing board. In any type of multicampus system, local campus boards, whose authority may be formal but limited or purely advisory, may also exist.

TABLE 1 *Number of public governing and governing-coordinating boards for senior colleges and universities, 1958–59 and 1968–69*

	Number of boards		
Type of board	*1958–59*	*1968–69*	*Difference*
Governing (one campus)	101	114	+13
Governing-coordinating (multicampus)	63	84	+21
TOTALS	164	198	+34

SOURCE: 1958–59 data from Martorana & Hollis (1960). Data adjusted: (1) to eliminate seven governing boards comprising only two-year colleges and (2) to eliminate two governing-coordinating boards with only two-year colleges. 1968–69 data from Association of Governing Boards (forthcoming).

	Number of systems		
Type of system	1958–59	1968–69	Difference
Multicampus systems comprising all *higher* education in a state*	14	19	+5
Multicampus systems comprising only a portion or segment *of higher* education in a state	49	65	+16
TOTALS	63	84	+21

*Note that these do not include statewide coordinating agencies which have *only* coordinating functions; coordinating agencies, including the systems noted in the table, increased from 25 in 1959–60 to 47 in 1970. [Preliminary data from Berdahl (forthcoming).]

SOURCE: 1958–59 data from Martorana & Hollis (1960, pp. 15–23). 1968–69 data from Association of Governing Boards (forthcoming).

On the basis of specific and formal structural criteria, we classified the multicampus systems to isolate the nine considered here. Of the multicampus systems identified in 1968 when the study began, only 11 met four specific criteria:

1   Each had responsibility for only a portion of higher education in the state.

2   Each had more than one four-year campus.

3   Each had a systemwide executive with the title of president or chancellor.

4   This executive did *not* have specific responsibility for one of the campuses.

These 11 systems are the *multicampus universities.*[2]

Our criteria are admittedly arbitrary. Other kinds of multicampus systems have much in common with those we have designated multicampus universities, and different criteria for categorizing multicampus systems may prove more fruitful for later analysis. But our goal is to identify multicampus institutions which are as

[2] Both the California and Minnesota State College systems are, by the definition of their states, not universities. We have not differentiated them here, although important differences are obvious. The problems of governance among institutions with several campuses have many similarities, whether or not the campuses are entirely collegiate, university, or both. Although we use "university" in this study to refer to a campus which offers advanced professional or graduate degrees, specifically the Ph.D., the definition is not universal. Many institutions throughout the nation with responsibility only through the master's degree are designated universities. Finally, a desire for brevity has led us to avoid the stylistic awkwardness in continually referring to multicampus universities and colleges.

similar as possible in their governing structures, rather than to compare different kinds of multicampus systems. In this context, the validity of the four standards becomes more obvious at the conclusion of the study than was evident at the start. The formal criteria have a basis in the realities of governance.

1 *The university is responsible for only a portion of higher education.* We assumed that there was an important difference in the environment of governance between those systems which were responsible for all senior public institutions in the state and those having less than universal responsibility. Specifically, we were concerned with the problem of "layering" arising in the states in which a coordinating agency is interposed between the multicampus system and state government. The evidence of this study clarified this common problem, which the multicampus universities share.

2 *The university is responsible for more than one senior (four-year) campus.* We investigated systems in which there was more than one senior campus to examine the interaction of campuses with similar or overlapping programs. We assumed that if there was only one four-year campus with two-year "satellites," the junior partners in the academic hierarchy would be controlled by the four-year campus. A parallel dominance is likely in a system comprising only one comprehensive senior campus and one or more smaller professional campuses. Examination of the governance of systems consisting of *only* two-year campuses is a specialized endeavor and one under separate investigation.[3]

3 *The system executive has the title of* president *or* chancellor. In many of the multicampus systems, excluding the single-board states, the principal systemwide administrative officer is designated *executive director, director, executive secretary,* or some other similar "nonacademic" title. In contrast, the chief executive's title in multicampus universities is *president* or *chancellor,* a designation carrying status and prestige in academic governance. We assume that the difference in title denotes a difference in authority and responsibility. A director or executive secretary, we anticipate,

[3] See, for example, Kintzer, Jensen, & Hansen (undated). A pending study is Palola & Oswald (forthcoming).

is primarily a staff officer of the governing board; campus executives tend to have direct relationships with the board. In contrast, a systemwide president or chancellor is a *chief executive,* to whom the campus executives are responsible. The reality of this latter premise is supported by our study, but we have only limited evidence to validate our impressions of the role of the director or executive secretary. Brief correspondence with a few such officers indicates that they do not regard themselves as "chief executives," but that they may nevertheless exercise significant administrative responsibility in specific areas (e.g., budget preparation). In any event, we have no reason to doubt the substantive reality of the authority inherent in the president-chancellor title.

4 *The system executive is not simultaneously the chief administrative officer for one of the campuses.* In a large number of multicampus systems, typically those containing only one university campus and one or two collegiate campuses, the system executive also doubles as the head of the senior campus. In contrast, the system executive of the multicampus university, as we have defined it, does not directly administer a particular campus. We assumed that the responsibilities of an executive officer and staff responsible for *both* system affairs and campus governance would be quite distinct from the relationships existing in a system in which system and campus responsibilities were not combined. This distinction is also symbolized in the multicampus universities by the designation of the campus executive as chancellor or president (the title *not* employed by the system executive in the particular university), rather than the title of dean or provost, which does not imply as great a degree of executive authority. (Separate medical campuses in the University of Texas system are headed by deans or presidents.)

These four criteria applied to eleven multicampus systems in 1968. We did not visit two of these, Louisiana State University and the Minnesota State Colleges. As noted, the nine systems investigated were the Universities of California, Illinois, Missouri, North Carolina, Texas, and Wisconsin, the State and City Universities of New York, and the California State Colleges. Even among these nine, application of the criteria is sometimes clouded. The State University of New York, for example, with direct responsibility for all public four-year colleges and universities outside New

York City and substantial supervisory authority over some 30 community colleges throughout the state comes very close to being a statewide system, as does City University in the unique environment of New York City. The title of "chancellor *and* vice-president" held by the chief executive of the Madison campus of the University of Wisconsin implies that that executive has some systemwide authority. Nevertheless, a key finding of our investigation is that the nine multicampus universities have much in common. They are, in the words of Theodore Caplow, "the same type" of organizations.[4] They belong to the same organizational set.

Although multicampus systems, generally, have had a long history, the emergence of the multicampus university, as we have defined it, as an important institution of academic governance is fairly recent. In terms of our formal definition of a multicampus university, the period of establishment ranged from 1945, when the University of North Carolina first employed the title of "chancellor" for its campus executives, to 1967, when the chancellor of the University of Texas ceased to be the chief executive of the Austin campus as well. All the nine universities in this study had more than one campus prior to 1960, and some of the universities had comprised several campuses for decades (the Universities of California and North Carolina, for example). A few, too, had witnessed the appointment of separate system and campus executives with the academically prestigious title of chancellor or president in the 1940s and 1950s (the Universities of California, North Carolina, and the State University of New York). But not until the 1960s did the multicampus university as an educational and organizational concept truly come of age. It was in this decade that the organizational framework of the existing systems was firmly established, and the newer systems were created.

The nine multicampus systems loom large in the statistics of higher education. At the end of the 1960s, they enrolled more than 900,000 students, some 17 percent of all students in public four-year colleges and universities and 27 percent of those enrolled for

---

[4] Caplow (1964, pp. 201 ff.) defines an organizational set as two or more organizations of the same type, each of which is continuously visible to every other. They are "of the same type" if there is (1) a prestige order that is recognized by most participants, (2) interchangeability of *some* personnel, and (3) *some* activity common to all members of the set. The nine multicampus universities in the study generally satisfy these criteria in several areas of governance, and we believe the concept of organizational sets would be most useful in further research.

advanced degrees. They awarded almost one-quarter of all the bachelor degrees given in public higher education and nearly 30 percent of the doctoral degrees. Twelve of their campuses were among the 100 colleges and universities awarded the largest amounts of federal support for "academic science," receiving a third of the total amount granted to public institutions among the top 100 institutions.

Finally, we note that between the time we commenced our study in 1968 and its conclusion in 1970, the multicampus university was adopted as the basic form of organization for the major senior institutions of four additional states. The Universities of Indiana, Nebraska, Massachusetts, and Tennessee now fit our criteria, and we have no doubt that other states are studying the multicampus university as a possible answer to the organization of higher education. The conditions under which this choice would be wise is a matter to which we return in the final chapter. But in 1970, there is little doubt that the multicampus university is an organizational alternative of extraordinary significance.

**THE RATION-
ALE FOR THE
MULTICAMPUS
UNIVERSITY**
The origins of the nine multicampus universities are to be found in the history of each institution and the life of the state in which it is located. Each university is the unique product of a series of events, circumstances, and personalities set in a distinct economic, social, and political environment. We touch briefly on the context of each of the nine states and universities in Chapters 1 and 2.

Despite their diversity of origins, however, the fundamental rationale for each multicampus university is the same. Although seldom expressed explicitly—there have been few philosophers of the multicampus university—a common set of assumptions underlies its origins and continued existence. Briefly stated, two propositions may be advanced:

1 In contrast to a single statewide system of higher education, multiple goals, evidenced by alternative approaches in academic plans and programs, can be better achieved if the state divides responsibility among separate institutions.

2 However, in contrast to a system of completely autonomous campuses, these differences can be coordinated and sustained more effectively if campuses are grouped under common governing structures.

In sum, the multicampus university is designed to promote specialization, diversity, and cooperation—a division of labor and alternative approaches to education in a coordinated, intercampus context.

Thus, it is suggested, for example, that the peculiar values of research-oriented university campuses can best be protected if they are grouped together but separated from responsibility for exclusively undergraduate campuses (as in California or Missouri) or that the state colleges can best play their important role as teaching institutions if organized into a separate system (as in California). Or, even if the multicampus system is "comprehensive," encompassing both university and college campuses, there are values to society in having competing institutions, whether in other multicampus systems (as in New York and Wisconsin), or in separate campuses (as in North Carolina), or in both systems and campuses (as in Texas and Illinois). In short, a belief in pluralistic approaches or, indeed, in the values of educational competition undergird the notion of separate institutions. At the same time, this pluralism is controlled, for the institutions are joined together in multicampus universities.

This study constitutes an evaluation of these assumptions. Repeatedly, we assess the effectiveness of the multicampus university in promoting specialization, diversity, and cooperation. We cannot, from the evidence of this study, compare the record of the multicampus university with that of other organizational alternatives, whether single-board states or autonomous campuses. We can, however, hold the multicampus university up to the light of its own standards.

DISTRIBUTION OF AUTHORITY: THE EXPLORATORY INSTRUMENT In any college or university, particularly a public one, authority is distributed along a continuum, stretching, for example, from the action of a chairman to have an item included in a departmental budget to the governor and legislature, where the total university appropriation is finally determined. This is a study of that continuum. Our primary attention is to that section represented by what we variously term the multicampus system or central administration and its relationships to the campuses and to the external environment of the state and federal government. The continuum is not, to say the least, neat and orderly. For example, ties between a campus and the state budget office or the campus and federal and foundation fund administrators may often be more critical than ties to the system executive. We are, of course, interested in the impact of such "external" factors upon internal governance. Similarly, within the multicampus university, relationships between the system executive and his governing board or between the campus executive and his students may reveal more about the ties between the two executives than any explicit analysis of that particular relationship itself.

In both organization theory and ordinary conversation, distribution of authority appears in a number of guises. For example, distribution of authority suggests a *division of labor.* In narrow areas, it may well be just this: The multicampus administration develops a universitywide academic salary plan; the campus administration makes individual salary decisions in accordance with the approved plan. At a broader and much less precise level, the campus executive is responsible for "local" political relationships; the system executive, for representation of the university to the state.

A second aspect of distribution of authority is that of *decentralization* or *delegation* of authority from one level of an administrative hierarchy to another. It is particularly useful to consider changes in the distribution of authority over time *within the same organization* in these terms. We found it less helpful for comparative purposes in this cross-sectional study.

A possible third way of looking at distribution of authority is the real but elusive *distinction between policy and administration.* In theory, and with an eye on a hierarchical organization chart, one might assume that the governing board and the multicampus administration are primarily concerned with policy and the campuses with the implementation of that policy. However, this model generally is a caricature of reality. There is almost no agreement over a wide range of university affairs as to what is "policy." More importantly, regardless of the definition, a great deal of fundamental academic policy is the province of the faculty, individually and collectively. In many areas of university life. the apparent hierarchy is inverted. While we sometimes trace decisions or proposals from their beginning at the departmental level through to the multicampus level and beyond, we do not here explore the most important (for good or ill) of all academic organizations, the department itself.

A possible fourth way of looking at distribution of authority is in terms of *institutional autonomy.* Governing boards, administrators, faculty, and students seek more "autonomy" to solve whatever the current problem may be. Unfortunately, there is no generally accepted definition of autonomy which is coextensive with the diverse organizational forms of higher education. We need not offer such a universal definition here because of our focus on a limited category of multicampus systems. We can use any public campus that has its own governing board as a model of an autonomous campus and compare it with the constraints and opportunities which arise on a campus in a multicampus university. The multicampus administration can be seen as an independent variable which acts upon both the campus and the governing board to change the structure and processes of each. The other campuses in the system are also such a variable. A decision which necessarily would be made by a single campus or its governing board or a combination of these may, in a multicampus system, be influenced or made by the central administration. In a multicampus system there is an added level of administration and the added consideration of other campuses. To the extent that the authority of an individual campus administration or faculty is circumscribed by the multicampus central administration, the autonomy of the campus is limited by the rules or procedures of the system. Or, in contrast, to the extent that the central administration sets policy or makes decisions that would be the responsibility of the governing board in a single-campus institution, the role of the board is altered. We find this concept of *conditional autonomy* useful. Its originator, James Thompson (1967, pp. 58 ff.) defines and employs it with precision and clarity to which we do not pretend. Its use in this context is suggestive only.

To recapitulate, we are examining the distribution of authority within and surrounding a defined educational organization. Our primary concern is the authority of the systemwide administration of the multicampus university and the impact of this authority on other elements of university governance. All the many facets of distribution of authority are useful to some extent and for some purposes. Whether in terms of division of labor, decentralization, delegation of authority, policy and administration, or conditional autonomy, we are seeking the location of specific decisions in specific areas of academic administration.

ORIGINS AND METHODOLOGY In a very real sense, this study had its origins in 1948, when the senior author (then a graduate student) was employed by the Public Administration Service to participate in an administrative survey of the University of California. This consultant's report, although never published, was one of the early statements of the special governance problems of a multicampus university. Subsequently, with the inauguration of Clark Kerr as president of the university in 1960, the senior author was asked to coordinate the reorganization of the administration for the purpose of separating the central offices from direct responsibilities for the campuses. Finally, from 1965 to 1967, the senior author again assumed responsibility for a reappraisal of university organization, with an emphasis upon an expansion and clarification of the authority of campus executives.

Each of these three events in the life of the University of California drove home the lack of available information about the organizational pattern of other multicampus systems. Specifically, a search of the literature as late as 1968 revealed almost no information about the internal governance of multicampus universities, despite their unquestioned and increasing importance on the educational scene. This gap in knowledge and understanding, the interest of administrators, faculty, board members, and government officials in several states, and the encouragement and support of the Carnegie Commission on Higher Education all led to the decision that the inquiry should be made. The steps in the investigation were as follows.

In the fall of 1967, we developed the rough, structural classification of multicampus universities to determine the specific systems to study.

In the spring of 1968, we asked the chief executives of nine of the multicampus universities which satisfied the initial criteria for their assistance in the study. We requested both documentation relating to their organizations and their opinions concerning which major educational and organizational issues were raised by the particular multicampus structure. In addition, we were fortunate to be able to sit with and serve as staff to five of the system executives who met in the summer of 1968 for the express purpose of discussing multicampus organizational problems.

In the summer of 1968, we developed an outline of factual matters relevant to the governance of a multicampus university. This outline was subjected to review and criticism by a number of interested administrators, whose comments and suggestions were taken into account as we planned interviews. We emphasize that it was never our intent to answer all the questions or issues implied by the outline. In this exploratory study, we were ". . . looking for provocative ideas and useful insights, not for the statistics of the profession."[5]

In the early fall of 1968, we arranged visits to each of the nine systems, sending a copy of the outline to the chief executive and to a campus executive. To the extent that preliminary information permitted, we indicated by name or position the persons we wished to interview, requested that a schedule be arranged, and suggested that these persons be furnished with the appropriate section of the outline. The particular campus within each multicampus system which we selected for the study was generally a "second" campus rather than the "flagship" campus—for example, we interviewed officials and faculty of the University of Texas at Arlington, not at Austin; the University of Illinois at the Chicago Circle campus, not at Urbana. Nevertheless, in the course of visits to system offices, we were able to interview virtually all the "main" campus executives.

The visits during the fall of 1968 and the early spring of 1969 usually consisted of three days at the central administrative offices of the multicampus university and another two days at the campus. Together or separately, we spoke to about 150 administrators at the system level and over 100 at campuses in each of the systems, a total of over 250 persons across the country active in the governance of multicampus universities. Aside from administrators, our only regularly scheduled interviews were with faculty members active in systemwide faculty organizations, if any, or in campus faculty organizations. Without exception, the prearranged schedules were extended to reach other faculty or administrators, who gave us useful information. In the course of the visits, we talked to few students, and even fewer state officials. With one exception, we did not meet governing board members. We did not meet with statewide coordinating agency members or staff.

The interviews were largely unstructured. An open-ended interview schedule was continually revised and expanded to meet local conditions. Each interview lasted about an hour and a half, and

---

[5] "The aim of the experience survey is to obtain insight into the relationships between variables rather than to get an accurate picture of current practices or a simple consensus as to best practices. One is looking for provocative ideas and useful insights, not for the statistics of the profession. Thus the respondents must be chosen because of the likelihood that they will offer the contributions sought. In other words, a selected sample of people working in the area is called for" (Selltiz, Jahoda, Deutsch, & Cook, 1967, p. 55).

generally involved only one respondent. These interviews were almost always enriched, however, by our being able to attend various meetings such as those of a governing board, a portion of a state budget hearing, meetings of faculty governing groups, and several administrative "councils" consisting of top-level system staff or campus executives meeting with the system executive. During the interviews we requested and obtained such documents as minutes of committees, correspondence, memoranda. We asked to be placed on a number of mailing lists to receive board agenda, administrative memoranda, and the like.

After completion of the field work in the spring of 1969, we analyzed the transcribed interview notes and reviewed each section of the outline and the pertinent interviews and documentary material for major gaps in information to be filled by correspondence or telephone. This process of continual checking and rechecking continued as we prepared draft chapters, which were sent to key persons in each of the nine systems for criticism and verification. Extensive and valuable written commentary on these initial drafts added significantly to the field investigation.

Our goal throughout the study was not to produce a detailed and accurate survey of each phase of administration in each university but, rather, to see the overall picture, the broad dimensions of multicampus organization. We are highly aware of our ignorance of many details of administration, but we are confident that we have grasped the essential elements of governance. For example, if our data indicated, as they did in one instance, a disagreement between system and campus offices on whether a campus executive's authority to appoint faculty was limited to a ceiling of $10,000 or $12,000, we were content with the uncertainty—itself revealing something about the administrative process. In another university, to suggest a second example, a heated debate at a campus faculty meeting on whether to invite the system executive to address the group ended without decision. We knew little of the participants, and never learned how, if at all, their specific problem was solved. But we did learn much from the meeting of the dynamics of relationships between faculty and universitywide administration.

Organizational structures and processes formally and by tradition allocate specific decisions to particular parties within the academic enterprise. But such formal and traditional allocations interact with personal aspirations and interests and also with social and political factors. The perceptions and attitudes of knowledgeable people concerning the distribution of authority told us how formal and informal authority interacted and was distributed in each of the multicampus systems. These perceptions, opinions, examples, and attitudes were grist for the mill of this study. They enabled us to form overall impressions useful for comparative purposes across all nine multicampus universities.

Limited time and resources restrained our almost unlimited curiosity. On the other hand, this unlimited curiosity and a very real concern with goals, directions, and values initially led to the study. Both curiosity and concern sustained us during some dark days when the paucity of quantitative data and the overwhelming mass of subjective evidence seemed to present an insuperable obstacle to rational analysis. The approach to this exploratory study may be no more unorthodox than similar ventures, but it will not satisfy those interested in ". . . only those facets of reality susceptible to uncovering by established methodological precepts" (Hacker, 1970). During one visit, a leading organizational theorist who had recently turned his hand to academic administration remarked with candor on our methodology that he "didn't know that anyone did this sort of research anymore." We have done "this sort of research" because we knew of no better way to investigate the hitherto unexplored world of the multicampus university.

LIMITATIONS, DISCLAIMERS, AND QUALIFICATIONS We like to think of the present study as bold, open-ended, and unstructured; others, we admit, have been less than hesitant to call it overambitious and overgeneralized. Fortunately, choice between these extremes is not required for recognition of several limitations and qualifications, some of which have been mentioned earlier.

Limited comparisons among the nine multicampus systems
We emphasize the difficulty of comparing activities among *public* organizations located in different states. We offer impressions that a university in one state may have greater authority over a particular area of academic administration than does a university in another. The evidence supporting such comparison is sometimes conflicting and almost always qualified by the impact of state law and politics. The text will, we trust, always make these limitations explicit.

Limited comparisons — the single campus and the single board
A more serious limitation arises from the fact that we have studied only a subset of the several multicampus systems, a point noted above. If one considers the organization of higher education on a

continuum with a single campus under an individual executive and governing board at one extreme and all campuses in the state under a single system executive and governing board at the other, it is apparent that we investigated neither extreme.

Exclusion of these extremes can be rationalized in terms other than the usual plea of time and resources. The administration of an individual campus has been the subject of many investigations since James A. Perkins (1960) pointed out that administrative theorists were interested in all forms of organization except the academic organizations which housed them. Corson, Millett, Barzun, and others have generalized about the administration of individual campuses.[6] Single-board states, in which there is one governing board for all higher education, have also received substantial attention from Glenny, Pliner, Berdahl, and others.[7] This ground has been plowed deeply and well, and here again we will refer to this existing literature if comparisons are ventured.

Nevertheless, it remains true that an adequate comparison of these alternative organizational forms—their strengths and weaknesses, their underlying assumptions, and the external conditions under which each can work effectively—has yet to be made. This study provides evidence to evaluate the effectiveness of one alternative; it is not a comparison of alternatives.

Limited comparisons—two borderline cases
We have previously indicated that two other types of multicampus systems, closely related to the nine multicampus universities, are not included in the study. These two related organizational structures did not quite fit the criteria for inclusion in this study, and we found very little information about them.

The first of these types consists of universities in which the chief executive of the system is also the executive of the "main" campus. Several of the nine multicampus systems in the present study grew from this organizational form, and we found many opinions concerning the transition. For smaller systems, such a structure may be a reasonable alternative to the category under investigation here. In any event, we do not consider this type as merely a transitional form. Although we discuss those transitional problems which came

[6] Barzun, 1968; Corson, 1960; Millett, 1962; Brown, 1969.
[7] Berdahl, 1971; Glenny, 1959; Palola, Lehmann, & Blischke, 1970; Pliner, 1966.

to our attention, we disclaim any intent to weigh the merits of this particular category of multicampus system against those of the nine in the study.

The second borderline organizational category is a group of campuses under a single board where a systemwide administrative officer lacks an "academic administrative" title of president or chancellor and where campus executives have more direct ties to the governing board. This grouping of campuses under a single board served by an executive secretary or director may be an option open to larger multicampus systems, but here we lack even the data on transitions available for the other category of borderline organization. What we know about these types of multicampus systems is very limited indeed.

Limited time

As noted earlier, we spent only a week at each of the nine multicampus universities in the study. Although we always felt the need for additional time, we do not believe that the time actually available and used was too short. It was more important to see more multicampus universities within the period available than it was to spend more time at a fewer number of systems. Some pervasive variables — for example, pressure for enrollment of "disadvantaged" students, cutbacks in research funding, student unrest, and the growing politicization of the university — which were at play upon all nine systems were kept constant in this fashion.

Only two investigators

Limitations of time were compounded by the limitations of using only two investigators. But here, too, there were offsetting advantages which we feel justify the research strategy. Just as it was important to view the nine universities in one temporal framework, so was it desirable for the two of us to observe, evaluate, and synthesize the evidence directly, without the intervention of other investigators or the complication of a "team" effort. For every loss in detail, we feel there was a gain in personal understanding arising out of our attempt to view the entire picture first hand. Interrelationships among seemingly discrete functions which became obvious to us, we suspect might have eluded a larger, more formal investigation. In any event, we are personally gratified that we adopted this approach, despite its obvious shortcomings.

Varying stages of development of the multicampus systems
Comparisons among the nine multicampus systems are complicated
in two respects because of the differing ages of the systems. A
change of lines and titles on an organization chart at the end of
one academic year does not result in a substantially different kind
of organization at the beginning of the next. Indeed, the full effect
of a new organizational structure may only be apparent after an
entirely new generation of faculty and administrators is in office,
and there is evidence that this is the case.

Equally difficult to deal with is the establishment of the multicampus systems at different times in history. The University of
North Carolina, for example, was established for the explicit purpose of saving the state money during the Depression of the 1930s.
Most have come into being during recent periods of affluence. Some
were established when a state's rural population was larger and a
more dominant political factor than in recent times; others are a direct organizational response of the university to the "urban crisis."

Although we will explicitly point out these two "chronological"
problems, we are under no illusion that we have discerned all
shades of the influence which age may cast on the practices we
were investigating.

The flagship campuses
Six of the nine multicampus systems visited had a main, or *flagship,* campus. The impact of these upon the multicampus universities will be discussed in the chapters which follow.

Using the term, however, as descriptive of a campus with a
national reputation for excellence suggests another important
limitation: We were studying multicampus systems and not campuses. Some of the flagship campuses—Madison, Chapel Hill,
and others—are names to conjure with in higher education. It is
not improbable that Madison and Chapel Hill have more in common with each other *as campuses* than do the Universities of Wisconsin and North Carolina *as multicampus systems.* The influence
of such prestigious campuses on a multicampus system is considered at length, but we cannot assess the influence which these
campuses have on each other or on higher education generally.

Anonymous comparisons
Quite deliberately, we do not usually identify particular structures,
processes, quotations, or examples with a named multicampus
system or campus. Our desire is to direct our analysis and the

reader's attention to the multicampus university as a unique institution, not to the specifics of each individual system. Furthermore, we feel there was a net gain in the quality of the evidence we received by our assurances of a certain degree of confidentiality. Nevertheless, it is possible that the anonymous examples of problems, difficulties, and friction may cause more discomfort than if the source of each were identified. Very few of the more serious administrative difficulties were unique, and we suspect that an example drawn from one university may be seized by two or three others as clearly based on their local situation. For example, although state law, politics, and history limit generalizations about the devious course which budget requests must follow in the different multicampus systems, administrative and faculty attitudes and opinions on the local brand of deviousness were remarkably similar—to no one's surprise.

**ORGANI-
ZATION OF
THE STUDY**
The study is divided into three parts. Part 1, Chapters 2 and 3, considers the *environment* of multicampus university governance. While the line between internal and external factors in academic governance is one that can rarely be drawn with certainty, Chapter 2 emphasizes the latter, primarily the impact of state government and the overall statewide organization of higher education. Chapter 3 deals with internal factors, providing a broad look at the organization and history of the nine multicampus systems themselves.

Part 2, Chapters 4 through 7, is concerned with multicampus governing *structures.* Separate chapters consider governing boards, the central administration, and systemwide faculty and student organizations. These chapters cannot avoid some discussion of problems and practices which multicampus universities share with those which have but one campus. However, our concern and emphasis are on the peculiar structures to which the governance of several campuses has given rise. We must caution here, as we do elsewhere, that the internal governance of the campuses is *not* considered. For example, the relationship between a systemwide faculty organization and faculty authority at the campuses is critical to our study. But we delve no deeper into *campus* faculty organization, or lack of it, than is essential to uncover this relationship.

Part 3, Chapters 8 through 13, discusses the *processes* which make up academic governance in the multicampus setting. These six chapters concern academic plans, budget administration, admissions, faculty and administrative personnel, public and governmental relations, and business affairs.

In each of these chapters, attention is concentrated on the particular role of the multicampus administration in the process of university governance: What difference does it make to the campus, to the governing board, to state officials that these processes are conducted in the context of a multicampus university? What is the contribution of this added administrative level which is the special characteristic of such a university system?

Part 4, Chapters 14 and 15, presents our conclusions. Chapter 14 summarizes and assesses the evidence of the study, with particular emphasis upon three "dimensions" of the multicampus university—its origins, its organization, and its size. The chapter concludes with an evaluation of the strengths and shortcomings of this form of university as it appeared to us in 1968–69.

Finally, in Chapter 15 we pose some of the critical issues facing higher education in the 1970s and describe the conditions under which we feel the multicampus university can contribute to their resolution. The pages to follow annotate the rich potential for effective governance in the concept of a multicampus university. The achievement of this potential will require more dedicated thought, leadership, and support than is now in evidence. This study is designed to stimulate and inform such dedication.

Part One

The Environment of Governance

2. Higher Education in the States

What forces shape the multicampus university? Faculty entrepreneurs? Angry student militants and the public's response to them? The intricacies of federal support? Each reply and others as well would find an advocate, and most observers recognize a multiplicity of factors. The most pervasive influence is at the same time more obvious and more subtle. More obvious because each multicampus university is a *state* university. It is more subtle because in every state the historical, economic, and political influences—more often implicit than explicit—are currents that run deep and resist direct investigation. Crucial influences in any one state, moreover, may be unique to it.

Assuredly, the internal affairs of individual campuses, particularly large, major campuses, are profoundly influenced by national trends and marketplaces. Nevertheless, the state and region loom large in the relationships which each campus in a multicampus system has with its central offices, with its sibling campuses, and with state executive, legislative, and coordinating agencies. The nine systems in this study are very much the product of the seven states in which they are located. The economy, politics, and traditions of these states have had and will have far more to do with the present and future status of these systems and even their most prestigious campuses than the particular governing structures and processes with which this study is concerned.

THE SOCIAL AND ECONOMIC CONTEXT The nine multicampus universities are located in seven states: New York and North Carolina on the East Coast, California on the West; California and Texas bordering Mexico, and New York and Wisconsin bordering Canada; Illinois, Missouri, and Wisconsin in the Midwest, and Texas and North Carolina in the South. There is no typical state, and these seven are as varied a selection as any.

Population Factors In population, the states range from the two largest in the nation, California and New York, with 20 and 18 million persons respectively, to Missouri and Wisconsin with less than 5 million. In area, the variation is even greater, from the state of Texas to the city of New York, although the small area of the latter is more than balanced by its population density. It is not surprising to find multicampus universities in the larger states where both the need and the demand for several campuses have been most apparent. That such organizational form is not limited to large states, however, is equally clear. In addition to the smaller states in the study, Tennessee, for example, has adopted this pattern recently, and it has even been considered for Nevada.

Higher education is less often influenced by absolute population than by the rate at which such population has been achieved (Table 3). The obvious impact of this growth and shift of population need not be belabored. The trend to urbanization, particularly, is considered in the following chapter where city campuses are discussed. The increasing mobility of students undoubtedly softens the impact of population pressure for particular states, but it by no means eliminates it. There has been an outward migration of students from states such as New York, which have been slow in the establishment of public campuses; other states—California, Wiscon-

TABLE 3
Population shifts in seven states, 1950–1970

State	Total population (in thousands)			Percent increase	Percent urban ‡	
	1950*	1960*	1970†	1950–70	1950	1960
California	10,586	15,717	19,697	86	80.7	86.4
Illinois	8,712	10,081	10,974	26	77.6	80.7
Missouri	3,995	4,320	4,636	16	61.5	66.6
New York	14,830	16,782	17,980	21	85.5	85.4
North Carolina	4,062	4,556	4,962	22	33.7	39.5
Texas	7,711	9,580	10,989	42	62.7	75.0
Wisconsin	3,435	3,952	4,367	27	57.9	63.8

*U.S. Department of Commerce (1969, table 13, p. 14).
†Preliminary returns from the Bureau of the Census as reported in *Congressional Quarterly Weekly Report* (1970, p. 2195).
‡U.S. Department of Commerce (1956, 1967).

ɜin, and North Carolina—have attracted large numbers of out-of-state students (U.S. Office of Education, 1968, p. 71).

Economic Factors Administrators of the multicampus universities often contrast the willingness and the ability of the state to give financial support. As Table 4 indicates, the seven states are spread from one extreme of per capita income to the other, from second in the nation to forty-third. They cluster somewhat above the national median in per capita support of higher education, but somewhat below it in support per $100 of personal income. The figures in Table 4 do not appear to distinguish these seven states from any others that might have been randomly selected. Among these particular seven, however, New York, first in per capita income, is seventh in support per $100 of personal income, doubtlessly reflecting its historical reliance on private institutions. On the other hand, North Carolina is seventh in per capita income and second in the extent of support per $100 of personal income. New York "exports" more students than any of the other seven states, and North Carolina "imports" more.

Social Factors Census and economic data of particular states are easier to compare than are subjective impressions of the social milieu of higher education in them. According to Logan Wilson (1963, p. 106), regional, social, and economic differences may explain the extent of political "interference" more than the form of state government, and his impression seems confirmed by Hartnett (1969, pp. 22–23) with respect to the attitudes of governing boards toward academic freedom. The seven states in the study left us with seven highly subjective and untested impressions of public attitudes toward the multicampus universities, ranging from substantial support to general neglect and occasional hostility. It is not easy to separate public attitudes from those of political leaders; moreover, public disenchantment with student disorder and violence casts a pall over any such attempt. System executives, however, are well aware of the need for public support, and the awareness is deeper than a veneer of good public relations. One executive, expressing qualified optimism about the future, was pleased that "the people in this state *care* about higher education."

Broad and continuing social factors have long been at work to shape the multicampus universities in the seven states. The "Wis-

TABLE 4
State support
for public higher
education in
seven states,
1967–69

Per capita income, 1968*			Per capita support, 1969–1970†	
Rank in study	*Amount*	*National rank*	*Rank in study*	*Amount*
New York	$4,133	2	California	$39.32
California	4,012	4	Wisconsin	39.21
Illinois	3,994	5	Illinois	36.87
Wisconsin	3,407	18	North Carolina	34.65
Missouri	3,220	26	New York	34.20
Texas	3,016	31	Texas	30.94
North Carolina	2,606	43	Missouri	27.65

*U.S. Department of Commerce (1969, table 469, p. 320).

†American Association for Higher Education (1969).

‡Office of the Vice-president for Planning and Analysis (1969, table 8b), listing sources as U.S. Department of Commerce: "Personal income derived from 'Survey of Current Business,'" Office of Business Economics, Washington, D.C., 49(8):14 (August 1969). Operating expenditures for higher education derived from *The Chronicle of Higher Education,* Editorial Projects for Education, Baltimore, 4(5): 1 (October 27, 1969).

NOTE: 1968–69 state personal income figures not yet available for certain states.

consin Idea," the strength of public higher education in North Carolina, and its past weakness in New York are well known.[1] But these factors do change: The social factors influencing higher education in 1970 are not those of 1950, and no state is immune to these shifts. Change is continuous, perception of it differential, and analysis across time difficult. Proposals for less selective admissions policies or higher tuition may appear as sudden or extreme concessions to the political left or right. But a sometimes expedient response should not disguise the possibility of a firm foundation in changed public attitudes.

[1] Salisbury (1965, p. 364) remarked on state traditions: ". . . the traditional posture in the state toward education—the value placed on good schools—provides a context within which legislators operate and that context has much to do with the level of appropriations. California, Kansas, and Michigan are simply more generous toward public higher education than Missouri or Connecticut, and variations in the quality of their football teams will not explain the difference."

Support for public higher education			
		Per $100 of personal income, 1967–1968‡	
National rank	*Rank in study*	*Amount*	*National rank*
9	Wisconsin	$.96	14
10	North Carolina	.82	20
15	Texas	.74	27
20	California	.73	30
21	Illinois	.71	32
27	Missouri	.64	38
33	New York	.60	39

THE POLITICAL CONTEXT The titles and general responsibilities of political and educational officers and agencies in the seven states present a surface appearance of uniformity. Each has a governor, a legislature, coordinating agency, and other public and private campuses in addition to their multicampus universities. Any appearance of uniformity collapses, however, on the most casual investigation. In each state, the interplay of power and prestige, formal and informal, has complex and unique characteristics. Selecting a site for a new campus or meshing campus priorities for new buildings can assume peculiarities among the political and educational participants normally associated with the mating dances of rare birds; administrators involved are sometimes as much at a loss to explain the utility of the rituals as would be a great crested grebe.

Generalizations about political behavior across seven states are necessarily limited, particularly from the specialized vantage point of this study. It is far easier to point out substantial differences than to uncover real similarities. Each legislature and each executive branch has its own traditional patterns of doing business, patterns which do not change when issues involve higher education.[2]

Common Areas of Policy Despite sometimes striking differences in political practices, procedures, and current issues, the key policy position of higher education in all states is a common factor.[3] At least six "educational issues always seem to require resolution in an explicitly "political" context.

1 *The budget.* The budget, both capital and operating, by size alone commands the attention of the governor, the legislators, and their administrative aides.

---

[2] We do not see constitutional status as a significant *current* issue in governance, and it is not included in this discussion. The nine multicampus universities fall into four categories: (1) The University of Texas and the California State Colleges appear in the statutes as state agencies. (2) The Universities of Illinois, North Carolina, and Wisconsin and the State and City Universities of New York have varying degrees of independence as "statutory corporations." (3) The University of California is a "constitutional corporation." (4) The University of Missouri also has some constitutional prerogatives, but to a more limited extent.

The constitutions of California and, to a lesser extent, Missouri, have undoubtedly been barriers to intervention, arbitrary or otherwise, in these states. However, these barriers are being lowered by increasing state interest in fiscal accountability and by statewide coordinating agencies. Like the benefits of municipal home rule, those of constitutional status still exist, but more as an inhibition on casual legislative interference than as an absolute guarantee against substantial state intervention.

We saw few operational or educational distinctions among the universities arising out of their legal status. And one system executive of a university with "only" statutory status indicated that he preferred it this way; the lack of constitutional protection forced his university into "bringing the legislature along so that it would have pride in their university."

[3] Eulau and Quinley (1970) provide an informed insight into this matter: "On the whole . . . higher education has low political salience for state legislators because articulated demands from a broad section of the population are missing. . . . The legislator as an individual and the legislature as a whole can more readily play the role of 'trustee' in matters of higher education than would otherwise be possible. Lack of interest on the part of ordinary citizens, alumni, and special groups gives the legislature much freedom of action."

Eulau and Quinley talked to legislators, and we did not. The administrators and faculty with whom we did talk, however, were well aware of the legislature's role in university governance. It is not clear they would agree that higher education has "low political salience."

2 *Increased demands.* All states are responding to a felt demand for higher education as not merely a desirable, but a necessary, public service for all qualified applicants. Responses vary, as does the meaning of "qualified."

3 *Student activism.* Student activism, whether or not a symptom of a newer and deeper generation gap, nevertheless focuses attention on the university campuses as symbols of emphasis on moral values. Instant self-righteousness is unlikely to cure the world's ills; assuredly, however, it reminds governors, legislators, and academic administrators that students would like to see cures attempted.

4 *Public service or social action.* In each of the seven states, the college and university campuses have an impact on the state and local communities in addition to that of educating their youth. There is growing recognition that the campuses are and always have been "agents for social action," whether that term means municipal reform or aid to the state's agricultural interests, to select only two examples. Political issues and questions predominate over academic ones in this area. How does the university act as such an agent? Who determines the meaning of "social action"?

5 *The university as an economic force.* Each multicampus university is a major statewide employer, builder, purchaser, and investor. Its employees, architects, contractors, suppliers, and bankers form a clientele with their own political thrust.

6 *Institutional location.* In most of the seven states, the major campus of the multicampus university symbolizes a public commitment to intellect and culture: Chapel Hill is a "historical monument"; Austin is "sacred ground." This symbolism benefits other campuses in the multicampus university, but it is a mixed blessing for the system as a whole. Being on a pedestal is quite conspicuous, and staying there sometimes requires stepping on the fingers of others who would like to share the position. It is difficult to translate a symbolic position into larger appropriations without a suitably discriminatory formula, but fighting off those campuses against which the formula discriminates can tarnish the image of disinterested intellect.

Closely related to the symbolic stature of the major campus is its location, or that of the multicampus central offices, or both, at the state capital. The political implications in having the "local community" of a campus consist of the state's governmental establishment are obvious. The citizen whose peace is disturbed by either youthful exuberance or revolutionary fervor may be the director of the state budget office. Central office location as opposed to that of a campus produces other arguments. Proponents of location at the state capital argue that it increases ease of communication and facilitates coordination.[4] Opponents are concerned that the central administration may become "politicized" and lose the character of an "intellectual establishment." Evidence is fragmentary and inconclusive. In this era of leased lines and jet travel, the interaction of a multicampus university with the state government seems far more dependent on primary political considerations—i.e., campus unrest, the strength of farm interests, and personal relationships between university administrators, the governor, and key legislators—than on location.

Selection of a site for a new campus often proved to be an excellent lens through which to view higher education and state politics. Anyone who believes that locating a campus is a purely "educational" or "academic" decision has never observed the process. On the national scene, Greenberg (1967, pp. 246–268) found the selection of Weston, Illinois, as the site of the 200 BEV accelerator to represent a "new politics of science," new because of the explicitly political context. His discussion of the new *federal* politics of science would be quite familiar to veterans of the older *state* politics of campus site selection.

The Governor   Moos and Rourke (1959, p. 234) introduced their discussion of the relationships between campuses and state governors with the following paragraph:

> The state governor today is the most prominent single official in a college's relation to state government. Not only does the governor lead the way in shaping the general fiscal policies that influence higher education, but also his power to appoint college governing boards, his role in many states as an *ex-officio* board member, and the resources of his personal staff all combine to place him in a commanding position to affect the activities of state colleges and universities.

Although details in particular states have changed, their generalizations are as applicable to the multicampus universities as to individual campuses.

[4] Both the state capital and the flagship campus are mentioned in what appears to be the single instance in which factors relating to location are made specific: "The Central Administration shall be based at the University of Texas at Austin, to benefit from the proximity of State Agencies and to take advantage of economies made possible by shared use of personnel and facilities of The University of Texas at Austin . . ." (Texas Board of Regents, January 23, 1960, with amendments to May 31, 1968).

The power of the governor vis-à-vis the state legislature varies from state to state, and over time. In California, the budget is basically his instrument, and a line-item veto gives him considerable power to enforce his will. In North Carolina, the legislature plays a much stronger role. In all states, the governor's personal strengths, inclinations, and policies are of equal if not greater importance to the multicampus university than his formal powers. The establishment of the State University of New York by one governor and its rapid development under another are closely related to their personal and political strength. While no governor is inimical to the broad goals of higher education, there are obvious differences in specific ends and means.

Although the strength of the State University of New York has been built on that of the governor's office, it seems equally true that the strength of other multicampus universities might be attributed to gubernatorial political weakness. In brief, nothing in our study indicates that the relative political power of the governor, as such, is related to the political health of the multicampus university.

In all states, albeit to varying degrees, governors are both personally interested and personally active in budgets for higher education, qualifying Moos and Rourke's (1959, pp. 235–236) 10-year-old generalization that governors were ". . . highly restrained in the exercise of their stronger fiscal authority." In contrast to the smaller states, they had noted:

In the larger states—New York, California, or Pennsylvania for example—the governors are not often concerned with the detailed finances of state colleges and universities but rather with the total figures that fit into the over-all state budget. The governor of California rarely concerns himself with the inner workings of educational finance. . . .

Among the seven states in the study, the size of the state has little to do with the interest which the governor takes in the details of a multicampus budget.

Our view of the states at one moment in time obscures the fact that the role of the governor changes with events and personalities, both in the statehouse and in the university. An activist governor interested in making higher education his "monument" can lead in one direction, while his successor may be distinguished by his indifference to the same institution. Regardless of the direction taken, however, the governor is everywhere assuming a more central role in the affairs of the multicampus universities. The reasons are clear. Increased public attention and interest in higher education—whether positively directed at its increasingly crucial role in society or negatively aimed at its increasingly noisy and disruptive one—compel the governor to engage himself in problems largely unknown to his predecessors. How the governor chooses to exercise this new role can be critical. Second, the university's budget, in virtually every state, is one of the largest items in the state's budget and, importantly, one relatively free from restrictions. Many aspects of health, welfare, highways are earmarked in state budgets; there is little flexibility in their funding. Governors must look elsewhere to alter spending patterns, and the university's appropriation looms large as a target.

The governor and the governing board
Informal rather than formal authority characterizes the impact of the governor on governing boards. His presence on or power to appoint members of the board is undoubtedly his most direct and continuing contact with it. Board members of the University of Illinois are chosen at general elections, and those of the University of North Carolina are elected by the state legislature. In all the other systems, members are appointed by the governor (or, in the case of the City University of New York, by the mayor). The governor of North Carolina presides over the board of the multicampus university nominally and in reality. The governor of California sits as a member of both multicampus boards, the University and the State Colleges, and the incumbent in 1970 attended with an unprecedented regularity. In contrast, Illinois' governor, also an *ex officio* trustee, rarely participates in board activity.

The governor as chief of police
Whether a governor is enthusiastic or indifferent to a multicampus university, he cannot always avoid being pulled into a conspicuous position. As the head of the state National Guard, his alone is the decision to use troops on the campus. Whether he acts at the request of the academic administration or not, his decision has a profound effect on governance. With specific reference to the multicampus university, a crisis which requires troops can obliterate all normal lines of authority or patterns of doing business. Only with difficulty, if at all, can a system executive remain removed from the problems of a single campus.

It is unfortunate to write of this military aspect of governmental relationships as though it were more than a passing phenomenon. Hopes that it may be temporary should not obscure the current difficulties, however. In five of the seven states in the study, governors had called out the National Guard to keep order on a campus during the period from 1968 to 1970. The use of the guard is one interaction between higher education and state government that was nonexistent 10 years ago. The command and coordination not only of the National Guard, but of state, county, and municipal law officers as well, is clearly a factor in the governance of higher education to be explored "in peace" for guidance "in war."

State Executive Agencies The personal role of the governor, whether he is commenting on the budget, appointing board members, or quelling riots, is a highly visible one. State administrative agencies, on the contrary, tend to penetrate and influence university governance without publicity. There is no deliberate secrecy; the continuing, day-to-day activities of fiscal, purchasing, and personnel agencies are hardly newsworthy, however influential they may be on the governance of higher education. Politics, not governance, is news. However, three overall generalizations about administrative agencies emerge from the study.

First, it is not just the public at large, but the faculty, students, and sometimes campus administrators who are uninformed, misinformed, or confused about the operations of state administrative agencies. This uncertainty is often settled by "fixing blame" on whoever is either visible or close at hand—what one administrator called the "whipping boy" theory of academic administration. Governors are favorite whipping boys, and relatively few problems at the campus level *cannot* be related to "unrealistic budget constraints." For problems which cannot be so characterized, the central administration becomes responsible in the eyes of the campus: "It doesn't make sense but that's the way *they* want it." *They,* of course, are the systemwide officers at University Hall, Thurlow Terrace, or 80th Street. But in reality, the critical points of decision are often the state administrative agencies. They are a very real part of university governance, but widespread ignorance of their activities and the additional layer of academic administration in a multicampus system often prevents their being recognized as such.

Second, despite varying degrees of impact, one or more administrative agencies in all states can be considered participants in the governance of the multicampus university. These agencies—fiscal, purchasing, civil service, and others—have political interests of their own which, willy-nilly, become those of the multicampus university. For example, a state civil service agency cannot amend its rules to meet the special needs of the university without carefully assessing their impact upon the state employees' association.

Third, although the governor's cabinet is usually an extension of his office, the state's permanent bureaucracy leads its own life within broad limits of executive policy. These limits are so extensive that second-level staff contacts between system administrators and agency staff, particularly in fiscal and personnel areas, appear as influential as most explicitly political relationships. In short, understanding the governance of a multicampus university requires realization that state officials and agency staff are often an integral, albeit distinct, part of that governance.

The Legislature

An executive budget and the governor's prominence give credence to the belief that the governor is the dominant political figure in the relationships between the multicampus university and the state. As a single political actor, he undoubtedly is. On the whole, however, political relationships with the legislature appear to be more pervasive and demanding of the time and attention of the multicampus university than those with the governor. At least, they were mentioned more often.

The individual legislator

An individual legislator of political consequence has been in the state capital for a long time. He has seen the rise and fall of many budgets for higher education, and his views on these budgets and other policy areas are fairly well known. His views usually remain stable. College and university relationships with such key legislators are universally regarded as durable and valuable.

In addition, every legislator, regardless of his length of service, his interest in higher education, or his place in the legislative pecking order, is a complaint and service bureau for his constituents. He must explain why places at the prestigious campus of the state university can be found for "long-haired radicals" from another state, when a constituent's daughter, president of her high school class, cannot even get into the freshman class. If an intern was rude to a patient in a teaching hospital, the legislator will hear about it. The examples are endless. The geographic spread of the multicampus university increases legislative concern and contact to give many individual legislators important if sporadic roles in governance. If a campus is located in a legislator's district, there is direct interest. If a campus is not, he generally wants one.

The legislature as ultimate coordinator

Legislatures, through the budget process, are, in fact, the ultimate coordinating agencies in the states. They are not seen as such, however, by the campuses of the multicampus universities, and this negative finding is of consequence. The campuses do not, for instance, see the formal statewide coordinating agency as necessary to "protect" them from political intervention by the legislature. In part, this can be attributed to the fact that despite complaints about disorder and jockeying over campus location, there is little evidence of legislative favoritism towards a particular campus in the appropriation procedures. If any legislator or groups of legislators discriminate or attempt to discriminate in the funding of existing campuses because of their location, it has not come to our attention. (In two states, however, predominately rural legislatures may have delayed programs at urban campuses.)

Legislative strategies in the exercise of this coordinating role vary from activism to restraint. In Illinois, the legislature has delegated many of its responsibilities to the coordinating agency and, with respect to matters not delegated, generally accepts its recommendations.[5] In two other states, in contrast, the very existence of the coordinating agency is a subject of debate by a legislature jealous of its own prerogatives in the governance of higher education.

Within the overall responsibilities of the legislature, many policy issues appear to lie fallow most of the time, becoming politically critical only in specific situations. State support in relation to tuition or long-range building plans are examples, but the catalog of such specific legislative interests is endless. Although each such interest looms large when its particular time has come, the basic organization of higher education is always a central concern.

What is the role of the coordinating agency? The mission of the multicampus university? Such broad questions are policy questions for ultimate legislative decision in virtually every state. The survival

[5] See footnote 8, which describes the shifting Illinois scene.

of more than one multicampus university depends on the answers. Can the City University of New York survive as an institution apart from the State University? Can the prestige of Berkeley or Chapel Hill, which have not yet been diluted by the existing multicampus university structures, survive inclusion—as has been proposed—in one embracing all higher education in the state? Can the legislature continue to fund different universities, campuses, and programs at markedly different levels, necessary on educational grounds but fraught with political difficulties?

Legislative staff

The legislators who raise such questions do not rely entirely upon intuition, or advice from those affected by the answers, for information. Like the executive bureaucracy, legislative staff frequently have had longer experience and wider acquaintance with the affairs of higher education than many legislators and university administrators. Some legislative staff exercise substantial power and often without consultation with university officials. While lack of consultation is to be deplored, highly informed executive and legislative staffs are the essence of good government. It is inevitable that they will exercise influence, if only an implicit veto by failure to approve recommendations, and we found frequent examples of such power.

The Political Context: A Summary Tensions are inevitable in politics, and multicampus universities are very much a part of politics. On the other hand, it is not clear that all the tensions found are necessary or productive.

The nine multicampus universities in this study are not the only institutions of higher education involved in politics. Governors appoint the boards of other public educational institutions, and legislatures allocate funds to them as well as to the multicampus university systems under scrutiny here. Nevertheless, the multicampus universities do present unusual political characteristics.

First, they are large, and size alone accentuates all the political relationships noted above. Whether or not a multicampus university exercises more political muscle, it is always suspected of doing so. For such an advantage, it pays a price: the concentration of attention from governor and legislature alike. Size also complicates whatever claims to prestige or "quality" the multicampus university may have. While other segments of higher education may tolerate the claims of a single campus as "the quality institution" in the state, they discount them when made by a multicampus university which is not averse to enrolling as many students as possible on as many campuses as possible.

Second, the *quantitative* difference in enrollment and the number of campuses and their locations create a *qualitative* difference. A multicampus university serves the people of the state from widely spread campuses. A new multicampus outpost brings real and imagined but almost always intangible benefits to the youth of a particular area. It also brings equally intangible political complications for the multicampus university. Regardless of whether the locally elected legislator is friend or foe, the whole range of system activity is now properly his interest also. While some state legislators are urging the location of the next campus in their district, others whose districts include one are attacking the taste of local dramatic productions. Individually and as a group, these legislators are of great value to the multicampus university. They can also be an immense problem. Relationships with them are a vital function of the central administration.

Third, state government in all seven states is a functioning part of the university governance. We have maintained the tradition here that the governor, the legislature, and their permanent administrative staff are "external influences." Realistically, however, state government is not external to the public multicampus university, but rather another level of its governance. Characterizing virtually any interest which governors and legislatures take in higher education as "interference" does little to further understanding of governing processes. The central focus of this study is on the boundary between the campus and the multicampus administration and governing board. The agencies of state government are active participants in this context, not as outsiders, but because they are part of the governing structure.

**HIGHER EDU-
CATION IN
THE STATES** By our definition, none of the nine systems includes all public institutions of higher education in its state. All types of private campuses share the academic scene as well. In each of the seven states, a coordinating agency attempts to relate the activities of the public campuses, and in some it has a degree of authority over private campuses also.

**Public Higher
Education** Change and variety obscure the organization of public higher education in the seven states. Indeed, the word "organization" itself is

overdrawn, with its implications of conscious plans and decisions. Despite the seeming order of the discussion below, the pattern in any given state reflects a host of historical events and unplanned developments, many of which have faded from memory. Table 5 indicates the number and types of public college and university campuses in these states, but rapid change and ambiguous defini-

		Universities			
		In multicampus system			
State	With separate boards	Number of campuses	Name	With separate boards
California	0	9	University of California	0
Illinois	0	3	University of Illinois	0
		2	Southern Illinois University	
		1	Regency Universities	
Missouri	0	4	University of Missouri	8
New York	0	6	State University of New York	0
		2	City University of New York	
North Carolina	0	4	University of North Carolina	12
Texas	4	3	University of Texas	7
		1	Texas Agricultural and Mechanical University	0
Wisconsin	0	2	University of Wisconsin	0

TABLE 5 *Numbers and organization of public four-year colleges and universities in seven states, 1968–1969*

SOURCE: U.S. Office of Education (1969), adjusted to reflect (1) probable changes in status and (2) numbers of campuses in multicampus systems.

tion limit its timeliness. The diversity in overall organization illustrated by the table will remain, however.

A further complication intrudes in the attempt to categorize "college" and "university" campuses. To determine whether a particular college campus will become a university is not easy when those whose recommendations will guide the final decision

| Colleges | |
| In multicampus system | |
Number of campuses	Name
18	California State Colleges
4	State Colleges and Universities System
1	Regency Universities
0	
11	State University of New York
9	City University of New York
0	
5	Texas Senior Colleges
2	Texas Agricultural and Mechanical University
2	University of Wisconsin
9	Wisconsin State Universities

are themselves uncertain. It is sufficient, here, to say that the distinction is based on the granting of a doctoral degree, or on reasonably certain plans for so doing.

Patterns of Organization: Segmental, Regional, and Mixed There are two distinct aspects to segmental organization, both of which are fundamental to the study and to an understanding of Table 5. First, as used here, a segmental *state system* of higher education is one in which the multicampus university has exclusive jurisdiction over the doctorate among the public institutions in the state, which—by definition—are not all found within that system. Second, under our nomenclature, a segmental *multicampus university* is one in which *all campuses* within the university system uniformly either grant or do not grant the doctoral degree. The implications of this latter point are discussed in the following chapter. Here, we are concerned with only the first aspect, the overall organization of higher education in the state.

The pattern of statewide organization in four states with five multicampus universities is clearly segmental. In California, Missouri, Wisconsin, and North Carolina, only the multicampus university, as we have defined it, can award doctoral degrees. The California State Colleges, included in this study, offer work only through the master's degree (although they do join with the University of California in granting *joint* doctorates and in 1969 were given similar authority to grant doctorates jointly with private institutions). Similarly, in Wisconsin, the State University system does not offer a doctorate, nor do the individual campuses, each with its own board, in North Carolina and Missouri.

Public higher education in the remaining three states is not segmentally organized; that is, more than one multicampus system or separate institution of higher education offers the doctorate. However, the pattern in the three states differs markedly. Public higher education in New York, with the two multicampus universities (State and City) can be described as "regional." With immaterial exceptions, each university system is responsible for all college and university campuses within its respective area, geographically divided by the city limits of New York City. On the other hand, in Texas and Illinois, the organization of higher education is neither segmental nor regional. In each state, there are public institutions of higher education other than the multicampus university which offer the doctorate, and there are no territorial boundaries within the state to any of the systems or institutions.

State *segmental* organization imposes a formal, structural distinction between research-oriented and teaching-oriented campuses which cannot be altered except by the state legislature. *Regional* organization, on the other hand, requires a multicampus university to encompass campuses with both orientations but geographically restricts its responsibilities. The *mixed* pattern of Illinois and Texas does not restrict the doctorate to one system or institution; neither does it limit the jurisdiction of any system or institution to a particular part of the state. The following discussion is addressed to each of these three patterns.

Segmental. State segmental organization—the pattern in California, Missouri, North Carolina, and Wisconsin—is seen by those who favor it as protecting both the research and teaching orientations of higher education. However, some observers view the campuses with research orientation as being "protected" and the campuses with teaching orientation as "contained."[6] Whether protection or containment is the aim, state segmental organization is said to make it easier for the state to maintain the distinction between differently oriented campuses. However, ease of differentiation is obtained at a cost. A rigid state segmental structure intended to contain unjustified ambitions of college campuses to enter into doctoral instruction can bear just as heavily and rigidly upon legitimate aspirations in that direction. Moreover, the almost impossible burden of distinguishing between "unjustified ambition" and "legitimate aspiration" is on the legislature. In large and complex colleges, productive research-oriented faculty look upon state segmental organization as a formal and unrealistic barrier. The glamour of the name "university" and the research orientation that it implies are not the only spurs to ambition. Differences in salary scales, sabbatical privileges, office space, and miscellaneous support such as secretarial help also lead the "second-class citizens" at large colleges to resent the segmental pattern of higher education.

The legislative response to such pressures often draws the line

---

[6] A former chairman of the California coordinating agency saw the different segmental orientations as causing struggles ". . . between and among segments themselves as major 'corporate' entities vying for advantage, favor, and finance" (Coons, 1968, p. 149). A report to a joint committee of the California legislature suggested elemination of the three-tiered structure based on such segmental differences (Joint Committee on Higher Education, 1968).

between colleges and universities with a very broad political brush. If one or two state colleges become as complex as university campuses, then the university title may be awarded to all college campuses (as in Wisconsin) or at least to other college campuses whose qualifications are not so clear (as in North Carolina). Delegation of such decisions to the coordinating agency is possible, but it has not occurred, although legislation along this line has been proposed in California.

In two "segmental" states, California and Wisconsin, all the colleges form another multicampus system. In the other two states, North Carolina and Missouri, each institution has its own individual board. The reasons for this difference are not readily apparent, but one implication is evident. In both North Carolina and Missouri, the coordinating agency appears to be filling a leadership vacuum for the state college segment. An often-mentioned benefit of multicampus organization is the ability of the system executive to take positions which a campus executive cannot take without coming into conflict with his peers. In Missouri and North Carolina, the coordinating agency is felt to be the spokesman for the overall interests of numerous independent state colleges. This role of the coordinating agency is not unlike that which it might undertake for private campuses, which similarly lack a governmental spokesman. While this paternalistic role may benefit both the private campuses and the public colleges, it is, by the same token, potentially disadvantageous to the multicampus university. In any event, the differing coordinating agency roles in states with solely autonomous campuses, or solely multicampus systems, or both is an important aspect of the overall governance of higher education which is often unrecognized.

Regional. The organization of New York has theoretically been designed to avoid some of the difficulties raised by rigid segmental boundaries. Faculty members whose home campus has a teaching orientation can be given opportunities to supervise graduate work at research-oriented campuses within the multicampus university. Similarly, students at college campuses can benefit from periodical instruction from faculty whose appointment is primarily with a university campus. A regionally organized multicampus university can isolate some graduate work from any campus, as has the City University of New York. In theory, faculty and students can retain orientation to predominantly undergraduate campuses while still benefiting from the research-oriented graduate center. Students as well as faculty can utilize more than one type of campus. So go the arguments, although there is sparse evidence of implementation of these concepts.

"Second-class citizenship" is personal as well as organizational, and it was suggested that an organization combining both college and university campuses might alleviate some of the stigma for matriculating individuals as well as for institutions. Common or broadly overlapping salary schedules for faculty or admission standards for students might eliminate invidious comparisons. At least, the distinctions would not be on a rigid system-versus-system basis, as is most pronounced in California.

If the New York pattern solves some of the problems of state segmental differentiation, it has hardly solved them all. The difficulty of distinguishing a college from a university in borderline situations is a prime source of tension for the segmentally organized state. The ease with which these can be distinguished, however, is a source of tension for the regionally organized state. A major university campus differs from a college campus in a number of respects, but in particular in being nationally and usually internationally competitive in some fields. A major university campus does not seem to suffer either in prestige or in the material necessities of such competition by its inclusion in a system in which all campuses have university status—for example, Berkeley, or Urbana. Whether such a major campus can remain or become competitive in an organization such as CUNY or SUNY—with *both* college and university campuses—remains to be seen. Assuming fixed resources, pressures to equalize support levels and admissions standards may be accommodated only at the cost of diluting the status of the major university campuses. Admittedly, it is premature in both New York systems to raise this as more than a possibility. Both are so new and distinct that comparisons with other systems are somewhat dubious. Nevertheless, the potential problem is real. With the present ease of interstate mobility of prestigious faculty and able students, even a slight decrease in the attractiveness of a particular campus can have adverse implications.

In short, observers of the two New York university systems express concern that the critical distinction between "equity" and "equality" cannot be maintained. The former term implies the maintenance of qualitative distinctions among campuses in terms of salaries, support costs, and admissions standards, but it is feared these cannot continue to exist within a single system. Instead, a tendency toward indiscriminate equality, with an inevitable leveling among campuses, is a possible and pessimistic alternative. If the university system cannot accept one or two campuses as being "more equal" than the others, the academic marketplace does and will continue to do so to entice away faculty and students.

Mixed.   Segmental and regional organization for higher education in five of the states provide two general designs for dealing with institutional aspirations. Texas and Illinois offer a third alternative. In neither state is the multicampus university in the study the only public institution offering doctoral degrees.

In Illinois as of 1968, five college and six university campuses were organized into four multicampus systems, only one of which, the University of Illinois, is part of this study. In Texas, 14 colleges and eight universities were distributed among 10 single campuses and three multicampus systems, one of which, the University of Texas system, we studied.

In Illinois, unlike Texas, a relatively elaborate theory supports the state's overall organization. Omitting two-year campuses, a "balance of systems" concept, based on an institutional "typology," is as follows (Illinois Board of Higher Education, 1966, p. 12):

1   The fully developed, complex, multipurpose university. This type of institution offers work, usually at both the undergraduate and graduate levels, in most of the recognized fields of knowledge, has a diversity of professional schools, and is extensively involved in research and public service (University of Illinois).

2   The rapidly developing, complex, multipurpose university. This type of institution retains some probative restrictions related to geography, advanced professional programs, and typological priorities (Southern Illinois University).

3   The liberal arts university. This type of institution is one having a program of graduate education leading to the doctorate in a significant number of fields, but whose breadth of offerings is restricted to the liberal arts and sciences and other related undergraduate programs, with only a limited number of associated graduate professional schools, usually education or business administration (Northern Illinois University and Illinois State University).

4   The state university and state college. This type of institution has a more limited scope of offerings, usually does not have professional schools ex-

cept in the field of teacher education, and offers the doctorate in only a very limited number of fields or not at all.

The absence of any similar or all-inclusive typology for higher education in Texas is not surprising, for as one college administrator explained, "Political interests in Texas don't really control higher education, they just push it around." Politicians and educators alike appear more inclined to keep all their options open. What, at first blush, seems to be a complete lack of overall statewide organization for higher education in Texas may be just that, but it is not entirely irrational. State support for *all* college and university campuses, including those of the University of Texas, is uniformly distributed according to detailed formulas based on the number of students and the level of instruction. These formulas make no distinction between the Austin campus of the University of Texas and the smallest of the four-year college campuses. But, in addition to the appropriations determined by these formulas, the state provides its two major institutions with an endowment. The University of Texas (more specifically the Austin campus) as the principal beneficiary (two-thirds of current income) and Texas A & M as a secondary beneficiary (one-third) share the income from over 2 million acres of oil-producing land in west Texas. Without attempting to fit *all* campuses in the state of Texas into the Illinois organizational typology, the University of Texas would appear to be a "fully developed" and Texas A & M a "rapidly developing" institution.

By devious routes, Texas and Illinois may have reached a common solution to the problem of differentiating among colleges and universities. The University of Illinois is ". . . 'The University' of the state of Illinois" (Illinois Board of Higher Education, 1966, p. 14). There is little doubt that the Austin campus, but not necessarily the entire University of Texas, occupies a similar position in that state. The predominant research orientation of the University of Illinois is protected by elaborate classification that goes far beyond simple segmental differentiation. In Texas, explicit discrimination in financial support shines like a beacon to distinguish the university at Austin, also research-oriented, from all other higher education.

While scholarly despair over the typology in Illinois or the lack of any at all in Texas may be justified, the two contrasting patterns make a difference to the multicampus universities. For example, in Illinois the legislature approved in 1969 a recommendation of the coordinating agency to assign a new campus at the state capital to the "liberal arts" multicampus system, *not* to the University of Illinois. Although the coordinating agency's recommendation appears to have been based substantially on the political influence of private higher education as well as that of other public systems, it was buttressed by considerable discussion about the value of "free-standing [i.e., autonomous] institutions" in a "balance of systems" (Illinois Board of Higher Education, 1967). The organizational typology would not, of course, have prevented the assignment of the new campus to the University of Illinois, a logical choice on strictly academic grounds. The typology, however, did ease the way for a decision based, at least in part, on noneducational grounds.

In Texas, a somewhat contrary result has occurred. If the logical growth and development of the University of Illinois has been restricted by too elaborate a conceptual scheme for higher education, that of the University of Texas seems to have been rushed for want of one. Legislation in Texas in 1969 authorized three new general campuses and four new health units for the University of Texas. The time, energy, resources, and imagination needed to build, staff, and plan these new campuses will be immense. In 1969, the University of Texas, aside from its medical campuses, was not a large multicampus university. It was still in the process of developing a suitable central administrative structure and clarifying lines of communication with the three existing general campuses. It was not clear that the university, as a system, would be able to provide the necessary aid to so many new campuses. As in Illinois, the Texas decision seemed politically determined, and probably no theoretical structure for higher education could have prevented the addition of these new campuses to the system. But the lack of any structure or model for development in Texas assuredly made the political decision easier.

The opinions of the multicampus administrators in Illinois and Texas were by no means in complete agreement with our own as to whether the new campus decisions were correct. From the point of view of each of the multicampus universities, however, the political decisions may have been the proper ones. There are advantages to the University of Illinois in keeping its lines of communication short and avoiding the growing pains of an adventurous new campus in a state capital. Moreover, the same strong coordinating agency which was instrumental in denying to it the additional campus at Springfield can probably be relied upon to protect the university's nationally prestigious position. In Texas, on the other hand, the University of Texas has neither the advantages nor disadvantages of a strong coordinating agency; it relies entirely on its own political base and must build up that base whenever possible. The new campuses will undoubtedly aid in this end.

Two-Year Campuses The term *two-year campus* covers as many different kinds of campuses as does the term *university*. At one extreme, a two-year campus can be explicitly vocational, technical, and "terminal" in the sense that neither the students nor the other campuses expect the students to continue beyond the two-year program. The agricultural and technical campuses of the State University of New York and the technical institute at North Carolina State University at Raleigh are in this category. At the other extreme, the two-year campuses of the University of Wisconsin are considered lower-division extensions of the liberal arts college at Madison, with the explicit assumption that students will transfer. Qualifications temper both of these extremes, and by far the greatest number of two-year campuses in the seven states are dual-purpose community colleges intended to serve both groups of students.

Two-year campuses affect the multicampus universities in three ways. First, in New York, Wisconsin, and, to a very limited extent, in North Carolina, some two-year campuses are governed by one of the multicampus universities in the study. These are discussed more fully in Chapter 3. Second, the articulation or transfer of students between two-year campuses and the multicampus universities is an issue in all states and is discussed in Chapter 11. A third facet is considered here: To what extent are these two-year campuses a political factor for the systems in the study?

Briefly, the two-year campuses do not appear to be of any substantial political significance to the organization and operations of the nine multicampus universities. In two or three states, *local* pressure on a college or university campus to accept transfer students from a nearby two-year campus has encouraged the coordinating agency to study the problem. Such local pressure, however, has nowhere risen to the level of statewide political interest or concern.

Organization in the seven states

In the seven states, the governance and coordination of two-year campuses involve complex allocations of authority. Accommodation to local control, still the dominant mode of governance, and dual financing by the locality and the state explain much of the complexity. Four general patterns of organization are evident: (1) In New York, most two-year campuses, including those in New York City, are under local boards which share authority with the State University of New York. The governing board of the City University of New York is also the local board for the two-year campuses within the city limits. "Complex" is the gentleman's word for the intricacies of governance of two-year campuses in New York City.[7] (2) In Illinois, California, and Wisconsin, most of the two-year campuses have local boards which share authority with a statewide board other than the state's board of education. (3) In Missouri and North Carolina, the two-year colleges have separate local boards which share authority with the state board of education. (4) In Texas, local boards share authority with the coordinating agency.

Two-year campuses and politics

A safe prediction is that the two-year campuses will become increasingly active and influential in state politics. More voters or their children are enrolled on two-year campuses. A growing number of state legislators have one or more two-year campuses in their districts. At the level of federal politics, the national association for two-year campuses in Washington, D.C., is tending to treat the traditional higher education "establishment" with somewhat less respect than senior members of the family think proper (Bloland, 1969, pp. 158–160). The ability of the two-year campuses to exert political influence is increasing even as their need for such influence is being felt.

It is easier to predict rising political power than to discern the uses to which it will be put. Two probabilities emerge. First, the two-year campuses will require and doubtless obtain new or substantially increased state support to supplement or replace the predominantly local support of the past. In part, this continues the shift in orientation of two-year colleges from local school districts to "higher education." The main factor, though, is the inadequacy of the local property tax base, a factor portending sweeping changes for intergovernmental relations generally. The *exact* impact that

---

[7] In a consultant's report presented to the New York State Department of Education, Peat, Marwick, Mitchell and Co. (1969, p. 6) recommended, among other things, ". . . that the community colleges in New York City be governed solely by the Board of Higher Education, and that the present legal relationship to the State University Trustees be discontinued."

greater state support of two-year campuses will have on the multi-campus universities is beyond speculation. The general impact, however, is clear; there is going to be another and powerful claimant for the educational dollar at both state and national levels.

Secondly, the two-year campuses will increasingly be in a better bargaining position vis-à-vis the colleges and universities over the articulation of students. The multicampus universities will be under growing pressure to admit applicants they are sent rather than unilaterally specifying qualifications.

However, the two-year campuses do not presently have a strong position in the politics of the seven states comparable to that of other institutions. Nor are the nine multicampus universities quite as interested in the two-year campuses as the probable future educational and political strength of the latter might justify. If the two-year campuses are going to educate most of the nation's undergraduates, the universities will undoubtedly have to become more concerned as to how that education is being conducted.

Private Higher Education

All seven of the states have privately controlled campuses of distinction. The influence of this private sector on the multicampus universities in the study varies greatly, although active proposals for state aid or support of some aspect of private higher education exist in every state. The implications for the multicampus universities are readily apparent.

Table 6 points out distinct variations among the seven states. For example, the proportion of four-year college and university students in public institutions ranges from 40 percent in New York to nearly double that in California, Texas, and Wisconsin. The table does not, of course, indicate subtle variations in public attitude and commitment to public or private higher education. In New York, a full-fledged public university to compete with Cornell or Columbia did not even exist until the 1962 merger of the State University of New York and the then private University of Buffalo. On the other hand, both the Berkeley and Los Angeles campuses of the University of California have long enjoyed national reputations at least equal to any of that state's private institutions. The historical commitment of California, unlike that of New York, has been a commitment to *public* higher education, and not necessarily a commitment to higher education generally. In contrast, the state of New York, from about 1961 to 1967, provided individual students with funds for tuition at either public or private campuses in amounts

TABLE 6
Numbers and enrollment in public and private four-year colleges and universities in seven states, 1968–69

State	Public			Number of university campuses
	Number of university campuses	Number of college campuses	Enrollment	
California	9	18	385,235	4
Illinois	6	5	150,173	5
Missouri	4	8	87,507	2
New York	8	20	211,723	12
North Carolina	4	12	72,785	2
Texas	8	14	215,137	4
Wisconsin	2	11	120,956	1

SOURCE: U.S. Office of Education (1969), adjusted to reflect: (1) anticipated change from college to university status where known and (2) the numbers of campuses in multicampus systems where these were not separately counted.

"about two and one-half times all the other states combined . . ." (Select Committee, 1968, p. 26).

At least four specific aspects of the influence of the private educational sector on the multicampus universities are evident in the seven states.

First, *fiscal survival* has on occasion given a private campus little alternative except to come under public control. Two campuses joined multicampus universities under such circumstances.

Second, *medical education* appears to be a special case and is at the cutting edge of public aid for private higher education. Expensive, professional, and prestigious, a medical school is considered a hallmark of a "real university." Unless private medical schools are supported, expensive plant and experienced staff will be lost and the manpower crisis in medicine deepened. The alternative to public support for a private medical school is often location on a public campus, but whatever the distinction the public campus may gain by adding a medical school must be balanced against the inroads such an addition might make on campus resources. Even for the particular public campus involved, it is not easy to decide whether to take over an existing private medical school or to encourage public support for it. Moreover, medical school objectives can differ from those of the multicampus board and central staff.

Private		Percentage
Number of college campuses	Enrollment	of students on public campuses
81	114,521	77
72	123,980	55
36	43,761	66
108	323,405	40
29	38,248	65
37	64,627	77
27	32,267	78

Third, there is a fairly clear dichotomy in *attitudes toward public support* of the private sector. Administrators in older, larger, or stronger multicampus universities and their campuses either publicly or privately favor (or do not oppose) such aid. They appear confident that public higher education will be the dominant sector in the future. Administrators in the newer and less secure multi-campus universities, on the other hand, seem more inclined to dispute such aid.

A fourth finding is the opinion of several system administrators that *coordinating agencies are more supportive of the private sector* than is necessary or desirable. This situation is not unlike the leadership role which the coordinating agencies often seem to perform for public colleges outside a multicampus system and points up again the ambivalence of agency relationships in states with both systems and autonomous campuses.

COORDINAT-ING AGENCIES   In each of the seven states, a governmental agency has a primary function of "coordinating" higher education. Table 7 indicates their composition and major areas of authority; clearly there is little or no agreement on the specific authority denoted by "coordinate."

Nevertheless, as diverse as they are, coordinating agencies have this in common: an involvement—in some measure—in the govern-

TABLE 7 *Composition and authority of seven statewide coordinating agencies, 1968–1969*

					Master plans	
	Number of board	Appointed by	Represent higher education			
State	positions	governor	institutions	Other	Prepare	Revise
California	18	6[1]	12[2]			x
Illinois	16	10[1]	6[3]		x	x
Missouri	10	6[1]	4[4]		x	x
New York	15			15[7]	x	x
North Carolina	15	8[1]	7[5]		x	x
Texas	18	18[1]			x	x
Wisconsin	17	9[1]	8[6]		x	x

Composition of coordinating agencies — *Method of selection*

[1] With Senate consent. (North Carolina, with House consent also.)

[2] Three are appointed by the governor as representatives of private colleges and universities; six are members of governing boards of the University of California, the California State Colleges, and the community colleges. The remaining three are the president of the University of California, the chancellor of the California State Colleges, and the chancellor of the community colleges, all ex officio. Legislation in 1970 reduced the number of representatives of institutions of higher education from twelve to four and added the superintendent of public instruction, ex officio and without vote.

[3] Representatives of governing boards of the University of Illinois, Southern Illinois University, the state colleges and universities, regency universities, and state junior colleges, and the superintendent of public instruction, ex officio.

[4] Heads of the various types of institutions, appointed by the governor.

[5] Two from the board of the University of North Carolina and four from other institutional boards. The four institutions are designated by the governor on a rotating basis and the respective boards name the representatives. One is appointed by the governor from the membership of the state board of education which governs technical schools and community colleges.

ance of the multicampus universities. Moreover, all are central figures in the political milieu of higher education. The chairman of one such agency (Heineman, 1966) states the matter clearly:

The . . . [coordinating agency] . . . in seeking to fulfill the role conferred upon it by the legislature, must never lose sight of what it is, and what it is not. The . . . [coordinating agency] . . . has no built-in constituency, no traditions, little public awareness of its purpose and function, and operates on monies appropriated by the legislature. The coordinating and planning processes for which it is responsible are in the most real sense political ones involving powerful social agencies, such as colleges and universities, with

Authority of coordinating agencies							
		New campuses and programs				Admissions	Transfers
			Approve new degree programs			Establish	Establish inter-
Review budget request		Approve new	Under-		Profes-	admission	institutional
Operating	Capital	campuses	graduate	Graduate	sional	policy	transfer policy
x[8]	x[8]	x	x[10]	x[10]	x[10]	x[11]	
x	x	x	x	x	x	x[12]	
x	x	x[11]	x[11]	x[11]	x[11]	x[11]	x[11]
		x	x	x	x		
		x	x	x	x		
	x[8]	x[9]	x	x	x	x[11]	x[11]
x	x	x	x	x	x		

A 1969 statute added seven members, the governor and the chairmen of finance, appropriations, and higher education committees of both houses.

[6] Six are chairmen and one a member of boards of the University of Wisconsin; the state colleges; and vocational, technical, and adult education. A seventh is a member of the board of county teachers colleges; this is a transitory membership since the county teachers colleges are being phased out. The state superintendent of education is also a member.

[7] Elected by legislature on joint ballot. The Regents also have responsibility for elementary and secondary education.

[8] Review of selected items.

[9] Two-year colleges only.

[10] Approve programs according to administratively established procedures.

[11] Recommending authority only.

[12] Minimum standards.

SOURCE: Pliner, 1966, and correspondence with chief executive officers of coordinating agencies.

their historic intellectual independence and autonomy, and their loyal alumni constituency on the one hand, the central public policy formulating authority of the governor and the legislature on the other.

The statement illustrates not only the political qualities of the coordinating agencies, but their ambiguous nature. At one and the same time, they are expected to be both agencies of the state to control higher education and a spokesman for those to be controlled. In addition to the conflict inherent in these two roles, the coordinating agency is also generally expected to take a third role as a completely neutral arbitrator between the various elements of higher education. That the coordinating agency's position is merely ambiguous and not totally impossible is attributable to the possibility that rarely are any of these conflicting expectations very strongly held, even by the coordinating agency itself.

As an agency of the state, the coordinating agency suffers from the need of an independent political base. It lacks alumni, parents, students, faculty, football teams, and local community support. In addition to or perhaps because of this lack of support, it is generally less prestigious than multicampus or campus boards. On the other hand, as the spokesman for higher education, it lacks credibility with its supposed constituency. With limited exceptions, therefore, the coordinating agency is politically vulnerable, relying upon the governor and key legislators to support most of its activities. The price of support in more than one state is that the agency serves as budgetary agent for the governor, or perhaps staff to a legislative committee. In either case, political vulnerability weakens its ability to meet its other responsibilities.

Most of the coordinating agencies, however, do not appear to be effective agents of either the governor or the legislature. Only in Illinois do the powers delegated to the agency appear sufficient to carry out a broad legislative mandate to coordinate, however that term might be defined.[8] Lack of authority as both symptom and cause of political vulnerability is not peculiar to higher education, but three specific coordinating agency characteristics are pertinent to the relative political positions of the agencies and the multicampus universities: (1) The boards of the coordinating agencies are generally less prestigious than those of the multicampus universities. (2) Coordinating agencies lack traditional patterns of organization and authority based on single campus operations. (3) The coordinating agency's staff members lack a

---

[8] Writing in April 1970, a long-time observer of the Illinois political scene who will remain anonymous wrote as follows: "In some ways on this day, I think it might be well if you came back and started over in Illinois. The game really seems to have changed. Today the Governor in his budget message cut the higher education appropriations significantly from that recommended by the Board of Higher Education. This was done even though it was 'his' Board, as he has 'his' man as chairman, and the new executive director is pretty much 'his' man. Our new Bureau of the Budget for the first time is feeling its oats, and has made its influence felt on higher education, particularly in the new budget. In addition, the Governor announced in his budget message that tuition would be raised—in the past he played a more subtle role behind the scenes. To repeat, the name of the game has changed here."

clear career pattern. All three shortcomings can be attributed, at least in part, to the recent origins of most coordinating agencies.

Prestige

To the extent that the prestige of the members of any board is a political asset, seven multicampus universities have an advantage over coordinating agencies. The only clear exception in both age and prestige is the venerable New York Regents, which antedate the governing boards of the State and City Universities by more than a century and a half. In other states, with the possible exception of Illinois, the governing boards of the multicampus universities enjoy both greater prestige and political influence than the boards of the coordinating agencies. Prestige appears to derive more from the tradition and strength of a major campus than from size, while such factors as geographic dispersion give the multicampus university political influence, or at least political visibility.

Lack of tradition

The lack of traditional patterns of organization and authority involves more than merely age. A coordinating agency finds itself not merely new, but new also in the context of governing patterns with origins that are lost in antiquity. The result is a problem in "organizational role definition" or, more sharply, an "identity crisis." At the campus level, the administration is fairly clear about its own activities and how they should be handled. There is less clarity at the multicampus university level, but at the level of the coordinating agency there is little clarity at all. The coordinating agency and its staff are still another step removed from the campus and the constraints and guidance of daily operations and traditions of academic administration. Statutory duties, rarely precise, offer no substitute for tradition as a guide. While the multicampus university has only slightly more precise guidance, it is relatively free to experiment internally with organization and authority allocation. The coordinating agency, on the other hand, operates in the milieu of the state capital. Indeed, its powers border closely on those of the legislature itself, which is unlikely to look with favor on any derogation of these.

Uncertain career lines

Coordinating agency staff members are neither members of the academic bureaucracy nor part of the administrative hierarchy of state governments. With one exception among the nine multicampus universities in 1970, all system chief executives had teaching or administrative experience, usually both, at one or more major campuses; they and their staffs (with the possible exceptions of business officers) consider themselves to be "academics" and in some measure "representative" of the faculty on their campuses. Almost without exception, no staff member of a multicampus university above a position bordering on the clerical is subject to civil service. On the other hand, a common description in the seven states is that coordinating agencies are staffed with "small-college people" or that, because of unrealistic civil service requirements or salary scales, major positions remain unfilled. Civil service is a term that academic administrators seem to use to frighten their children, for regardless of technical appropriateness by way of qualifications and salary, a civil service position is—by university definition—not an *academic* position. Exclusion from the state civil service is a status symbol in academic administration and one which keeps some qualified academics and professionals from working with the coordinating agencies.

If the staff of the coordinating agency is out of the academic career ladder, it is also virtually isolated from that of the state governmental bureaucracies. A budget analyst with the state coordinating agency defies easy status characterization. In part, this matter of status or prestige is irrational, but in part it is the product of the newness and ambiguity of the coordinating agencies.

Coordination and the Multicampus University

On the face of it, the need for coordination of a number of separate campuses with separate boards should be much greater than such need for two or three multicampus university systems. Thus, it is argued, a multicampus university with its ability to attract competent specialists to its central staff can do for itself and its campuses what the coordinating agency would normally be expected to do for separate campuses. For example, in a state with a dozen individual campuses, each with its separate board, the coordinating agency might perform a valuable task in bringing expertise to bear in sifting and analyzing information both for the legislature and for the campuses themselves. But in a state with a multicampus university, the system might better be able to do this for its own campuses, while suprasystem questions involving high-level political decisions frequently call for the judgment of the governor and the legislature.

Another implication of coordination that expressly affects the multicampus university is the additional layer of administration and paper work. Without exception, system administrators reported that they had to go to their campuses to obtain detailed information which the coordinating agency, not the multicampus system, would utilize. Even the information needed by the system was increasingly produced on forms and at times required by the coordinating agency. With due respect to the possible future use of computers in extensive information systems,[9] the bulk of the data is still gathered and processed by hand. At the campus level particularly, the hands are few and the demands many. Within a system with direct responsibility for its campuses, information is sought on a selective basis with knowledge and consideration of campus capacity to produce it. Central administrators seldom feel they possess sufficient information, but generally they try to avoid overburdening the sources at the campus. However, coordinating agencies are reported to ask for more information than the systems themselves feel they require. Whether, as was sometimes implied, these agencies engage in endless and detailed surveys which fail to balance the cost of the information against its possible utility cannot here be confirmed or denied.

Another facet of the separation of responsibility from information and its implications for the multicampus university is the use which coordinating agencies make of advisory committees consisting of faculty members or campus administrators. The problem is somewhat akin to all-university faculty participation in system governance, discussed in Chapter 6. The generally negative attitude of campus executives to having "their faculty" act as part of an all-university governing structure is paralleled here in the attitudes of system executives. The latter indicated some discomfort in finding a faculty member from one of the campuses meeting and negotiating directly with the statewide coordinating staff. Within the multicampus university, some form of faculty participation in university-wide academic governance is almost universally recognized as legitimate, however irritating the particular form or extent might be to the campus executives. Similar legitimacy does not attach to faculty participation in the activities of the coordinating agency, at least in the minds of the system executives. The system executive who utilizes the advice of campus faculty is responsible for the

---

[9] The reader is referred to Rourke and Brooks (1966).

action taken. The coordinating agency, on the other hand, can select a site and fix ultimate enrollments with faculty advice, but it is not responsible for the operation of the campus, as is the system executive. Faculty participation at the level of the coordinating agency is sometimes seen as undermining institutional integrity, an attempt by the coordinating agency's staff to build an academic constituency at the expense of the multicampus university.

The use or misuse of such advisory groups was illustrated by the following explanation of them given by a member of the board of the coordinating agency (Heineman, 1966):

Faculty members serving on . . . [advisory] . . . committees enter the dialogue as important independent spokesmen for higher education. Unlike some college administrators, faculty members—whether from public or non-public colleges—generally commit their professional expertness without strong bias toward the more parochial aspirations or objectives of their institutions. . . .

The value of independent and expert advice cannot be doubted, but there is a fine line between nonparochial and nonrepresentative. System executives are concerned that faculty participation in coordinating agency decisions as "important independent spokesmen for higher education" can be construed as representation of the university itself. Such concern is not unjustified, for in one state the staff of the coordinating agency has made just such a claim.

In sum, just as there are different kinds of multicampus universities, there are many different patterns for coordinating agencies. At one extreme is an agency responsible for the oversight of a number of separate and autonomous campuses, each with its own governing board. (This, for example, is the pattern in Ohio, a state not included in this study.) At the other end of the continuum is a coordinating body in a state in which all four-year or university campuses are themselves organized into multicampus systems, with no separately governed campuses (the pattern in California, New York, Wisconsin, and Illinois). In the middle are those states in which both multicampus systems and autonomous campuses exist (the pattern in Texas, Missouri, and North Carolina).

Inherently, the middle position would appear to be the least stable. At the two ends of the continuum, with either all autonomous campuses or all multicampus systems, a viable division of labor might emerge, although none is yet apparent with respect to the multicampus systems. But a coordinating agency forced to deal with *both* systems and separate campuses is potentially subject to institutional schizophrenia, unable to make the necessary distinctions between the two kinds of institutions. For the multicampus university, the concern is that modes of operation appropriate for coordination of autonomous campuses will be applied to it, that its resources and experience will be ignored and its authority reduced.

The above models and continuum can only be posed as possible courses of development. In 1970, there was little to differentiate coordinating agency–multicampus university relationships in the seven states. All were unstable and in flux. If a more stable division of labor is emerging in the four states exclusively organized in multicampus systems, in contrast to the three states with both systems and autonomous campuses, it is not yet evident.

The Uses of Coordination

This study, with almost no contact with coordinating agency members or staff, is by no means an adequate way to obtain a balanced view of this important part of the governance of higher education. No claim is made that such a view is given here. Coordinating agencies have had and will have their own champions. The "coordinated" will resent the "coordinator" under the best of circumstances. Our information, which comes from the former, is not all unfavorable to the agencies, however, and three items may add balance.

First, in certain cases the coordinating agencies have made allowance for the fact that it is a *multicampus* system they are coordinating, not individual and autonomous campuses. For example, if the coordinating agency has approved a specific academic program for one campus of the system, then the program can be extended by the system to additional campuses.

Second, the argument that multicampus universities can do most of the things that a coordinating agency does is meritorious only if these universities perform in fact as theory indicates they should. This is rarely the case. Academic planning is an activity which neither the systems nor their campuses have often undertaken on their own initiative. There is some indication that the central administrators of the multicampus universities occasionally welcome planning requirements set by the coordinating agency as an "excuse" to encourage plans by the campuses.

Third, the political vulnerability of the coordinating agency is not an unmitigated misfortune. Academic tradition and prestige often put constraints on needed flexibility. The credibility of a multicampus university both with its own campuses and with the public at large is surely attributable to a major extent to its being created in the pattern of most universities in most places. For the same reason, however, it may be less suited to solve those problems in higher education which do not fit the traditional mold. There may not be any broad solutions, of course, and there certainly are no simple ones. But if innovation is required, it may be the less prestigious coordinating agency that will prove productive. The very vulnerability of the coordinating agencies to political forces may force them into forms and activity more in keeping with the changing times.

The Single Board: Coordination and Governance "Single-board" states have what is usually designated a "governing" form of coordination. This approach to statewide organization of higher education places all campuses in a state (generally excluding two-year colleges) under one governing board and does not utilize local campus boards in other than a strictly advisory capacity. Single boards had a spurt of popularity some years ago, dropped out of fashion, but may be making a comeback. (Five states have adopted the pattern in the last decade, for a total of nineteen.) While our investigation did not include any single-board states, the State University of New York approximates single-board operation in many ways. In addition, in two states — California and North Carolina — recommendations for a single board were made by the coordinating agency or consultants from 1968 to 1970.

The existence of single-board states, however, does reinforce our impression that the description of coordinating agencies as "coordinating" or "governing" is an exercise in futility. Glenny (1959), Pliner (1966), Paltridge (1965), and Berdahl (1971) have done great service in capturing and categorizing the variety of these state agencies. To understand their impact on the campuses of a multicampus university, however, the word *coordination* might well be abandoned.

In our view, "coordinating" is misleading because it indicates that there is something which the state agency does that the multicampus university does not. Governance, the term we prefer, is certainly broad enough to embrace coordination, and does not fragment or confuse the slender lines of authority that can be traced from governor and legislature to professor and student. We have already made the point that certain state administrative agencies concerned with the budget, purchasing, civil service authorities, and the like, are often part of the governing structure of higher education. The same argument is even more applicable to the coordinating agency. Since the question of whether a campus is permitted to offer a degree in fine arts is answered in different states by the campus, by the multicampus university, or by the coordinating agency, it borders on sophistry to pretend that in the last instance the coordinating agency is not exercising governing functions. Similarly, with such questions as admission standards, building programs, campus enrollment ceilings, and faculty salaries, there are levels of governance. While the distinction between them can be of immense importance, the step in the hierarchy between a multicampus system level and the statewide coordinating agency level does not require a different name any more than the step between campus and system.

FEDERAL PROGRAMS The impact of the federal government on individual campuses has been the object of other studies. There are, at this writing, however, no comparable studies of the ways state governments have organized to receive federal funds, nor of the influence such organization may have on higher education within the state. Federal programs and procedures can be crucial in the relationships among the individual faculty members, their campus, the multicampus university, the coordinating agency, and state government itself.

Federal funds are often allocated to campuses or multicampus universities through an agency designated by the state to plan on a statewide basis. Where the coordinating agency of the state acts as the designated agency, there is little doubt that such designation has enhanced its authority (Cox and Harrell, 1969, p. 63). For example, with extremely limited planning facilities and staff, the coordinating agency in one state has requested extensive and detailed information from all institutions of higher education. Any doubt about the ability of the coordinating agency to analyze such a great amount of information disappears in the light of the federal funding involved (Select Committee, 1968, p. 40):

The current appropriation within the . . . [coordinating agency] . . . for higher education planning purposes is less than $145,000.

There is a separate planning group funded through the Federal Higher Education Facilities Act with six full-time staff members, a coordinator, and several consultants. A grant of $265,000 for the current year is provided specifically for a detailed facilities inventory on each campus and related collection. As matters stand the state is undoubtedly obtaining more useful planning information from this limited source than from the small state funds noted above.

Where designation of a state agency is required, by federal law, the coordinating agency appears to be the primary choice. In one state, the governing board of the multicampus university is the designated agency for two federal programs, both generally concerned with continuing education and extension. Such designation is particularly appropriate because of centralization of these functions at the multicampus system level. On the other hand, in another state with less, but still substantial centralization, the designated agent is neither the multicampus university nor the coordinating agency, but rather a separate and specially formed state board. A third form of designation exists in a state in which the multicampus university is the designated agency for the administration of certain federal funds, but has delegated the authority to one of its campuses.

By far, the bulk of federal funds not channeled through a designated state agency are research grants or contracts. Organizational structure, whether multicampus or coordinating agency, has little influence on these. The faculty negotiates most of them as individuals, and for all practical purposes, the faculty "owns" them despite some procedural control at system level.

Federal funds for general support are a continuing and controversial subject. Should funds go to individual students as scholarships to be used at any campus? To the states for internal allocation? To the institutions directly? The answers to such questions require knowledge of the differential impact of alternative federal strategies on the organization of higher education in each state—matters beyond the scope of this study. The patterns of interaction between the coordinating agency and the campuses and multicampus universities change with the flow of federal funds, as does the particular balance in each state between public and private higher education. The way in which support is given can be as critical as the amount. We can only suggest that federal funding is complex and probably has unintended consequences which do not take into account the variety of ways in which higher education, public and private, is organized within the boundaries of each state.

SUMMARY   Nine dynamic and changing multicampus institutions have been
selected for study at a particular moment of time in accordance
with gross structural criteria. They are also firmly embedded in
particular states, each with the traditions, economy, and politics
like no other. In each state, the patterns of organization and
authority of higher education, existing and proposed, are major
political issues. Politicians and academic administrators alike
clearly understand that the structure of higher education is not
neutral. Through the interplay of the various groups and individuals, differing values and goals are implicit in the differing ways
in which a state organizes higher education. However, the precise
goals or values which attach to particular forms of organization are
not known. Allowing only one multicampus university in a state to
offer a doctorate may represent a commitment to quality in the form
of research and graduate education. If the balance of public higher
education is also organized as a multicampus university which does
not offer the doctorate, then it represents a commitment to quality
in the form of a teaching institution. The only generally accepted
definition of *quality* is that which is applicable to the graduate,
research-oriented major university. Harvard, Yale, Berkeley, and
Madison are all in this category. What is a quality teaching institution, however? *Private* campuses in this category may not
abound, but some can be named without difficulty — Swarthmore,
Oberlin, for example, although even their teaching missions are
limited ones. The name of a *public* campus in the same category
does not readily come to mind. Old Westbury or Santa Cruz, perhaps, but these new public campuses reach for the same goal as
their prestigious private counterparts: national repute. Some other
definitions of quality, we suggest, would be more appropriate for
the far greater number of teaching institutions — New Paltz, Chico
State, and Greensboro — and for the variety of educational goals
they hope to serve.

    This study does not rate campuses or multicampus universities
along the lines of the Roose-Anderson Report (1970) in its ranking
of graduate programs. Such rating or evaluation, however, is often
close to the surface of any discussion of organization of higher
education within a state. The major university campuses in multicampus systems generally fear inclusion under a governing structure with the rest of higher education (i.e., as in a single-board
state). These graduate, research-oriented campuses have a vague,
abstract feeling that the value of the term *university* will be diluted,
and more tangible concerns that the commitment to research may

be jeopardized and fiscal support levels dropped for the benefit of the undergraduate, teaching-oriented institutions. On occasion, too, teaching institutions are concerned that their interests will be lost or submerged if they are administered along with the research-oriented campus or campuses. In several of the multicampus universities, these concerns are being weighed. In the State University of New York, particularly, the challenge of successfully framing, encouraging, and maintaining differing definitions of quality is most clearly presented.

The organization of higher education in the state is assuredly an important factor in the future of the nine multicampus universities which are the object of this study. Is the overall structure segmental or otherwise? Are all campuses included within a multicampus system or are there autonomous institutions? How strong is the coordinating agency? What organizational changes are being proposed? Do two-year campuses aspire to become four-year institutions and the colleges to become university campuses?

As important as these organizational questions are and as crucial in a specific situation as they might be, they are secondary to the social, economic, and political climate in which the multicampus university exists. The questions whose answers seem truly determinative to the future of the multicampus systems are beyond those of formal or informal organizational structure. How rich is the state and how willing to support higher education? What is the state's population? Is it growing? What is the age distribution? What sort of political leaders with what sort of attitudes are likely to be produced by the state's social and political climate? What elements in the economy depend on research and trained graduates? These at a minimum are some of the basic determinants of the future of the nine multicampus universities in the seven states, indeed, of higher education in the 1970s.

3. Organization and History of the Multicampus University

No easy distinction separates the *external* pressures and influences exerted on a multicampus system by its environment, considered in the previous chapter, and the *internal* pressures of a system's own organization and history. Here, we indicate major factors influencing governance which are part of the general context of the nine universities.

We do *not* attempt to trace the individual histories of the nine multicampus systems in detail, but we do point out the major turning points in the development of each university as these were brought to our attention. The resulting generalizations do not, however, serve as the major and separate historical study which each system deserves but few have received.

The question of *what* a multicampus university is cannot be separated from the question of *when* whatever existed previously became such a system. By our definition, a multicampus university came into being when a *separate* systemwide chief executive with the academic-administrative title of president or chancellor was interposed between the campus executives and the governing board, or—as sometimes happened—when a separate executive on the main campus was interposed between the system executive and the campus administration. In a sense, this definition is an artifact to allow exploration of the allocation of governing authority in selected universities on the assumption that they are similar. Because it grossly understates the richness and complexity of the multicampus structure as a continuing institution, we emphasize the changing structures and processes rather than those existing at the time of the study.

Perhaps the most striking characteristic of the multicampus universities is the tentativeness of their organizational form, a tentativeness not always or merely the result of newness. Almost all systems are on shakedown cruises of one kind or another, even the older and more established ones. One was described as having been on a shakedown cruise for the past four or five years, changing its organizational course so frequently that both seasoned administrators and determined students of higher education were anxiously awaiting arrival at a safe harbor.

Our definition of a multicampus university, based largely on the title and separateness of the office of the system executive, was satisfactory to most observers. However, while accepting the definition as adequate, many had their own concepts of just when their system had become or would become a "true" multicampus university. Although subject to almost endless refinement and combination, the six concepts listed below are fairly exhaustive. Not all these six were found in all systems, and most definitions had much to do with the autonomy of campuses. We ourselves are not convinced that our definition, as useful as we believe it to be, is any more useful or correct than these others. The "true" multicampus university, then, is said to become such:

1 *The single executive budget.* When the system executive has a "decisive" role in budget formulation, probably when a single executive budget for the entire university is introduced.

2 *Appointment of campus executives.* When the system executive recommends the appointment of the campus executives, and none are appointed without such recommendation.

3 *Line and staff.* When all administrators at the campus report to the campus executive, and all lines of authority from campus level to multicampus level run through the campus executive.

4 *Campus administrative authority.* When the campus executive has specified authority commensurate with his responsibility and status. Definitions of the specific areas of such authority and whether it should be "substantial" or "total" produce endless argument. Major suggestions are: (a) academic and administrative appointments and promotions; (b) budget transfers of all but most critical items; and (c) flexibility to organize the campus administration.

5 *Symbolism.* (a) When the system executive moves his office or residence away from the flagship campus. (b) When the football team of a newer campus within the system beats that of the flagship campus. (c) When the campus executives are not (or are) representatives to prestigious national educational groups.

6 *Faculty authority.* When the *campus* faculty controls its own academic destiny, free from detailed regulation by either the system administration or any systemwide faculty organization. Or, paradoxically, when the *systemwide* faculty organization has control over *its* academic destiny.

In common parlance, and for our purposes, *both* the multicampus university *and* each of its campuses are "educational" or "academic" institutions. Applying usual measures of authority appropriate for an individual campus with its own governing board to only one of these — the system as a whole or any campus — to determine the authority that it "should have" strips the other of its claims to being an academic institution. *Both* campus *and* system must share this traditional authority in a true multicampus university.

The criterion of faculty authority above is suggestive. If the campus faculty which conducts academic programs has little or no influence over their initiation, content, or termination, then such campus lacks, we believe, an essential element of an institution of higher education. If, to the contrary, the campus faculty has *complete* control over such programs, then the multicampus system — the sum of *all* campuses *and* the central administration — is simply a state budgetary category.

The generality of the six concepts obscures their true complexity. For example, when does a campus have more authority over appointments? When the campus executive has all his recommendations for faculty appointments approved without question by the system, even though he lacks formal authority? Or when he has complete formal appointing authority for all nontenure appointments, but tenure appointees are carefully screened at the multicampus level?

The possibly theoretical question of how much autonomy or authority a campus should have in specific areas is a very real one that assumes concrete proportions in the situational and personal relationships between system and campus executives. The latter may well reveal more about the actual operations of a multicampus university than formal rules and policies. For example, one system executive talks about another:

His theory of administration? He never had any theory! When he was at the campus he wanted authority at the campus. Now that he's at the system level, he wants authority there. That's his theory.

A system executive discusses a former campus executive who left to become head of an institution in another state:

It didn't take more than a couple of weeks after he took over the campus for us both to know that he wanted to run the show by himself. He's doing that now, and believe me, he's happier and I'm happier.

These statements suggest that the true multicampus university depends more upon specific allocations of authority than on our structural definition. We do know, however, that titles are not totally irrelevant. The designation of a president or chancellor, as well as being a status symbol in the academic world, both assumes and vests substantial authority in its holder. It became clear early in the course of the study, however, that the multi-campus systems selected on the basis of the structural criteria were very diverse institutions indeed.

The following pages point out significant diversities and similarities and relate these to changes over time. We commence, however, with a disclaimer: We neither know nor could find agreement on when either the branch campuses of a system originating from a single campus became so independent, or the central administration of a system originating in an aggregation of existing campuses became so strong, that a true multicampus university came into being.

THE ORIGINS OF THE MULTICAMPUS UNIVERSITIES

The nine multicampus universities developed in two distinct patterns: *Consolidated* systems resulted from the aggregation under a new central administration and governing board, of previously existing campuses. *Flagship* systems resulted from the extension of an established campus into a system either by the creation of new campuses or the absorption of old ones.[1] The different origins are reflected in the title of the system executive. With one exception (University of North Carolina) the title *chancellor* is used in the consolidated universities, while the title *president* is retained by the several campus executives. In contrast, again with one exception

[1] The word *flagship* can be misleading, and it is important to remember that it describes history and origins, not necessarily the current status of the campus. For example, UCLA sails a course of its own and has left its imprint on other campuses, but its faculty committee structure can be traced to the Berkeley influence of the 1930s. More descriptive than *flagship*, the term *colonial* has pejorative connotations. We left it unused lest it reappear on picket signs at more than one of the campuses which were visited.

(University of Texas), the titles are reversed in the flagship systems. Typically, when the head of the main campus moved to leadership of the system, he retained his old title of president, and the new campus executives became chancellors.

It is not accidental that Texas and North Carolina are the exceptions. Inclusion of North Carolina as a consolidated system understates the importance of Chapel Hill, a campus so prestigious that it was described as a "state monument." Alternatively, the inclusion of Texas in the second category, with Austin as its flagship, obscures the fact that its growth has been less an extension of Austin than an attachment of campuses to Austin. Furthermore, consolidated systems, once established, have frequently assumed responsibility for the creation of new campuses, a development characteristic of expanding flagship systems. In contrast, the merger of a previously existing autonomous campus into a flagship system has elements of a consolidated system.

Both *organizational* and *administrative* questions are critical to this study. The first revolves around numbers, types, and sizes of the constituent campuses, and how these became part of a system; the second involves the establishment of the multicampus administrative structure as here defined — separate system and campus executives. A generalization may relate these two facets. The organizational substance of a system — its numbers and types of campuses — generally results from *external* pressures and needs. On the other hand, the administrative form or structure is attributable to *internal* factors. Rapidly expanding demands for admission require establishment of new campuses, and this pressure of numbers is reinforced by local or regional political pressure. Most systems consisted of more than one campus for some period of time before a separate system executive was appointed or ceased serving as a campus executive.

The Consolidated Systems

Of the nine multicampus universities, four originated as aggregations of previously existing campuses. Subsequently, each then established or acquired new campuses much like the flagship systems.

The University of North Carolina was formed by the shotgun wedding of three previously independent campuses at Chapel Hill, Greensboro, and Raleigh. Economy was the explicit reason and, in 1931, a crucial one. The first major act of the new system was to reallocate major academic programs. Engineering went to North

Carolina State College at Raleigh; business administration to the University of North Carolina at Chapel Hill. Initially, a president was appointed for the university, with each campus headed by a vice-president, a title changed in 1934 to dean of administration and in 1945 to chancellor. From its beginning, the multicampus system has had a small—indeed minimal—central administration. Many major decisions of resource allocation were—and are—negotiated directly between the campuses and the state, with relatively little system participation.

"A loose confederation held together by the legislative budget commission" is one description, for this state agency holds much of the authority found elsewhere in governing boards and system executives. When the study began, there were four campuses, including one established at Charlotte in 1965, but two more were added late in 1969. North Carolina differs from the other consolidated systems primarily because of the prestige of its main campus at Chapel Hill. Of the consolidated systems, only City College in the City University of New York system has a comparable status and history *within* its system. A second unusual feature of the North Carolina scene is the strength within the system of the North Carolina State campus at Raleigh. Only UCLA in California is a stronger "second campus."

The California State Colleges were united by the California Master Plan legislation of 1960 under a single board and separate system executive, designated chancellor. The 14 campuses then in existence had been administered by the state Board of Education. Despite detailed state fiscal constraints, these campuses were then headed by strong and relatively autonomous campus executives—presidents. The level of state control has been modified to give greater authority to the board and the system executive, but a high degree of state supervision still remains. The original 14 campuses grew to 19 by 1970, and several are comparable to many universities in size and qualifications of faculty and students. Under the California Master Plan, however, these campuses cannot award doctoral degrees on their own, a controversial limitation.[2]

The City University of New York is of complex origin. Both City College and Hunter College were originally under the city

[2] Joint doctoral degrees with either private universities or the University of California can be authorized by the coordinating agency.

Board of Education, and then had separate boards which were merged in 1926 into the Board of *Higher* Education. Until the name was changed to City University in 1961 and authority to award doctoral degrees given, the complaint at the campuses was similar to that in the California State College system: they had the ". . . largest pool of Ph.D.s [in the nation] not yet being used as a faculty for doctoral work" (Holy, 1962, p. *lx*). In addition to the older, well-known campuses—City College, Hunter, Brooklyn, and Queens—there were six other four-year and six two-year campuses in 1969, along with a unique, physically separate, systemwide graduate center and an affiliated medical school. Half of City University's operating income is furnished by New York City and half by the state, and the State University of New York has certain supervisory authority over the two-year campuses. As in the California State Colleges, the strength of the campus executives (presidents) was quite substantial before appointment of a separate system executive (chancellor) in 1960. These campus executives are still meeting as a collegial body with authority over many questions, but the office of the system executive has gained increasing authority in the recent past.

The State University of New York comes very close to being a "single board" for the entire state, a type of multicampus system not included in the study. Only the geographically distinct City University prevents the State University from comprising all public campuses in New York State. While this exception is of immense significance, some elements of the governance of the State University are undoubtedly more often associated with single boards than with multicampus structures constituting only a part of all state higher education. In 1948, a variety of two- and four-year campuses—none a university—were placed under a new board and new system executive, designated a chancellor. In 1969, the State University consisted of 30 campuses, of which four either had or were approaching intended university status. Eleven others were four-year liberal arts campuses, two were medical centers, and seven were specialized professional schools. The State University also governs six two-year colleges directly and, in addition, has limited supervisory authority over 31 locally governed two-year colleges. By 1969, only two of the directly governed 30 campuses enrolled more than 10,000 students. (In the California State Colleges, in contrast, 10 campuses exceeded the enrollment figure of 10,000.)

Characteristics of the consolidated systems

The four consolidated multicampus systems have certain features not shared with the flagship systems. First, and perhaps the most obvious characteristic of the consolidated systems, is the location of the central offices. Three have central offices clearly isolated from any campus. On the other hand, of the five flagship systems in 1969, all maintained system offices either on or adjacent to the main campus, as did North Carolina, which resembles the flagship systems in many ways. Location has implications other than simple distance, of course. Only in North Carolina, of the four consolidated systems, does the public, as well as faculty and students, identify the central administration with a particular campus. Such identification, however, is found in all five flagship systems.

The second characteristic relates to the governing boards. All four consolidated systems have local advisory boards or standing committees, special or liaison, of the governing board for each of their campuses. Although these local governing arrangements vary so greatly that the contrasts are at least as striking as the similarities, the fact remains that they do exist. Comparable boards or committees do not exist in the five flagship systems, and no consideration has been given to separate boards as new campuses have been added. While these local arrangements in the consolidated systems are a heritage of the independent pasts of the older campuses, they are more than mere relics. Three of the four consolidated systems are considering strengthening the local governing boards or committees. No flagship system, on the other hand, is giving serious consideration to establishing them.

None of these local arrangements seriously influenced the development of the multicampus systems. Historically, their usefulness has been largely what the campus executive has wished it to be. Current proposals to give such local boards or committees a more substantial governing role are based on hopes of what might be, rather than any clearly proven value in the past. Because of history, however, these hopes can be built on existing structures.

These two structural distinctions are readily visible, although their consequences are less so. Even less apparent are the implications of shifts in authority that have occurred when a new central administrative structure is interposed between the state and relatively independent campuses. Three related but still distinct impressions came to our attention. Essentially, all three arise from the difficulties of inserting a new layer of authority—the system administration—between the campuses and the state agencies with which they have previously dealt directly.

The first problem is simply *finding* an area of authority with the appearance of legitimacy for both the state and the campuses. This problem can be seen most clearly in contrast to the situation of the flagship systems. In a flagship system, when the major campus establishes a new campus, the central administration and commonly the faculty of the flagship campus are recognized as having proper authority over virtually any activity at the new campus. While the new campus may resent this authority and quickly become restive when it is not delegated, there is rarely the feeling that the central administration should not exercise it in the first place. Such feeling is not uncommon, however, on the campuses of the consolidated systems.

Prior history of direct dealing with state agencies has complicated the beginnings of a consolidated system in a second fashion. State constraints on salaries, purchasing, or construction, while by no means previously accepted without complaint, nevertheless are *externally* imposed. With the advent of the multicampus structure, the same or somewhat less burdensome constraints become *internal*—a family affair. Although the integrity and competence of "Sacramento," "across the river," or "downtown" (i.e., the state governmental offices) are rarely questioned, campus faculty and administrators clearly suspect that no state agency can ever really understand higher education. Red tape and delay are expected evils, but it comes as a shock that these evils do not cease when Professor Chips leaves the campus to become Vice-President Chips at the system level. The shock may last about ten years.

A third factor affects campus executives in at least two ways. First, new system executives inevitably and early stake out claims on personal contacts with the state government and often with the governing board. While most campus executives see this as a proper division of labor, some have clearly resented their system executive's claim to be the primary if not the sole channel to government. Second, new campus executives are generally more amenable to the authority which recruited them—the system executive— than are those whose tenure antedates that authority.

The Flagship Systems The five remaining multicampus universities, designated as flagship systems, had their origins in a single main campus from which the larger university developed.

Growth took three basic forms: (1) The main campus set up branches—two-year, four-year, or professional—clearly subordinate to it; the branch-campus executive generally had a title such as dean and reported to the president of the main campus. As the branch campuses grew in size and number, pressures arose from both the branches and main campus for separate campus executives with authority and a more prestigious title. Typically, the main campus executive assumed leadership of the entire system, retaining his title as president, while chancellors were appointed to head the campuses. (2) The multicampus system itself, not its major campus, created a new campus. (3) Either the major campus or the system acquired or had attached to it an already existing campus, public or private. Four of the five systems in this flagship category grew by means of all three of the above forms, the fifth by two.

University of California. The flagship campus, Berkeley, established specialized medical and agricultural branches relatively early in its history. A two-year branch in Los Angeles quickly emerged as a separate four-year and graduate institution. Other campuses were either established around specialized activities (e.g., San Diego around the Scripps Oceanographic Research Station), built from the ground up (e.g., Santa Cruz), or acquired from the state college system (e.g., Santa Barbara). While the university had several campuses headed by deans and provosts for much of its history, the pattern of a decentralized multicampus system, with considerable campus autonomy, did not develop until the 1950s. This was signaled by the use of the title *chancellor* for the campus executives, which first occurred in 1952 for the Berkeley and Los Angeles campuses, and was extended thereafter to all. In 1969, there were nine campuses (one of which was concerned with the health sciences) and no immediate plans for expansion.

University of Illinois. The flagship campus at Urbana long maintained a separate medical center in Chicago, which was first headed by an executive dean and later by a vice-president. Following World War II, an undergraduate program was established in Chicago ("Navy Pier"), which was initially headed by a dean and then a vice-president. This program was succeeded by the present Chicago Circle campus program in 1965. Substantial administrative authority for the campus at Urbana was delegated to the provost. The two campus executives in Chicago and a new executive in Urbana were given the title of chancellor during the years 1966 to 1968. Most administrative services were then reorganized during this period to reflect the chancellorship system on the three campuses.

University of Missouri. For many years, the flagship campus at Columbia included a specialized engineering school, which was geographically separated from the main campus although organizationally part of it. The dean at Rolla who headed the school did so with no greater or less authority than other deans located on the main campus. Almost simultaneously in 1963, a new campus in St. Louis was developed out of and on the site of a former two-year college and the private University of Kansas City was acquired. By 1964, the executives of all four campuses had the title of chancellor under a president freed from all direct campus operating responsibilities.

University of Texas. In addition to the flagship campus at Austin, the university for many years maintained several medical and health branches. The heads of these reported to the president at Austin. A mining college, established in El Paso in 1913 as part of the university, gradually emerged into a general academic institution. The Arlington campus was acquired from the Texas A & M System in 1965. During the 1960s, the system executive served on occasion as head of the Austin campus; his title was variously chancellor and president, the former term being in use in 1969, while the general campus executives, including the one at Austin, were designated as presidents. In 1969, the legislature authorized the university to establish seven new units, a general four-year campus, two upper-division campuses, and four schools in the health professions.

University of Wisconsin. Madison, the flagship campus, was the only campus of the university for most of its history, although after World War I numerous lower-division, two-year branches were established throughout the state. In 1956, the Milwaukee campus was acquired from the state college system, the campus executive having the title of provost. In 1963, a provost was appointed for the Madison campus, and in 1964, the title of chancellor was given to both four-year campus executives as well as to the executive officer of the two-year center system. By 1969, two new four-year campuses, each headed by a chancellor, had developed out of six of the two-year centers. Each of the seven remaining two-year centers was headed by a dean.

The influence of the flagship campus

The unique and dominant feature of these five systems is, of course, the flagship campus. These campuses were first in historical terms, and, in most cases, the main if not the only public university in their states for many years. At some point, a single chief administrator was the executive of both the flagship campus and the system as a whole. Although, by definition, this duality has disappeared, in 1969 central administrative offices were always just across the hall, down the street, or in the next block from the office of the flagship campus executive. Nuances of history and personality have created subtle variations in each system, but the general pattern is one of substantial and continuing influence from the main campus.

In the chapters which follow—those concerning administration and academic plans in particular—the influence of the flagship campuses will be considered in detail. The influence operates on the multicampus system as a whole and upon each campus. For example, we have already noted that North Carolina's Chapel Hill campus could easily be included in the category of a flagship campus for most purposes. This is true not only because of popular identification of the system executive with that campus, but to a lesser extent because of the continuing impact of Chapel Hill on the *system,* if not the other campuses. The same is true of each of the five flagship systems to one degree or another.

Flagship campuses are more than simply the oldest and largest institutions of the particular system. They are also major influences in higher education throughout the United States. Jencks and Riesman (1968, p. 168) make the point that graduate education is almost wholly nationalized in both public and private campuses, and comment:

The University of Wisconsin and the University of North Carolina, for example, are certainly different from one another, but they are nowhere nearly as different from one another as both are from the other institutions in their respective states.

The authors were undoubtedly referring to the Madison and Chapel Hill campuses of the two universities.

Again, a recent journal article (Carter, 1969) mentioned "Rice, Duke, and the University of North Carolina" as "rivals in quality" to the Austin campus of the University of Texas. The article, five pages long, devoted a single sentence to all nine other units and campuses of the University of Texas.[3] Madison, Chapel Hill, Austin, and each of the other flagship campuses indeed compete in two worlds. In one world, each is closely related to the state which supports it and to the region from which it draws its students—at least most of its undergraduates. In this locally oriented world, it competes with other public campuses for state funds, and with them and nearby private campuses for students. This same competition takes place internally where the flagship campus is forced to compete with its multicampus siblings. The second world is the broader, national one. It involves relationships with the federal government, for the flagship campuses are "federal-grant" universities. Faculty and graduate students dependent on federal research funds come from all over the country and often the world. In this national arena, the flagship campuses compete with each other and the national educational establishment for resources.

The impact of this overlapping competition among the flagship campuses themselves cannot readily be assessed in this study. However, three implications which their national status has for the university system and its campuses are apparent. First, in each flagship system there is a definite tendency for administrators and faculty alike to look to the values of graduate education and its research orientation—the values of the older, main campus—as establishing a single definition of quality for the entire university. Second, national competitive pressures seem to be transmitted through the flagship campus to the other campuses, pressures which in some instances are unrelated to local and state conditions. Academic salaries, for example, may be determined on a national scale for the flagship campus and then extended to the other campuses either "to keep peace in the family" or out of the conviction that all should be in fact equal to the flagship campus. Third and finally, there is a very real spillover of prestige from the flagship campus to the others and indeed to the system itself.

A recurrent theme of this study is that these features are a mixed blessing. Within the systems themselves, however, the implications

---

[3] In the University of California system, however, UCLA had clearly emerged as a "rival in quality" to Berkeley. In a somewhat different fashion and to a lesser extent, North Carolina State was a "second campus" which had doubts about the continuing dominance of the system's main campus at Chapel Hill.

of having such a campus were generally described as positive for all except the main campus itself. At only one or two flagship campuses was specific concern expressed over a drain of resources to other campuses. A more general attitude was that flagship campuses bring more to the system than it brings to them. However, a perceptive executive at one flagship campus suggested that while the balance of payments might be currently turning against his campus, he could look "down the road a piece" to the time when he would need the system's broader political base. A system executive commented to the same effect: "Remote campuses are an 'outpost line' against incursions from the state even though the flagship campus does not appreciate this benefit."

New Campuses Of the nine university systems, only one has not established a new campus within the recent past. Subsequent chapters describe ways in which birth pangs of new campuses have been eased by the larger university system. Here, five general observations are important. Within a multicampus university:

1 A planning organization is in existence to undertake or assist in both academic and physical planning for a new campus.

2 A new campus presents an opportunity—perhaps realistically the *only* opportunity—for innovation or reform.

3 Variety and experimentation have a better opportunity—not always fully realized—to flourish within a broader educational and administrative context, which can act as a shield or buffer during formative periods of growth.

4 Despite its value as a buffer, the multicampus university itself can be a determinant in perhaps less desirable ways, perpetuating both educational and administrative patterns or anachronisms.

5 Age appears as a factor in governance only in the flagship systems. In consolidated systems, all campuses, whether encompassed by the original consolidation or established later, seem on an even footing; more importantly, system policies and procedures have been developed without the influence of a single dominant campus. In the flagship systems, on the other hand, the age and size of the "second campus" in the system is a factor in the pattern of system relationships with all other campuses. For example, UCLA, Milwaukee, and Chicago Circle have all had an impact on their system administrations, the flagship campuses, and, in California and Wisconsin, on newer campuses in the university. Each has reached size, promise, and sophistication to justify the measure of independence evi-

denced by the title of chancellor for the campus executive. But reorganization of a second campus alone is impossible, for the substance of independence also brings pressures for parallel changes at the flagship campus. The system executive must withdraw a step from the flagship campus and allow it to establish a separate chief executive. Moreover, both formally and informally, these second campuses often serve as models for newer campuses which usually have more in common with them than with the older, flagship campuses.

This development of systemwide patterns from earlier second-campus relationships is going on in all the flagship universities. In one, an administrator from the second campus noted that his colleagues were fighting battles with both the system and the flagship campus for increased autonomy; new campuses within the system would benefit subsequently without having to pay the same price in terms of time, energy, and a loss of personal goodwill.

Absorption and Transition of Existing Campuses The creation of *new* campuses such as Old Westbury, Santa Cruz, or Green Bay is difficult, to say the least. However, differing aspirations of the campus and system can be resolved by the institutional experience, procedures, and practices of the multicampus university. Bringing an *existing* campus into a multicampus system or changing its educational purpose is more troublesome. Often both transitions are contemporaneous, compounding the difficulties. Furthermore, the resolution involves the traditions and experience of *both* the system and the campus. These problems appear under two general categories: (1) change of educational mission from "college" to "university" and (2) transition from private to public control or from one system to another.

Transition from college to university

All the multicampus universities (excluding the California State Colleges) have had campuses at one stage or another of the transition from a college with a predominantly teaching orientation to a university with a research and graduate orientation. In general, the major implications—aside from the obvious one of universitywide control over academic programs—have been in the area of personnel: (1) the prior existence of the campus practically ensures that a substantial number of faculty and administrators prefer to teach and work at a relatively small liberal arts college than to do research at a large campus oriented to graduate education. Not all professors are partisans of Jencks and Riesman's "academic revolution"

(1968). (2) Campus administrators—campus executives in particular—are not always familiar enough with the mores of the graduate education and research "establishment" to guide their campus. (3) Faculty qualifications for appointment, promotion, and tenure in the two kinds of campuses now joined by the transition often differ sharply, and doing justice to both the continuing individual and the changing institution is always a delicate task.

The role of the multicampus system is to advise, encourage, and control. The problems which such campuses face are often alleviated by sympathetic and sophisticated universitywide administration.

Another form of transition is similar to that of moving a campus from college to university status, one where several campuses in different systems are in various stages of transition from predominantly local and regional orientation to a broader role in the national scene. At one outstanding urban campus, portions of the faculty who had previously been seriously concerned with local continuing education and extension seemed to be isolated from their newer, research-oriented, and more cosmopolitan colleagues. Similar schizophrenia was evidenced at a rural campus by a lengthy faculty document which criticized a planning instrument as too oriented to agriculture in view of the new and broader campus mission. On the same page as this general criticism, however, the document was more specific. It criticized the characterization of students as a "product as though they were a crop of rice."

Transition from without to within the system

The second form of transition is that of a campus moving from outside the system into it. Among the nine universities, examples of such transition have involved both private and public campuses. Public campuses were occasionally part of another system of higher education prior to their merger into the multicampus university. In general, the problems of entry of a *public* campus into an existing multicampus system are shaped primarily by a contemporaneous transition from college to university status. At the time of the study, only North Carolina had proposed that an existing public campus be added *without* changing its liberal arts, undergraduate orientation to that of a full-fledged university campus.

The transition of a *private* campus into a public multicampus university is unavoidably difficult. Both of the examples in the study (Kansas City and Buffalo) contained elements of personal and institutional trauma, based largely upon the prior campus history of relatively informal methods of governance and fiscal accountability. Although a number of years have passed since the two mergers, some suspicion still remains on the part of the faculty as to universitywide intentions in particular academic areas. On the whole, however, *academic* questions have been fairly easily resolved. Freshman English is freshman English, whether a campus is public or private. *Business* and *fiscal* areas, on the other hand, are another matter. State civil service regulations and centralized purchasing procedures can be troublesome and arbitrary, even for those who have known nothing else. For administrators or faculty whose only experience has been in private higher education, these bureaucratic phenomena, together with the added complexities of the system itself, sometimes assume nightmare proportions.

In short, while in both instances the transition relieved serious financial pressure, some have considered the cost in loss of autonomy to be too great. This attitude has been particularly fostered by those who were on the campus prior to the mergers, for institutional memory of the "good old days" runs deep and long.

Despite the dictation of these mergers by financial necessity, the multicampus universities and merged campuses seem to have benefited, although not everyone admits it. For the campuses, the association has brought immediate financial support, but more crucially, the security of substantially greater long-term stability because of public support. For the systems, the formerly private campuses have introduced new or at least different concepts of campus and systemwide governance. In one instance, the private campus has exemplified to the multicampus system that higher education need not be managed like any other state agency and has initiated liberalized system business procedures. Less tangible but equally important have been the long traditions of academic freedom which one campus brought to a relatively new system.

The origin of the multicampus system, whether consolidated or flagship, is relatively less important to a campus than the way in which it joined the system. In two specific instances, the important key to understanding the relationship of a particular campus to the central administration was said to be that the campus had "never been under" the major campus in the system. In one instance the conversation was about a consolidated system and in the other about a flagship system.

The Separate Graduate School

The organization of graduate education was not a criterion by which multicampus systems were selected for the study. Such organization is very closely related, however, to our criterion of separate system and campus executives. Just as the separate campus executive is an index of prestige and greater local *administrative* authority, so the separate, campus-based graduate school usually evidences greater local *academic* authority.

Many systems—particularly those arising out of a flagship campus—controlled graduate education by a single, universitywide graduate school for some time after several campuses were authorized to conduct such programs. Such single graduate schools, universally and quite naturally dominated by flagship campus faculty, were of substantial benefit to other campuses in the review of academic programs and other graduate affairs. Like many other benefits handed down from above, however, such dominance created restiveness in those benefited. Establishment of a separate graduate school has been clearly viewed as an educational declaration of independence by faculty at a newer campus. The independence, it should be noted, is not from systemwide review, for this is always present for some purposes in every system. The independence is from the detailed—"humiliating," in the opinion of one campus dean—review of local programs by faculty from the *flagship campus.* The separate graduate school formally places the graduate faculty of all campuses on a par.

The thrust of most campuses in the systems is to be as much like an individual campus under a separate governing board as possible, and the separate graduate school issue illustrates this. This factor, as much as actual resentment of flagship faculty, may have brought about separate campus graduate schools. The same pressure for campus control of graduate education is found in the City University of New York, which has established a single universitywide graduate school, an organizationally and physically separate structure under a provost (changed to president in 1970). This experiment has been under attack by campus faculty and administrators, even though the City University—a consolidated system—lacks a flagship campus.

The Urban Campuses

A striking feature in six systems which have both a major campus and the system staff in a small city is a newly acquired or established urban campus. When several of the older campuses were established, it was thought desirable to insulate the young from the temptations of city life. In three instances, even location at a state capital did not mean location at the major population center of the state. In the 1960s, in contrast, universities were actively seeking urban campuses.[4]

The prime example of an "urban branch" in the minds of those at new city campuses is the Los Angeles campus of the University of California. Enrollment at UCLA is not only greater than at the "mother campus" at Berkeley, but its medical school enrollment alone almost exceeds that of the university's separate medical campus in San Francisco. Perhaps more indicative of maturity than size alone, federal obligations to UCLA for research and development in 1969 exceeded those to Berkeley.

Although the present study is not pointed toward the "urban crisis," our visits to city campuses were not accidental. These campuses, quite as much as the major campus, are where something new is happening. Not only have they benefited from the incremental growth that permits innovation, but they seem to have greater willingness to take advantage of such permission by moving out of traditional educational channels.

The cities, whatever shape they take, will determine the country's future, and the form they assume may well be influenced by the educational institutions they contain or spawn. Urban campuses have great problems in faculty, in students, in curriculum, and in community relations. Yet these same problems are also great opportunities, some of which have implications for the multicampus university.

In three systems (Illinois, North Carolina, and Texas), universitywide urban research centers or institutes are located at or directed from an urban campus, and in two of these, such intercampus research activity was described as the first such universitywide effort in any field. While it is not clear that cooperation is any greater in those programs within a multicampus system than between separate campuses anywhere, universitywide urban cen-

---

[4] That universities are becoming "urbanized" has been noted by others. William M. Birenbaum (1969, p. 28), for example, states: "Most of the country's outstanding universities are now urban-based. Those which aren't are reaching out for the nearest city as rapidly as they can: Illinois at Urbana for Chicago, . . . Wisconsin at Madison for Milwaukee, Missouri at Columbia for St. Louis and Kansas City, etc. The conditions which allowed many of these institutions to become great, like Cornell in Ithaca, for example, no longer exist."

ters or institutes appear to be new responses to new needs made possible by the multicampus structure. Indeed, the Milwaukee campus has been given an explicitly urban orientation.[5] The system-wide staff monitors requests for new programs and faculty qualifications to be certain that they are suitable for the urban mission of the institution.

Teacher education at the University of Illinois, Champaign-Urbana, has been given an added and increasingly necessary dimension by sending its student teachers to the Chicago Circle campus for experience. In this instance, as in some other university-wide activities elsewhere, neither initiation nor operation of the program seems to have been greatly influenced by the multicampus administration. The common board, common procedures, and personal exchanges within a discipline, however, have undoubtedly facilitated the program.

These few examples of multicampus accomplishments are neither exhaustive nor do they purport to set out the extent of campus activity. With respect to the latter, inner-city community relations programs of one urban campus, although easily characterized as high-risk ventures, have been accepted by central staff located at a rural campus. No instances were reported of an urban campus being inhibited in its responses to the urban crisis by multicampus administrative or faculty structures. Emulation of the research orientation of the major campus—the single most popular hallmark of quality—remains an internal inhibition, however.

Despite these examples, the multicampus systems do not yet appear to have related the peculiar advantages of their structure to the problems of urban society. While it is recognized that the resources of several campuses are greater than the resources of one alone, marshaling these scattered resources and aiming them effectively at the blight, pollution, and dissolution of the cities on a *universitywide* basis presents an unsolved problem. For example, one system announced that substantial funds would be available for "urban problems" and solicited proposals from faculty to be considered on their merits. However, ultimate allocation among the campuses was in almost direct proportion to enrollment, in order to keep peace in the family. Moreover, systemwide reordering

---

[5] The campus executive at Milwaukee in 1970, appropriately, was Chancellor J. Martin Klotsche, author of *The Urban University* (1966).

of individual campus priorities in the interest of overall program balance was regarded as undue interference with local autonomy.

MULTICAMPUS ORGANIZA-TION: TYPES OF CAMPUSES AND SYSTEMS In the nine university systems, curricular offerings range from an explicitly vocational program in cake decorating to the most advanced graduate seminars. Some campuses are dedicated to undergraduate teaching, while on others the basic orientation is toward graduate education and research. The nine universities, however, are not of interest simply because of diversity—any random selection of public campuses would produce an equally mixed bag—but because, implicitly or explicitly, their common multicampus structures are attempts to contain, to give direction to, or to accommodate the inevitable variety which different campuses present.

While no two campuses in any system are alike, they can be categorized as colleges or universities, depending upon whether they offer or have pending plans to offer the doctoral degree. The existence, mix, and distribution of each of these types has an impact upon the governance of the university system. An additional impact results if there are two-year colleges as well. Related matters discussed here include three specialized activities—medical education, agricultural experiment stations, and extension and continuing education—each of which is organized on a universitywide basis in at least one multicampus system.

The existence of a doctoral program as a basis of classification is somewhat arbitrary. Widely accepted and easily understood, however, this criterion of advanced graduate and professional education reaches the heart of almost all academic plans and programs. In California, Missouri, North Carolina, and Wisconsin, the doctorate differentiates the statutory missions of the public campuses. At this writing, only the multicampus university can award the doctorate in these states, even though other public campuses in North Carolina and Wisconsin use the word *university* in their names. Our use of the doctorate as a criterion is justified, for the reality of the "academic revolution" with its emphasis upon graduate education and research is everywhere apparent; counter-revolutionaries are few and scattered.

Nevertheless, despite its general applicability, the criterion of the doctorate has a major fault: it obscures and understates, simply by not recognizing the proper significance of graduate work below the doctoral level, particularly first professional degrees in such fields as architecture, social welfare, public administration, business administration, and public health. In offering such professional programs, with qualified faculty and library resources, many colleges are universities as the term is often used, regardless of their title.

The criterion of the doctorate is closely related to the development of the multicampus university as defined for this study in a way which was not immediately obvious. Throughout the country, there are a number of multicampus systems in which the executive of a university campus is also the chief executive of one or more college campuses in a system.[6] To our knowledge, no such system contains a university campus (i.e., one granting doctoral degrees) other than the main one. This is not accidental, for once a campus within a system is authorized to award a doctorate, once university status is in prospect, a dynamic comes into play which creates pressure for the particular type of system of interest here—one with separate campus and system executives, each with the academically prestigious title of chancellor or president. The drive for a separate campus executive seems inseparable from the whole thrust of graduate education and research: the increased cost of facilities and equipment, the higher salaries that the graduate faculty can command, the need to support graduate students, and the politics of extramural support. These pressures can be contained for a long period in some instances, but we suggest a general instability—born out of symbolism as much as administrative reality—in the governance of a university campus either by a campus administrator with a lesser title than president or chancellor or by a system administrator with responsibilities for another campus.[7]

Segmental Versus Comprehensive Systems: The Mix of Campus Types

In the preceding chapter, states were classified on the basis of whether the responsibility for awarding the doctoral degree has been limited to only one multicampus system. We called such state organization *segmental* and found it in California, Missouri, North Carolina, and Wisconsin, four states embracing five systems in the

---

[6] The University of Minnesota in 1968–1969, for example, had two campuses other than the main campus which were headed by provosts. Neither offered the doctorate.

[7] Fourteen years passed between the time that UCLA awarded its first Ph.D. in 1938 and the time a chancellor was appointed in 1952, but the period of incubation is probably foreshortened in this faster-moving era.

study. In three states—Illinois, New York, and Texas more than one university or university system can award the doctorate, a pattern of state organization we called *not segmental* for want of a better term.

Here, our concern is with the nine multicampus universities, not the seven states. Despite possibility of confusion, the term *segmental* is used to describe a multicampus system which comprises only one type of campus, either university or college. If a system has both university and college campuses (for example, the City University of New York), then it is termed a *comprehensive* system. The description of the states is not related to the description of the campuses. For example, the University of Wisconsin is designated a comprehensive system, having both college and university campuses, although the organization of higher education in the state is segmental, with only the university granting the doctorate.

Segmental multicampus universities

Of the nine multicampus systems, four are segmentally organized. All campuses of the Universities of California, Illinois, and Missouri are authorized to award the doctoral degree; none of the campuses in the California State Colleges can grant the doctorate, although "joint doctoral" programs are permitted in cooperation with both the University of California and private institutions.

Comprehensive multicampus universities

It is easier to identify the campuses remaining as two- or four-year colleges than to predict the transition of a campus from college to university status. The five systems which are classified as comprehensive—the Universities of Texas, Wisconsin, and North Carolina, and the State and City Universities of New York—all have definite plans to maintain differences between types of campuses. These five systems, encompassing both colleges and universities, are of two distinct kinds. Three are primarily university systems to which colleges have been attached; two are primarily college systems to which universities have been affiliated.

The comprehensive systems: universities plus. In 1969, the University of Texas comprised three university campuses and seven professional units. The University of Wisconsin includes the two university campuses at Madison and Milwaukee, two college campuses at Green Bay and Parkside, and seven two-year campuses. The University of North Carolina includes four university campuses at Chapel Hill, Raleigh, Greensboro, and Charlotte,[8] and two additional college campuses which have recently been assigned to the university. In addition, a two-year technical institute is administered by a university campus.

Campuses in each of these two systems are in some measure in competition with other campuses outside the system because offerings are at a parallel level. The university campuses are the only public ones in the state with jurisdiction over the doctoral degree, but there are other college campuses and other two-year campuses. Without suggesting that the graduate-research orientation of the university campuses makes them any better than the colleges, assuredly it makes them different. The difference is the primary conceptual basis for the separate system in each state. But what makes the college or two-year college campuses within these systems different? Will a student at a college campus in one of these two multicampus systems receive a better undergraduate education than at a college campus outside the system? This was publicly suggested in one state. In addition, a political advantage was put forth: An outpost in a remote part of the state justifies a multicampus *university* system in establishing or maintaining two-year or four-year college campuses.

We offer no opinions about whether or not these systems, more particularly their college campuses, are effectively serving the needs of their states. Indeed, we assume that they are. We do not assume, however, that the particular pattern of organization is transferable beyond the bounds of each state. One system executive condemned what he called the "uncritical acceptance of the California Master Plan scheme" with its strict segmental division between college and university systems by states which did not understand the reasons behind it. Similarly, the reasons for the organization of the two multicampus universities in Wisconsin and North Carolina, consisting of university campuses to which other types of campuses have been attached, are historically and politically unique within the seven states and nine systems in the study.

---

[8] Although the Charlotte campus is not presently authorized to award the doctorate, it is anticipated that this will take place.

The comprehensive systems: colleges plus. The organization of higher education in the state of New York is far too complex for simple description here—or perhaps anywhere. Our characterization of both the State and City Universities as "colleges plus" is based on their relatively recent origins out of existing campuses, none of which offered the doctoral degree at the time of consolidation. In the State University, the merger of the private University of Buffalo into the system in 1962 was its "plus." In the City University, the Graduate Center offered its first doctoral programs in the same year, and moved to separate facilities in January 1964 — a plus for this previously collegiate system.

The most striking feature of both New York systems is their inclusion of *all* public campuses within their specific geographic limits. The State University governs all campuses outside the limits of New York City with the immaterial exception of three specialized schools. The City University not only operates solely within the city limits but even restricts freshman enrollment to city residents.

A second feature of the two systems is the manner in which they interlock in governance. The State University is responsible for approving the budgets, academic programs, and selection of the presidents of all two-year community college campuses in the state. Other authority is in local governing boards. In 1969, the state provided one-half of the capital budget and one-third of the operating budget for these community colleges, and the balance of the support was local. In effect, the trustees of the State University serve as a coordinating agency for the community colleges and as a governing board for the senior colleges, university campuses, and certain agricultural and technical schools. Community colleges within New York City are governed by the City University Board of Higher Education and are considered part of the university. But they are also subject to the same supervision by the State University as all other community colleges.

The governance of the two-year campuses in New York City is unnecessarily detailed. For some purposes, both the City University and State University claim the two-year colleges. Two-year campus administrators of the city system were said to carry "inside information" between the systems, because they attend meetings in both. Each university was critical of the way the other handled responsibility for the two-year campuses. While aware of uncertainty and confusion, we have no way of assessing their importance. However, the dual responsibility suggests that some facet of governance might be neglected by both.[9]

In the State University, two formerly college campuses have been changed to universities; one university campus, formerly private, has been merged into the system; and a fourth university campus has been built from the ground up. Eleven four-year colleges offered undergraduate and master's level work in 1970, but plans expressly precluded giving university status.

In the City University, as noted above, the organization of graduate work at the doctoral level is complex. The physically and administratively separate Graduate Center is responsible for doctorates in the "paper and pencil" disciplines, and particular campuses as "chosen agents" have such responsibility in disciplines which require laboratories and extensive equipment. It is unclear whether the trend is toward more development at the Graduate Center or at the campuses. Strong factions support both alternatives. Many faculty and campus administrators are not content with having doctoral programs controlled away from their particular campus or with the transfer of key faculty loyalty downtown to the center. On the other hand, the center makes possible the creation of a critical mass of specialized faculty which could not readily be matched at any one of the campuses.

Segmental and comprehensive: a summing up

In the balance of the study, the relative merits of the segmental and comprehensive systems will be assessed. However, each alleged advantage of one approach is countered by an argument for the other. In specific processes of governance, these will be seen more clearly. Here, we pose some initial questions. Prestige and money, both institutional and personal, are involved in the answers.

Segmental proponents, arguing for a system composed exclusively of college *or* university campuses, claim that each segment has a specific role and mission and that in a comprehensive system these segmental differences are lost. In particular, it is asserted that college and two-year campuses lose their identity if included in a system with a major university campus. Proponents of comprehensive systems reply that, to some degree, teaching, research,

[9] See note 7, Chapter 2.

and public service are goals in all segments and that mere difference in emphasis does not justify relegation of all but the university to a different status. Why, we heard, should a philosophy professor at a university be paid more than one teaching the same subject to the same number of students at a college campus?

Proponents of the segmental system argue that competition can be healthy and constructive and that all segments benefit by the need to justify their diverse programs to the legislature. Proponents of the comprehensive system, on the other hand, respond that competition can better be handled within the educational establishment where specialized knowledge produces more "rational" decisions.

These arguments and others appear in later chapters and are reviewed in the conclusions. The issues are important, for they involve a final phase in the historical development of the normal schools, which first became teachers colleges and then liberal arts colleges.[10] To what extent and how should these now either become university campuses or be "retained" as college campuses? Can either goal be better achieved in a separate segmental system including all such colleges or in a comprehensive system including both college and university campuses? Central to the answer is the extent to which the governor and the legislature choose to involve themselves in the decision, with respect to both individual campuses and the systems as a whole. In the segmental systems, explicit questions relating to varying levels of support between segments remain with state fiscal authorities. In the comprehensive systems, although governing boards sometimes have nominal power to shift resources among segments, the pattern is much the same. In fact, none of the comprehensive universities have authority to change either the mission or the basic support pattern for individual campuses without legislative authorization.

It was everywhere suggested that educational values or purposes can be realized in the multicampus context. However, it may be equally true that multicampus structures serve not the educational or academic purposes of the campuses as much as the administrative ones of the state.[11] All nine systems are devices for the alloca-

[10] The growth and changing functions of such colleges are the subject of E. Alden Dunham (1969).

[11] One flagship campus executive saw the *educational* value of the multicampus structure as "marginal, but it's of real political benefit to all of the campuses including the big one."

tion of resources. Some have the basic responsibility to divide such resources among relatively equal (or unequal) units. Others are organizational bins intended less for the exercise of judgment in the distribution of funds than merely to contain campuses to which the legislature itself would make the distribution. If educational judgment is brought to bear in the allocation of resources, then educational purposes are being served. On the other hand, an administrative structure acting only as a conduit for state funds and state control is difficult to justify in academic terms.

We attempt to infer the intent of the state from the three-way relationships between it, the campuses, and the multicampus university. We speculate about the effectiveness of the multicampus systems to serve these purposes of the state and the implications of such purposes for the educational goals of the system and its campuses. Whether a system is segmental or comprehensive is at best a slight clue to the answers we are seeking.

The Two-Year Campuses

The important future of two-year campuses in the overall educational structure of the states contrasts with our impression that the actual impact upon their system of those which were part of multicampus universities is very small indeed. With the possible exception of articulation, discussed in Chapter 11, the very great differences within even the limited range of two-year colleges in four of the nine university systems in the study forestall useful generalization.

In the University of North Carolina, an explicitly vocational and terminal two-year agricultural institute is operated by and on the North Carolina State campus. Staffed by regular campus faculty, only the inability of the students in the institute to transfer into a four-year program gives it the character of a separate entity.

At the other extreme, the two-year centers of the University of Wisconsin are explicitly intended to transfer students to the four-year campuses. Each of the seven centers is headed by a dean, and the seven are centrally administered by a chancellor. The new four-year campuses at Green Bay and Parkside are the outgrowth of six previously existing two-year centers. The creation of the unusual four-campus complex at Green Bay would probably not have been possible but for the previously existing two-year campuses.

No attention is given here to the six two-year agricultural and technical colleges in the State University of New York. With respect to the 31 community colleges (as of 1969) with local sponsoring boards, however, the State University's supervisory powers are exercised somewhat apart from its governance of its university and collegiate campuses, and the two-year campuses seem to have little visible influence on the multicampus governing structure and processes.

On the other hand, the governing board of the City University is also directly responsible for the six of these 31 community colleges located in New York City. For most purposes, therefore, they are an integral part of the City University, and through them it is able to serve a public not eligible to attend its four-year campuses. One may speculate that these campuses also preserve the traditional academic standards of the four-year campuses by absorbing less scholastically qualified students.[12]

While other influences of the two-year campuses on the four university systems undoubtedly exist, the three-way administrative interface between the central administration, governing board, and the four-year and university campuses appears relatively unaffected by the presence of the two-year campuses.

Medical Education, Agriculture, and Continuing Education Three special academic areas found in almost all nine systems complicate attempts to stretch traditional, single-campus organizational patterns across several campuses: (1) medical schools, which sometimes have their own campuses; and (2) agricultural experiment stations; and (3) continuing education and extension sometimes engage the central staff in actual operating functions. Like the two-year campuses, these three special areas intruded upon the study rather than being the subject of it, yet each area has such important implications for the multicampus structure that it deserves more extensive investigation.

Medical education

Despite wide differences in the organizational structure of medical education across the nine systems, two distinct trends are apparent. First is the more or less horizontal expansion of medical education into the life sciences at the graduate level. Second is a more or

[12] In 1970, pressures and proposals for some form of open admissions for all campuses of the City University were mounting. That such pressures had been relieved to some extent in the recent past by the two-year campuses may be indicated by the fear that open admissions might turn the City University campuses ". . . into four-year community colleges, with all academic distinction being remorselessly extinguished" (Kristol & Weaver, 1969, p. 45).

less vertical expansion into undergraduate education. Each trend has implications for multicampus governance, although it is difficult to relate the trends to system organization of medical education itself. Four rough categories are apparent: (1) two systems do not directly govern medical schools; (2) two systems have medical education entirely on separate campuses; (3) three systems have medical schools as an integral part of particular general campuses; and (4) in the remaining two systems, medical education is found both on separate campuses and as part of general campuses.

The absence of medical schools in two systems is explained in one instance—the City University of New York—by the relatively recent emergence of advanced graduate education of any kind, and in the other—the California State Colleges—by a mission which explicitly excludes such work. In both instances, however, interest in medical education is very much in evidence. The proposed Health Professions Complex of the City University involves both two-year and four-year campuses and an affiliated hospital.[13] This proposed plan seems an excellent way for a multicampus university to mobilize its resources to meet increasingly diverse manpower problems in the medical field. In the other system, individual California State College campuses maintain working relationships with local medical facilities for the training of paramedical personnel, but the multicampus staff is not involved in what are essentially locally organized programs.

Three of the multicampus universities, Wisconsin, Missouri, and North Carolina, have a single medical school as part of a general campus. Two of these are considering an additional medical school as part of another campus. The presence of a medical school on a campus complicates governance in one obvious fashion and in another that is less so. The high cost of medical education is the most evident problem. In both instances in which a new medical school at a general campus was proposed, local faculty

[13] The organizational relationship between the City University and Mount Sinai appears to be one of a kind. We asked one system administrator whether the City University "had" a medical school. He replied: "Whether we 'have' a medical school is a moot point. Mount Sinai is affiliated with us. Its name is now 'The Mount Sinai School of Medicine of the City University of New York.' Its president is a member of our Administrative Council. We must approve all curriculums and faculty appointments. Their faculty are elected to our doctoral faculty, and we operate many joint programs. They do, however, retain exclusive authority and responsibility for their own finances. The most interesting aspect of our affiliation is the establishment of a new kind of relationship between a public and a private institution."

and administrators were fearful of possible diversion of resources from existing academic programs. Decisions reached *off* campus concerning the most costly *on*-campus program were suspect. Attitudes were mixed, however. One campus was first concerned that it would not get the medical school which it considered desirable as a matter of academic planning as well as prestige. Serious second thoughts about possible diversion of resources did not come until the new school was obtained.

The less obvious problem is based on the traditional, perhaps notorious, independence of medical schools in their public and governmental relations. Like some schools of agriculture, they often maintain substantial public relations activities which seem only nominally under the control of either campus or multicampus administrations. Although not unique to the multicampus structure, the implications of such independence are compounded by the longer lines of communication between the system executive and his staff and the medical school dean and his.

The location of medical schools entirely on separate campuses in two other systems, Illinois and Texas, does not seem to inhibit cooperation with the general campuses. This, of course, is most evident where a medical campus and a general campus are relatively close together. In Chicago, the newer general campus and the older medical campus—only a few blocks apart—have not been organizationally joined under a single administration for, among other reasons, fear of disturbing longstanding relationships between the medical campus and the strong basic science departments at Urbana.

In Texas in 1969, several widely scattered medical campuses were under the general supervision and line direction of a senior central staff officer. In all but name, this senior officer was the system executive of a multicampus system consisting solely of medical and health-related campuses.[14] Systemwide academic programs as well as new admissions procedures had been proposed to identify interested undergraduates; substantial integration of undergraduate education and medical education was being explored.

While the coordinated programs of the Texas medical campuses

[14] The administrative pattern was abandoned in 1970. All campuses, medical and otherwise, now report directly to the chancellor; the position described here, "the executive vice chancellor for health affairs," has been abolished. We are unable to report upon the operational differences which may develop between these two patterns.

provide an impressive example for all multicampus universities and other academic areas, qualifying factors limit more general applicability, both in Texas and in the other states as well. Fiscally, medical education is less subject to restrictive state budget formulae and its benefits more from direct federal support. The goals and mission of medical campuses, while increasingly broad, remain narrow in comparison to those of university campuses. The state organization of higher education is such that the University of Texas has almost a monopoly on public medical education, allowing it to define the limits of its own activity. Administratively, deans and department heads in medical schools have generally been stronger than their counterparts in a general university campus vis-à-vis the faculty, and this facilitates effective administrative coordination. As important a factor as any, perhaps, is the separate location of the medical campuses away from the general campuses. Where medical education takes place at a general campus, lines of authority and communication between a central medical administrator and the medical school executives are broken by the authority of the campus executive.

The two systems in California and New York, in which some medical schools are governed by general campuses and others are organizationally separate, illustrates the difficulty of imposing strong administrative coordination in this area. Several highly qualified medical and hospital specialists at the multicampus level in California serve in a staff capacity but do not direct activity in the health fields. The older medical schools find this desirable, but the executive of a campus just beginning its own medical program expressed a clear need for more direction and advice based on the experience of the system and the existing medical units. A faculty member at an older unit saw an equal need:

. . . I would like to suggest that more use be made of the established faculty on this campus in aiding the new medical and other health science schools on other campuses. Appointment of some university professors in health science fields might be a valuable step in this direction. Distinguished scientists who had their base on an established campus such as this one could then spend time lecturing, organizing, and advising on the newer campuses, to the benefit of all concerned. Faculty members on one campus can now lecture on another, but time for such lectures is limited. The type of faculty members I am talking about would have lighter commitments on the parent campus so that they would have time to spend more prolonged periods on other campuses.

Of the nine systems, three have more than one medical school, but only in Texas was there a full-fledged attempt at coordination as of 1970. In the second system a position for high-level coordination existed but was unfilled. In the third, coordination was the task of functional specialists at the middle rather than the senior staff level. In all, however, it is clear that increasing systemwide attention will be paid to medical education, major aspects of which transcend details of academic governance; the extremely high costs and traditionally low "productivity" of medical schools require greater rationalization in the face of increasing fiscal constraints and a quantifiable and critical manpower shortage.

Agricultural experiment stations

Five of the nine multicampus universities (California, Illinois, Missouri, North Carolina, and Wisconsin) are land-grant institutions, and a sixth (State University of New York) has partial governing responsibility for land-grant activities at an otherwise private campus. In all but one of the five, direction of agricultural experiment stations is the responsibility of a single campus of the university, rather than of the system executive and his staff. Although the activities of the experiment stations are of university-wide importance, they do not appear to present problems unique to the multicampus structure. In the one system in which this aspect of governance is centralized—the University of California— a senior central staff officer is the chief administrative officer of the experiment stations.

This single exception to campus direction is more attributable to the early dispersion of agricultural education to several campuses in California than to any administrative rationalization. However, the similarity of the administrative arrangement to the strong coordination of separate medical campuses which existed in Texas is noteworthy. Both the need for and the possibility of more centralized "research management" in these two applied fields may, to some extent, account for the comparable organization. Agricultural education as opposed to experiment station research remains under the control of the general campuses in California, however, significantly distinguishing it from the coordinated medical activities of Texas. In addition, experiment station personnel in California are jointly appointed by the multicampus director and the campus executive, with the latter being the more significant in the review process. In Texas the multicampus officer independently reviewed medical campus personnel decisions and was clearly higher in the governing hierarchy.

Extension and continuing education

The broad policy question of defining the mission of a university campus—particularly a research-oriented campus—in extension and continuing education was seen as an urgent one by numerous respondents during the study. Of almost equal concern were practical questions of accommodating its administrative organization to the multicampus structure. Despite high-level recognition of these issues, continuing education and extension generally lack high universitywide priority.

Low priority seems attributable to three related factors, the two most prominent of which have nothing to do with the multicampus structure itself. First is the lack of "academic respectability" from which the field suffers, and second, the lack of substantial public financial support, if any. The third factor, peculiar to the multicampus structure, is the difficulty of administering any intercampus activity—a difficulty which in most of the systems leaves agricultural extension to the campus with the school of agriculture, and general extension within almost total control of individual campuses.

Two systems, Wisconsin and Missouri, are notable exceptions to the almost totally decentralized administration. Both combine agricultural extension with general extension activities and have built upon the strength and financial support of the former to encourage the latter. Their administrative structures differ substantially.

In Wisconsin, extension is under direct control of an executive officer of equal rank with the campus executives. Most of the faculty have career lines separate from the campus faculty, but many hold joint appointments. An extension "presence" existed on each campus in 1969 in the form of a campus staff officer, 60 percent of whose salary came from extension funds and 40 percent from the campus budget. One such officer described his status on the organizational chart as being "connected by a dotted line to everyone."

In Missouri, a senior multicampus *staff* officer is responsible for intercampus coordination and promotion of extension activity. His task is made possible by substantial budget authority, although he does not directly administer an exclusively extension faculty as in Wisconsin. In neither system have traditionally adverse faculty attitudes toward extension been overcome, but in both there was confidence that progress was being made.

Educational programs utilizing radio and television are considered part of continuing education and extension in most of the nine university systems. Operating control of this activity, however, is generally not decentralized, even in the systems in which all other aspects of extension have been. Central operation, if not with the multicampus administration itself, has been delegated to a specific campus. In one system, the enthusiastic promotion of education by radio and television is the primary—almost only—systemwide extension activity. In another, these media are considered peripheral, if not frivolous.

The decentralization of extension activity to the campuses, as in most of the systems, has a cost for the responsible campus liaison administrators. While favoring decentralization, the view was often expressed that extension does not have necessary support at the multicampus level. Indeed, in one system, campus extension officers with substantial control over "profit" from continuing education had pooled their campus resources to fund a high-level multicampus coordinator!

Three special situations: a comment

The three activities considered here are so diverse that generalization may be forced. The programs exemplified the lack of generally accepted principles for specifically multicampus governance. For example, where extension education has been decentralized to the campuses, there is no consistency about whether campus jurisdiction should be territorial or programmatic. Principles of academic governance derived from the experience of traditional single campuses can be stretched or squeezed to fit the multicampus mold for most activities *on* a campus. Where the activity takes place *off* campus, however, the lack of specific multicampus concepts is evident in the absence of elementary agreement on how to administer the three areas of special concern here.

The development of principles for multicampus governance of these activities is awaiting broad policy answers to even broader policy questions: What are the respective roles of the state and federal government in medical education? What land-grant activity remains relevant in an urban nation? What should be the respective responsibilities of different types of campuses for education beyond their traditional boundaries of both territory and students?

Regional Organization   Both as a matter of theory and as a studied proposal, regional organization of campuses in a state has had substantial recent attention.[15] However, only the two multicampus universities in New York can be characterized as regional, and these only if the term is used so broadly as to lose real meaning.

Examples of generally informal regional coalitions for specific purposes are found in all nine systems, but these rarely involve more than one campus in the system and appear to have little or no impact on multicampus governance.[16] That such impact might be felt, however, is exemplified by a private consultant's report in New York on the feasibility of a regional organization in the Mid-Hudson area. The proposed organization would include one four-year campus of the State University, four public community colleges, and 14 private two- and four-year campuses (Campus Facilities Associates, 1963, p. 121).

The only example of explicitly regional structuring of campuses *within* a multicampus university is the Green Bay campus of the University of Wisconsin: three two-year campuses are organizationally part of a four-year campus. This recently established "system within a system" illustrated in its announcement a strength which might be that of most multicampus systems: "A student may move freely from one to another campus. One who does is not considered a transfer student." The same catalog, however, lists courses with titles that point to a serious potential danger in regional organization: "Recreation Resource Planning in the Upper Great Lakes Region" and "Peoples and Cultures of the Upper Great Lakes Region." If not carefully regulated, the regionalization of campuses may enhance student mobility within the region but limit it even within the state.

---

[15] For example, see California Joint Committee (1968, pp. 49–50).

[16] This is true even of the well-known and quite formal "Research Triangle" which consists of Duke University and the Chapel Hill and North Carolina State campuses of the University of North Carolina. Over ten years old, it does not appear to have had any appreciable influence on multicampus system governance.

THE CAM-
PUSES: NUM-
BERS, SIZE,
AND
LOCATION

Much of the diversity characterizing all aspects of higher education in the United States is accurately reflected in the nine multicampus universities. The number of campuses in such systems in 1969 ranged from three to thirty (excluding the locally governed community colleges subject to supervisory authority by the State University of New York). The enrollment at the campuses varied from 33,000 students at one extreme to 85 at the other. Many campuses are well over 100 years old, but one was registering its first students on the day of our visit. Campuses in the nine systems include both terminal, two-year vocational schools and prestigious, research-oriented universities of international renown —and virtually all types in between.

Leadership and Autonomy

Table 8 indicates the numbers of each type of campus in the nine multicampus universities in 1969 and notes changes since the Martorana and Hollis survey 10 years earlier. The distinction between university and college as shown on the chart is based upon whether the campus either offers a doctoral degree or has firm expectations of offering such a degree in the near future. Two-year campuses come in a great number of forms, most of which are discussed later in the chapter. Separate professional schools— those not connected to a general campus—are almost exclusively medical schools, but also include other health science campuses.

Although the present discussion isolates the implications of the number of campuses in a system from those arising from enrollment, this isolation does not exist in fact. Increased enrollment is a condition of an increased number of campuses, but, as noted in the preceding chapter, political pressure for geographical dispersal of campuses reinforces, and may be more important than, the effect of added enrollment per se.

While the concept of "span of control" has ceased to be classed as a principle by organization theorists, it has reality and applicability in the context of the multicampus university. One system executive questioned whether academic or educational leadership can be exercised with more than six or seven campuses in the system. He was speaking of his leadership, but expressed an additional doubt that a qualified staff could be maintained to handle more than such a number. Despite his comment, academic leadership—executive guidance of educational policy—is apparent in some of the larger multicampus universities. The abundance of

TABLE 8
Numbers and
types of
campuses in
nine
multicampus
universities,
1958–59 and
1968–69*

Multicampus system	University		Four-year colleges		Professional
	1958–59	1968–69	1958–59	1968–69	1958–59
University of California	2	8	3		3
California State Colleges			14	18	
University of Illinois	1	2			1
University of Missouri	1	4			1
State University of New York		4	12	11	10
City University of New York		1	4	9	
University of North Carolina	2	4	1		
University of Texas	1	3	1		3
University of Wisconsin	1	2	1	2	

*1958–59 data are from Martorana & Hollis, 1960. 1968–69 data were developed by the authors.

†The six two-year colleges in the State University of New York were agricultural and technical colleges in both years and are included in the table. In addition to its governance of these six two-year colleges, the State University also has certain supervisory authority (in 1969) over 31 community colleges which are governed by local boards. None of these are shown as being part of the State University. On the other hand, 6 of the 31 are in New York City, and their local board is the Board of Higher Education, the governing board of the City University; these six are included as part of the City University.

value judgments surrounding the definition of leadership may put the issue beyond resolution. In any event, it is clear that the *style* of leadership changes with the number of campuses.

While such style is related to the number of campuses, the difference from one extreme to the other is one of degree rather than kind. On the face of it, a system executive with three campuses to worry about would seem to have little in common with one concerned about 18—little, that is, other than inclusion in the present study. (This, indeed, was rather pointedly suggested to us.) The facts appear to be to the contrary. A day in the life of each is quite similar, as are the educational, organizational, and political problems with which they must deal. If a system executive is seen as primarily concerned with representing the campus to the outside

| 1968–69 | Two-year college | | Total | |
	1958–59	1968–69	1958–59	1968–69
1			8	9
			14	18
1	1		3	3
			2	4
9	6†	6†	28	30
1	3†	6†	7	17
			3	4
7			5	10
	8	7	10	11

world, then the number of campuses in the system may be irrelevant to his activity. On the other hand, the number is quite relevant in his relationship to each of the campuses.

Burton Clark (1962, p. 162) has stated that a "loose meandering" style of leadership may be the only way to govern academic organizations, because of the need for and, usually, the fact of faculty independence. If correct with respect to the single campuses of which he was writing, then such style may be exaggerated in the multicampus context. We found, as the balance of the study will indicate, that academic administration at the multicampus level is characterized by soft, directed mediation and face-to-face resolution of problems of resource allocation. Exercise of authority in the nine multicampus universities probably resembles that in any large, single-campus multiversity, but it is greatly complicated by the dispersed locations of the campuses and their claim to autonomy. Distance and the status of a separate campus executive weaken the already soft administrative style needed for a single campus.

The Location of the Campuses

Geographic dispersion of the campuses has two aspects: the actual distances between the campuses and the central offices and the simple fact that there is any distance at all. The latter is far more important than the former. The inconvenience and inefficiency of *any* geographic separation, not the extent of it, reduce the opportunity for frequent personal contact which some have suggested is the *sine qua non* of academic leadership.

Whether an absolute necessity or not, if there are a large number of campuses in a system, the lack of face-to-face contact makes the system executive's job more difficult. Even in a small system, one system executive's attempts to maintain close contact with a relatively few peripheral campuses were criticized by the faculty at the main campus, where they thought him a "stranger." The larger the number of campuses, the greater the problem.

The implications of geographic dispersion go beyond the system executive as an individual. Absence of easy personal contact between central and campus administrators is a frequent concern. It is particularly disturbing in the related, although quite distinct, areas of public and governmental relations, where quantitative hierarchical allocation of authority is more complicated. However hard the public relations officer of a multicampus university with 10 or 20 campuses may try to develop the necessary and very personal trust and confidence of his campus counterparts, he or they will probably become more familiar with air terminals than with each other.

Among the nine systems, the City University of New York is, of course, an apparent exception to the problems arising from geographic dispersion. City traffic and public transportation substitute an explicit time dimension for distance: "How long does it take to get there?" The problems of distance seem less, but it would be a mistake to believe that they do not exist.

Number of Campuses and Campus Autonomy

The number of campuses is the most easily observable characteristic of a system. Generalizations to the effect that numbers of campuses have an effect on campus administration and on faculty participation are not supported by this study.

First, regarding campus administration, Moos and Rourke (1959, p. 212) suggest that governance of several campuses means that the governing board cannot give full attention to any one of them; the resulting "power vacuum" is filled by the campus administrators.[17] This is not the case among the nine systems. Although most campuses have substantial institutional freedom or are moving in that direction, it is not because of a power vacuum. Rather, the increasing autonomy is the deliberate choice of all participants. A power vacuum may exist in other types of multicampus systems whose governing boards lack a central administrative structure, but where the system executive assisted by his central staff can gather and organize information for board action, this is not the case. Moreover, we learned not to underestimate the capacity of the governing board to delve into the details of specific issues at any campus.

Other possible factors may inhibit growth of authority by the campus administrations at the expense of the governing board and central administration. If a system is small, the relationship between the system executive, the governing board, and three, four, or five campus executives can be an intimate one. The campuses may well have more autonomy in such a small system simply because the board and system executive have personal confidence in each campus executive. On the other hand, in the larger systems, where a power vacuum is most probable, detailed controls can preclude the informality and flexibility of administration upon which the autonomy of any public campus depends. This is particularly true in areas of business and finance. A campus may have greater freedom from arbitrary interference by the central administration and board because of the large size of the system, but, for the same reason, the freedom is often narrowly bounded by formal, detailed, and often inflexible rules and regulations.

In short, the price of a decentralized administrative structure—of campus autonomy—can be an increase in uniformity as well as formality. The risk is one of rigidity and leveling, and leveling

---

[17] Martorana and Hollis (1960, p. 19) are even more explicit, but our findings do not support their views: ". . . Depending on the size and complexity of the units, such a board should be responsible for not more than 6–9 institutions. With a larger number, a condition develops which may be termed 'presidential control,' as opposed to 'board control,' of the institutions in the system. This encourages too great an assumption of authority in the administrative head of each unit and weakens the vital principle of lay board control to which this country is fully committed."

generally downward. One system executive described his hardest task as finding ways to be "unfair" and to maintain "inequality," when such was a desired course in any of the countless facets of educational programs. On an individual campus, the campus executive can discriminate among a host of individual budget and personnel decisions. Initiative and excellence can be rewarded and stupidity penalized. At the multicampus level, however, large-scale campus-by-campus budget allocations are highly visible, and both internal and external pressures constantly push the sometimes false equity of uniformity.

Second, regarding faculty participation, Thad Hungate (1964, p. 220) has suggested that the faculty "cannot adequately partipate in management" in a multicampus system because of their isolation from the governing board. Although many decisions in the multicampus university are made at a systemwide level, seemingly removed from easy access to faculty, we did not find that this caused faculty participation in governance to decline. Several structures for faculty participation at the system level exist, and the system frequently has stimulated improved faculty organization on the campuses. In general, within the schools and departments in all nine universities, the faculty has retained or increased its traditional authority to initiate and control educational policy. Neither at system nor at campus levels is faculty participation related to the number of campuses.

THE CAMPUSES: ENROLLMENTS, CEILINGS, AND QUOTAS In the preceding chapter, the distribution of enrollment between public and private higher education was seen as one determinant of system administration. Here, and in a more specific way, we consider the impact of enrollment *within* a multicampus system.

Enrollment and the Budget Enrollment figures and state budget support are directly related in every state, although the precise relationships seemed almost always to be in dispute.[18] With respect to the development and organization of the systems, however, two points concerning budget formulas can be made: (1) The *rate* of growth is as important as absolute size; (2) the *mix* of students by class level is as important as the rate of growth.

The almost one-to-one relationship between budgets and enroll-

---

[18] The great variety of formulas defining such relationships are discussed in some detail in Chapter 9.

ment in all states is so obvious that it tends to obscure a more subtle relationship: Additional funds attributable to enrollment growth form a basis for incremental change in academic programs. Whether change means meeting the needs and demands of disadvantaged students or of research-oriented faculty, numerical growth helps to solve funding problems unrelated to enrollment per se. Constant (albeit differential) growth of enrollment in all systems since World War II may have obscured this aspect of its impact. At one campus, however, a system-imposed enrollment ceiling has only recently been reached. In prior years, the system executive explained to the campus that its "extensive" growth was approaching an end as the ceiling came closer and that thereafter "intensive" growth would be required. A campus administrator complained that "intensive" growth had a fine, sophisticated ring to it until the enrollment ceiling arrived; at that point the campus discovered that it could be defined as growth without money.

Intensive growth is not really growth without money, for the campus academic plan estimates that the number of graduate students will increase as undergraduate enrollment decreases; the budget formula provides for additional funds as the graduate proportion increases. In general, state support in almost every instance is related not merely to the gross enrollment but also to its levels. Whether graduate education *should* or *does*, in fact, cost more than undergraduate instruction are questions to which we do not address ourselves here. It is clear, however, that state appropriations are more generous on a formula basis for graduate education, and that the university which is increasing graduate enrollment is at a distinct advantage, at least in terms of its gross budget increase.

Major budgetary questions which face each system executive must be answered in terms of enrollment and graduate enrollment. The older campuses need growth—particularly in graduate enrollment—to provide the funds felt necessary to keep current with the knowledge explosion. Yet every new or growing campus requires its share of budgetary increases. In few other areas do fiscal policy and long-term academic planning intersect more clearly.

Enrollment Ceilings and Quotas The important implications of enrollment both for budgeting and as a foundation for educational change have led to a variety of attempts to control it. For convenience, we class interim enrollment limitations as *quotas* and ultimate limitations as *ceilings*.

Overall quotas or ceilings are not generally applicable to the multicampus university as such. Where these exist for the campuses, they are only infrequently added up to derive and impose any universitywide total. Specific campus quotas (short-run) are quite common, as expected, although campus ceilings (long-term) are not. Quotas usually result from fiscal and other factors that sometimes involve space, or a combination of limitations, or, very rarely, a deliberate long-range policy decision concerning a desired rate of growth. In 1969, ultimate ceilings for specific campuses were found in only two systems. In California, these have been internally determined by the system itself; in Texas, by the coordinating agency. Only on two campuses in the first system have such ceilings actually been reached.

In the history of a multicampus university, both ceilings and quotas are critical factors. Both can cause a spillover of students from one campus to another, giving the second campus an increment of growth to allow some progress along educational frontiers which the older campuses may be either unwilling or unable to explore.

Campus enrollment: balance within the system

Differences in campus enrollment within a system are either transient because of growth or permanent because of deliberate planning. Whether one or the other, the existing imbalance at any given point of time has implications for all concerned. Campus enrollment characteristics indicate two kinds of systems: (1) In three or four systems, one campus will continue to dominate the system in size of enrollment. (2) In five or six, no one campus will dominate; campuses will be more equal in size, or such equality is anticipated. In both cases, present and future patterns are based as much on lack of planning as on any specific plans.

Table 9 indicates the relative sizes of the three largest campuses in the nine multicampus universities. In four of the five flagship systems—the Universities of Illinois, Missouri, Texas, and Wisconsin—the largest campus is twice the size of the next largest one. The exception is the University of California, in which both UCLA and Berkeley have reached ultimate enrollment ceilings according to existing university plans. Among the four consolidated systems—the California State Colleges, the City and State Universities of New York, and the University of North Carolina—only the State University of New York exhibits similar disproportion.

Generalization about the *third* largest campuses is difficult because of their diversity and varying ages. However, the virtual equality in the enrollment of the three largest campuses in two consolidated systems—the California State Colleges and the City University of New York—is in marked contrast to the pattern of all other systems. Moreover, the third largest campuses in each of these two systems is almost twice as large as the third largest campus in any of the other seven in the study.

Although complicated by issues of campus role and mission, the absolute size of a campus at any particular moment of time has less impact on morale and aspirations than its planned ultimate size. Where campuses are equal in size or planned to be virtually so, there seems to be less potential for intercampus conflict than in those in which a single campus will remain dominant. And within these latter systems, when a single campus is *explicitly* recognized as dominant, there is less potential for conflict than where the future is in doubt. In all cases, however, prospective, not existing, enrollment is the critical factor, complicated by uncertainty.

While governing boards often spend the bulk of their time with the problems of the largest campus of a system, the same is not true of the central staff. The major or flagship campuses, old and established, have both the experience and the bureaucratic apparatus to handle most problems other than those which require board approval or those which the board will not leave alone because of their controversial nature. The older and larger the campus, however, the greater the number of formal matters before the board and the greater probability of controversial matters. Newer campuses, on the other hand, more often look to the central staff for advice about their growing pains—recruitment of faculty and administrators; planning, both academic and physical; and a multitude of other matters.

Relationships between the system executive and his campus executives are assuredly complicated by the large and dominating size of the flagship campus. The head of such a campus has added prestige. Similarly, because of size and history, such campuses naturally draw the attention of the board and the public. The relations of the flagship campus with other campuses are sometimes strained. It is not clear how much of the tension, if any, should be attributed to the transitional factors of size and extent of activity at the flagship campus, or how much to the less tangible factors of historical prestige and political strength. Simple propinquity is undoubtedly responsible for much of the confusion in

TABLE 9
Enrollment
of nine
multicampus
universities and
comparative
enrollment of
their three
largest
campuses,
1968–69

System	Number of campuses	Total enrollment	Percentage (and number) of students on	
			Largest campus	Second largest campus
University of California	9	122,239	23% (28,288)	23% (28,132)
California State Colleges	18	259,450	12% (32,178)	12% (30,077)
University of Illinois	3	51,161	67% (34,353)	28% (14,152)
University of Missouri	4	44,482	46% (20,601)	20% (8,891)
City University of New York	17	156,921	15% (24,125)	15% (23,089)
State University of New York	30	118,066†	18% (20,601)	9% (10,102)
University of North Carolina	4	37,403	43% (16,233)	31% (11,688)
University of Texas	10	58,466	58% (33,797)	21% (12,158)
University of Wisconsin	11	62,333	56% (34,670)	27% (16,768)

*The University of Illinois Medical Center in Chicago.

†The 31 two-year community colleges with local governing boards are not included in the overall enrollment of the State University of New York.

‡The University of Wisconsin at Green Bay opened in 1968.

SOURCE: U.S. Office of Education, 1969.

roles between major campus and system executives, but not all. The disproportionate size of the major campus is often a contributing factor.

SUMMARY Across the nine multicampus universities, the one constant is the changing nature of their campuses and administrative structures. Even the oldest and most successfully established are in a state of transition, but as diverse as the systems are in origin and as mixed as their methods and rates of growth have been, these changes have common characteristics. With the exception of the rapidly expanding University of Texas and—to a lesser extent—North Carolina, systems appear to be entering into a period of consolidation, of completing and implementing plans for new campuses rather than

Third largest campus	Percent of all students in the system enrolled on 3 largest campuses
10% (12,619)	56
10% (27,176)	34
5%* (2,656)	100
20% (8,719)	86
13% (19,615)	43
8% (8,876)	35
16% (6,068)	90
17% (10,170)	96
3%‡ (1,796)	86

developing new plans, and of adjusting to a possible flattening curve of enrollment growth on existing campuses.

In addition to these common demographic trends, three organizational developments seem destined to mark the history of the multicampus universities in the 1970s.

1 *Pressure for a single board.* In three states, there is substantial pressure from a variety of sources to replace the existing multiple academic governing structures with a single board, usually the board of the more prestigious multicampus system. The reasons vary. In California, it is claimed that statewide coordination is ineffective because of competition between segmental systems, that only a single board can avoid "artificial" distinctions among campuses. Similar reasons have been urged in North Carolina,

where the issue is compounded by possible organizational "segregation" of predominantly Negro campuses. In New York, political and educational considerations buttress purely fiscal ones, as the City University system finds substantially increased state aid a virtual condition of its survival. [19]

2 *Decentralization.* Discussions of superimposing a single governing board are sometimes interrupted or joined by proposals for local boards for each campus. Such proposals, considered in detail in the following chapter, vary from strengthening existing advisory boards, through creating local boards with substantive governing power, to a total restructuring of higher education to provide for regional boards.

3 *Coordinating agencies.* In all seven states, tension exists between the statewide coordinating agency and the multicampus universities. This tension, much of it inevitable, is important to the state's overall organization and is also a factor in the internal governance of multicampus systems: the establishment of stable governing patterns within the university system is inordinately difficult where the system itself is uncertain of its authority vis-à-vis the coordinating agency.

These three trends are inconsistent in many respects, but share the thread of being primarily political. More accurately, all three are pressures for change from *outside* the multicampus universities. *Within* the systems, the educational pattern—as opposed to the organizational pattern—appears relatively stable. The comprehensive systems which encompass two- and four-year colleges as well as university campuses are showing little sign of internal pressure to break into segments. Similarly, the segmental systems seem generally content with their more specific missions. In both categories, however, there is evidence of the almost inherent, internal dynamic that pushes college campuses to seek university status.

An additional trend points to more balanced enrollment among campuses within each system. Whether or not ultimate enrollment ceilings are restricting growth of particular campuses, the smaller are growing vis-à-vis the larger. In several systems, newer campuses are reaching a competitive position with the older, major campuses, or will soon be in that position.

---

[19] In 1971, the governor of North Carolina endorsed a report calling for the "deconsolidation" of the university, the creation of separate institutional boards, and the establishment of a new statewide "planning and coordinating agency," the University of North Carolina System. In Wisconsin in 1971, the governor proposed consolidating the two existing segmental systems under a single statewide governing board.

The newer campuses are not competitive in enrollment alone. In educational programs, and particularly in graduate education, these campuses are proud of their recent accomplishments and ambitious for the future. In numbers of graduate students, therefore, as well as overall enrollment, it can be anticipated that the campuses of most multicampus systems will look more alike. However, it is also possible that greater distinctions between campuses within systems will appear along lines of graduate and professional specialties. In any case, the multicampus university of the 1970s will be more a system of equals than a system dominated by one or two main institutions.

Part Two
The Structures of Governance

4. The Governing Board

Most educators agree that the distinction between public and private higher education is rapidly disappearing.[1] Nevertheless, the distinction remains one of critical importance for understanding the authority of public governing boards. Subject to broad legal limits, the governance of *private* campuses is firmly and totally in their governing boards. On the other hand, the state, acting through its governor, its legislature, and a baker's dozen of state agencies, is everywhere enmeshed in the governance of the *public* campuses.

Issues raised by the existence of the state as the source of authority are treated both here and in the following chapter in discussion of the system executive. The impact of the state has equal implications for both board and system executive. The divided treatment emphasizes the frequent ambiguity that governmental involvement in the governance of public higher education can cause. The allocation of authority between the board and the executive officer of a single campus university is probably no more precise, but, in the multicampus system, the effects of vague allocation are reinforced by an "uncertainty factor." Once any decision leaves the physical boundaries of the campus, our study suggests, few at the campus know precisely where it ends up. The campuses rarely think of the state as the locus for a decision unless they are in direct contact with it. More often, they look to or blame a particular central staff officer or the system executive. The paradox is that the state, which has both the authority and the choice of delegation in the first place, is usually the last to be held accountable for failing

[1] The generalization that public and private higher education are converging is supported in detail by looking at federal support, as did Clark Kerr (1964, p. 133), or the federal constitutional rights of students, as did Clark Byse (1966, pp. 305–317). See also Gladys M. Kammerer, (1969, pp. 289, 291), who sees a need for a clear look at the distinction.

to exercise or delegate it. At the other end of the line, the system executive who can exercise only such authority as both the state and the governing board delegate is usually the first to be blamed.

Two conclusions emerge from the locus of ultimate authority in the state. First, in every state and for every multicampus university in the study, there are some powers of university governance which the governing board does not have but which remain with the state and its agencies. Second, because *ultimate* authority is not generally in the governing board, the allocation of authority between the board and the administration is often unclear, a problem by no means confined to geographically distant campuses.

COMPOSITION AND STRUCTURE Governing boards have been subject to substantial comment and analysis, virtually all of which is as applicable to the multicampus boards as to those governing only single campuses. Except to the extent that the mechanics of governing more than one campus require different procedures, the multicampus boards operate through such time-honored procedures as regular monthly meetings and a variety of committees. Members of these boards are like those on boards of single campuses insofar as selection, tenure, and general beliefs and attitudes are concerned (Martorana & Hollis, 1960; Hartnett, 1969); they are equally subject to the criticism of those whom they govern.

That five of the nine multicampus boards closely resemble those of single campus universities is obviously attributable to their origins as such. On the other hand, four of the nine had the opportunity to avoid the traditional pattern but chose not to do so. Even had they sought guidance to patterns of governance beyond the traditional, however, little would have been found. Differences between boards in the public and private sectors, and minor variance in particulars, have been overshadowed by uniformity.

However, traditional governing boards are everywhere undergoing extensive reexamination. The previous acid criticisms of Veblen (1957) and Beck (1947) have little practical effect in contrast to current pressures discussed here. The multicampus universities are being subjected to the same pressures felt throughout higher education.

A first and common pressure is the rapidly rising interest in faculty and student participation in academic governance. In the late 1960s, at least two private universities added representatives of younger alumni to their boards, and one called for a faculty representative from an outside campus. That these private campuses could so easily revise their board structure in comparison to public institutions is not surprising.[2] However, among public institutions, there is an important distinction to be made about such changes in the multicampus as opposed to the single-campus university. Pressures for *systemwide* faculty and student participation have probably been less pronounced and adequate responses to them more difficult than in a single-campus university. Both reduced pressure and greater difficulty in response stem from the same cause, the isolation of the board (and the central staff) from faculty and students. Less pressure for representation on the board is felt because the board is not identified as an important governing structure vis-à-vis the local campus administration. A fine distinction between representation and tokenism is apparent: one or two young alumni or academic professionals on the board of a single campus can be representative of faculty and student interests. In a multicampus university, however, the numbers and dispersion of the campuses can make such participation appear artificial and contrived. Who "speaks for" 200,000 students or 10,000 faculty members? Of what significance is alumni representation, if the delegate is always from "another" campus?

Second, in addition to the "political" pressures for participation, a common pressure arises from the growing number of faculty and students. Again, growth is not unique to the multicampus systems, but multiple campuses involve larger numbers, and in dealing with them substance can be diluted by procedural formalities.

The third pressure — for possible restructuring of the governing boards to include local boards — is peculiar to the multicampus systems. The traditional academic governance pattern of one board for each campus seems to have had little or no influence on the initial structuring of the multicampus universities. More recent pressures for local boards have arisen from the local campus and community, while in other cases, the governing board and the central administration have been the source of this pressure.

EXERCISE OF BOARD POWERS   Although growth of a multicampus university *might* change the manner in which the governing boards exercise their powers, the increase in the size and number of campuses has not been matched by a shift in the conduct of the governing boards.

The proper role of a governing board has everywhere been said

[2] Harold Orlans (1962, p. 169) suggests that greater management flexibility of private universities enabled them to respond immediately to federal research needs during World War II in a way that the public universities could not.

to be that of setting policy—the development of general guidelines or rules for the central administration and the campuses to apply in individual situations. Most boards are deeply involved, however, in specific decisions. Writing of boards for single campuses, Moos and Rourke (1959, p. 307) commented that the ". . . quest for an authoritative statement on the position of . . . [governing boards] . . . is a perennial one." More than ten years later, the quest seems no closer to completion. Martin Trow (1970a, pp. 7–8) suggests that the role of the boards is everywhere in flux, with trustees losing power to external authorities, on the one hand, and to faculty and administration, on the other.

Despite uncertainty and ambiguity, the multicampus university board exercises two kinds of powers, usually categorized as *coordinating* and *governing.* We consider all such powers as part of the governing process, whether they are exercised by the state government, the board, the coordinating agency, or the administration and faculty. Most powers exercised in the multicampus context by all of these groups are those traditionally associated with higher education generally. On the other hand, some can be found only in a multicampus university, for they are unique to an academic organization with more than one campus.

For example, approval of a new academic program, at least its funding, is a traditional board function at any institution. Exercise of this authority in a multicampus system, however, has the additional and not incidental effect of allocating the approved program to a specific campus. Although board actions cannot be readily categorized, the governing boards appear to exercise those powers peculiar to a multicampus university with a broader "policy" view of their responsibilities than they do in the exercise of powers traditional to all governing boards.

Traditional board functions, however, are handled in the detailed manner for which most boards have long been criticized. At every system we heard stories about board involvement in the tedious detail of some local administrative matter. The criticism which Parkinson leveled against high-level bureaucratic concern with minutiae appears equally applicable to multicampus governing boards. This criticism was heard more often, however, than an answer to it. If the governing board is not usually qualified to assess the efficiency of the acquisition of costly, sophisticated, and highly specialized scientific equipment, most members can determine if a proposed building is too costly. Public and private boards of directors use the building as a rule of thumb to measure the effectiveness of a $5 million purchasing program. While perhaps not the best solution, it is common and not unreasonable.

Although there is some justification for a governing board's interest in detail, it does not extend to the depth and breadth of such interest. Two related cases are illustrative. The activities of the student union on one flagship campus are managed by a campus committee composed of students, faculty, and administrators, and committee minutes are forwarded each month to the university governing board which has authority to reverse any action taken. Exercise of such authority in two cases exemplifies the inability of governing boards generally to extricate themselves from detail. (They may also illustrate the tendency of multicampus board members to keep their fingers in pies at the flagship campus.)

The first case involved the proposed location of a radio antenna on top of the student union building for use by the campus radio club. The governing board overruled the campus committee to permit the campus radio club to install the antenna, subject to quite specific stipulations concerning the structural condition of the roof. In the second case, the multicampus board overruled the committee to deny use of the union building for the annual national meeting of the Students for a Democratic Society. The board should not, we suggest, have been involved in either decision.

The location of a radio antenna on a student union building should come to a governing board only because of major aesthetic or fiscal considerations, neither of which seemed present in this case. The board simply decided that the student union committee had made the wrong decision, but even if it had, the exercise of the governing board's power was inappropriate. If the board undertakes to review all the decisions made during a given month on any campus, it will have little time for anything else.

The problem of a meeting place for the Students for a Democratic Society is quite another matter. Here, the question is not whether the SDS should have been permitted to meet in the student union, but whether the governing board should have made the specific decision. The proper function of the governing board should be, we suggest, the framing of a general rule under which the campus will be guided to the proper decision. Framing such a rule poses a number of difficulties, but requirement of specific guarantees of financial responsibility together with a more general statement concerning probability of violence or disorder might have solved the problem.

Undoubtedly, the governing board's review of the student union committee was a holdover from its governance of only a single campus. There appeared to be no review of similar activities at newer campuses. Such interest in the flagship campus is quite common, although rarely as formal. One campus executive complained that student disorder on the flagship campus meant more stringent but wholly unnecessary rules for his remote one. Aside from controversial matters, however, turnover of board membership does tend to turn the board's interest to the system as a whole as habits of working only with a single campus fade.

At least five of the nine boards have agenda filled with so many items that serious attention to most of them is not even considered a remote possibility. For example, hundreds, sometimes thousands of promotions, transfers, appointments, and changes of status for faculty and other employees require formal board approval in more than one system. Nor are the boards unaware of the difference between policy and administration. The true situation, we suggest, is that the multicampus university boards, and probably most governing boards, simply do not fully accept the policy-administration distinction. It seems unlikely, moreover, that anyone can do much about it. One member of a governing board in the study publicly commented:

The statute creating the board says that it shall govern the university. . . . It doesn't say that it shall oversee the administration. It expressly says that the board can hire and fire professors, appoint administrators, approve salaries, and make all other rules and regulations. That doesn't sound like it's only a policy board.[3]

Although both organization theorists and practicing administrators alike might agree that this statement is primarily commendable for its candor, it is probably more representative of board attitudes than is generally admitted. Statutory authority to govern includes whatever detail the board may wish it to. It is an attitude with which academic administrators will have to live for a longer time than most want to believe.

The attention the governing boards give to immediate and de-

[3] Quoted in Carter (1969, p. 1154).

tailed matters brings uncertainty to day-to-day administration at the several campuses by removing decisions from the place where they are most operational. Equally serious, perhaps, is the unerring accuracy with which most governing boards seize upon details. It precludes their giving attention to the hard policy decisions required for general rules and planning. Few systems have a reasonably accessible, complete, and current set of general rules. This lack is partly attributable to the rapidity with which organizational structures are changing. It is also attributable to the cluttered agenda with which many boards are faced each month.

A board can be a strong policy board, making general rules and delegating substantial authority for implementing these rules to the central administration and campuses. It can, on the other hand, operate in a highly centralized fashion as an administrative board, reserving virtually all decisions to itself. Both extremes exist. We are not persuaded by the reliance found in more than one system on statutes that do not permit delegation of the board's authority. Were change desired, the boards and the administrators working with them seem quite competent to see that the law is either amended or interpreted to allow a desired change *within* the system.

That they will do so, however, is problematic. One seasoned system executive suggested the particular dilemma confronting the boards of multicampus universities:

It's hard for a lay board to be effective in policy setting in many areas of academic life, and it is even more difficult for a board to evaluate the effectiveness with which many university policies are implemented. Therefore, boards tend to become managerial and involve themselves in administrative detail. But in a multicampus system, this becomes increasingly impossible; the very scale of the university prevents any systematic concern with management. Thus, board business tends to be dominated by the personal interests of members and crises of the moment.

We cannot assess the general application of this comment. It is clear, however, that in the 1970s the conditions under which higher education will be governed are changing with respect to the extent and source of funds, the needs and composition of the student body, the attitudes of faculty toward unionization, and suggestions that the campuses be local "instruments of social action." While these changing conditions are not inevitably on a collision course with traditional governing board practices, the boards will undoubtedly have to exhibit greater adaptability if they are to counter Trow's characterization of their "loss of control over 'their' university" (1970*a*, p. 10).

THE BOARD AND THE CAMPUSES

Although previous studies have given attention to the history, theory, and structure of governing board operation, there have been virtually no investigations of boards in the multicampus context. With respect to traditional board powers, a specifically multicampus study would probably produce little of interest. On the other hand, the need of one multicampus board to relate to several campuses produces diverse and potentially significant new relationships in academic governance.

Martorana and Hollis (1960, p. 48) stated that governing functions which were explicitly multicampus in nature were ". . . in the sense of interinstitutional programming and long-range planning . . . much less stated, accepted, and implemented . . ." than those which were traditional to a single campus. They suggested that

. . . loss of contact between the board and the several units of the system other than the main campus often leads to a view of the former as being "stepchildren" of the latter with a loss of a sense of educational mission on the part of the smaller units of the system.

Ten years later, this same lack of substantial interest in interinstitutional programming and long-range planning is often evident, but within the nine systems there is little tendency to treat peripheral campuses as "stepchildren." Lack of attention to the governing functions specifically relating to more than one campus— for example, long-range interinstitutional planning—does not appear to result from neglect of the smaller outlying campuses in favor of the flagship campus. The boards' continued attention to the main campuses, upon which Martorana and Hollis comment, seems both transitional, arising out of force of habit, and required by the greater volume of activity at a large campus.

Nevertheless, several boards are attempting to be innovative in their contact with the campuses. The necessity of governing more than one campus is, of course, an artifact of the multicampus structure. To the extent that traditional one-campus governing practices can be separated from specifically or predominantly multicampus activity, the boards seem to be pursuing an active interest in the latter. Several systems have inherited formal structures for interaction with dispersed campuses, and in these, also, efforts are being made to improve the older policies and practices.

Five possible explanations for this "multicampus" board activity were offered. Three pressures on the boards are internal, in that they concern the relationship of the board with campus faculty, students, and administration. Two external pressures are more concerned with the community in which the campus is located.

Internal Influences

Internally, the board needs contact with the campuses to make rational decisions within its proper area of authority. While the board may not be involved in day-to-day operations at the campuses, the members feel a need to be generally aware of such matters as the location of proposed buildings, streets, and parking lots. Need for campus information is not exhausted, of course, by recitation of campus physical characteristics. Governing boards of single-campus institutions have an intangible "feel" that is acquired by seeing a campus and its faculty, students, and administration, month after month over a period of years. This "feel" is also needed by a multicampus board and central staff. The central staff have, in fact, a much greater opportunity to know the campuses than does the board, although the staff members sometimes fail to take advantage of this opportunity—which for them is a responsibility as well.

The second internal factor is a mirror image of the first: If board members have to know the campuses to make more informed decisions, faculty, students, and often administrators need contact with the governing board if its decisions are to be regarded as legitimate. The board represents the unity of the multicampus university in many ways, even if, as is unfortunately and occasionally the case, unity comes from considering the board as a common enemy.

The third possible internal consideration is the currency of belief in participatory governance. One system executive noted that the faculty has a "political model" of the university which contrasts and conflicts with the governing board's "business model." Although "participation" is a popular political slogan, it is not as strong an influence in fostering board-campus relationships as its popularity might indicate. The urge for "participation" is being felt most strongly at the campus level.

**External
Influences** A fourth and external influence on the board's exploration of new relationships with the campuses is responsive to a belief that the local community should be represented in university governance. In some instances, it was suggested that the local community should have limited, defined authority over a local campus and perhaps a voice before the universitywide governing board. There is surprisingly little evidence that any concept of participatory governance has influenced relationships between multicampus boards and the communities in which the campuses are situated. Students and faculty sometimes want to participate, but local citizenry, with one notable exception, do not appear particularly interested. The exception, arising out of recurring crises at San Francisco State College, relates as much to city-state debates over responsibility for law enforcement as to questions of university governance. It is noteworthy, too, that the exception involves the one system in our study which formally provides a local but purely advisory board for each campus.

The second external factor is the necessity for the multicampus universities to broaden and deepen public support. A few systems seem to be reaching out for this additional support, to balance pressures on their campus executives. A local board can be an ally of the campus executive or a counterpressure upon him, as faculty and student participation in campus governance increases.

**RESPONSES
WITHIN THE
MULTICAMPUS
SYSTEM** These five pressures, while not mutually exclusive, are found in varying measure in almost every one of the nine universities. The responses of the governing boards have varied.

**Appearance at
Board Meetings** *Campus executives.*   At the meetings of the governing boards, the campuses are represented by the regular attendance of all campus executives in all but the State University of New York, in which the number of campuses alone precludes it. At the inception of two other systems, the system executives attended board meetings alone, apparently to establish their own position as the interpreters of board policy to the campuses. In both, however, the campus executives were subsequently invited to attend.

The presence and participation of the campus executives at board meetings is believed to lead to their greater identification with the system and so to strengthen universitywide policies. In at least one system, however, this rather abstract consideration assumes more concrete terms: The campus executive, not the system executive, responds to board criticism. Were all board members models of self-restraint, "putting campus executives on the spot" would have few ill effects. But board members are not such models, and the presence of the campus executive sometimes encourages the board to probe into details further than their major policy responsibilities appear to warrant. In only one system is there a formal scheduling of appearances for the campus executive to explain his campus activities. This scheduling has been adopted as a substitute for the prior practice of holding board meetings at different campuses.

In their contacts with the board, campus executives generally act as individuals, rather than as a group. Only in the California State Colleges have relatively formal procedures been established to permit campus executives to make their collective wishes known to the board through their own spokesmen, although informal procedures sometimes produce the same result in other universities. In this same system, a similar voice at board meetings has been given to faculty and students. In another board, criticism of one campus executive elicited outspoken support for him from the other campus executives. Although campus executives would undoubtedly gain strength by presenting a united front, they could in the process lose whatever advantage there is in having the system executive interposed between them and the board. On the whole, the informal and individual representation by campus executives seems adequate. In the rare situations when a board might seriously threaten a crucial common value, such as academic freedom, however, the unity of the campus executives can be of determining weight.

Faculty. No instance was reported of campus faculty *as such* being represented at the board meetings. Representatives of a universitywide faculty organization regularly attend board meetings in three of the systems, although there are provisions for formal participation in the meetings in only one. However, campus faculty sat with board members on committees in at least two instances where questions were raised about faculty authority which the board had previously delegated to them. On one occasion, the board was concerned about the qualifications of outside lecturers; in the other, about the procedures for enforcing rules of student conduct. System and campus executives alike generally agree that campus faculty opinion should best reach the board through administrative channels. Direct faculty contact with the board is not without cost.

While the presence of administrators at board meetings gives the board an opportunity to delve into the details of academic management, direct board interest in the details of teaching and research is a much more sensitive matter.[4]

Students. There is student attendance and participation in board meetings on an informal basis in three systems. Student representatives, unlike the faculty representatives, are officers of campus student organizations rather than of those set up on a universitywide basis. In a fourth case, the system has established formal procedures for listening not only to students but also to the campus executives and the faculty. The relatively easy access of student officers to the governing board can be particularly annoying to campus deans and directors who never get closer to the board than reading about it in the newspaper.

The limited time available to the governing board at its general or committee meetings is a major barrier to regular contact with faculty and students. One administrator commented that the desirability of student consultation with the board on specific problems is often offset by student attempts to convince board members that their "entire philosophy of life is wrong." This built-in "generation gap" is widened by concentration of faculty and student interest in areas such as curricula, admissions, and rules of conduct, which are primarily oriented to specific campuses. The difficulties of finding systemwide areas of concern for faculty and students are detailed in later chapters.

The Board at the Campus In all but two systems, the governing board meets at different campuses during the year, although there is substantial variation in the relationship of such meetings to the campus itself. In at least one instance, the campus simply provides the facilities: The board's contact with the campus is limited to what the members may see between the airport and the board room. At the other extreme, another system held meetings for two days, the first of which was devoted to reviewing activities at the campus on which the meeting was held. While board meetings at the cam-

[4] A study of campus governance by a student-faculty committee in one system characterized the lack of contact between the faculty and the governing board as "intolerable." A philosophy professor replied, "Intolerable? Heraclitus said, a long time ago, that 'the channel up is the channel down.' Dig this channel if you want to discover what 'intolerable' can mean."

puses is one of the more obvious means by which the need for board and campus contacts can be met, this system's practice of devoting a day to the host campus was being abandoned. The abandonment suggests that these meetings were not without cost, and such is the case.

Three costs of holding regular board meetings at the campuses were given. The first and most obvious is the time and expense of travel to often fairly remote locations. Also, not all campuses have adequate meeting rooms, press facilities, and the like—a far from trivial matter where board meetings have become important public and political events. Moreover, these campus meetings take many of the central staff away from easy access to information which the board might and usually does require on short notice. The time and expense of transportation and housing are of significance not only for the board but particularly for campus executives required to be absent from their campuses for two or three days each month.

A second cost, most applicable to the practice of using a full day for discussing the affairs of a single campus, is borne by the campus administration. During our visit to one campus, a local administrator explained that pressing items of normal campus business were delayed because everyone was busy preparing for the board meeting. A board officer, on the other hand, commented that campus effort to prepare for a local board meeting does little harm because it is not required every month. Not enough evidence is available to assess this unquestioned cost against the undoubted value.

A third reason why several systems are less than enthusiastic about campus board meetings is an unfortunate one. Even if a campus has adequate physical space, communications, and other facilities necessary for a meeting, it may not offer security from physical disruption of proceedings by campus militants, as has occurred in at least two instances. Extension to all campuses of the style of architecture termed "riot renaissance" to ensure the safety of the board is an expensive yet still insufficient solution. A windowless, soundproof room on one campus is just a windowless, soundproof room, regardless of location. Although this consideration has caused one system to abandon its previous policy of board meetings on the campuses, most boards still hold them, and expect to do so.

Another way of maintaining contact with the campuses is found in visits by board members to campuses on a formal or informal basis. Most systems encourage informal visits to the campuses by board members, but we were unable to assess the extent, value, or costs of these. North Carolina, with a large board, has a formal visiting committee whose subcommittees visit the campuses annually and render written reports. In the past, we were told, such visits had been a relatively pleasant formality in which visiting board members accepted the best face that the campus could show and allowed the campus administration to write the report. Currently, however, the visiting subcommittees are being encouraged to form more independent judgments, even to the extent of preparing their own reports. In one recent example, a subcommittee report that students at the campuses were unhappy with academic calendar arrangements over the Christmas holidays resulted in a board request for an administrative investigation to find a remedy.

In the University of California, relatively informal committees have made similar visits, and arrangements are made for presentations by faculty, students, and administrators. These meetings are designed to give board members an opportunity to hear directly what is on the minds of those at the campuses and to report back to the full board. The meetings appear to have met with varying degrees of success. "At one campus, even the Eagle Scouts found a militant radical to attend the meeting," complained one board officer.

There is no easy or obvious solution to keeping board members aware of activity at several campuses. The more formal such contacts, the less likely they are to be timely and, indeed, they might be formalities in the pejorative sense. The less formal, the more likely that in an era of confrontation they will be counterproductive. Several systems have shown interest in promoting informal contacts between faculty members and board members. The experience of one multicampus university was instructive: When board members arrived late for a cocktail party because of unforeseen complications at their business meeting, the faculty had been present for some time and was warmed up for discussion. The meeting was not deemed a success.

Campus Committees The nine boards of the systems in the study are generally organized into standing and special committees. A few such committees have particular implications for the multicampus structure, and these fall into categories: general committees and special committees.

One of the general committees is the previously mentioned visiting committee in the University of North Carolina. While these campus subcommittees made up of board members are of considerable influence in their advisory recommendations to the full board, they are not an integral part of the governing structure. In the City University of New York, in contrast, three or four members of the board constitute a committee for each campus. All matters relating to a campus are reviewed by the committee, and a campus executive can place matters on its agenda to get them before the entire board. The campus executives saw these campus committees as helpful in giving them a specific board member or members with whom to consult in times of crisis. At board meetings, the campus executives found that their campuses benefited from an additional spokesman.

On the surface, it would appear that the existence of the campus committees described above and their direct contact with campus executives would subvert the usual board to system executive to campus executive line of communication; we were advised that this is not the case. The system executive maintains soft but apparently quite effective liaison with the campus committees. His office receives copies of their agendas, and officers of his central staff are assigned to attend all meetings of specific campus committees. In any event, it was suggested that only rarely does a board member raise an issue on behalf of a campus on whose campus committee he sits and that such issues as are raised are easily resolved.

City University furnished the only example of operating campus committees among the nine governing boards. The structure has a respectable past, but the campus committees are increasingly unable to keep up with the growth of the number of the campuses. Their future does not seem bright.

Special campus committees have been established in at least two other instances. In North Carolina, separate board committees exist to approve the design and to select architects for buildings at each campus. Each campus executive works with the board's building committee for his particular campus and also with state building authorities, almost to the total exclusion of the central administration and the full board itself. This practice is less attributable to deliberate design by the governing board than to the extensive controls imposed by the state in all areas of governance. In Wisconsin in the recent past, the board has established two special committees, one to determine the mission of a new campus and a second to serve as its building committee. Here also, the campus executive deals directly with committee members.

Too little evidence of any kind was obtained to permit clear assessment of the value of campus committees. There does, however, seem to be unanimity of opinion on the part of the campus executives that the committees, whether special or general, are often of help and never a hindrance.

RESPONSES BEYOND THE SYSTEM Although only one of the nine systems has local boards with governing authority, purely advisory local boards exist or have been proposed in several, and one system is giving serious consideration to establishing local boards with substantial governing authority.

Local Boards: Governing and Advisory Four of the nine systems had their origins in the merger of previously independent or relatively independent campuses, and these origins have influenced the subsequent relationships of the governing boards to the several campuses. Two of these four are North Carolina with its visiting committees and City University with its campus committees. Of the other two systems, the State University of New York retains relatively independent local governing boards for each four-year and university campus, but these have quite limited powers. The California State Colleges have advisory boards for each campus.

The local campus *governing* boards found in the State University of New York (excluding the community college boards in this discussion) are relics of the former independent status of the campuses. The local board members are appointed by the governor in the same manner as the members of the system's governing board itself. The system executive is consulted, but his advice may or may not be taken. These local boards have three major statutory responsibilities: participation in the selection of a campus executive, the formulation of rules for student conduct, and the approval of an academic plan. The system does not attempt to control the local boards within their areas of responsibility; indeed, the central staff appears more interested in the independence and autonomy of the local boards than are, in fact, the boards themselves. On the other hand, because of the prestige of the system executive and the specialized experience of his staff, the local boards often seek and follow their advice.

Local *advisory* boards are found in some form in virtually every system, if only for a particular professional school within a campus.

However, only the California State Colleges have established such a board for each campus. These boards, formally appointed by the system board, are solely advisory. Members are recommended by the campus executives, who face understandable pressure to re-appoint their predecessors' selections. These local boards serve whatever purpose the local campus executive may choose, but in an era of rapid turnover of campus executives, any given board often consists of members selected because of their suitability to a previous campus executive. Although this particular defect is being corrected by limiting terms of appointment, their permanent role is yet to be defined. One campus executive rather wearily described his board as "just one more public" with which he had to deal.

The most striking thing about these local boards, governing in one system and advisory in another, is the similarity of their role, despite their varying formal authority. In both instances, the system executives consider the existing local boards a nuisance, perhaps, but neither a real asset nor difficulty. The campus executives, on the other hand, are of two minds. In both systems they believe that local boards can be of value, if there were only enough time to organize them and get the right people as members. At the same time—sometimes in the same conversation—such boards are viewed as an added chore. In short, a local board is of value and influence to the campus and to the multicampus system only to the extent that the campus executive can effectively make use of it. Examples of effective local boards exist in both the State University of New York and the California State Colleges. One campus executive of a new campus in a large town was obtaining financial and moral support from his board. Another with an older urban campus was organizing the board into working committees and attempting to make it more representative of the areas from which students were drawn. In both instances, the direction, initiative, and continuity of effort were those of the campus executives. The system, other than in providing the structure, has little influence on the apparent success of the local boards. In contrast, during a crisis at another campus which lasted over a period of several months and involved both racial violence and a faculty strike, the local board was never seriously, if at all, involved.

Another common factor is the composition of the local boards in both the State University of New York and California State College systems. Despite differences in the method of appointment, the membership appears to be a minor league image of the overall board—the "right people"—politically, economically, and sometimes socially. In several instances, campus executives in urban areas want local boards more representative of the students at the campus. Again, however, such wishes are inevitably qualified by concern over the cost in his own time and energy of local board involvement. Campus committees of the multicampus board require overtime effort on the part of board members, and local boards consisting of other citizens make a similar demand on the campus executives. Two proposals in other systems that were pending in 1970 indicate that, despite such additional effort, consideration is being given to local boards which will combine the campus committee concept with local participation.

Local Boards:
Two Proposals

Existing methods of relating the multicampus board to the campuses in all nine systems have been determined by history rather than current needs. With the possible exception of the State University of New York, where local boards are authorized to approve rules for student conduct for their campuses, none of the local boards substantially influences the activities of the system board or central administration. The two proposals discussed here, therefore, represent instrumentalities of governance which are quite new in the context of the study and, if not entirely new,[5] at least unfamiliar to higher education generally. Neither proposal was far enough advanced in 1970 to permit assessment.

Stronger advice. The first but least-developed proposal, suggested informally within the California State College system, would strengthen existing campus advisory boards without changing their advisory character. These campus boards consist of important local citizens, but are not only without authority but without any

[5] Local boards exist in a variety of forms. One interesting example is the local "Planning Committees" of the Texas Senior Colleges, a multicampus system not included in the study. Three members of the multicampus board itself are designated as a "Local Committee" for a campus; they and the executive director of the system constitute four of the thirteen members of the campus planning committee. Four campus administrators are members: the campus executive, his chief fiscal and academic officers, and his architect. A faculty member and a student are committee members. Three local citizens make up the total, and of these three, one is the local mayor or his representative and another represents the local chamber of commerce. The planning committee is advisory to the multicampus board.

clear channels of communicating with anyone other than the campus executive himself.

The proposal would maintain the advisory role of the local board, but place on it, as a liaison member, at least one member of the multicampus governing board. All major policy matters pertaining to a specific campus would be considered first by its local board, which would then give its recommendations to the campus executive for transmittal to the multicampus board. The local board would not, however, be restricted in the matters which it might consider on its own initiative. The suggested reorganization appears to result from a desire to strengthen the hand of the campus executives by bringing them closer to both the multicampus board internally and the local public externally, balancing the relative influence of faculty and students.

Campus executives view the proposal with some misgivings. They see probable conflict between a strengthened local board and their own faculty and students. Even at the early stages of discussion, faculty organizations have expressed fear that a stronger campus board might weaken their influence at both campus and multicampus levels. The governing board of the California State Colleges has relatively less formal authority than most other boards in the study, especially in the area of finances, and much of the authority which it does have has been delegated to the campuses. Vocal and active systemwide employee organizations keep close tabs on the authority the board possesses, and campus faculty organizations are relatively strong. The interests of both campus and system faculty groups might be upset if the existing but innocuous local boards were given additional functions, even though these would be only advisory.

Finally, individual members of the governing board have expressed reservations regarding the proposal. Their objections center around the logistics of meeting schedules and time demands, loss of board authority, and political efforts to establish independent local boards.

Thus, despite its merits, the proposal would seem to face substantial obstacles in being accepted or implemented.

Beyond advice. The second proposal, formally recommended in the City University of New York, is also built on an existing structure—in this instance, the standing campus committees of the governing board. A 1968 system planning document mentioned "the growing interest in strengthening the ties between the colleges and the communities in which they are situated." Local but merely advisory boards were explicitly rejected as not an "effective means for continuing involvement in the development of . . . policy" at the campuses.

A board committee was subsequently charged with developing a new method to strengthen such ties. Its report criticized the existing campus committees, noting the difficulty the board was having in "offering counsel and assistance" to campus executives and also the limited "public participation in the governance" of the system. The committee's suggestion that individual public boards be established for each campus was tentatively approved and referred to the campuses for further study.

The proposed new campus boards would have 13 members: two alumni, two students, two faculty members, six public members, and the campus executive. All members would be appointed by the multicampus governing board from nominations by appropriate student, faculty, and alumni groups or, with respect to the public members, from recommendations of public and community organizations. At least one public member would be a member of the multicampus board and would serve as chairman of the local board.

Initially, the proposed local boards would be advisory because of legal restrictions on delegation of board authority. Ultimately, the local board would have final authority over matters relating solely to the campus—for example, approval of all staff appointments except that of the campus executive himself, approval of courses, formulation of policies governing student affairs, and community relations. The multicampus board would "place its major emphasis on the coordination of [The City University] as a system, rather than upon the governance of the individual [campuses]."

Although the representation of faculty and students is to be balanced by public and alumni representatives and the campus executive, this second proposal does not seem based on the need to strengthen the hand of the campus executive. Rather it seeks a broadened public support for the system as a whole through local community involvement with the campuses.

In its suggested authority allocations, the multicampus board appears to be giving to the local boards authority which is clearly administrative in its emphasis on specific decisions—for example, "hiring of nonacademic personnel" and "changes in courses, credits, numbers, etc." Two reasons for this type of allocation were suggested. First, the statute under which the multicampus board operates is said to prevent the board from delegating "any of its powers to any other individual, board or body." Whatever specific effects this inability may impose, it appears to have habituated the board to continuous concern with the details of most aspects of campus academic administration. The habit is undoubtedly reinforced by the campus committee structure, which affords board members an even closer look at these intricacies. Over the years, this attention to the specific rather than the general has led to an apparent belief that such detailed considerations are necessary and proper board responsibilities. For example, designation of a course number is considered such, but because of system growth it has become a function which the multicampus board itself can no longer perform adequately. Therefore, it is proposed to be delegated to a new local board, although it is, we suggest, more properly a matter for strictly faculty and administrative concern.

Second, although advice of legal counsel in the City University system may have loomed large in the centralization of authority in the multicampus board, its short history indicates considerable concern for the maintenance of central authority for its own sake. Establishing a multicampus structure with a central administration over previously independent campuses has not been an easy task in any of the four consolidated systems. In this instance, too, the board of City University may have a natural reluctance to let its so recently hard-won authority go completely. The limited authority to be delegated to campus boards under the proposal is of a type that most boards in the study have already delegated to either the system executive or the campuses. By placing one of its own members on the local board as chairman, the overall board evinces unwillingness to relinquish even these small areas of board authority.

This proposal for a local board composed of faculty and students as well as public members is undoubtedly one of the most innovative structures to come to our attention. It is flawed, however, perhaps fatally, by the unwillingness or inability of the multicampus board to delegate substantial authority over general decisions, rules, and policies to the proposed local boards and to delegate detailed administrative authority to system and campus executives. Nevertheless, the proposal is one to be followed with interest. The creation of new institutions of campus governance, as well as new forms of statewide coordination, are certain to be key issues of higher education in the decade of the 1970s.

The Old Boards

In three systems, the governing boards of previously independent private campuses remained in existence after those campuses merged into the larger multicampus universities. In the State University of New York, one such continuing board (Buffalo) has assumed the functions of a local board with limited governing board powers typical of all campuses. In the other two instances (Kansas City and the California College of Medicine), the boards have survived primarily as fund-raising organizations. Although the major problems of a merger in each of these three survivals were highly individual, two generalizations are possible.

First although in each of the three cases financial difficulties of the private campus had led to the merger, the surviving board retained control of some funds for at least a transitional period. The terms and conditions of restricted endowment funds seem the primary reason for this retention, although negotiations leading to each merger also have played a part. One of these boards dealt directly with the campus executive to fund physical facilities for a new academic program which was not one of the priorities of the multicampus board or administration. In part at least, the replacement of the campus executive, a local cause célèbre, was the result of the tension created by his close relationships with this surviving board. Although the difficulties between the central administration, the old campus board, and the campus executive appear to have been mainly those of differing styles and personalities, the ability of the local board to control certain funds was assuredly an important factor.

The second generalization is that the types of individuals sitting on the board of a private campus that survives as a local board can be quite different from those on the board of the university system. The differences are such to form—possibly unavoidably—a foundation for conflict which will disappear only when the local board members accept the realities of public control and the authority of the multicampus administration.

5. *Administration*

The chief executive and the central administration of a multicampus university are unique in educational organization. Every college or university in the country has a governing board, and each has a campus administration, but only the multicampus university has an intervening administrative layer between the campus executive and the governing board, and one with authority and prestige.[1]

Although the central administration is our focus, this chapter covers administration generally, and many actors in this broader area are found outside the central staff. Undoubtedly, the most crucial external group is that of the campus executives. Whether organized collegially or not, theirs is generally the strongest voice next to that of the system executive. Others, not so clearly identified as "administration," are also included, principally the officers of the governing boards whose functions complement, duplicate, or parallel those of the central administration. In addition, other persons and groups essential to the success of the system executive are discussed elsewhere: universitywide faculty and student organizations, for example, are two such influential groups.

In short, the governing structures of a multicampus university are not as neatly categorized as our chapter headings might imply. We have noted one system executive's complaint that his governing board had a "business model," the faculty had a "political model," and that he and his campus executives were without simple

---

[1] As previously noted, not all university and college systems with several campuses have a systemwide executive with both the authority and prestige suggested by the title of chancellor or president. These systems are excluded— by definition—from this study. Single-board states are similarly omitted, even though headed by an executive officer with a title such as chancellor. In addition, there are several single-board states with several campuses in which there is, in effect, no chief executive at all; campus executives report directly to the board.

alternatives to either. Our "administration model" is really a set of oversimplified assumptions about the downward flow of authority from the state: the state grants the governing board a broad range of authority, a substantial portion of which is delegated to the system executive officer, who himself delegates authority both to the campus executives and among his own staff. Under these assumptions and from the appearance of the usual organization charts, authority flows like a mountain waterfall, cleanly and clearly from one pool at a higher level to another at a lower. These assumptions, of course, are almost outrageously incorrect in all nine multicampus systems. Their organization charts, if any, rarely convey information more profound than the names and titles of the players. The assumptions and charts *are* a beginning point, however, and in a sense this entire study annotates these. We have indicated that substantial power is not always delegated to a governing board by the state. Here we note that a second major qualification to the organization chart model is the omission of faculty authority and influence.

Although there is nothing new in recognizing faculty participation in administration, it remains true that their influence is much greater than persons outside academe generally realize. Sometimes their authority is formally delegated; more often it is informal and traditional. Whether tolerated or resented, whether enhancing academic freedom or clamping a dead hand on progress, whether good, bad, or neither, "faculty power" confounds and complicates strictly administrative lines in every multicampus university. The interest here is on the administrators, but the faculty is everywhere in the wings. A few wait in the right wing, an academic procession resplendent in caps and gowns; a few in the left, a bearded and sandaled picket line. Most, however, remain in their offices, classrooms, or laboratories, talking to each other, to students, to congressmen, or perhaps to themselves. Many are only vaguely aware of details about the administration of the multicampus university, although all are, in fact, deeply involved in it.[2] Here we mention

---

[2] Dykes (1968, p. 42) surveyed faculty participation in the governance of a single campus and concluded that ". . . academicians hold an exceedingly simplistic view of the distribution of influence and power in their own community. The faculty . . . attributed to the administration vastly more power than it actually possesses. The constraints imposed on the administration from within and without the university were only dimly perceived, and the potency of countervailing forces was vastly underestimated."

their involvement only in passing, leaving more detailed discussion for the following chapter.

THE CHIEF EXECUTIVE OF THE MULTICAMPUS UNIVERSITY

The administrative as well as educational keystone of the multicampus university is its chief executive officer. In terms of personal characteristics, he is not unique. The executives of the nine university systems do not differ markedly in either education or professional experience from their single-campus colleagues. No real difference had been anticipated, although one could certainly have been justified. On the face of it, the talents and temperament required to meet—perhaps confront—faculty and students on the campus immediately after breakfast every morning differ substantially, in degree if not in kind, from those needed by the more isolated system executive. In this context, the system executive's concerns might be characterized as strategy and the campus executive's as tactics. However, this commonplace military analogy, which distinguishes the type of individuals best suited for different levels of command, is a poor one in the traditionally, if not currently, less bellicose field of academic administration. The strategic plans of an army group or theater commander consist of *his* broad and relatively long-range plans, which his subordinates implement. In contrast, the strategy of a system executive often entails enticing his "subordinates" into letting him know what *their* long-range plans are.

System executives resemble their campus counterparts in their professional careers: Of the nine who were in office in 1969, five had held faculty or administrative positions at one of the campuses in the system, and four of these had been campus executives, three at the major campus. Of the remaining four system executives who had come from outside, one had previous service as a campus executive, and the remaining three had been deans or other academic officers on a campus.

By combining the experience at several multicampus universities over time, it is possible to hypothecate a pattern in system executive recruitment. In systems which originated from a single, flagship campus, the executive of that campus became the chief executive officer for the newer campuses as these were established, without relinquishing his authority for the main campus. Later, a separate executive officer was appointed for the peripheral campuses and, shortly after, for the flagship campus as well. The original campus executive became a system executive almost by right of succession.

When it eventually became necessary to replace him, many of the bonds which formerly connected the flagship campus to the central administration had been weakened: dual staff responsibilities had been separated; attrition had reduced personal relationships; the newer campuses demanded increasing attention from the system executive. The final stage was reached when the executive of the flagship campus was no longer the most obvious or inevitable choice as a replacement. The new system executive would be appointed from outside the flagship campus or even outside the system.

With minor exceptions, this cycle has been completed in two of the five flagship systems and partially so in the remaining three. The resignation of two flagship system executives in 1970 permits a further testing and refinement of the hypothetical pattern.[3]

For the four consolidated systems, on the other hand, no such pattern can be divined or projected. The recruitment of the chief executive in each appears to be a case unto itself. Regardless of the means of recruitment of system executives, however, and for all nine systems, educational leadership, broadly defined, rather than administrative skill, narrowly defined, will continue to be the prime criterion.[4]

The Personalization of Authority

The naïve assumption that the system executive is fully aware of administrative details at all campuses in the system appears to be shared by faculty, students, the general public, and the governing board in all multicampus universities. Most of these appreciate that he requires staff to compensate for lack of time to handle all aspects of university affairs. He is still expected, however, to be familiar with numerous details, an expectation regularly demonstrated at each meeting of the governing board. The identical expectation exists, of course, with campus executives, in or out of a multicampus system. While impractical at any sizable campus, it is even more so than for a multicampus system.

---

[3] In 1970, President John Weaver of the University of Missouri was appointed president of the University of Wisconsin, the first move of a system executive from one multicampus university to another. In 1971, Chancellor Albert Bowker of the CUNY System accepted appointment as Chancellor at Berkeley.

[4] In 1970, the appointments of system executives in both the Texas and SUNY systems were not made from the ranks of campus executives. Instead, the chief deputy to the system executive was promoted; in both cases, the primary administrative experience of the chief deputy had been in systemwide, rather than campus, administration.

Is the "organizational lag," which has been said (Gross, 1963) to distinguish academic administration from that of business, in evidence here? Although executive committees or even "ad hoc gatherings of experts" have not yet replaced all captains of industry, the latter are assuredly harder to identify today than 40 years ago.[5] A university, however, is still characterized by many as the lengthened shadow of its chief executive. It is not easy for the system executive to avoid the impossible expectations which this imposes, even by explicit shifting of the burden to another person. Successful delegation of authority is difficult. Like the political executive, the head of the multicampus university may ease his workload, but he cannot relieve his responsibility. No one can speak for him.

His problem differs from that of the campus executive. At the campus, deans and department chairmen are officers with fairly clear authority and responsibility, which they exercise independently of the campus executive. Whether formally true or not, they generally speak for themselves, not as agents of the campus executive. The immediate staff of the campus executive also tends to be faculty-based, facilitating both staff members' recruitment and lines of communication within the campus. Locating a chief deputy for the campus is generally a matter of selecting among a number of senior deans, all with experience and credibility at the campus. Tradition and sound administrative practice combine to make it possible and acceptable for the campus executive to delegate important aspects of his authority both to a chief deputy and to other subordinates.

A system executive's problems in recruiting and retaining a chief deputy are far greater. Neither tradition nor a stable of experienced academic administrators are available to him. Nor are the conditions the same. The system executive's tasks are a level away from friends and colleagues and might not attract a person who would accept a position as the "number two" man at his own campus. Moreover, it is not only faculty and students who have to be satisfied with the surrogate, but campus executives as well. These are often and understandably reluctant to deal with anyone other than the chief executive. It is not, we believe, coincidence

---

[5] Bennis (1966, p. 12) sees the executives of the future as coordinators of "adaptive, temporary systems of diverse specialists. . . ." His concepts are popularized in "Organizations: The Coming Ad-Hocracy," a chapter in Toffler (1970, p. 112).

that in two of the four systems with the most success in making the task of the system executive manageable as of 1970, the chief deputies to whom the system executives delegated authority had themselves been former campus executives—in both cases, however, from outside the state.[6] In the other two of these four systems, the multicampus structure was relatively new, and the deputy retained the prestige of his similar prior position at the flagship campus.

The remaining five systems appear to be groping toward the solution of a prestigious deputy, but it is not easy to reach. It requires finding an executive as competent as the system executive and convincing him to take a job perhaps less prestigious than the one that he might be holding or could obtain. It requires finding a person ready to make a career break from his campus and its academic and professional ties, a move not necessary for the chief deputy at a campus. Both time to find a number-two man and money to pay him are essential. Two or three systems have just barely enough senior administrators to cover all bases, possibly reflecting a smaller number of campuses or less need for the prestigious second-in-command. Two other systems have formal deputies or number-two vice-executives, but they do not yet appear to have attained the high prestige of those noted above.

In two systems, a division of the chief executive's administrative load has been attempted through the establishment of a senior staff officer directly responsible for some but not all campuses in the system. These segmental staff officers, discussed in detail below, were primarily distinguished from chief deputies by the limitation of their authority to specific campuses. While we see little future for segmental specialists, it can be predicted that a prestigious deputy to the system executive will play an increasing part in the multicampus scene.

The Division of Labor   Although reached by different routes, the system executive's tasks in each of the multicampus universities are approximately the same. As a generalization to be immediately qualified, he is—in relative terms—primarily responsible for *external* affairs and the campus executive for *internal* ones. The system executive's responsibilities go beyond acting as a conduit for opinions and suggestions from the

[6] In 1970, both men became the executives of multicampus systems in other states.

campuses. His tasks are to initiate policy and planning recommendations for the governing board and often for the legislature and to determine how laws and policy decisions are to be implemented. The campus executives, on the other hand, concentrate on campus activities, emphasizing the academic side of university administration—a side sometimes neglected, to be sure, in the press of contemporary educational crises.

In general, the multicampus structure divides the traditional duties of a single-campus executive to permit specialization and avoid overlap. This division of labor is found in all nine multicampus universities and, despite numerous qualifications, provides a useful overall view of the internal relationship between the system and campus executives. It also helps explain how they represent themselves to the outside world. The internal-external division of labor between system and campus executives is not, however, a division between administrative activity and educational activity, but between internal and external *administrative* activity. Most educational activity is well under the control of the faculty, and reallocating the traditional tasks of a single-campus executive does not undo such faculty dominance. In a multicampus system therefore, the campus executive has more interest in educational activity, but only because he is closer to his faculty and students than the system executive.

There are, however, three important qualifications to this generalization. First, the system executive's concerns with more than one campus are not traditional. In essence, this entire study explores these nontraditional duties of the system executive. Second, external affairs do not belong to the system executive alone. Campus executives have a real interest, not only in the local community and local legislators, but also in any statewide or national matter which explicitly impinges on their campuses. Third, internal affairs are not the exclusive province of the campus executives but concern the system executive as well.

Almost universally, interviews revealed that system executives consider their primary task to be *educational leadership,* and that to be effective they must maintain interest in the internal operations at the campus level. The meaning of educational leadership was suggested by one system executive's criticism of coordinating agency staff. He believed that the function of the coordinating agency was budgetary only, and that they had neither the capacity nor responsibility for handling substantive questions of curricula and degrees. He characterized the coordinating staff, however, as "professional educators who aren't content to cut the budget but have to make their name in academic matters." He felt that the agency staff had pushed itself into educational issues where proper levels of decision should be within the system. On the other hand, there was little doubt in his mind that a wide variety of academic matters at the campus level were the proper subject of *his* interest —for example, the expansion of a library or continuing education at the campuses. Without such concern for internal campus activity, he could neither encourage diversity and cooperation nor require specialization among the campuses.

Another example of interest in matters internal to the campuses was suggested by one system executive who believed that acting as spokesman for the faculty was one of his prime duties. He observed that, "Unless I represent them, the faculty voice doesn't sound at the system level." Another executive saw himself as the representative of the students at the multicampus level. And in still another instance, it was the system executive to whom campus faculty grievance committees reported on questions of tenure and dismissal, formally bypassing their campus executive. Yet again, a system executive had the final authority to approve the extension of an existing degree to a new campus program. In sum, in all multicampus universities, system executives are directly involved in the internal affairs of the campuses. Each, indeed, can be an educational leader only because of such involvement.

Under the division of labor posed above as a useful generalization, however, the campus executive should be the educational leader at his campus. If every campus had two leaders, there could be tension between them, and this is indeed the case. Conflict is rare, but tension is always present. Otherwise perceptive administrators can sometimes be blind to the implications of the two overlapping executive positions. When a campus executive complained that his personnel appointments were "being reviewed by clerks" at the multicampus level, the system executive denied the accusation. "I review them myself," he said, shifting the tension from a bureaucratic level to a personal one.

The division of labor is far from orderly where the system executive intervenes in internal campus processes. Yet his intervention is vitally necessary. Only the system executive can, as one so stated, provide a forward thrust in educational planning which will bring the governing board, the legislature, the governor, and public support along with it. Without active involvement in internal campus processes, such forward thrust, if it exists, will be ill-informed and lack credibility.

Central Office Location Some years ago, the central offices of the California State Colleges were located on a street named Imperial Boulevard. Although long since removed to newer offices at another address, the central administration remains "Imperial Headquarters" to the faculty at the campuses. Less trivial, though sometimes hardly less accidental, aspects of central office location significantly affect the system executive and his staff.

In 1969, six of the nine central administrative offices were located on the major campus of the system; indeed, two occupied the same building as the campus administration.[7] Location of the central offices at the main campuses is not an accident, of course, but derivative of the transitional nature of the growth of the multicampus structure. Although little can be said about informal individual contacts between system executives and other campus executives, there are aspects to living in the same town which are impossible to overlook. For example, confusion over mail and telephone calls may grow more serious with the increasing volume of communications.

Bureaucratic annoyance at misdirected mail is minor, however, compared to very real confusion in the minds of faculty, students, and public when system and campus administrations seem to overlap. One campus executive, referring to his system executive's informal social contacts with students, said that "he butters 'em up and then turns 'em loose on me." The complaint was good-humored, but a complaint nonetheless. There were similar stories at all six campuses.

In more recently established systems, the confusion is often not just in the eyes of the beholders. The reluctance, conscious or otherwise, of individual members of the central staff to relinquish previous operating authority is matched by some hesitancy on the part of flagship campus administrators to let them do so. With the best of intentions and the most precise delineation of authority,

---

[7] Several years before, in one multicampus university, the newly appointed campus executive refused to share a suite of offices with the system executive. The nominal headquarters of the campus shifted to the faculty study of the campus head. Weeks transpired before the system executive reluctantly agreed to the symbolic break which separate offices implied.

personal ties between staff members and the campuses of their prior affiliation can ultimately be broken only by attrition.

Furthermore, it requires more than one or two generations of system and campus executives to solve identity problems which arise outside of the academic community. To the state as a whole and to older alumni, the system executive often remains the head of a flagship campus. At an alumni meeting, one flagship campus executive, the chancellor, was greeted and, after a quick look at his name card, introduced by old grads as "Chance." The system executive of another large university was regularly given personal credit for the athletic triumphs of one campus and personal blame for "revolutionary" activity on another.

In the community where both campus and central offices are located, the problem is not confusion over who is in charge, but perhaps the opposite. Town is well aware of Gown's hierarchy for social purposes, even if it does not appreciate all the nuances of decentralized authority. The traditional residence of the flagship campus executive sometimes has been continued as that of the system executive and remains a local social landmark, if not an architectural one.

The problem of central administration location at the flagship campus has two other facets. First, it is much easier to recognize the confusion than to do anything about it. Central offices have been moved to another building in one or two instances, or across the street from the campus in two others. Although these were recognized at the time as halfway measures, moving farther away raised the equally difficult problem of where to go. This quandary is sometimes colored by external pressures to relocate at the state capital, a move which both system and campus executives generally oppose. Also, there are unquestioned advantages to having the central offices near a campus; as tersely stated by one administrator: "It helps us remember it's a university we're trying to manage." More down-to-earth advantages include the use of campus housekeeping and library services and the convenience of borrowing faculty for specialized assignments.

In 1970, some of the above concerns were evidenced by the move of system headquarters offices of the Universities of Missouri and Texas away from the main campus. The universitywide offices in Columbia are about 1½ miles from the main campus, those in downtown Austin, several blocks away. In 1971, a similar move will be made in North Carolina, with the opening of a new system office building about ½ mile from the Chapel Hill campus.

A second issue of location seems a historical anomaly. All central offices sharing a location with flagship campuses are in areas which, if not precisely bucolic (e.g., Berkeley) are nonetheless not in the major cities of their states. While the relocation of the central administration into the heart of the major cities is undoubtedly not the answer, it remains true that some crucial problems of the major cities do not seem as pressing in Urbana as in Chicago, in Madison as in Milwaukee, or in Columbia as in St. Louis. Or, if urban issues are seen clearly, perhaps they are felt less intensely. Urban campus administrators riding subways or stalled on freeways, and surrounded by thousands of young people who are poor or black, frustrated or discouraged, are likely, we believe, to be under quite different pressures from those of a geographically isolated central staff. The differing pressures are usually reconciled, but it takes skill and patience to do so. The problem will be a continuing one, for much of the future of the multicampus university rests with its urban campuses. The problems as well as people are concentrated in the cities.

DELEGATION AND DECENTRALIZATION OF AUTHORITY

In the preceding chapter we stressed the sometimes neglected distinction between public universities and private universities, whose governing boards are completely autonomous. Governing boards of the nine public systems are all subject to some degree of control by the state. The distinction is equally important here, for the authority of the system executive and the central staff is, with few exceptions, derived from the governing board. Any governmental restrictions on or qualifications to the governing board's authority are automatically applicable to the multicampus administration. Lack of delegation by the state often results in undeserved censure of the system executive for failure to grant authority to the campuses. On the other hand, delegation by either the state or governing board of specific authority to someone other than the governing board or system executive can lead to equal confusion and uncertainty.

The Authority of the System Executive

Formal provisions delegating authority from the governing boards to system executives vary greatly. The traditional language of the policy-administration dichotomy is generally employed. The procedures of one system state that the governing board ". . . formulates University policies but leaves the execution of those policies to its administrative agents, acting under its general supervision." The system executive is the "chief officer of the University" and he ". . . may act with freedom within the lines of general policy approved by the board."

In another university, the system executive is called the "principal executive officer," but in this instance the policy-administration distinction is avoided, as he is instructed to ". . . formulate the educational and administrative policies of the University." The multicampus structure is also recognized in the authority given to the system executive to ". . . coordinate all activities of the institutions of the University." As broad as this delegation is, it does not match that of another system head who is given ". . . full authority and responsibility over the administration of all affairs and operations. . . ."

The apparent spirit of these broad allocations of authority to the system executives is narrowed, however, by specific board delegations. Examples are legion of detailed limitations upon the power of the system executive to appoint personnel, to transfer funds, to enter into contracts, to make purchases, or otherwise to act independently as a chief executive. These limitations are pointed out repeatedly in the remainder of this study. Suffice it to say that the division of labor between governing board and system executive bears little resemblance to explicit and general statements of policy such as those quoted above. Most governing boards can be characterized as management boards, not policy boards, and a substantial part of the system executive's time is spent seeking board ratification of specific management decisions. In most instances, this is not regarded as a serious obstacle to effective university governance, but in none is it regarded as desirable.

For more than one system executive, the transition from a campus administrator with operating authority to a multicampus executive with largely recommending powers has not been easy. "I've delegated all the authority I have to the campus executives," was one lament. "The only power I have is to persuade the governing board." This is, of course, an overstatement based on formal rather than effective executive authority. The preparation of a universitywide executive budget, for example, is a power of immense significance, despite the fact that it requires ratification by the governing board. The budget process requires countless executive decisions, only a few of which are ever effectively reviewed by the governing board. Nevertheless, lack of formal authority dramatizes the precarious role of the system administrator. If he has authority, he is under pressure to delegate it to the campuses. If he needs more, the governing board is often reluctant to grant it.

Delegation by the System Executive

With few exceptions, redelegation of the system executive's authority either to members of his central staff or to the campuses is not restricted. In one or two instances, it was argued that it is not possible for the system executive to redelegate without explicit statutory authority. It is our impression, however, that where legal barriers were offered as a reason for a centralized operation, there were other clearly understood, more cogent, but rarely articulated barriers—e.g., a wish to monitor centrally certain campus activities.

Within the central administration itself, precise allocation of authority is difficult to determine; delegation from the system executive to other system officers is more often informal than otherwise. This is not unexpected, because only rarely does a decision at the multicampus level fit neatly into the province of a single staff officer. Decisions are usually committee decisions less by design than by necessity. Formal delegations to staff officers are more likely to be found, however, when authority is delegated to chief deputies or officers responsible for segments.

Delegation of authority to the campuses is usually less difficult to identify, but it is not always easy to relate formal delegation to reality. The difficulty of identifying authority in specific officers of the central staff is relevant here. In the five flagship systems (those which originated from a single major campus) many staff officers had exercised authority first at that campus and then as systemwide administrators. Exercise of authority is a habit which does not disappear immediately upon publication of new administrative directives. Orders and inquiries often follow well-worn channels of communication which several of the newer systems have formally abolished.

If we are not surprised that it takes more than a stroke of the pen to decentralize a university system, we are surprised at the lack of agitation for it by campus executives. Many campus executives seem content with the status quo and are not seeking a significant increase in authority from the system executive. Two rather general factors explain this absence of pressure. First, the temper of the times is such that most administrators do not want to be heroes standing alone before enraged faculty, students, taxpayers, legislators, budget analysts, or perhaps the whole world except other academic executives. The second explanation is related to the first. The complexity of academic administration has increased to the point where substantial decentralization requires campus staff far greater in numbers and skills than in the past—budgeting and physical construction specialists in particular. One campus executive, for example, stated that he knew little about physical construction, had no one on his staff who did, and doubted if he could find anyone as competent as those who were doing the job at the multicampus level. Campus executives realistically seek moral and technical support more than the theoretical benefits of autonomy.

Delegation to Others than the System Executive

While most authority within the multicampus university flows downward by delegation from the system executive, several areas exist in which campus executives, faculty, and members of the central staff have been directly delegated authority by the state or the board. In one instance, statutory delegation by the legislature to the faculty of authority over student disciplinary proceedings was said to have inhibited attempts by the university to bring students into this process. In another, a similar delegation by the governing board to faculty resulted in rather awkward negotiations between the two bodies from which the central administration was almost excluded. In the business and financial areas, statutory delegation occasionally has unusual implications. In one instance, where a systemwide business officer holds authority under a statute rather than under the board or system executive, his authority was not considered broad enough to permit redelegation.

An important aspect of apparent allocation of authority to someone other than the system executive occurs in North Carolina, where jurisdiction over a great many administrative areas has been retained by the state. State agencies deal directly with the campuses, and to the extent that the state's authority has been delegated to anyone, it is informally delegated to the campus administrators. Their regular, direct contacts with state agencies give an appearance of decentralization within the university, because so few ultimate decisions are within the central administration's narrow range of authority. Such appearance belies the fact, however, that neither is there authority at the campus level. Many delegations of authority can and do skip normal lines of communication.

Uneven Delegation to Campuses
Whether from the board or system executive, several examples of differing delegations of authority to sibling campuses within the same multicampus university came to light.

First, as expected, a newer campus is often given more limited authority than an older one. In part, this is attributable to initial lack of qualified and experienced faculty and administrative personnel. In part, too, it can be attributed to initially limited confidence in an untried campus executive. Here, however, it is occasionally difficult to delineate administrative boundaries between a new campus, the flagship campus, and the central administration. The development of the multicampus university can be marked by a separation of: (1) the system administration from that of the flagship campus, (2) the flagship campus from the newer campus, and (3) the newer campus from the system administration. Initially, newer campuses always have less authority than the flagship campus in areas such as personnel or public relations, but paradoxically, they often achieve greater independent authority in these areas before the flagship campus. The administration of the latter is more often than not enmeshed with the central administration in a number of ways. As an interim arrangement, the same person may serve as the public relations officer for both the central administration and the flagship campus, for example. When a separate public relations or personnel man for the flagship is finally selected, it is not improbable that he is the former assistant to the university-wide officer, and that they will share the same offices.

In several systems originating from a flagship campus, most senior officers of the central administration have been operating officers of the major campus. It is understandably difficult for them to relinquish their operating functions for this campus and become "only" planners and policy makers, while sitting at the same desk and dealing with the same people.

Less comprehensive authority is delegated to newer campuses not merely because of their lack of experience, but also because it is crucial that the system maintain initial control to encourage diversity or direct specialization. In three multicampus universities in the late 1960s, system executives retained substantially more control over faculty and administrative appointments at newer campuses than they did at older ones. Only in one, however, was this discrimination formally evidenced by a written delegation. Neither in that system nor in the other two did it appear that the differential delegation was a matter of common knowledge, although it was recognized that more attention was given to academic and administrative appointments at the newer campuses. The lack of explicit statement was brought out in pointed fashion when two campus executives separately confided that each alone had been delegated the same authority in this area!

THE CENTRAL STAFF: A COMMUNITY OF BUREAUCRATS

It is convenient and usually unobjectionable to speak of the central administration as though the officers form a homogeneous group with identical organizational characteristics. This, however, is far from true. The central staff is midway between the campus administration, on one hand, and the coordinating agency staff on the other—less bound by traditional academic practices and operational determinants than the campuses and, at the same time, freer from governmental constraints than the coordinating agency. This greater flexibility means that few senior central staff officers fill administrative positions with clearly predetermined duties. Boxes on the organization charts are expanded, deleted, and rearranged to fit the qualifications and personal characteristics of the individual officer.

Central staff officers can be categorized as *board officers* and *administrative officers,* broad, overlapping categories which we have not attempted to refine. Any refinement would probably be more descriptive of the individuals than of organizational position. A brief glossary, however, to explain our use of several terms does indicate the direction of possible refinement.

Board officers have direct responsibility to the governing board, at least for some purposes bypassing the system executive. A pure example is a trust officer whose sole duty is the management of endowments. He has little or no contact with the campuses, or even with the system executive except through the finance committee of the governing board. More often, however, such officers have responsibilities which do require regular contact with system or campus administrators.

Administrative officers, by far the largest portion of the central staff, are generally solely responsible to the system executive. In some instances, a single officer might be both an administrative officer under the system executive for one purpose, such as business management, and a board officer for another, such as fiscal control.

Functional specialists are either board or administrative officers with responsibilities in particular academic or administrative areas. All board officers are functional specialists, as are most administrative officers, for example, the counsel and treasurer of the board, or a director of physical planning, or personnel specialist.

Segmental specialists, on the other hand, are exclusively administrative officers, responsible for a particular class of campuses, such as two-year colleges or medical centers.

The authority of most board and administrative officers can be generally characterized as *staff* authority. They advise the board, the system executive, or both; usually, if they exercise any authority directly with the campuses, it is in the name of the board or the system executive. Within the nine university systems, both boards and system executives have delegated some of their executive authority, however, and there are several examples of *line* authority being exercised by central staff officers in their own right under such delegations. Universitywide functional specialists in the business areas such as physical planning and purchasing afford common examples of such delegated line authority. Much less common are examples of line authority being exercised by either segmental or functional specialists who would be considered academic as opposed to nonacademic administrators.[8]

Board Officers   So long as board officers perform functions only for the board itself, there are few implications for the multicampus structure. Even here, however, conflict between administrative staff and board officers can and does arise over who should draft regulations or sign contracts. Similar conflict can occur as easily in a single-campus structure, but it would not be a source of confusion to geographically distant campuses. The staff officer of a single campus might be irritated with the interference of the board officer

---

[8] In another context, our suggested distinction between line and staff met with the following rebuttal from a system administrator: "[It is a] fiction that an education officer is either *staff* or *line,* terms that were developed in military and big business. This is nonsense in higher education, and many officers have both functions, which is sensible." Granting that staff and executive responsibility can overlap, we still find the distinction useful.

(or vice versa), but each would have a clear understanding of the other's activities. In a multicampus university, on the other hand, the geographic removal of *both* the central administration and the board officers from a campus increases the uncertainty which the campus has in determining where responsibility rests. Such uncertainty is aggravated where conflict exists within the central staff.

Secretary to the board

There are no implications for the multicampus system in the organization of the office of secretary to the governing board. Functions of such offices do not differ materially from those found in any university. In two instances, the secretary is explicitly an administrative officer, part of the system executive's staff. In two other cases, he is substantially independent of the administrative staff. In general, even when formally independent, the secretary relies heavily on the administration for information and staff assistance and is in effect an arm of it. We found no reason why the board secretary should not be a part of the usual central administrative staff, complementing rather than duplicating and sometimes confusing the channels of communication down from the governing board.

Treasurer

Treasurers of the multicampus universities—involved with the custody of funds and occasionally with endowment management —typically have little direct contact with the campuses and few unique implications for the multicampus governing structure. In one instance, there were as many treasurers as campuses, one at each location. These seemingly honorary and almost hereditary positions are held by local bankers, and seem to be largely a historical accident. In another system, the state treasurer is the ex officio treasurer of the board. Because of stringent state financial controls, this unusual arrangement facilitates delegation of financial authority to the campuses. In only one multicampus university is the treasurer involved with administrative matters and, thus, in system-campus relationships: delegation by both the board and the system executive over such matters as real estate and residence hall financing has thrust the treasurer into important aspects of university governance.

Counsel

Typically, treasurers and secretaries engage in few activities with peculiar implications for the multicampus structure; their work relates to the governing board rather than the campus. This also was true of the board's counsel in quieter times, but no longer. His responsibilities to the board have become no less, but those to the campuses have increased immeasurably. His relationships to the board, to the system, and to campus executives are discussed at length after discussion of the central staff and its procedures.

**The Adminis-
trative Staff**
The composition and activity of the central administrative staff are generally shaped by the same factors and constraints as those influencing the administration of every public campus. At the multicampus level, physical planning, budget formulation, review of academic programs, and other specific processes are often campus administration writ large. Planning and policy responsibility for several campuses, however, requires different emphasis and new roles.

Coordinators and catalysts

Whether a central staff officer's duties are limited to a specific administrative function or to a specific class of campuses, he has two roles. As a *coordinator,* he must determine whether physical, fiscal, or academic programs of one campus are consistent with those of other campuses and the system; he encourages diversity and enforces specialization. In his second role as a *catalyst,* he promotes intercampus cooperation for new activities or programs not possible for a single campus alone. The roles are never mutually exclusive and the balance between them is determined by the officer's specific area of specialization, his level of authority within the central staff, and his own interests and talents.

The ways in which functional specialization and level of authority influence this balance are described, implicitly at least, in the subsequent chapters on specific governing processes. Most members of the central staff have responsibilities limited to a single function such as physical planning. Here, however, our interest is in the system administrators concerned with several functions for all campuses or all functions for a specified group of campuses.

In all systems, of course, the system executive himself is the prime example of coordinator and catalyst. Although his major responsibility is that of representing the system to the public, his also is the ultimate authority for intercampus activity, whether explicitly so or because of his power to make recommendations to the governing board. A prestigious chief deputy, if one has been appointed, can have similar authority over internal system affairs and act as a coordinator and catalyst—as an overall educational leader.

Only two instances were found of staff officers who had titles and authority evidencing their primary responsibility as coordinators and catalysts. In one of these, a senior staff officer was designated "vice-president for universitywide activities." His office gathered under one individual's responsibility numerous activities which in other systems are handled, if at all, by different staff members. The functions of this office are sufficiently important to detail here, even though many will be mentioned again. Six objectives were listed in a planning document:

1   *Consultation and cooperative planning* involved plans for systemwide activities on the part of students, faculty, and campus executives, including regularly scheduled meetings as well as formal organizational activity such as the all-university faculty senate and the student advisory group.

2   *Personal and professional growth* involved conferences and workshops similar to the activity under objective 1, but oriented to educational matters rather than to governing processes.

3   *Sharing faculty talent and research facilities* was self-explanatory, and included proposed visits between campuses by faculty.

4   *Sharing in the arts* was similar to objective 3 but with emphasis on the creative arts. The intent was not merely to exchange talent within the system, but also to bring in artists from the outside, and to take university talent into the inner city.

5   *Publication of scholarly and educational writings* In this system, the university press was a systemwide operation.

6   *Coordination of admissions program* Essentially, this was the systemwide admissions office.

This office of universitywide affairs was "established especially to focus [on efforts] to achieve identity and unity within the University," a goal common to all nine systems. How successful it has been in achieving all the stated objectives could not be determined. Beyond the high-sounding phrases, however, specific activities are operating and believed effective. If institutional "identity and unity" are evidenced by these specific activities across campus lines, then this multicampus university is more than a collection of discrete campuses. This officer did not, however, appear to be emphasizing the role of catalyst.

In contrast, the role of catalyst was emphasized in another system by a vice-president for public service. This administrator organized, or at least was present during the organization of, new educational or research programs requiring intercampus cooperation. Campuses organized along traditional academic lines (and most are) do not always welcome injection of educational ideas from outside. It was the task of the catalyst to overcome this barrier. Not all system executives feel the need for a staff officer to seek out new ideas. One stated quite bluntly that too many good proposals from the campuses could not be funded. But so it is in all systems. The role of the catalytic central staff officer is not to look for better ideas than those from the campuses, but rather for the kinds of ideas that a *single* campus will not or cannot propose.

With the exception of the segmental specialists, central staff officers in other systems lack titles to identify them as having overall and general responsibilities as coordinators and catalysts. Several undertake these important roles, but usually within the limits of their specific functional areas. Coordinator is becoming an increasingly popular title for junior administrators, but none appears to have the status to influence multicampus governance.

Segmental specialists

We have already noted that certain system executives have delegated full authority over matters of internal governance to a prestigious chief deputy. More limited approaches have been attempted in two systems. Both interposed a senior staff officer between the system executive and campuses of a particular type—medical, university, two-year, etc. Both systems, therefore, had a segmental staff officer to whom a campus executive might report, but here the similarity ends. In one, the delegated authority was too uncertain; in the other, too great.

In the first, the authority of the segmental staff officer was both limited to internal matters—budget review, for example—and shared with other staff officers in functions such as personnel, planning, and finance. This organization gave campus executives a point of entry into the central administration which they otherwise might not have had because of its large size and the necessarily extensive outside activity of its executive. As one might expect, campus executives made varying use of what seemed to be the internal "management consultant" available to them. The exact authority of these segmental staff officers vis-à-vis the functional staff officers was unclear, and the staff was in the process of reorganization during the period of the study. The then existing arrangement had value as an interim device, for it was sufficiently complex, ambiguous, and flexible to allow experimentation with internal staff procedures, as was the case. The permanent usefulness of the organizational pattern, however, seems dubious.

In contrast, the second multicampus university had relatively clean lines of authority. Two segmental staff officers, one responsible for general campuses, the other for health-professions campuses, exercised virtually all duties of the system executive both inside and outside the system. For those campuses within his orbit, the segmental staff officer was the system executive for all practical purposes. The only other officer at the level of the segmental officers was responsible for business and finance. This system, however, was also in process of reorganization, and in 1970 this administrative pattern had been effectively abandoned.

As evidenced by subsequent changes, neither organization with its particular form of segmental staff officer was stable. In the first, the overlapping authority of the segmental staff with functional staff was fluid indeed, changing shape almost as we examined it. Senior officers on the central staff were quite clear in their own minds that the organization chart was really just a formality required by law and that their positions were not intended to be encumbered by too specific lines of authority. It is uncertain, however, just how far down into the staff itself this somewhat sophisticated idea had penetrated or shouid be allowed to penetrate. Moreover, the uncertainty was a minor source of confusion at the campus level.

For quite different reasons the other system with two segmental staff officers was equally unstable despite more certain allocation of authority. This organizational pattern was vulnerable because the qualifications of the segmental staff officers paralleled those of the system executive. It is difficult to locate, recruit, and retain even one such person to act as the system executive's chief deputy.

Finding two or more such deputies is more difficult but not impossible. But the most improbable task is locating two who will happily share the equal status that such organization presupposes.

Internal Staff Procedures Specific internal staff procedures arise from the geographical dispersion of the campuses—the physical isolation of the central administration from the operations which it plans or in some instances directs. Isolation requires a formal structure to ensure that matters brought up from the campuses are placed in the hands of someone in the central administration for action or advice. In a single-campus institution with its own board, an interested faculty member, dean, or custodian can lurk in a local administrative corridor until satisfied. Not so where the central administration is 400 or 500 miles away, and follow-up letters may follow the original inquiry into a hold box.

There is general agreement, not always evident in practice, that governing a multicampus university requires more conscious effort to organize staff activity and to order its priorities. Internal staff procedures at the nine systems vary extensively, but variation seems largely dependent on the system executive's leadership style. Freedom from traditional day-to-day campus operations means that these do not impose any particular structure on the central administration. System executives are much freer to implement their own methods than are campus executives.

The size of the central staff bears an expected relationship to the number of campuses in the system, although there are exceptions. Unexpectedly, however, the degree of formality of internal staff procedures does not have a similar relationship, a finding most apparent at the extremes: In one of the largest systems we were told that often the system executive reached decisions after discussions with members of his staff who "just happened to be in his office or standing outside the door—sometimes not even the guy whose problem was involved." At the other extreme, in a much smaller system, regularly scheduled luncheon meetings of senior staff and the system executive were quite informal in spirit, but it was nevertheless clear that they were orderly and planned business meetings.

Although the number of campuses does not appear to influence formality of staff procedure, the large size of a central staff is a problem. Quantitative data on staff size are notoriously unreliable, and we do not use them here. Titles and responsibilities vary across the nine systems, and segregating the system staff from that of the campus on which they are located adds further uncertainty. In three university systems, however, the central administration numbers well into several hundreds. In these, the system executive has real and symbolic leadership problems vis-à-vis the university-wide staff, not unlike the campus executive with his faculty.

Although the staff leadership problem is most prominent in larger multicampus universities, it exists everywhere. In smaller systems, for example, campus executives and staff alike felt that "less was accomplished" when their regular meetings were chaired by someone other than the system executive. The deputy can divert some of the personal pressure from the system executive, but not all. There are occasions on which only the system executive can preside, and regular administrative meetings seem to be one of these.

Staff loyalty at the system level is highly dependent on personal ties to the system executive. The bonds of common campus origin and closely related daily operations that hold campus administrations together are largely absent at the system level.

Staff Relations with Campuses Not the least of many intractable system problems is whether and how the central staff can keep in contact with the campuses. Two contradictory points of view were in evidence. Not only at the campuses, but sometimes within the central staff itself, complaints were expressed that officers did not "get out to the field" and that they were unaware of what was happening at the campuses. One long-time campus executive repeatedly cited the example of a senior staff officer who had never visited his campus—an officer whose tenure was so short that the paint barely dried on his door before he moved on. The opposite position was equally clear: "We really got tired of one staff officer who kept coming out here to count the paper clips."

For the campus, the sad choice is between possible loss of local control because of frequent central staff visits or uninformed staff decisions. The system staff faces a similar dilemma, which each system met in a slightly different way. Although no continuum of system response can be identified, there are possible extremes. One staff officer explained by telephone to a campus executive that if the latter did not like a particular universitywide decision, he was free to find another campus! In contrast, another, sensitive to individual preferences, carefully distinguished between campuses when writing to his campus counterparts: At one campus, the executive wished copies of such correspondence; at another, the original; and at a third, nothing.

Although these examples are drawn from different systems, the two administrators might well have been sharing adjacent offices. While there may be a uniform tone to system-campus contacts, the real character of a staff officer's relationships with the campuses is up to him. Within reasonable limits, he determines the content of his position, including the style and substance of campus contacts.

As of 1970, only one system had adopted a formal scheme for maintaining staff contact with the campuses, and even this exception was the concept of a single officer. The plan appeared unusual and imaginative, but had been in effect too short a time to permit assessment. The central staff officer for academic affairs had five or six subordinates (coordinators) whom he used, in the terms of one campus executive, as "visiting nurses." On one day each week, a coordinator would visit each campus and listen to whoever came to talk about a problem—any problem. The campuses were taking a "wait and see" attitude, for there was general uncertainty about the functions the coordinators were to serve.

Although specific difficulties had not arisen during the short life of this program, the attitudes of the campus executives ranged from lack of enthusiasm to reasonably well-veiled hostility. The executive of the flagship campus—also the location of the central administrative offices—was defending a difficult perimeter, and the coordinator from the central staff was an incursion which he clearly believed to be quite unnecessary. These campus visitors were said to serve two primary purposes: First, they provided a "system presence" on each of the campuses as a tie to students and faculty —a psychological tie as much as anything else. Such "presence" was believed to promote a feeling of universitywide unity or identity. Second, the visits were seen as a practical method for the system administration to obtain a "feel" for campus activities. The question of how this "feel" was to be disseminated within the central staff, beyond the small group of visitors themselves, was still unresolved.

The visiting program was ambitious in scope, perhaps too much so. Attempting to project the image of the whole central administration on the campus is a great deal to ask of a young junior administrator. Nor did he always seem a proper conduit for all campus problems. In administration, as in academe generally, specialization lends legitimacy, and the visitors' lack of specialization was probably a handicap. The experiment left us with the impression that a sense of identity with the multicampus university as such is not something which can be too openly cultivated, however worthy the goal.

In all systems, of course, there are many examples of staff visits to the campuses. Two are noteworthy because they were undertaken on a regular and recurring basis, and, in a limited fashion, they also were intended to create a "system presence" and promote unity. In one university, the senior staff officer for physical planning has a subordinate whose formal title belies his broader duties as a troubleshooter. He does not merely respond to pressing problems, but "rides circuit" to all the campuses, primarily to talk about the inevitable problems of minor repairs and maintenance. However, his authority extends beyond these particulars, and although it is not great, it was said to be sufficient to smooth over many local difficulties as well as build goodwill for the central staff. The second example is furnished by the visits of lawyers from the general counsel's office. These also are on a regular basis and are not designed to solve any specific problem. In one of the two systems in which attorneys make such visits, we were told (by the attorneys) that these "set a good example for the rest of the central staff."

University Counsel: A Study in Centralized Operations

Each particular area of university administration furnishes its own rationale for the allocation of authority. Later chapters detail both predominantly centralized activities, such as physical planning and business and finance, and others that are generally decentralized, such as research management.

All but one central administration has legal counsel, and in each of these eight, legal services are centralized. This uniformity across all systems would itself merit further attention, but equally intriguing is the dissatisfaction of almost all campus executives with the centralization. While they concede—even reluctantly—the virtues of a centralized business or physical construction office, campus executives want their own lawyers.

The relationship between the system executive and a general counsel who reports directly to the board, as well as to him, can be complex.[9] In any university, responsibility of the counsel to two masters can produce tension, but in a multicampus university, the counsel's service to the campuses adds another client and another dimension. In an increasingly crowded and interconnected world, system and campus executives find it difficult to take any significant action without treading on legally protected toes. They bootleg advice from faculty lawyers and find themselves obtaining advice through two equally legitimate lines of professional authority.

Fortunately, examples of actual conflict are rare. Unfortunately, the possibility of it is always just below the surface. In several instances, relationships between the governing board and the system executive were at arm's length, although not rising to the level of active hostility. Moreover, in one instance at the time of the study and in another at an earlier date, board-appointed counsel resembled ambassadors from one polity to another—the counsel was the "board's man at the system central offices." The undesirability of this arrangement speaks for itself: The campus and system executives had no one to whom to turn for legal advice.

Casual reading of virtually any newspaper highlights the dramatic increase in the need for legal services to unscramble rights and liabilities of students and faculty. In multicampus universities, this need arises on geographically dispersed campuses to conflict with an almost universal belief among attorneys that their services can be most effectively performed only from a centralized location. In every system there are problems; they exist in the one system in which neither the board nor the central administration employ a lawyer, and in another which retains a platoon of them.

---

[9] The organizational question of the joint responsibility of the legal counsel to the chief executive and the governing board is present in virtually all the multicampus universities, but it is not peculiar to them, and we do not dwell on it here. Suffice it to say that in four of the eight university systems with legal counsel, his appointment is made by the board upon recommendation of the system executive, and he is regarded as responsible to both. In three he, like most administrative officers, is solely responsible to the system executive. In one system only, the appointment is made by the board without necessary reference to the system executive, and the symbolism of the distinction is not unimportant. In all cases, an effective working climate depends upon the personal relationship between the two officers.

Three principal arguments support a centralized legal office:

1 Law, unlike other areas of academic administration, does not allow a margin for error or difference in judgment between the campuses. An act is either legal or illegal, and individual educational theories or campus autonomy are simply irrelevant to legal constraints.

2 Lawyers have independent professional status with the time-honored impedimenta of customs and beliefs, one of which is that lawyers can be more effective if they cluster in a group. The better part of a lawyer's training comes from his association with other lawyers. Centralized legal services allow for both individual specialization and group consultation. Both multicampus university counsel and private corporate counsel are in general agreement that such centralized organization is more effective.

3 The position of the state attorney general as the trial lawyer for the university constitutes an additional reason for centralization in five of the nine universities. It appears likely that both the university and the attorney general may wish a single point of contact and responsibility, rather than have the state official deal separately with each campus counsel.

Most campus executives, on the other hand, deny the benefits of centralization. They suggest that the uniformity of the law and legal advice across all campuses is an artifact of centralized legal services, not a reason for it. They argue that the best-trained and most highly specialized counsel is of little use if he is neither available when needed nor intimately knowledgeable about the particular campus.

With the very minor exception of a lawyer at one campus who reviewed routine contracts, there was no exception to the centralization of university law offices at the time of the study. In every system, the university counsel (whether he reported to the board or the system executive or both) had direct control over all lawyers advising the campuses. In only three systems did campuses have specific attorneys assigned to them. In two of these, attorneys were physically located at the central offices but made regular visits to specific campuses. Visits were not directed to any particular local problem but were intended to make general legal advice available locally. In the third system, lawyers were resident on the campuses to which they were assigned, but were directly responsible to the university counsel, not to the campus executive. The first two multicampus universities were large, as were their legal staffs. The third was one of the smaller in the study.

The assignment of centrally controlled attorneys to individual campuses is intended to improve legal services by giving counsel greater familiarity with campus personalities, programs, and facilities. We have no reason to believe that such familiarity has not taken place, and similar programs are being planned or considered elsewhere. It would be a mistake, however, to assume that these efforts are considered sufficient by the campus executives. Two complaints were expressed, and a possible third can be inferred. First, campus executives do not believe that periodic visits by centrally located counsel solve the problem of *geographic* isolation of advice from the campuses. Correspondence, long distance telephone calls, and jet commuter planes are insufficient to make advice available on short notice when it is most needed.

Second, campus executives are dissatisfied with the *organizational* isolation of legal advice. Having a lawyer at the campus irregularly when one is needed, periodically whether needed or not, or actually in residence makes less difference to a campus executive than the fact that the lawyer is not *his* lawyer. Although the lawyer-client privilege is a technical rule of evidence, the principle supporting it encourages the seeking of legal advice by requiring confidentiality of the conversations. System executives may be concerned that their consultations with the university counsel may not be held in confidence if he reports to the board. Campus executives are similarly concerned, but with the added care that the central administration as well as the board might be privy to their discussion.

Although the attorneys are cognizant of the problem, there is no general agreement as to just what "confidentiality" means in this virtually unexplored area of academic legal services. In one system, for example, we were told that a telephone call from a campus dean discussing imminent student unrest would not only be considered confidential at the time, but might remain so even if the attorney's advice were not taken. In another system and at the opposite extreme, counsel regularly exchanged information not merely about legal affairs but about all campus administrative matters. In this latter situation, it was quite possible to find a net systemwide gain in free exchange of information; but any gain was at a cost to the campus executive's desire to keep—at least temporarily—certain information on his particular campus.

Third, we infer that most campus executives would prefer their own lawyers for two reasons only peripherally connected with legal services as such: for prestige and as an "extra hand," an additional staff officer with legitimacy as a generalist.

The organization of legal services is noteworthy because law and lawyers will play an increasingly important role in higher education in the future. Pressure of numbers and fiscal constraints will demand finer legal distinctions between, for example, resident and nonresident (Carbone, 1970), student and nonstudent, to name but two. One administrator (Kauffman, 1966, p. 145) has noted the belief that "loss of an educational relationship has meant increased attempts to find a legal relationship." Also, the dissatisfactions of campus executives about legal services seem clearly to require an early resolution of the organizational problem. At both levels, executive officers will have to make decisions which depend upon continuing and, from time to time, immediate legal advice. It is probable that the campuses of most multicampus universities will have resident counsel in the foreseeable future. However, the exact organizational relationship of these attorneys to the campus executives is unpredictable. The three experiments with campus counsel noted above are too recent and too limited for extrapolation.

Whether legal services are decentralized, system and campus executives, as well as the governing board, will require counsel in whom they have confidence. The areas of policy and administration in which they are free to act without possible legal liability are constantly shrinking. Moreover, system and campus executives need freedom to develop, weigh, and discard proposed courses of action with advice of counsel but without the inhibition of possible premature disclosure of alternatives to "hostile" board members. The issue is not one of concealment from the board, but rather avoidance of unnecessary debate and discussion of immature plans. Academic executives are not noted for initiating radical or illegal proposals, but with 14 or 15 campus executives in a multicampus system, the odds favor one of them periodically putting forward a controversial one. Controversy cannot—should not—be avoided, but to the extent that it can be anticipated before reaching the board and the public domain, the system benefits.

CAMPUS EX-
ECUTIVES AND
THEIR ADMIN-
ISTRATIONS

The specific administrative structure of the campuses is effectively within the control of the campus executives. In only one instance were systemwide requirements for uniformity of administrative patterns across the campuses such that they aroused complaint. Even here the complaint was misdirected against the central administration, for the limitations were imposed, in fact, by state budget authorities. The case illustrates a broader problem. The central administration had originally drawn up the details of the limitations as flexible guidelines to convince the state budget office that more campus administrators were needed. Subsequently, however, most campuses, and indeed the system as a whole, changed character, requiring more and different campus administrators than the original guidelines allowed, but the latter were being used to frustrate both needs.

The central administration in almost all systems retains an ultimate veto by requiring its approval of major campus administrative appointments. However, the veto has not impeded the local design of structures different from those of sibling campuses. Campus administrations are different within the multicampus systems, and the differences are often imaginative. One perceptive system administrator suggested that one of the primary advantages of the multicampus structure was that it could afford to be a laboratory in which individual campuses could experiment with administrative structure. He thought of administration in terms of diversity, and saw the central administration encouraging variation and acting as a shield against imposition of uniformity from above. Uniformity was clearly suggested by the report of one statewide coordinating agency:

> *We recommend,* because of inadequacies in administrative staffing that continue to exist, and because of inequities among comparable institutions, (1) that wide variation in administrative organization be eliminated in institutions comparable in size, academic programs, and statutory functions. . . .

Even if the multicampus structure can inhibit the imposition of uniformity, two related and less formal constraints are applicable to all campuses. First, the content of campus administrative activity is similar, despite variations in form. Secondly, there are always a limited number of administrators to respond to the needs. Universally, budget requests for administrative support are cut back by state agencies and legislatures on the grounds that it "takes money away from education." Expanding responsibilities, matched with a limited staff, do not lead to uniformity, but they do limit the range of possible structural variation.

Selection The head of one system said that he never knew how a campus executive was going to behave until it was too late to do anything about it. His method of selection may or may not have been representative: "You have to find someone you can get along with, regardless of anything else." It is not easy to select campus executives nor is it always easy to get along with them. The multicampus structure has implications for both problems, since the relationship between the system executive and his campus counterparts is unique. A campus executive must be selected with all the attributes of a single-campus head, yet must be willing to accept the real and symbolic authority of the system executive.

The importance of the title of the campus executive cannot be overestimated. The significance of the use of president or chancellor as the title of the system executive has been noted, and the use of these titles is equally critical at the campus level. One campus executive said he would not have accepted his position had it not carried with it substantial independent authority. Yet in addition to such authority he also insisted upon—despite the objections of the system executive—the title of president rather than vice-chancellor or provost. The campus executive wanted his leadership role recognized by the title. Here is another example of Wilson's (1942) emphasis on prestige as a crucial factor in academic life.

Even with the title, however, it is evident that the post of campus executive in a multicampus university differs from that of its single-campus counterpart. The division of labor between system and campus executive requires a willingness on the part of both to forgo a portion of the authority traditionally belonging to an academic chief executive. For the campus executive, acceptance that the system head bears the major responsibility for relationships with the governing board and the state government is not always easy. While most favor the division, more than one thought, "We could do better on our own." Regardless of the prestige or size of the campus, the campus executive is in a sense subordinate. He is also sought by a large number of governing boards of single-campus institutions able to offer "number one" status, even if on a smaller campus.

The recruitment and retention of able campus executives is perhaps the most critical task of the system head. On the one hand, he must provide them with both the substance and symbolism necessary for effective campus leadership; on the other, he must be sensitive to his own base of power, both within and without the university. The effective exercise of this balancing act represents educational statecraft at its best.

In general, the selection of the chief executives of existing campuses is based on an initial agreement between the system executive and the campus faculty, each in effect having veto power, with subsequent governing board ratification. The formal rules of most multicampus universities provide that the board make the appointment of campus executives upon the recommendation of the system executive, and in all systems this practice is followed. However, board appointment of campus executives is far from being a mere formality, as it often is with respect to lesser appointments. Although its activity is nowhere as great as in the selection of the system executive, board interest is substantial. System executives devote a significant measure of time and energy to "selling" governing board members their recommendations for these key positions, and it is clear that behind-the-scenes negotiation often occurs.

The use of faculty committees to screen candidates for the position of campus executive is a common practice within the multicampus university, as it is at single-campus institutions generally. In two systems, other campus executives from within the system are also committee members. In one of these, campus faculties select committee members and twice appointed an executive from another campus. The other system has a complex committee arrangement comprising, in addition to the executive of another campus, members of both the governing board and the local campus advisory board, as well as faculty, students, and central staff.

Obtaining faculty advice when selecting the chief executive for a new campus—one without its own faculty—is more difficult. Here, the multicampus university has a unique capability to structure an academic input to both the system executive and the governing board, not as easily available to a single-campus institution. In one case, for example, the systemwide faculty government presented a panel of names from existing campuses from which the system executive selected an advisory committee. In another, he directly appointed such a committee without the benefit of nominations. In only one system did the universitywide faculty government itself directly select the advisory committee members. In all cases, the faculty advisory committees were regarded as an important step in nominating distinguished candidates for consideration as campus executive, in facilitating their recruitment, and in legitimatizing their authority once appointed.

Meetings and Formal Contacts One central staff officer was certain that the scheduled regular meetings of campus executives with the system executive were a most important aspect of multicampus governance: "That is where the really crucial decisions are made." A campus executive in the same university was equally certain that they were a waste of time. Their disagreement went far beyond simple differences of opinion in that particular system.

System administrative activity oriented to the preservation and maintenance of the *system* as such can be distinguished from system activity directly oriented to the *campuses,* a distinction discussed in the short section to follow. It is pertinent here because the need for campus executives to meet as a group with the system executive often collides head-on with the demands on the campus executive at his own campus.

One- or two-day monthly meetings of all campus executives are common. Such regularly scheduled meetings are held in all but one system, usually before or after those of the governing board, although in two systems, meetings have been deliberately scheduled for other times of the month.

In three instances, system executives meet jointly with their staff and campus executives and only briefly and informally with the campus executives alone, either before or after the more general meeting. Two of these joint meetings of campus executives and staff which we attended presented an interesting contrast. Both were quite informal in tone, but in one, campus executives sat at the head table next to the system executive, and the central staff occupied chairs in an outer ring. In the other, only the system executive himself had a fixed seat, and campus executives, central staff, and miscellaneous others entitled to be present were scattered about the room.

Suitable recognition of the status of the campus executives might well entail formal seating at joint sessions with the senior staff officers. It is not unknown in other kinds of organizations. The question of regular seating, however, is assuredly of less consequence than whether the campus executives meet formally and separately with the system executive without other systemwide staff present at all, as is the case in five other systems. Status is not unimportant. In one of these, although the most central staff officers believed that joint meetings should be held, a more senior officer opposed this: "What they don't realize is that the campus heads are playing ball in a different league."

Three considerations other than recognition of status account for whether or not the campus executives alone meet with the system executive without routine attendance by the central staff: (1) Size is an obvious consideration. The five systems holding separate meetings all have more campuses than the three in which the campus executives meet with the central staff. The quantitative difference is reflected in our impression of a qualitative difference as well. Senior central staff officers in the smaller systems consider themselves to be part of a "family" which includes the campus executives. It is not clear that campus executives share this feeling. (2) In one system at the time of the study, and historically in another, the campus executives acted as a collegial executive. The regular presence of the central staff would have been an intrusion. (3) The campus executives as generalists have different interests and tasks compared to the central staff as specialists, with resulting difficulties in holding common meetings relevant to both groups.

The two systems in which the campus executives acted as a collegial executive were both the result of consolidations of relatively independent campuses. In one, the first act of the new system executive was to eliminate all the previously exercised collegial authority, as well as to prohibit direct contacts between the campus executives and the governing board and legislature. Later attempts to revive a limited form of collegial authority met with little success for a number of entirely unrelated reasons. Within the group of campus executives itself, those at the older, established campuses were not averse to a weak central group. (A similar preference to "home rule" by faculty is mentioned in the next chapter.) The organized systemwide faculty did not believe that campus executives should have any authority (collegial or otherwise) in which faculty could not share. Finally, and quite apart from any dispute over who might exercise delegated authority, substantial questions existed as to whether the law permitted any delegation.

In the second system, the newly appointed system executive sat first as *primus inter pares* but quickly accumulated authority both by virtue of his own personality and by enlarging an informed central staff. His position was enhanced as new campus executives were appointed on his recommendation. In this system, however, the formality of a collegial executive still remains. That it is probably only a formality was indicated by the strongest of the campus executives who said that the group rarely votes, and then only when the system executive "knows that he has the votes." This campus executive himself preferred to deal directly and individually with the system executive. Although voting is rare, he considered the interests of his campus to be sufficiently distinct from the others that pressure of numbers, if not an actual vote, would be against him.

With one outstanding exception, noted below, the most prevalent attitude among campus executives is that their meetings are not as productive as they could or should be. A tendency to deal with administrative minutiae and, particularly in the two comprehensive systems, a lack of common interests were given as reasons. Campus executives universally conceded, however, that they would not want to be left out of the discussions. An apparent tendency in larger systems for executives of similar campuses to meet together either on a formal or informal basis is too recent in all instances to assess its effectiveness. No ready explanation of why the meetings of campus executives have met with less than total success is apparent, but numbers and similarity of campuses seem important. First, some form of critical mass is involved; the numbers of campus executives in the nine systems vary from 3 to 30. Where a system has only three or four campus executives, a telephone call can probably serve most purposes in a more timely fashion than a regular meeting. On the other hand, where there are 15 or more, the group is somewhat too large or diverse for easy communication either by telephone or at a meeting. Second, the collegial meetings of campus executives and the system executive are of greater importance in those systems in which the campuses are enough alike that their executives share common problems.

Both these hypotheses are supported by the experience of the one university system in which the monthly meetings of the system executive with the campus heads are regarded as a critical process of university governance. The meetings involve less than a dozen persons, and the campuses each have a university mission. Agenda are carefully prepared and minutes constitute an important record of system-campus communication. Central staff officers participate occasionally on an item-by-item basis, but are generally excluded.

In every system, the system executive's deputy—no matter how high his prestige—is generally not an acceptable substitute for the system executive himself at these regular meetings. Campus executives recognize that demands on the system executive's time often preclude his giving personal attention to individual campus problems, but when the problems of all campuses are the topic of discussion, it is universally felt that his time should have no greater priority. System executives rarely ignore this fact, and exceptions were noted with concern by their campus colleagues.

COMMITTEES, COUNCILS, AND MEETINGS
The numbers and variety of committees or similar groups concerned with multicampus administration are enormous. Even in the smaller systems, determining committee responsibilities and status would require a major investigation. Furthermore, such information is not always readily available even within the central administration. Thus, the brief generalizations offered here are based on random evidence.

First, "important" committees at the multicampus level generally consist of a majority of administrators or are understood to be otherwise administratively dominated. In contrast, faculty influence seems predominant in campus committee operations. Decisions with the most direct impact on faculty are at the department level, and this direct impact decreases as one moves up the administrative ladder, through the school to the campus and finally to the multicampus administration. For example, campus faculty committees may strongly influence departmental space requirements and the ordering of school and campus space priorities; however, their influence at the multicampus level in the meshing of such priorities among the several campuses appears negligible or nonexistent.

Second, cross-campus committees for discrete academic disciplines are clearly the exception. They appear as "standing committees" in only one system, as best as could be determined. It is the belief of the system executive that these committees give the system a cohesiveness and identity by utilizing the professional interests of the faculty. Generally, however, cross-campus disciplinary activities are ad hoc. In another system, the primary value of a universitywide meeting of natural science faculty was considered by them to be the opportunity to compare notes on differential campus enforcement of systemwide workload rules. The scholarly impact had apparently been nil.

Third, system executives expressed unhappiness over attempts by the coordinating agency's staff to work directly with the campuses. To a lesser extent, a similar defensive concern over institutional boundaries is present at some campuses toward regular cross-campus committees of academic-affairs administrators or graduate deans. Campus executives are more seriously concerned with formal systemwide faculty organizations, as will be seen in the following chapter, and far less concerned, if at all, with systemwide meetings of business and management personnel.

Fourth, system administrators in a variety of fields usually hold regular meetings with their campus counterparts to clarify policy, pass on specific information, and establish personal working relationships. Useful exchange of information, problems, and solutions result, but this value was most often described by the campus administrators as incidental to the formal agenda. Absence of tangible results does not necessarily indicate lack of success: Such arrangements, even though somewhat artificial, nevertheless create personal relationships to fill the gaps and ease the tensions of the formal authority structure.

In sum, multicampus committees or similar groups are generally recognized as inevitable by all, desirable by some, but subject always to the concern that they have too often become ends in themselves.

6. Faculty Government

Faculty, governing boards, and a major "trade association" in higher education agree that "agencies for faculty participation in the college or university should be established at each level where faculty responsibility is present."[1] In the face of such rare agreement, we must nevertheless ask, "Does the faculty have a responsibility at the *universitywide* level?" The answer is by no means clear. The nine multicampus universities are as diverse in their system faculty organization as in any other area of governance. Not only do organizational forms vary widely, if they exist at all, but their authority and responsibility cover a wide spectrum, including a relatively inactive advisory role, a role basically counter to the administration, and a delegated legislative role over major areas of university activity.

Nevertheless, it is clearly evident that formal faculty participation at the systemwide level is on the increase. Multicampus universities with a tradition of system faculty government are seeking to rationalize it. With only one exception, those universities without such an organization are in the process of establishing it. In no case is a university in the process of dissolving or weakening the existing systemwide faculty government. There is neither universal acceptance of the status quo nor general agreement that there should be a strong universitywide faculty organization. Where the oldest systemwide faculty organization exists, frequent rumblings were heard from both campus executives and campus faculty senates about cutting it down to size. In at least two other universities, flagship-campus faculty candidly admitted to us that they would "tolerate" a systemwide organization only as long as it does not have significant power.

---

[1] American Association of University Professors (1966, p. 13).

The development and operation of a multicampus faculty organization creates new, often troubling, relationships touching all participants in university government. Few dispute that the faculty voice should be heard by the system executive and the governing board, but there is no consensus about the issues to be included in such discussions. At the campus level, it is generally understood that faculty are responsible for the hundreds of specific decisions that mark academic life: the approval of individual courses, the review of student applications for admission or for fellowships, and the initiation and review of academic appointments. But at a systemwide level, where general policy issues are debated, the faculty role is uncertain.

It is convenient to think of faculty activity at the system level as of two types. The first is *advisory* and responds to the questions: How does the system executive obtain appropriate faculty advice on matters such as educational policy and academic programs which involve the entire university? Alternatively, how does the faculty ensure that its voice is adequately heard in the councils of the system? The answers to these two questions are not necessarily the same. What may be appropriate faculty input to a system executive may be regarded by the faculty as completely inadequate, and examples of such differences of opinion are not difficult to find.

The second type of faculty activity is *legislative.* It answers the questions: To what extent, implicitly or explicitly, has the faculty been delegated authority to approve—or to have the substantive recommending role—in matters of university affairs? What kinds of machinery has the faculty established to implement this authority?

The distinction between legislative and advisory authority does not accurately measure the strength of faculty authority vis-à-vis the administration and board at the system level. Indeed, one perceptive system administrator suggested that his board reacted favorably to advice while rejecting pleas for delegated legislative authority:

Much discussion on delegation has been on broad powers, which causes the board to dig in its heels. Yet when the systemwide senate advises responsibly on . . . specific programs, the board seldom objects.

Many issues involved in this discussion are present, in different ways, at the campus level or within single-campus universities.

But special problems exist in a multicampus system. One of the few references to multicampus universities appears in a recent study (American Association for Higher Education, 1967, p. 42):

Clearly, one of the major causes of faculty discontent has been the emergence of a hierarchy of boards and super boards which has moved the locus of decision-making away from the campus and the individual professor, and which has set the stage for invidious competition among faculty groups in the overall system.

We are inclined to disagree.

Strong faculty government at a campus is, in the words of one system executive, the result of ". . . groping over a period of a half century or longer," and its strength has not been weakened by either the multicampus structure or the coordinating mechanism. Campuses without a history of faculty government are all instituting it, most often with the help and encouragement of the system administration and systemwide faculty organization. In short, the authority of the individual professor or of the organized campus faculty is either retained or enhanced by the multicampus structure.

Some decisions have "moved away from the campus," and from the system as well, but these are in areas where the faculty has never had final authority, for example, in the establishment or location of a new school or campus. Many faculty are discontented and attribute their unhappiness to a multicampus governing board. (We would guess that none complain of the coordinating agencies because few know of them.) Blame is misplaced, because the state government holds the purse strings, and most complaints concern money or what money will buy, and the boards and agencies are usually on the side of the faculty. Even where boards and agencies do cut budgets, they are exercising authority which they have always had. The diminishing growth rate of support for higher education cannot be blamed on any emerging "hierarchy of boards and super boards." Rather, the increasing scarcity of resources for growth in all systems has transformed what would have been reasonable and acceptable demands 10 years ago into competing and unacceptable ones in 1970.

Nevertheless, special problems confront the faculty, administration, and governing board in establishing useful relationships at a systemwide level. Our concern is with such formal systemwide faculty organization or government as may exist. Excluded from investigation are a variety of informal devices which system executives have established to maintain contact with faculty for personal and professional, as well as institutional, reasons. We also exclude from this study specialized institutions of faculty governance, such as systemwide graduate councils and a host of academic and administrative committees. Finally, we omit discussion of issues confronting faculty government which do not have a special multicampus relevance. Thus, questions as to the extension of membership in the various university senates and faculties to librarians, full-time research personnel, and other parafaculty types on the one hand, or to students, on the other, are mentioned only in passing.

We use faculty *government* and faculty *organization* interchangeably. Government implies authority and power, yet some of the systemwide faculty machinery we describe has neither. On the other hand, a strictly advisory body—an organization—may be highly formal and representative. The distinction between the two terms is not always meaningful and is not maintained here.

AN OVERVIEW OF SYSTEM FACULTY GOVERNMENT Systemwide faculty organization differs from that at the campus. One system executive told us that the "faculty don't do well outside their own ball park." A second thought he knew why:

All-university faculty organization has less analogy to the campus organizations than most people think. When there are important questions for legislation at the system level, the governing board wants to do the legislating.

The organizational form and procedures of a campus faculty senate have been transferred to the system level in many instances. But expectations that the system executive and governing board will or can be as amenable as the campus executive to faculty power are transferable only at the risk of being rudely shattered.

The continuum of systemwide faculty organization in the nine multicampus universities ranges from the absence of any machinery at all to a highly structured and complicated representative government, replete with bylaws, regulations, committees, paid staff, printed agenda, and complaints about red tape. Within these extremes, the middle ground defies easy categorization. Age, sophistication, and general authority, however, do suggest five categories:

1   Two systems do not have any overall faculty organization (Missouri and Texas).

2   In another two, systemwide faculty government was initiated in 1968–69 (City University of New York and North Carolina).

3   Two consolidated systems have faculty organizations that have been in existence for several years (California State Colleges and State University of New York).

4   One system has a faculty agency to coordinate the several campus senates, which reviews universitywide matters through a process of joint referral (Illinois).

5   Finally, two systems have a long history of universitywide faculty participation in governance (University of California and Wisconsin).

However the systems might be categorized, the trend toward some form of systemwide faculty participation is obvious.

Absence of a Multicampus Faculty Organization   In the University of Texas, a systemwide faculty organization of any sort is neither present nor in prospect. The system executive spoke with some longing for the "good old days" when he was head of the flagship campus and faculty contacts were plentiful. But neither he nor the faculty of either the flagship campus or the other campuses was actively seeking to remedy the situation. Indeed, an intercampus graduate studies committee was in process of disestablishment. The reasons for this pattern are not clear, but may be found in the lack of traditionally strong faculty government at the flagship campus. The university can be characterized as board- and administration-governed, and only in recent years have faculty at the main campus pressed for greater participation. Nor do the newer campuses have any real heritage of faculty government. It is no surprise that internal pressures for a voice at the all-university level are muted, if not nonexistent.

The same description applies to another older multicampus university with relatively weak faculty participation in campus governance, the University of Missouri. But here, the system executive felt the need for faculty advice and was doing his utmost to promote the establishment of some sort of multicampus faculty organization. What form the organization might take remains uncertain, and multicampus faculty involvement is not universally favored even by the faculty. This lack of enthusiasm was most apparent on the new campuses, which saw such development as a threat to local autonomy. They feared domination both by the larger flagship campus and the system administration. At these campuses, the issue was highly colored by the fact that the flagship campus was not regarded as a model of effective faculty government.

Initial Organization of the Multicampus Faculty

In two of the nine universities, initial organizational meetings of the system faculty were being held almost simultaneously with this study. But the differences between them suggest difficulties of broad generalization. In one, North Carolina, a heritage of strong and effective faculty participation at the main campus had not engendered the desire to share this role with the other campuses. The system executive has met periodically with a small, informal advisory committee, but this is nowhere regarded as adequate to the times. Establishing a system organization is complicated by the differing missions of the two large campuses, resulting in a lack of common systemwide academic interests. The prospective system organization—a 36-man body—will be strictly advisory to the system executive and, in deference to pressure from the main campus, will not vote on substantive issues.

In the City University of New York, in contrast, the development of an all-university faculty senate of some 70 persons is seen as a necessary counter to a tradition of dominant campus executives and an increasingly significant systemwide administration. Both the faculty and the system administration feel the need for more direct communication concerning major policy decisions, previously channeled almost entirely through the campus executives. The issue is complicated by the undetermined status of the faculty organization in an increasingly complex collective bargaining environment.

Established Faculty Government: The Consolidated Universities

In two other large systems, the California State Colleges and the State University of New York, surface similarities in authority and organization mask significant differences. Both are consolidated systems, created by the merger of previously semiautonomous colleges. Both have large representative faculty bodies of approximately 45 and 75 members, which have been in existence for several years. Both bodies purport to be the "official" spokesman for the faculty in all-university matters. Both are advisory in authority, with no formally delegated responsibilities from either the governing board or the system administration. In both systems, the issue of collective bargaining is an active one, and the question of whether a faculty senate can be both an advisory and a bargaining agency is being debated. Both organizations have made important contributions to major policy decisions, have strengthened a sense of membership in a multicampus university, and have provided technical assistance to campus faculty governments.

In New York, however, the system executive has utilized the faculty organization as a major advisory and consultative group and as an important vehicle for internal communication to develop a sense of common universitywide interests. In the California State Colleges, the faculty organization and the system executive are often seen as adversaries, both by the public and by each other.

The reasons for this sharp difference between the two systems appear to be basically external in origin. In California, faculty expectations were high at the time the system was established. Frustration set in when, in faculty opinion, inadequate budgets and line-item scrutiny by state fiscal authorities continued. Frustration was shared by faculty, administration, and board, but the faculty could not easily give vent to its feelings against a traditional opponent. In New York, the recent environment has been much more congenial to the aspirations of the campuses, with increasing financial support and decreasing administrative control by the state. In the first instance, the system executive has been the bearer and administrator of bad news, in the second case, the harbinger of progress.

Established Faculty Government: A Tricameral Senate

In Illinois, the smallest (three-campus) of the nine multicampus universities, there is, on the surface, little in the way of systemwide faculty organization. In a sense this is true, but the parallel reality is that the governing board has delegated a great deal of authority over universitywide matters to the faculty. Rules require that all three campus senates attempt to agree on overall educational policy through a procedure of joint referral. In effect, each campus senate serves as a unicameral legislative body for matters affecting its own campus and as one chamber of a tricameral legislature for matters of universitywide concern. A coordinating committee composed of twelve representatives of the three campuses determines whether an action of any senate concerns more than one campus and, if so, transmits it to the other campuses. The committee's responsibility to promote agreement among the three senates is substantially supplemented by its authority to make independent recommendations to the system administration and governing board in the event of disagreement.

While this legislative procedure seems to work satisfactorily, more formal advisory machinery at a universitywide level has not yet been established, although a number of specialized faculty-administrative committees are in existence. Here, the small size of the system has been—surprisingly—an impediment, for the system administration has found it possible to obtain faculty advice directly from the campuses. We sensed an increasing feeling, however, that this direct contact will not be satisfactory for the long run and that even a three-campus university requires a more formal and direct communication link between the system executive and the faculty.

Established Faculty Government: The Flagship Heritage

The two remaining systems (the Universities of California and Wisconsin) have a long and active history of faculty participation in governance. Although the patterns are quite different at the campus level in each system, the ways in which both established systemwide faculty organizations are remarkably similar. Both created large, representative bodies (approximately 70 and 90 members, respectively), composed of faculty who are elected or appointed specifically for that purpose, plus certain ex officio members. Both universities have, in effect, an executive committee composed almost entirely of ex officio members holding other faculty government offices. Both are dominated in tradition and organization by the experience of their flagship campus, much of which has been uncritically accepted at the system level and on other campuses, even though not necessarily relevant to a multi-campus framework or to quite different campuses. Both have been delegated, or have come to assume, substantial authority and responsibility over major aspects of university policy. In each university, aspects of that authority are the subject of sharp controversy between the governing board and the faculty. In both systems, too, relationships between the faculty organization and the system executive are positive and frequent.

The similarities are not complete, however. In California, the older in terms of multicampus development, an elaborate committee structure at the system level parallels in almost every detail the equally elaborate campus structures. The newer system, Wisconsin, has not developed—and hopes to avoid—this phenomenon. In part, the differing organizational response of the two universities is a reflection of their campus senates. California has a highly centralized apparatus at the campus level, while faculty government in Wisconsin is dominated by a subcampus organizational pattern of broad subject-matter divisions. Similarly, in California, important academic legislation requires action at the universitywide level, while in Wisconsin, most of this is accomplished within the campus senates. Paradoxically, California is far more decentralized from an administrative viewpoint than Wisconsin, bearing out the finding that in the multicampus universities, administrative and faculty machinery are rarely considered at the same time, under the same circumstances, or by the same people.

THE ORGANI-ZATION OF SYSTEM FACULTY GOVERNMENT As suggested, the organization of faculty government in the multicampus university is marked by as much variety as similarity. This variety is seen in the definition of membership in the faculty, the pattern of representation in the systemwide organization, the internal structure of the organization and the respective roles of the system and campus executives within it, and the nature of faculty representation.

The Definition of Membership The definitions of faculty, in terms of eligibility to vote for or serve as a representative in the system faculty government, vary from detailed specification in the bylaws of one governing board to the generality in another that "regular" faculty are included. In some systems determination is up to each campus, and in others there is no definition at all.

In all cases but the one in which membership is fixed by the system, the definition includes all faculty from the ranks of instructor to full professor; in the single exception, only full professors are automatically eligible to vote or serve, with representation from the lesser ranks determined by their senior colleagues at each campus. Little consistency exists concerning the inclusion of other classes, such as lecturers, librarians, health service personnel, and student services staff.

Membership definition is directly related to the extent to which the faculty agencies, at either the campus or system level, are legislative rather than advisory. Where the faculty has been formally delegated authority, requirements for membership in the faculty government are more restrictive. Faculty organizations with a strictly advisory role, on the other hand, permit a broader and more flexible definition. Flexibility is most noticeable at the campus level, where, in several systems, membership in the local senate varies from campus to campus, with no requirement for universitywide approval. Within the same multicampus university, membership in one campus senate included the librarians and professional student personnel staff but no student representation, while on another campus, students were represented, but staff with non-teaching titles were not.

Patterns of Representation on the System Faculty Government

What is the appropriate electoral base for a multicampus representative faculty agency, the individual faculty member, or the campus? Whether the all-university faculty organization is primarily advisory or legislative, representation of the campuses presents a serious dilemma. Should each campus be represented equally in system-wide counsels, regardless of size, thus denying any special weight to the larger campus? Or should each faculty member be represented on an equal basis, permitting larger campuses to dominate the system organization?

The answer in six of the seven systems which have faced this question is a pragmatic combination of both approaches. The typical organization ranges in size from approximately 40 to 90 members (but in one case involving only 12 persons); each campus is guaranteed representation (ranging from one to six persons), with the remaining seats allocated on a proportionate or weighted basis. Representativeness in terms of any sort of "one professor — one vote" ideal varies widely, depending on the relative size of the campuses and the weighting formula. In no case, however, does this seem a major concern. Rather, the distribution of representatives symbolizes accommodation at a particular moment in time between the large and small campuses in the interests of the overall university system.[2]

In two systems, representation is complicated by the existence of a second faculty agency serving as an executive committee. Here, too, the issue of balance between campus and individual faculty representation is posed, but in both instances there is less emphasis upon proportionality than on equal representation of the campuses. In one instance, each of the six campuses has one representative (the chairman of the campus faculty), and the two largest campuses have one and two additional seats. In the other case, each of nine

---

[2] Several examples illustrate this accommodation: In one system, each campus is guaranteed one seat, regardless of faculty size, but no campus can have more than four. In a second, each campus has a minimum of three seats, but the largest campus has 38 representatives, more than the other campuses combined. In a third case, every campus is allocated two seats; campuses from 10,000 to 20,000 enrollment are assigned a third seat; and campuses of more than 20,000, a fourth.

campuses is represented on the executive committee by its local faculty chairmen, while five remaining seats are assigned ex officio to the chairmen of universitywide faculty committees, without regard to their campus affiliation. Thus, it is theoretically possible for one campus to be represented by 7 members out of a total of 15. Indeed, in a recent year one of the smallest campuses achieved the distinction of having 4 members on the 14-man executive committee. In both universities, the members of the executive committee are also members of the larger representative body, although not selected by it.

Apart from ex officio members, representatives to the system faculty government are, with only one exception, separately elected by the faculty for this office. In one instance, the universitywide council is composed of the members of each campus executive committee, itself elected by the faculty on each of the campuses. One variation to direct elections arises from a provision in one system that the method of selection to the all-university faculty body be a matter of campus option; almost every campus has chosen the electoral route, but at one campus the representatives are selected by the powerful campus committee on committees.

Ex officio representatives

Frequently, in addition to the separately elected faculty representatives, there are ex officio members. In every case but two, the system executive is an ex officio member of the faculty organization. In the two exceptions, one of the bodies is specifically designated as advisory to the system executive; the other is basically a procedural body, and the system executive continues to serve as chairman of each campus senate. In one instance, the system executive is authorized to select two persons from universitywide administration as ex officio representatives, while in another the chief deputy to the system executive is a member of the faculty organization. Finally, in one system faculty organization, the chairman of each campus faculty senate serves ex officio, as do faculty who chair important universitywide committees.

Although always members of their campus senates, campus executives are designated as members of the all-university faculty legislative body in only one instance. A separation-of-powers concept appears to be at work: the campus executive and the campus faculty separately present their views and recommendations to the system executive, governing board, or both. The idea that the campus executive should head his campus faculty delegation has been proposed in only one instance, although the concept would appear to be worthy of more consideration.

Committees As with legislative bodies generally, systemwide faculty bodies find committees necessary to conduct their business. In four systems, these committees are both numerous and highly structured. Of the three other universities of the seven with a system faculty organization, one was considering the establishment of standing committees but had not done so at the time of the study; two did not contemplate this development at all.

Typical standing committees include those on budget, educational policy (sometimes divided into graduate and undergraduate programs), and academic freedom. Appointments are usually made by an executive committee from among the members of the representative body. In one case, however, the universitywide committees are generally composed of the chairmen or members of the parallel campus committees; these ex officio members do not necessarily serve on the larger representative body, although they report to it. In this university, the chairmen of several important universitywide committees also serve on the system faculty executive committee. While this provides a tight communications link from campus committee to universitywide committee to executive committee, the workload implications for the individual members appear staggering.

In only one instance, Wisconsin, is the system executive the appointing power to universitywide faculty committees. In this case, the faculty-administration dichotomy, although not totally absent, appears to have been effectively bridged. Campus and system executives are seen, symbolically and actually, as the heads of the faculty. This is suggested, too, by the fact that the system executive presides over the meetings of the all-university faculty assembly. The partnership reflects a maturity of organizational development derived from a long history of effective executive-faculty relationships, first at the flagship campus and then at the system level. That such a pattern can be easily transported or accepted in other environments is questionable.

The Special Case of the Comprehensive University It is difficult to develop a systemwide faculty organization in a university composed of several campuses, even when they are basically alike in mission, faculty qualifications, and enrollment patterns. It is much more complicated when campuses, by design, differ on all of these counts. Within the nine universities, five are in this latter category. These multisegmental systems, which encompass two-year, collegiate, and university campuses, we have termed *comprehensive* universities. At each one, special problems confront faculty government.

The issue is best illustrated in three universities which include two-year campuses. In Wisconsin, these are grouped into a subsystem and classed collectively as a "campus," albeit one with several locations throughout the state. A separate faculty organization for this collectivity has been established, and it is represented on the all-university faculty body in proportion to the size of the total two-year faculty. Significantly, faculty ranks for the two-year system are identical with those in the university as a whole, although there are substantial differences in the distribution of ranks and salaries.

In the State and City Universities of New York, each two-year campus is treated as a separate entity, and each sends representatives to the universitywide senate in proportion to its numbers. In the State University, the universitywide senate includes regular representatives from six two-year agricultural and technical colleges, but only three observers from the more than 30 community colleges for which the university has general supervisory—but not governing—authority. In 1967, faculty of these community colleges themselves organized a separate systemwide faculty council to consider matters of common interest.

Because the relative proportions of two-year faculty are nowhere large enough to dominate the system organization, representation has not become controversial. The problem exists, however, as evidenced by occasional mutterings that the two-year staff do not share common interests and that traditional (but unnamed) faculty values will be "downgraded" by their participation.

The problem is not peculiar to the community colleges. A representative from one collegiate campus described a systemwide faculty meeting this way: "Every time someone from a four-year [college] campus wants to go deeply into a question, the university man changes the subject," for example, the free transfer of graduate students seeking a master's degree at the university. Faculty government reflects the same tension between desirable coordination and undesirable uniformity that exists in practically every aspect of the comprehensive systems.

In one such system, faculty leaders have attempted to accommodate these differences through the establishment, within the universitywide senate, of segmental caucuses which meet separately to settle problems of particular concern to the two-year, collegiate, and university campuses.

The advantages of a universitywide senate combining representation from all segments appear to outweigh the shortcomings. Experience is limited, however, and the continued viability of the arrangement is not assured, particularly in New York, where collective bargaining and the related role of the senate are matters of active concern in both university systems. It is highly predictable that formal collective bargaining will affect segmental elements of the system faculty in different ways and that each segment will have different responses. These differences pose a certain threat to the universitywide faculty organizations. Their reaction to this challenge will determine their future.

The Nature of Representation

Questions concerning patterns of faculty representation and organizational form are paralleled by classical political arguments over the nature of that representation and form. Does the all-university assembly or senate, or more particularly its executive committee, "speak for" the faculty? When can a system executive confidently report that his recommendation has the approval of the faculty in contrast to stating merely that he has consulted with them? Are the members of the campus delegation to an all-university senate to act individually or in concert? Are they to perform as instructed delegates or as a free deliberative body? Even assuming a preference for instructed representatives, on what basis will they receive instructions and from whom?

Problems of representation exist at any campus where questions are posed as to whether the faculty should convene as a "town meeting" or be governed by a representative body; whether the representative body should act itself on a given issue or poll the whole faculty by mailed ballot; or under what circumstances a faculty committee should advise the administration without seeking the view of the full body. In sum, given the nature of academic life, the answer of the individual professor to the question "Who speaks for the faculty?" quite often is "Nobody"—or possibly "Me!"

These uncertainties and disagreements pose a special dilemma in the multicampus universities for both the system executive and the universitywide faculty organization. One step removed from the campus, both are vulnerable to the charge of making decisions or recommendations without adequate consultation. Both find themselves "damned if you do, damned if you don't." As diligently as the system executive may try to determine the range and strength of faculty viewpoints, he can never be sure that his analysis of their views will be accepted. The all-university faculty council or executive committee can advise, but it is never free from the charge that it has failed to represent the viewpoint of the faculty as a whole, or of a given campus. "How dare the chairman presume to speak for this campus?" or "Why didn't the president refer the matter back to the campus for study?" are typical questions. Both point up the desirability of effective communication, but both also ignore the external pressures of time and events under which system decisions are made. "Effective communication" is not a universal remedy. As one faculty leader put it:

> The major problem is the incompatibility between the feeling of the faculty that they are insufficiently consulted in time to have appreciable effect and the realization of the administrative officers that they are not in a debating society—that decisions have to be made to meet deadlines.

The dilemma appears insoluble. Alternatives to present patterns —abandoning faculty consultation, on the one hand, or establishing permanent plebiscitary machinery, on the other—are neither practical nor desirable. Nor is it clear that multicampus faculty government can survive if extra weighting of faculty from small campuses is threatened, as indeed it might if the systemwide council becomes a true governing rather than an advisory body. Here, at least, a certain amount of inequity appears to be the price of unity.

However, certain lessons can be learned from the relatively brief experience of the multicampus universities which have faced these problems. System executives must accept full responsibility for their decisions and recommendations; they can never speak with confidence of faculty approval on any controversial matter, but can only report that they have attempted to take full advantage of available faculty advice. Campus executives must accept that "their" faculty is also the system executive's faculty, and that sharing symbols of leadership is an essential characteristic of the multicampus university. For their part, systemwide faculty organizations must remind themselves, the constituent faculty, and the system executive that they are advisory. But they have equal responsibility to assure that their advice is as informed and as representative as the situation permits. Finally, systemwide faculty bodies must limit their concerns to matters truly of an all-university nature and avoid the temptation to delve into questions which might better be handled at the campuses. Only by so doing can the universitywide body continue to be accepted as a legitimate spokesman for all the campuses and their faculty.

THE AUTHOR-ITY OF SYS-TEMWIDE FACULTY GOVERNMENT

A systemwide faculty senator has stated:

The simplest way to destroy faculty government as an effective voice would be to weaken or kill it at the all-university level on the assumption that there will be a strong central, universitywide organization and administration. I can imagine no worse calamity than for this to happen.

A campus executive stated:

The faculty on every campus is the responsibility of the campus executive, and the viewpoint of the campus should be a synthesis of all elements expressed through him. The present universitywide faculty government invites end-runs around the campus executive and requires elaborate coordination procedures that are expensive and likely to go awry. There is a need for some form of faculty interaction with the system executive, but this can be handled on an ad hoc basis.

These sharply contrasting comments by two experienced observers of the same university suggest the need for humility in generalizing about one multicampus university, much less nine. Formally and legally, authority for faculty participation in governance almost always rests on delegation from the governing board. More realistically, authority derives from traditions of faculty determination of most decisions about instruction and research, traditions which have come to be the badge of true university status. Regardless of university bylaws and regulations, for example, it is virtually impossible to imagine an academic appointment, or a decision to mount a degree program, that does not originate with the faculty. The governing board of any major university, even if it wishes to do so, has little real alternative other than to accept faculty authority as a *fait accompli.*

But the decision to create universitywide faculty structure is not preordained. Faculty government is not a universal characteristic of the multicampus university, nor is there agreement as to its form and mission. Each of the seven systems with universitywide faculty machinery has established it at its own speed and in its own manner. In every case, the decision has arisen out of the activities and wishes of the faculty on the several campuses, although the role of the system executive in supporting these wishes has been at times decisive and always essential.

In most instances, the constitution of the universitywide organization has been approved by the governing board, but in no instance has the board done more than ratify faculty action. In contrast, the governing board of one university has delegated to the faculty full authority to organize as it chooses. In another instance, state law directly delegates authority to the faculty to govern themselves, and this has been interpreted broadly and cooperatively by faculty and governing board. Regardless of varying approaches, however, the faculty generally have the right to organize in a manner of their own choosing at both the campus and multicampus levels. Potential for conflict among board, administration, and faculty over organizational form is, of course, present, but in 1970 conflict did not appear imminent.

Particular advisory and legislative functions of systemwide faculty government are based on policies of the governing board, most often revealed in the constitution of faculty organizations. Language is often general—for example, a statement that the all-university senate should "promote effective educational policies"—but sometimes specific—the faculty shall "advise the administration concerning the university budget." Delegations of authority to the faculty to act are less frequent, for most academic activity is based on unwritten practice, rather than formal action of the board.

In every instance, formal jurisdiction of the all-university faculty organization is specifically limited to matters of universitywide concern. One faculty constitution provides that the powers of the system senate "do not extend to matters exclusively within the domain of the campus faculties," while another states that the organization has "no authority over matters delegated to the campus." Yet another provides that the faculty of the university delegate its authority to the universitywide senate "to exercise authority in matters which concern more than one unit of the university or the university as a whole, and on which it is necessary to have a uniform university policy."[3]

This last phrase demonstrates the subjective, ambiguous, and

[3] If a question of jurisdiction arises, the universitywide senate has the power to decide if ". . . it is necessary to have a uniform university policy."

occasionally controversial nature of attempts to determine what sorts of matters are, in fact, universitywide in scope. Among the nine systems there is wide disagreement. In one, rules of student conduct are basically determined by each campus; in another, by the university as a whole. The situation is similar with policies on undergraduate admissions, new doctoral programs, and administration of faculty salaries. Nor is it possible to detect any common trend among the several systems in terms of greater or lesser authority for the campus senate vis-à-vis the universitywide body. The relative strength of each is a product of tradition and circumstance.

However, a trend of faculty organization (perhaps a prediction) is visible in the multicampus university. The systemwide faculty government is primarily an advisory rather than a legislative body. The power of the faculty to make *decisions* is either exercised at the campus level or not at all. Those decisions which require universitywide academic participation also require participation by the system administration, the governing board, or even the coordinating agency, and not just the faculty. This is the case in most of the multicampus universities; in only two, in fact, does any significant body of academic legislation require universitywide faculty approval. In Illinois, the joint approval of the three senates composing the total university is required. In the University of California, where universitywide faculty approval is required in such academic policy matters as grades, or degree requirements, there is general restiveness over existing requirements and, increasingly, the all-university senate has granted campus exceptions to its own rules or amended its policies to allow campus options.

Growing emphasis upon advisory rather than legislative functions might seem at first glance to imply a weaker faculty role. This is not the case. The nature of academic governance is such that the faculty's advisory role is, in reality, one of shared power. In most areas of university life, the faculty, the administration, and the governing board effectively have a joint veto; each must approve any important policy, none may order the other. This is as true at the systemwide level as it is on the campus. For the faculty, the responsibility to advise carries with it the power to consent and, not unexpectedly, even the advisory role of the faculty is not without controversy. "Who speaks for the faculty?" is a critical issue in the power relationships of multicampus university governance.

The problem centers around the three-way interaction among the system executive, the campus executives, and the faculty. To one degree or another, a common concern of the more than 20 campus executives interviewed was that their campus leadership inevitably would be undercut by too frequent, improper, unprogrammed (the modifiers were many) relationships between "their" faculty and the system executive. At the same time, even the most "home-rule" oriented of the campus executives understand that the system executive requires some direct and reasonably formal faculty contacts. They also recognize that the faculty has a legitimate need for communication with both the system executive and the governing board. More than one system executive spoke of his personal, in addition to an institutional, need to communicate with the faculty — to retain his feel for trends in scholarship, to maintain his academic credentials, to remind himself that it was a university he was heading. Institutionally, the faculty has to be provided with personal symbols of the multicampus university without which pressures for campus autonomy might become so strong as to threaten the system itself. Not the least of such symbols is direct faculty contact with the system executive, and a measure of his success is the development of effective avenues for this contact.

The foregoing, at least, is the conventional wisdom. Whether it has independent reality or will endure depends, more than on any other factor, on the skill and sophistication of the system executive. It is his responsibility to create the necessary faculty relationships at an all-university level for himself while at the same time protecting the campus executive's leadership at home. Insensitivity to the duality of this responsibility can be perilous. All system executives understand this, but not all are equally successful in maintaining the balance. More than once, campus executives recounted first learning of an important decision of the system executive from a faculty member (or worse yet, from a student) who had just attended an all-university meeting — perhaps one about which the campus executive knew nothing. At least a partial solution to successful system-campus executive relationships vis-à-vis the faculty organization appears to be affording the campus heads the last word in policy discussions before a final decision is reached or announced.

Collective Bargaining While generalizations are difficult, one portent (some would say dark cloud) looms on the horizon with critical implications for faculty government generally and for the multicampus university in particular. The issue is faculty collective bargaining, other aspects of which are discussed in the chapter on academic personnel. Under New York's Taylor Act, all public employees— including university faculty—may vote on *whether* they wish to be represented by a bargaining agent and *who* the bargaining agent should be. The question here is the relationship of the "official" faculty governing body to these two questions.

The experience of the two New York systems suggests that the answer is complex. In the City University, the universitywide faculty senate and the parallel organizations at each of the campuses took little part in the initial discussions about collective bargaining. They did not request that they be designated as the bargaining agent, nor, to all accounts, did they play a part in the elections to determine the "whether" and the "who." In the State University of New York, in marked contrast, the universitywide faculty senate formally and successfully requested state authorities to place it on the ballot as a "collective negotiating agency for the University professional staff."

Even the question of whether the senate *could* be declared a bargaining agent (an "employee organization" in the language of the Taylor Act) was disputed. The State University Federation of Teachers (an AFL-CIO affiliate) argued that the senate was ineligible to be recognized because it was not primarily concerned with working to improve the terms and conditions of employment. It also contended that the senate was employer-dominated by reason of its financial dependence on the university's budget. The state agency concluded, however, that the senate was eligible to appear on the ballot and that questions of employer dominance could be brought back to the agency under its power to hear "improper practice" charges against public employers and employee organizations. Subsequently, however, the senate withdrew as a contender, choosing instead to support a separate membership organization, affiliated with the National Education Association. This organization was eventually successful in the election which took place in early 1971.

Collective bargaining issues can confront any campus. Whether, as the State University senate originally asserted, its assumption of a bargaining role is a logical extension of faculty governance or whether, as others charge, it is abandoning its traditional role is beyond the concern of this study. On their face, collective bargaining practices and principles do not appear to be consistent with present models of faculty governance, whether legislative or advisory. Can a senate be both an effective advisor and an effective pressure group for faculty working conditions?[4] Can the system executive be the leader of the faculty and the spokesman for their employer? We have our doubts but are equally doubtful if the alternatives are necessarily more desirable or less complex.

However dubious the possible choices, it is evident that the role of faculty government will change under the impact of collective bargaining. Within the multicampus university, will senate concentration on collective bargaining so overshadow other aspects of systemwide faculty governance that new instruments of academic advice and consent will have to be created? Without it, however, will faculty interest and loyalty gravitate to the external bargaining agent, with an atrophy of the "official" senate? How will the different needs of two-year, collegiate, and university faculty in the comprehensive systems be accommodated? Will the system executive be forced into an entirely new role as an advocate for management, rather than as a link between the governing board and the faculty? As for the campus executive in the multicampus environment, will he be expected to be a spokesman for local faculty interests, in a possible adversary relationship with the system executive? Or will he be conceived as the campus representative of the "employer"? Clearly, new forces are loose, but their implications can now be only dimly comprehended.

System Government, Faculty, and the Campuses Although much is debatable concerning the role of systemwide faculty organizations, one fact appears indisputable: In all cases, they have strengthened faculty government on the new and emerging campuses. This nurturing of campus faculty organizations has taken several forms. Perhaps the most important, although the least explicit, is the example of the flagship campus. In three of the nine universities, a long and rich tradition of faculty governance at the flagship campus has been taken as a model for newer cam-

---

[4] The State University faculty concluded affirmatively in explicitly noting and unanimously turning down the concept that the "important question of collective negotiation" be turned over to any agency outside the direction and control which faculty governance provides. But note the above-mentioned modification of their original position.

puses, symbolic of full-fledged membership in the university. Indeed, the model has been slavishly imitated in each of the three systems. Although not required to be so, officers, committees, and procedures are carbon copies of the flagship structure, despite the concern of the new campuses over domination from "big brother" and inroads on campus autonomy. Emulation of the most available model is not surprising. That it has resulted in three, six, or nine duplicate and detailed versions of the same thing appears to be making too much of a good thing. No model is so effective that a new campus might not make it more relevant to local conditions and needs.

A second form of system encouragement has been the establishment of explicit universitywide requirements for campus organization. Bylaws of the governing board may specifically describe forms of faculty organization and participation, or authorize faculty activity, simply assuming the existence of a campus faculty structure to administer it. Alternatively, requirements for participation in the universitywide organization can be met only if there is a campus organization, a committee, senate, or council to provide ex officio representatives on the system governing body. Also, specification of an electoral procedure for representation on a universitywide body provides a stimulus for the creation of parallel campus organizations.

Finally, campus faculty organizations have been encouraged by leadership from the system executive and the systemwide faculty government itself. In more than one university, the system executive has been faced with the responsibility of changing the mission and character of former state teachers' colleges into more broadly based collegiate or university campuses. One feature of this transformation has been the establishment of effective faculty government at the campus. A stronger faculty voice has not always been welcomed by the existing campus executive, and system initiative has been necessary to redress the balance of faculty-administration authority at the campus level. Such initiative has often been reinforced by parallel activity on the part of the systemwide faculty. Both informal and formal "technical assistance" has been given to campuses by faculty experienced in the ways of academic governance. In one case, the all-university senate established visiting committees to study and report to both the specific campus faculty and the full senate upon the progress of local faculty government.

System encouragement of campus faculty organization is almost always regarded as desirable by faculty and administrators at both campus and system levels. Although such support and assistance are not unknown among autonomous institutions, the likelihood of their taking place does not seem as strong. Rather, the development of effective campus faculty government is a significant contribution of the multicampus university.

7. Student Organization

At the systemwide level, student participation in university governance is most notable because of its ineffectiveness or absence. Although multicampus student activity exists in some form in four of the nine universities, in each of these its history is short and undistinguished, and its future status and structure are in doubt. True, no university intends to give up existing systemwide student organization, but neither does any appear to be in the process of extending it. The five systems without student participation have varied proposals for the future, but these have neither the substance nor the urgency of similar plans for faculty government.

The uncertainty and frequent lack of universitywide student organizations are paralleled by the general absence of top-level multicampus administrators with primary responsibility for student affairs. Instead, the various elements of this broad concern are divided among virtually all the systemwide officers, with coordination provided by the system executive himself.

Our prior analysis of the governing board, the central administration, and the systemwide faculty structure is aided implicitly or explicitly by analogies to "the university"—one board, one campus, one administration, and one organized community of scholars. Such analogies become increasingly tenuous as the discussion moves from the boards through the administration and faculty to the present topic.

For example, the governing boards of the multicampus systems are almost indistinguishable from their single-campus counterparts. At the next level of this continuum, the central administration of each system is shaped by the history of that particular system, very much as though the traditional single-campus model has been trimmed here and stretched there on an ad hoc basis to fit the specific university. Systemwide faculty government, on the other hand, is much more rationalized in terms of the multicampus structure. Even where it is clearly the outgrowth of faculty governance at a particular campus, the specific multicampus structure is the result of careful study and deliberate action, often enshrined in a formal charter or bylaws. But what of student organization?

Analogies to "the university" are of little help in understanding the form or extent of systemwide student participation, for there are few well-settled patterns at any campus upon which to draw. Both the absence of systemwide participation and its relative ineffectiveness can be attributed to lack of campus experience.

For example, with only one exception, both the formal structure of governing boards and their members are fairly permanent fixtures. Not only is the composition and authority of these boards frozen in statutes or constitutions, but many individual members have watched a single campus become a multicampus system. Many system executives have been campus executives for some time, often within the same system, and many have witnessed the growth in enrollment and numbers of campuses during transition to a multicampus structure. There is parallel continuity in the central staff organization.

Where systemwide faculty organizations exist, the core of their multicampus authority and pattern of organization can generally be traced to traditional faculty interests at the campuses: faculty welfare, curricular matters, admissions, and general advice to the administration. In addition, even if the faculty organizational structure does not require it, the faculty voice is heard at the system level.

In sharp contrast to governing boards, administration, and faculty, students are transitory members of the multicampus universities and their campuses. Where student organizations exist at the campuses, neither their authority nor form can be easily translated to a multicampus level. Virtually all traditional aspects of student affairs are basically local in nature. With the advent of the multicampus form of university structure, such programs are left at the campus, with relatively minimal universitywide involvement.

Pressures of student activism are felt everywhere. All multicampus universities are confronted with problems of student dissent, and all are groping for solutions. But none is satisfied that its own arrangements are adequate. One generalization can be drawn. Disorder on the campus and public and governmental response to it usually involve a blurring of lines of authority and responsibility exercised by the governing board and system and campus executives. Both boards and system executives find it difficult to avoid "doing something about the mess on campus" when the press, the governor, and influential legislators demand it. Nevertheless, these pressures have not yet led to organizational or institutional responses unique to a multicampus system.

The brevity of the present chapter does not indicate either lack of student activity or of administrative interest in students. It does indicate that the *campus* is the primary focus of such activity and interest, however, and that there is little of either peculiar to the multicampus university.

THE FORMS OF UNIVERSITYWIDE STUDENT ACTIVITY   Although only one system executive expressed doubt about the utility of formalized student organization at the universitywide level, only four of the nine systems have structures for such participation. Among these four, the form of participation is similar. Students are represented at the system level by the campus student body presidents collectively, either alone or as part of a slightly expanded student delegation. These students meet periodically with the system executive to discuss university affairs. With one exception, these student groups do not have an internal organizational structure of their own. In all four cases, their authority is entirely advisory. Delegations of authority to student governments at the campus level over such matters as the expenditure of student fees or participation in student discipline are not duplicated at the systemwide level. Nor, on the face of it, do there appear to be parallel activities beyond the campus for which authority can be formally delegated.

System executives consider meetings with students both useful as an administrative device to obtain student opinion on specific issues and important as a way of reducing their own feeling of isolation from the grass roots of the academic enterprise. These meetings provide the system executive with a direct view into the campuses, a view otherwise screened by campus executives and faculty; and most system executives want a direct view.

In two systems, the initial pattern of student participation was one of relatively large delegations of students from each campus. In both, this pattern was being abandoned in favor of the smaller group of campus student body presidents. In one instance, it was believed that the smaller group would enable the system executive to establish better working relationships with students, and that, as part of a smaller group, the individual representatives would gain prestige on their campuses. In both cases, the students involved were of the opinion that, because of its size, the larger group was "just a social affair."

Although there is some sentiment favoring structural links between student representatives at the system level and campus student governments, neither the system executives, other administrators, nor—one suspects—the students themselves have any illusions about the actual representativeness of the student body presidents. At best, the latter are interested, available, and not patently unrepresentative. The implications of a possible lack of representativeness are magnified in the multicampus structure. A campus executive has far more opportunity to see a cross section of students. Moreover, in one system, the student presidents themselves elect a systemwide student leader who is authorized to "speak for" students at meetings of the governing board. In this case, there is obvious concern that a few score votes in an apathetic campus election may select the all-university spokesman for thousands of students.

As expected, the degree of formality of student participation varies with the size of the system. In one of the smallest, student body presidents meet monthly with the system executive and are invited to telephone him at any time. In this university, the system executive sees himself as the spokesman for student interests in the central administration and before the board. The other system executives, whether or not there is a systemwide student organization, consider some form of "open-door" policy for students to be desirable, although none have carried such policy into practice to the extent of the almost completely open communication first noted.

In another small system, a universitywide committee on student affairs consists of not only the student body presidents from each campus but the deans of students and campus faculty representatives as well. This mixed form of systemwide administrative committee seems most effective in a system with no more than five or six campuses. Committees of similarly mixed membership were tried in a very much larger system, but all campuses could not be represented by a particular type of member.

The constraint which the limitations of time place on contacts between the governing board and students also prevents greater contact between students and the system executive and inhibits effective student participation. One executive was tolerantly amused when an investigator of student government accused him of a "lack of interest" in students. He explained that it was not a question of interest but of priority. At the campus, contact with students is crucial, but at the system level, other responsibilities are of greater importance.

Campus executives, at least those with a system executive in residence on or near their campuses, are not generally enthusiastic about too much direct contact between him and their students. Campus executives consider themselves the proper representatives of the entire campus community—faculty and students. However, they appear somewhat more tolerant of systemwide participation by students than by their faculty, perhaps because it seems less threatening. One stated, "Students really don't want to talk to anyone less than the President of the United States." He implied that the least he could do was to let them talk to the system executive. Fortunately, he also appears to have an excellent understanding with the system executive as to their respective areas of authority.

In one of the larger systems, the representatives from each campus are the student body president, a member chosen by a select student group from each campus, and, depending on the size of the campus, one or two other representatives chosen by the campus executive. The selection of a delegate by the campus executive is not intended to give him a voice in the group, but rather to give the system executive greater assurance that the delegation will be, if not representative of all campus viewpoints, at least somewhat balanced. The representatives are expected to offer advice as individuals rather than as delegates from their campuses, and votes are not taken.

In contrast to the student meetings with the system executive in the smaller system, the meetings of this larger group are relatively formal, with the system executive conveying information and seeking advice on specific subjects. In one case, for example, a revision of the universitywide rules for student conduct, promulgated by the system executive, was presented to the student group. The administration considered the suggestions of the students to be valuable. Students, on the other hand, while recognizing their contribution to the wording of the rules, had other thoughts about both the procedure and the substance. Their complaints raised two points of general concern.

First, the students were disturbed because their advice was

sought on a draft of rules presented for the first time at the meeting itself. However, simply sending out copies of the rules in advance was not the simple solution it seemed. The framing of the policy statement by central administrative officers had involved numerous and seemingly interminable consultations with faculty, campus administrators (and by them with students), and board members. The sequence of such consultation was important and so was the manner in which word of what was being finally proposed reached the campuses and the public. In another system, an administrative decision over the controversial issue of whether student fees should be voluntary or not was released to the student advisory group and through them to the campuses before the campus executives themselves had learned of it. To the embarrassed campus executives, it made little difference whether the premature disclosure was an administrative error or whether the students had breached the confidentiality of the information.

The second source of student discontent in this example was the nature of the universitywide rules themselves. The difficulty illustrates the major problem of student participation: finding a valid area of student interest at the systemwide level. The rules upon which they were asked to comment were general policies applicable to all campuses. A workaday attempt to bring these rules up-to-date was being joined with an attempt to frame them in such a manner as to make it clear to the governing board and the public that "something was being done" about campus disorder. The students, on the other hand, were not at all convinced that the endeavor was worthwhile. At one extreme, their interest was in the specific rules by which each campus would implement the more general ones; at the other, it was in the philosophical underpinnings or legitimacy of the rules. To many of these students, the careful selection of sometimes intentionally and necessarily ambiguous words for administrative policy bordered upon sophistry.

Students can be influential at the policy level, without a formal universitywide structure. This was illustrated by their impact on the long-range academic plan of one large system. The central administration sought advice from administrators, faculty, and students at all campuses on a draft of a plan. Students at one campus (only) responded and were particularly critical of a section dealing with meeting the state's projected manpower demands. At their suggestion, this section was reworded to present a less quantitative and more qualitative approach to student careers. The spirit of the document was changed, and, in the opinion of all within the system, changed for the better.

Obtaining the full value of student opinions and insights at the systemwide level is not easy. In the example of the academic plan alterations, the system administration widely circulated the draft document and was willing to travel to the campuses to obtain student opinion. However, the student input was not, it should be noted, from the systemwide student organization but from an ad hoc campus group.

The value of student participation is not seriously questioned by administrators or faculty. But lack of continuity, absence of traditions of participation at the multicampus level, and the difficulty of identifying areas of general interest limit the usefulness of typical structures of student governance. The meetings of the system executives with the student body presidents serve the purpose of keeping a channel of communication open between the system administration and some students, and of giving some air of legitimacy to his directives and statements. There are, however, important limitations upon his ability to involve students effectively and directly at the universitywide level. The multicampus university and the system executive have a tremendous stake in overcoming the problems involved.

The stake is universally recognized. More than any single feature of academic life, student activism has dominated the agenda of most of the nine multicampus systems. Sit-ins and riots have blurred, if not obliterated, seemingly well-understood tables of organization and the respective authority of campus and system executives. Governing boards are often preoccupied with second-guessing both levels, to the exclusion of their primary policy-making function. And the autonomy of the university itself is inevitably undercut by the necessity to call upon both mayors and governors to preserve the peace.

These recurring crises have given rise to numerous proposals for closer working relationships between students and the governing board, administration, and faculty. However, the few such proposals that have been adopted have not had a significant impact upon the specifically multicampus aspects of university governance.

THE LACK OF SYSTEMWIDE STUDENT ORGANIZATION In 1970, five of the nine multicampus systems were without any form of universitywide student organization and the four which had such groups were not confident of their adequacy nor of how adequacy might be measured. The explanations given for the tenuous nature of systemwide student participation are varied but generally overlapping.

First, the governing board and the central administration stand at a geographic and organizational distance from the students. These systemwide governing structures are perceived by most students, if at all, as having little relevance to their immediate campus concerns. The trend of delegation and decentralization of administrative authority to the campuses has made the campus executive the major administrator with whom students are concerned. When one system executive found a number of students at his residence late one afternoon protesting a campus rule, he directed them to the home of the campus executive, and "by golly, they went." Students are appearing with greater regularity at governing board meetings and appearing before, if not sitting on, universitywide committees. Their presence, however, is almost always oriented to an issue of immediate concern rather than to the continuing processes of governance itself.

Second, lack of student participation in multicampus governance appears in some measure to be related to the absence of similar faculty participation. Of the four systems which had structured systemwide student participation, three also had active, systemwide faculty governing structures, and the fourth was in the process of establishing one. Of the five which had little or no student participation at the system level, only one had a tradition of strong faculty government at a multicampus level. We see no direct relationship between the two sectors, but the precedent of systemwide faculty organization may well have served as an example in three of the systems.

Third, both the multicampus structure and student pressure for participation in governance are comparatively recent phenomena in higher education. At the multicampus administrative level, problems are many and problem-solvers few. Unless the system executive is himself personally interested in systemwide student involvement, the forms and proposals for student participation can be easily set aside in favor of the daily demands upon his limited time. The increase of student militancy on the campuses is a dampener on board and administrative enthusiasm for student participation at the system level. It also provides more than enough problems to interfere with many pressing administrative and organizational plans, including—paradoxically—those for student participation in system governance.

Fourth, and of importance because it is often overlooked in more abstract discussions of this and other areas of systemwide governance, is the cost in time and dollars to students and administrators. The economics and technology of the multicampus structure are most clearly perceived as limiting factors only by those involved in the "nuts and bolts" of governance. We were told, for example, that all student-body presidents in one system had successfully exchanged information, plans, and tactics through a leased-wire system but that a change in the telephone connections had upset their lines of communication. In another state, a state legislator questioned the benefits of a cost incurred by system administrators traveling to distant campuses—the cost of student travel would undoubtedly have been questioned even more closely!

Fifth, Weinberg and Walker (1969, p. 77) have suggested that the form of student organization may be determined by the major relationships between the state and the university. To oversimplify their argument, two such major relationships are (1) governmental control over university structure and financing and (2) recruitment to political careers through party sponsorship of student aspirants. Where both of these relationships are strong (e.g., South America), student politics takes the form of factional competition among student branches of the political parties. On the other hand, where both factors are relatively weak or missing (e.g., the United States), student government is nonpolitical in the partisan sense and student political behavior, if any, is noninstitutionalized.

Although the arguments of Weinberg and Walker are addressed to higher education generally, they also seem broadly explanatory in the context of the multicampus universities. An important generalization about multicampus systems is the "division of labor" between the system and campus executives. Again as an oversimplification, this division allots to the system executive the task of external representation of the university to the legislature and public; the campus executive's role, on the other hand, stresses the more clearly academic aspects within the overall administration. The campus executive and his student government have shared interests. On the other hand, the system executive—indeed the central staff as a whole—have few *direct* interests in the immediate concerns of the students at the campuses.

Even the phenomenal increase of student interest in political issues has not been reflected in substantial changes in the forms of student participation in the governance of the multicampus university. Rather, consistent with the Weinberg-Walker thesis, this interest has bypassed even campus governance to take the form of noninstitutionalized and transient interest in specific aspects of policy rather than a structured interest in politics and political parties.

The Weinberg-Walker analysis suggests that the academic community alone may be unable to remold student participation for the better. If student government at the campuses is properly characterized as "sand box," and that at the system level as somewhat artificial, neither student apathy nor administrative ineptitude may be really to blame. The absence of formalized student participation at the systemwide level is perhaps the inevitable result of the relative independence in the United States of both the universities and the students from governmental control over or concern with their academic activities. That this relative independence will continue is not preordained; the prospect of the 18-year-old vote is closely related.

SYSTEMWIDE ADMINISTRATION OF STUDENT AFFAIRS The nature and extent of student participation in system governing structures—governance *by* students—represent but one facet of the multicampus organizational problem. Governance *of* students is an equally important aspect and relates to student participation.

In one way or another, responsibility for students is the task of all academic administrators whether at campus or multicampus levels. In general, however, administration of virtually all traditional student activities is local. Registration, admissions, financial aid, housing, and other auxiliary services all require some degree of face-to-face contact with students. In contrast, unless students are deliberately injected into them, such areas as academic personnel, academic and physical planning, and business and fiscal affairs can be administered without any contact with students at all.

Whether the system origins are in a flagship campus or in the consolidation of several campuses, the allocation of authority over student affairs between the campuses and the system follows the necessity for student contact rather than the logic of organizational form. Registrars, housing officers, and admissions officers at the campuses are often responsible to vice-presidents or vice-chancellors for student affairs, who are themselves increasingly important members of the campus executive's cabinet.

Although these campus student affairs officers are peers of the fiscal and academic officers in their campus administration, their relationship to the central staff contrasts sharply. Other campus administrators have a senior officer on the central staff to listen to their problems, coordinate their activity with the other campuses, and, most important perhaps, represent their particular interests within the central administration and often to the governing board itself.

In contrast, senior staff officers at the central staff level have little part in student affairs. In no system does a systemwide administrator at the cabinet level have student affairs as his primary duty. Various aspects of student affairs are scattered, for pragmatic reasons, among the junior and senior staff. In one system, the chief executive's special assistant handles "routine" student affairs, while a more senior officer assumes responsibility for those which rise to the level of his duties as the "vice-president for crises." Most systems have a multicampus director of admissions, but the "vice-president for crises," while by no means typical, illustrates the diffuse and ad hoc nature of much systemwide organizational behavior in this area.

Both the form and substance of systemwide student participation depend heavily upon the continuity and interest of a senior administrator. Where the students have an effective voice at a system level, the interested administrator is the system executive himself. In most systems, however, regardless of the existence or form of systemwide student participation, and regardless also of the real concern which all system executives have with student life, primary student contact with the system is through a junior officer.

We cannot seriously suggest that if a senior officer of the central staff is given primary responsibility for student affairs, effective student participation will ensue. On the other hand, it does not appear that student participation can exist at system level without interest and initiative at a high level in the central administration. Perhaps paradoxically, it is not students who appear most concerned about the position of student affairs in the central administration; it is the campus administrators.

In two systems, campus deans of student affairs expressed concern over the lack of administrative representation of students at multicampus level. In one, a high-level universitywide officer for student affairs had left the system and was not replaced. In the other, such a position at system level had been vacant for a number of years, reportedly because of lack of adequate funding. In both instances, the campus administrators saw the need for a senior systemwide officer both for coordination of intercampus activities and for representing their interests at the system level. In one university in particular, there is unhappiness because students in the systemwide student organization have greater access to the system administration, including the governing board, than do student affairs officers.

Whether the appointment of a senior universitywide staff officer with the student affairs portfolio would be advantageous cannot be answered across the nine university systems. That other senior campus officers have their system counterpart is not adequate justification in and of itself. Symmetry on an organization chart is not a virtue with pronounced significance for higher education. Nevertheless, it remains true that student affairs, however defined, will continue increasingly to demand systemwide attention. That these demands will lead to some form of organizational response is likely, but the exact response will vary with the specific factors shaping each system and the personal characteristics of the system executive. Increased universitywide attention is almost a certainty, but the form, whether a top-level member of the cabinet, more direct involvement of the system executive, or a continuance of the existing ad hoc and divided response, is beyond prediction.

Part Three

The Processes of Governance

8. Academic Plans and Programs

John Gardner (1967, pp. 315–319) has written: "We do not need more change as such. We need more *intentional* change—specifically, the kinds of change in our institutions that will enable them to adapt to the radically altered circumstances in which they are now forced to function." Indeed, the promotion of "intentional change" through academic planning is one of the most frequently given reasons for the establishment and continued existence of the multicampus university. For many, such planning, together with its operational counterpart—the budget—are the heart of system activity. The success of the multicampus university is measured by the effectiveness of universitywide academic planning and program review.

Despite the pervasiveness of this view, the multicampus university finds itself at an ambiguous and precarious midpoint between the micro-planning of the campus and the macro-planning of higher education in the state as a whole. The middle ground between these two poles is only dimly defined and neither well understood nor accepted.

The ambiguity is not unexpected. Academic planning and program review are at the center of a continuing struggle for influence that engages all groups with a stake in the multicampus university—students, faculty, administrators, legislators, special interest groups, and the general public, to name only the most obvious. A clear-cut allocation of responsibility for major policy decisions among the participants is probably impossible. Attempts to clarify and formalize responsibility are satisfactory for specific times, issues, and purposes, but these are never constant. There is a danger in artificial rigidification of an essentially fluid and dynamic process. The hazards for the investigator are obvious: When the parties at interest cannot agree on their respective authority or even on the meaning of basic terms (e.g., what a "plan" or "program" is), description is uncertain and evaluation dangerous.

Few disagree with the underlying cause of most of the uncertainty: The essence of an academic program rests in the decisions of individual faculty members, each of whom prizes his professional freedom as one of the defining characteristics of a scholar. To a degree unknown in any other complex organization, the basic employee—the professor—is an individual entrepreneur, free to shape his own working agenda. This is best illustrated, perhaps, by the freedom of the professor in the design of a course of instruction. There are limits, sanctions, and rewards for various kinds of activity, but the ultimate decisions remain with the faculty member.

It is not only unimaginable for a department chairman to "tell" a faculty member what to do either in the class or out of it; it is also difficult for a campus executive to have a comprehensive view of the work of his campus. Activities described in the course catalog represent only the tip of the iceberg. Only bits and pieces of critical information are available to help the campus executive make plans and assess programs. Moreover, he often lacks the authority necessary to carry these out.

None of this is peculiar to the multicampus university. At the systemwide level, however, the gap between the formal authority and actual responsibilities of the system executive and board looms even larger than at the campuses. The uncertainties and ambiguities at the campus level are compounded in the multicampus university by constraints and limitations imposed from above. New programs must be set in a context of statewide plans for higher education. No university can unilaterally decide upon and fund a major development without explicit approval of the legislature or, if legislative authority has been delegated, of the coordinating agency. Only rarely is it certain just what the legislature and the governor do, in fact, regard as their authority. The division of labor between the state, the coordinating agency, and the university and its campuses is in continual flux.

Statewide planning of higher education is the subject of a separate major research study elsewhere.[1] Our focus is on the special planning role of the multicampus university. Three aspects of academic plans and programs are discussed below. The first is long-range "master" planning, the attempt to define the goals of

[1] See footnote 6, Chapter 1.

higher education and the means of reaching those goals, integrating such factors as projected enrollment, admission standards, and the location of campuses. A second topic is specific program review to assess the capability and desirability of a campus to mount a program at the desired degree of effectiveness and quality in such terms as faculty, libraries, and physical resources. Finally, the chapter discusses universitywide programs, the extent to which the system itself undertakes or administers academic activities across several campuses.

THE ROLE OF THE MULTI-CAMPUS UNIVERSITY A basic premise underlying the multicampus university is that academic planning and program review should be the responsibility of an educational institution comprising more than one but less than all public campuses in the state. Coupled with this is the need for a *quality control* mechanism one step removed from the interested parties to ensure that plans and programs, if they exist, are being followed, and that "standards," assuming their relevance, are being maintained.

These premises do not go unchallenged. It is asserted that both the faculty and the governing board, who control planning and review in a single-campus university, lose their control in a multicampus system. At the other extreme, advocates of a single statewide governing board criticize the multicampus system as unable to curtail wasteful competition and duplication among the public campuses of a state. In the past, multicampus systems had little need to justify their organization. The University of Illinois was *the* University of Illinois, and few questioned that it was managing its affairs well; similar situations existed in most other states. Today, however, doubters in all seven states are much in evidence. Concerns are expressed by legislators, scholars, and the general public in terms of specific situations, and these cut through quickly to the general question, "Of what use is the multicampus university?" Some of the doubts about academic plans and programs and the responses to them are summarized here, providing a theoretical backdrop against which to describe the reality which we observed.

External planning and review functions can be, and often are, exercised by state authorities, both executive and legislative. However, the multicampus university—in common with all other universities—is based on the assumption that the widest possible range of educational decisions should be separated from the explicitly political arms of the state. In a free society, such matters as academic programs, courses, and degree requirements need to be determined by an "insulated" institution, buffered from direct political influence and from the short-term realities of the two- and four-year political calendar. Not only must the university be sheltered from shifting partisan winds but from the pervasive and omnipresent politics of patronage and pork barrel; colleges and universities are not rivers and harbors, and the value of this difference can be enhanced by assigning a large share of educational policy decisions to others than governors and legislators.

In theory, the multicampus university is peculiarly well-adapted to serve as a buffer. Hopefully removed from the internal pressures of the campus and the external politics of the state, planning and governing functions can be coordinated effectively. Budgeting and planning can be rationally integrated under the same institutional roof, and both require a specialized and sophisticated staff. The system should be able to support and justify the employment of specialists—a medical education coordinator, for example. The need for such specialized personnel will increase faster than the supply, and the university is probably a more attractive employer than either the state government or a coordinating agency. Furthermore, the competence and experience of the system, both among the campuses and within the universitywide organization itself, should be more available and easily shared in a multicampus context.

With respect to quality control, the multicampus university is in an ideal position to set academic standards and achieve compliance with them both for the process and the substance of campus decisions. Similarly, the campus executive may be strengthened in his efforts at planning, program review, and quality control, because local decisions will be reviewed. Campus executives and faculty as well may respond more positively to evaluation within the multicampus family.

Opinions that a multicampus university performs these functions better than a single campus or other governing arrangement are at best informed speculation. We are on firmer ground, however, when considering peculiarly multicampus matters. In academic planning and program review, three artifacts of multicampus structure should strengthen it in comparison to single campuses: *diversity* of campuses, *specialization* of campuses, and *cooperation* among campuses.

Diversity in this context means the different approaches which campuses may have to achieve the same general goals, e.g., undergraduate education, graduate or professional work. Within the multicampus system, the possibility of diversity exists because the system can promote and protect differing academic and administrative approaches. The most dramatic examples of this are seen in the innovative undergraduate college programs of Wisconsin, the State University of New York, and the University of California. Individual campuses can undertake educational experiments with assurance that success will reach beyond the campus boundary and that unanticipated costs will be shared by a larger entity. The possibility of diversity by no means assures it; one of the strongest criticisms of some multicampus universities is that their campuses are either imitations of a prestigious flagship campus or squeezed cookie-cutter fashion into administratively constructed standards.

Specialization is akin to diversity but designates differences in goals themselves. The most obvious examples are the health science campuses in California, New York, Illinois, and Texas. Perhaps more indicative of the future is the historic division of labor evidenced by the technical emphasis of North Carolina State and Chapel Hill's concentration on the liberal arts. A single-campus college or university can specialize, but it does so at the risk of competing for a limited number of students. A campus in a multicampus system cannot completely avoid such a risk, but it is minimized, for other campuses within the system are not allowed to compete.

Cooperation between the campuses of a multicampus system can marshal academic resources for tasks beyond the capacity of a single campus. The Graduate Center of the City University of New York most clearly illustrates such cooperation, but the Sea Grant Program of the Madison and Milwaukee campuses in the University of Wisconsin may be more generally applicable. Coalitions and cooperation between individual campuses on a voluntary basis are increasing, particularly in the private sector, but the multicampus structure can nevertheless provide a procedural umbrella to facilitate cross-campus activity within the system.

Proponents of a single-board system of higher education may grant the capacity of a multicampus system to permit, encourage, and maintain diversity, specialization, and cooperation. They can argue, however, that a single board has such capacities also: Whatever a multicampus system can do, a single board of higher education can do better. By definition, its responsibility for governing all public campuses in a state is broader than that of the multicampus system.

However, the undoubted advantage of greater breadth of responsibility carries a price. The multicampus universities evidence a belief at the statewide level in the desirability of a pluralistic—at least a nonmonopolistic—approach to the governance of higher education. Their existence as separate systems increases the odds that, for the state as a whole, alternative goals and strategies for public higher education will be examined and tested, which is in the public interest. The validity of this assumption rests, of course, not only on the multicampus university, but the activities of other systems and institutions within each state. We cannot assess this assumption in a study of only one element of higher education. But we can evaluate the process by which the goals of this element— the multicampus university—are developed and implemented and, by so doing, come to an increased understanding of the larger problem of the governance of higher education as a whole.

THE PLANNING CONTEXT The organizational structure within which academic planning and program review take place is not neutral. Institutional arrangements affect substantive outcomes, much as the assignment of a legislative bill to a particular committee may shape its character or determine its survival. Thus, whether the review and approval of a specific academic program are the responsibility of the campus, the university, the coordinating agency, or the state government may influence its fate. Within the multicampus university itself, one system executive suggested, there is a constant interplay of forces between the technical specialists at the central administration and the faculty at the campus level. "It's the experts against the faculty," and in a multicampus system, the former have the time and the information.

These structural arrangements involve far more than institutional loyalties, for the latter are closely related to a host of educational values. For example, a multicampus university with a monopoly on advanced graduate work may be less sensitive to pressures to introduce a "teaching doctorate" than one in a competitive situation. Again, a coordinating agency required to deal with competing systems may be forced by external pressures to balance the universities, rather than to stress quality control; two "average" professional schools rather than a single outstanding one might result.

If the structures are not neutral, neither are the planning documents. Although almost always offered as objective analyses by professional experts, most plans reviewed in the course of this study were value-laden and subjective, designed not merely to describe, but to influence and persuade. Such plans are often as interesting for what they do not say as for what is clearly set forth. In one instance, political reality dictated that there not be any formal plan at all. Such were the controversies surrounding the future of one campus that a clear exposition of precise goals could have rendered their implementation impossible. Only the hidden agenda had reality.

The most obvious factor shaping academic plans and programs for the multicampus university is its formal relationships to other academic institutions in the state, often expressed in constitutional or statutory language. In a previous chapter, we noted that in four states, California, Missouri, North Carolina, and Wisconsin, the multicampus university is segmentally differentiated from all other public institutions in that it alone has the authority to grant the doctorate or advanced professional degrees. Broad limits of specialization and diversity are mandated. However, segmental differentiations have been virtually eliminated at the undergraduate and master's level, with few formal distinctions between the multicampus system and other institutions in the state. In Illinois and Texas, even differentiation at the doctoral level has been eliminated. The remaining state, New York, has divided higher education into two large regional systems, each encompassing, for planning purposes, all the public institutions within its area.

Each of these three patterns, and there are wide variations within each as well, poses different relationships with the coordinating agency and with state government. In the first pattern of segmental differentiation, critical educational policy decisions are predetermined: legal and medical education as well as advanced graduate work belong to the university system to the exclusion of the balance of the state's public campuses. To the extent that segmental differentiation is absent, the potential for jurisdictional conflict among the several institutions increases, as does the need for a third-party arbiter to resolve their differences.

In addition to these basic institutional arrangements, many often unique environmental factors impinge on academic planning and program review. These seem far more significant than the formal constitutional or statutory framework, yet they are always difficult to evaluate or use as a basis for firm planning. Questions of economic growth, of population mobility, of public acceptance of taxation for higher education, are central to sound long-range educational forecasting, but neither universities nor states are effectively organized to measure them. Often, the pressures are conflicting.

For example, each university system is confronted with demands to become increasingly graduate-oriented, to concentrate on its unique "knowledge-creation" role, to become more differentiated from the collegiate institutions and more highly selective. Such a course is often urged by state financial authorities, coordinating agencies, the four-year collegiate institutions, and the universities themselves. At the same time, the universities face even more intense pressures—internal and external—to broaden their undergraduate programs, to accept larger numbers of persons lacking formal qualifications for admission, to engage in remedial work, and to become involved in social experiments that have little direct relationship to traditional university programs. One strategy for response calls for further segmentation and a clearer division of labor within the state's overall higher education system, the other for an even greater blurring of segmental lines. System options for specialization, diversity, and cooperation among its campuses are far fewer than examination of formal authority alone would indicate.

On a different front, with increasing pressures for state support of private schools, comprehensive academic planning including both public and private universities is being urged. New relationships are arising, not only between the state and the private schools but between the latter and the multicampus university directly.[2]

Within the multicampus university, parallel factors of the educational environment shape academic plans and programs. In a few states, Texas and New York, for example, universities are rapidly

---

[2] North Carolina's Research Triangle is a working example of one such endeavor. Midway between Chapel Hill, North Carolina State University, and Duke University (a private institution), the triangle constitutes a scientific center with cooperative relationships among all three campuses, including a large computer network.

adding new campuses and the foreseeable future is one of expansion. In most states, however, the number of campuses appears fixed for the time being, either by choice or by the policy dictates of legislatures and coordinating agencies. The academic planning role for the multicampus university is more certain, at least more obvious, in the first situation, in shaping new campuses and reviewing expansion.

One determining factor in academic planning and growth is the existence or absence of an enrollment ceiling on the major campus of the university. In the University of California, a limit of 27,500 students at any one campus has been reached on two, and has necessitated both internal reallocations within the university as well as targets and quotas for departments within each of the two campuses. In several other systems, in contrast, there is no immediate disposition to impose a growth ceiling on the main campuses, some of which have enrollments in excess of 30,000. As a result, these systems have not yet been confronted with the internal adjustments required by adherence to fixed campus enrollment. Continued growth has permitted the system administration to delay crucial decisions, most specifically on a forced distribution of students among the several campuses, with all the program adjustments that this entails.

The character of systemwide planning is also shaped by the extent to which the campuses are regarded as "general" or "specialized." In the University of California, which has adopted the former approach, each campus (excluding the San Francisco Medical Center) has the theoretical potential to approximate the main flagship campus in size and program diversity. This open-ended concept places heavy demands for program review on the system administration; there are few organizationally structured limits on what a campus may propose. Thus, the system has the continuing burden of developing a truly coordinated approach, of avoiding unwarranted duplication, and of encouraging desirable specialization. Similarly, although confronted with a very different problem, the California State Colleges do not differentiate among the collegiate campuses of that system. While campuses may have particular specialties, all have the same goals of general education. At the University of North Carolina, in contrast, many of these problems have been avoided by a policy of "allocation of functions," which has assigned specific and distinct program missions to each campus. Although the policy is changing to permit "complementarity of programs," the systemwide administration has been spared many difficult internal decisions over the years.

The modal pattern is midway between these two relative extremes. None, other than California, has gone so far as to class every campus as "general," with the open-ended connotations that term implies. But neither has any system put definite limits on the mission of each campus (excepting, of course, separate medical centers and two-year campuses). Rather, there is implicit recognition that the flagship campuses, where they exist, will continue to be dominant in the foreseeable future, that there should be some specialization among all campuses, and that, increasingly, both dominance and specialization will require classification by more formal statements of mission. But for the immediate future in almost every state, the pace of development is so fast and fluid and funding so uncertain that a clear-cut determination of the long-range role for each campus has been precluded.

This situation is somewhat modified in those universities which we have termed comprehensive. Here, two or three types of campuses within the university are formally recognized, and it is accepted as well as planned that one campus will continue as a two-year institution, another as a four-year, and a third as a full-university campus with advanced graduate work. But in these systems, while certain fundamental questions of academic planning have been resolved, questions of diversity and specialization among campuses of a similar type remain. So do problems of articulation among the segments within the university. In comparison with the segmental universities, the planning task in comprehensive systems is more complex and more manageable. The scope of academic plans and programs is materially increased by the inclusion of widely differentiated campuses within the same system. However, there are offsetting advantages in being able to resolve intersegmental issues within the family. Without exception, administrators of the comprehensive systems indicated their preference for this alternative over one which increased the need for negotiations with an independent coordinating agency.

In all seven states, an uneasy and unstable relationship exists between the multicampus university and the coordinating agency. Tension and disagreement between the two institutions have arisen over specific policies and programs, but, more fundamentally, over the basic authority and responsibility of each. Ernest Palola

(1968) observes from the vantage point of his research on statewide educational planning that ". . . agreement among state coordinators, campus administrators, and faculty is not very high as to who should have initiating, reviewing, recommending, or final authority across a rather wide range of topics—determination of institutional mission and role, program development, personnel policies, fiscal management, and the like." We found no evidence to contradict this finding.

Typically, the university has been reluctant to accept the coordinating agency as an equal partner in the governance of higher education. Nor, with the notable exception of Illinois, at least until 1970, have legislatures and governors been willing to rely on the recommendations of the agency. The coordinating agencies appear to be suffering an "identity crisis." Lacking the confidence of both the universities and the politicians, they tend to suffer from low prestige and inadequate staff. In at least two states, the continued existence of the agency was in doubt in 1970; in others, the agency had become closely identified as an arm of the executive branch of state government.

Despite this ambiguity—and in part because of it—the requirements imposed by a coordinating agency upon academic plans and programs are not insignificant. This is most obvious where agencies are required by statute to approve particular academic programs; but even in states where an agency is relatively weak, it is not without influence. Not all decisions of the coordinating agencies are accepted by the universities or by the state governments. But universities are loath to attempt to override them, whether legally binding on the system or not.

Examples of coordinating agency involvement include both minor and major aspects of educational policy. In Wisconsin, the agency vetoed the university's proposal that a specific department be authorized to award the doctorate on the grounds that the state did not need more scholars in that field than those already being produced at the Madison campus. In Illinois, the proposal of the university to establish a new campus in Springfield was denied by the agency, which assigned the campus to a competing system. And in California, a coordinating agency study of engineering education effectively altered system plans to expand such programs to new campuses. Questions of specialization and diversity in these instances were taken out of the hands of the systems and decided for them.

In most states, the question is not whether there is to be a co-ordinating agency, but the extent to which it will be autonomous from state government. The view of the multicampus university on this point is ambiguous. Will the coordinating agency's autonomy be at the expense of the state or the university? In either case, an increasing network of relationships between the university and the agency seems assured, and will affect not only systemwide activity but the character of system-campus relationships as well.

ACADEMIC PLANNING

While there is general agreement that all educational institutions should plan their development and a recognition that the multicampus university should be admirably equipped to engage in academic planning, widespread disagreement exists as to what the term encompasses.

The ostensible objective of academic planning — "ideal" planning — is to clarify the alternative goals of higher education and the various policies that might lead to their attainment. Theoretically, clarification of these goals and their implementation would be the relative responsibility of the different agencies charged with the overall governance of higher education in the state. For example, goals for a single campus might involve the distribution of students by discipline and by level; the relative emphasis to be given teaching, research, and public service; and the status of the campus as a local, state, or national institution. For the multicampus university, attention would be drawn to the number, size, and geographic spread of campuses; the breadth and specialization of undergraduate and graduate programs among the campuses; cooperation among campuses; and priorities involving both operating and capital expenditures. A coordinating agency might concern itself with the proportion of high school graduates who should be admitted, respectively, to the colleges and universities of the state; the overall responsibility of the universities and colleges for professional and graduate training; and the balancing of the needs of public and private higher education. For the state itself, long-range planning would lead to a carefully studied allocation of public resources to higher education — as opposed to other public programs.

Simply to state these few elements of a hypothetical long-range academic plan demonstrates the gulf between the reality and the ideal and the difficulty of clear assignment of responsibility among the parties. Many would argue that the ideal is either futile or undesirable: the "big picture" cannot be comprehended, much less guided, and attempts to do either may be illusory. In a time of multiple social and scientific revolutions, each affecting the modern university in widely differing and often conflicting ways, a long-range plan may be an impossibility.

While there is much justice in such critiques, decisions (or non-decisions) are being made with long-range consequences. Explicitly or implicitly, such decisions are based on predictions and value judgments about the future. Few ask whether there should be long-range planning, but many are concerned about its character: who does it, with what information, subject to what influences?

The answers to such questions are unclear. After an intensive investigation, Ernest Palola (1968) concludes that academic planning in the United States might best be described as "goal evasion," the *avoidance* of goal definition and its specification in operational terms. Instead of examining basic issues of educational policy, he states, most long-range planning is "quantitative, routine, means-oriented, based on limited research, without priorities and initiated by pressures external to the institutions."

For the multicampus systems, at least, his description appears too narrow. What is wrong with system plans is not the absence of qualitative goals, but their overabundance and the apparent impossibility of rational choice among them. Long-range planning is set in a context of apparent contradictions. "High-quality, mass education" means little to universities faced with tighter state budgets. Pressures from rising numbers of qualified high school graduates at one end and from society for highly skilled graduates at the other is matched by demands that the quality of both instruction and public service activities be upgraded; it is no wonder that academic planning moves uncertainly. "Goal inundation" rather than "goal evasion" more accurately describes system planning problems.

The technical quality of long-range decision making varies immensely; some critical decisions involve scarcely more than responses to immediate pressures or perceived needs, with little weighing of alternative strategies or ultimate consequences. In contrast, and often within the same university, other decisions are based on as careful a marshaling of evidence and alternative solutions as possible. One administrator suggested that the location of the responsibility for planning could cause variation within and between systems:

If the responsible organ is the Office of Institutional Research, then one would expect to find the process still of the "facts and figures" variety. If, on the other hand, there exists a separate "division of long-range planning" or something of that sort, there is no guarantee of a more substantive process—but at least some attempt is being made to escape the purely statistical design.

One generalization can be made. By and large, effective academic planning takes place in response to external demands from state governments or coordinating agencies. There are few examples of system-initiated academic planning, although once required to plan, some systems have moved beyond the formal, minimum requirements of the state. But for several of the universities, long-range planning, if any, has to be inferred from the one- or two-year cycles of the operating budget and the somewhat longer timetable of the capital outlay program.

The reasons given for this reluctance to look ahead, at least in formal terms, are numerous and go to the heart of university governance. One system executive, usually confronted with a complete turnover of his governing board every six years, spoke of both his difficulty in trying to see beyond the immediate future and the reluctance of new board members to be committed by their predecessors. Elsewhere, a senior administrator stated that any comprehensive plan which was not ratified by the faculty would be meaningless but that "the faculty of this university had never agreed." The net result was an absence of any identifiable long-range plan and no intention to develop one. In a third system, almost everyone agreed that any plan acceptable to all campuses would have to be so vague that it would not limit individual campus aspirations. Finally, one system executive suggested that it was the height of futility to try to plan far ahead because the legislature was jealous of its own prerogatives concerning higher education. Discussing this same system, another administrator stated, "The only universitywide plan we've got is when the president talks to the legislators in a smoke-filled room."

Within the nine multicampus universities, *formal* documentary evidence of academic planning is absent as much as it is present. In only four states are the university systems required to prepare formal academic plans. Generally, the process consists of the preparation of campus plans, their review and integration by systemwide staff, and the presentation of a universitywide plan to the governing board for its formal approval and subsequent transmission to the coordinating agency. This process is generally described as valuable, but not necessarily for the formal reasons which dictate the preparation of the plan. Campuses are forced to review their internal programs and bring inconsistencies to light. At the system level, the formal plans provide an opportunity to give campuses an early warning signal that particular proposals are unacceptable. As one campus executive described the procedure, "Getting a program into the approved plan gives us a hunting license. We have no guarantee we'll be able to establish the program, but at least we know we can try."

The academic planning process has its detrimental aspects. For example, in New York the four-year planning cycle with annual progress reports appears to frustrate rather than to aid a truly long-range view of the university. The endless production of reports led one planner to state, "We don't plan. We write plans."

System executives are by no means unanimous in advocating formal, long-range planning. Unstructured, informal, day-to-day decisions characterize a not uncommon administrative style. "I don't want to concentrate grievances by denying everyone's proposals at the same time in a formal plan. A system executive needs a little leverage. I don't have much to give away; saying 'yes' to campus proposals from time to time is one gift that I have to ration."

Academic plans are often more important for what they do not say rather than as positive statements of long-range goals. The multicampus university effectively screens out duplication and promotes coordination. But it often lacks the ability and the authority to go beyond this to establish positive goals with assurance they will be implemented. This limited achievement is no mean one. As one campus administrator suggested: "In a world of rapid change, about all the decision maker can do is avoid *bad* mistakes." While it may be difficult to accept the avoidance of serious error as the definition of success, the above discussion makes clear that, at best, serious obstacles to effective long-range academic planning are many and pervasive.

For one thing, each university is faced with immense sunk costs in terms of physical plant and staff, the latter often with tenure. It is often difficult to reshape buildings and personnel to meet changing educational goals. This is particularly so in a period of little growth, where new developments can take place only at the expense of existing practices and programs. There are also organizational barriers to effective planning. In every university there is difficulty in relating the relatively open-ended process of academic planning to the more specific requirements of the capital and operating budget. Each process has its own timetable, its own staff, its own dynamic; and they rarely are coordinated. In theory, academic planning should precede budgeting. In fact, both the physical and the operating budgets usually have priority. In more than one university, the long-range plan has been put on the shelf until "next year."

In part, this lack of coordination is a mirror image of state government. Each phase of the state's planning-budgeting process — with its own procedures, requirements, staff, and leadership — is on a different schedule. Even within the same state fiscal office, the capital and operating budget staff are not always in close communication. Nor, as previously suggested, is there clear delineation of the role of state government vis-à-vis the coordinating agency. The latter may review the academic aspects of programs, but the budget office reviews their fiscal requirements, and it is not obvious how, if at all, these are meshed. The divided authority of the administrative arms of state government is found also in the legislature. Separate committees often review the operating and capital outlay requests and render independent judgments, despite obvious interrelationships. Fragmentation and discontinuity at the state level cast doubt on the possibility of a long-range academic plan in the absence of a long-range state plan. Moreover, the annual budget cycle and only slightly longer legislative and gubernatorial terms virtually guarantee that such a state plan will not be developed, even assuming it might be desirable.

The long-range future of higher education depends, not on formal plans, but on the support which the citizens of the state — as represented by their political leaders — wish to give higher education. The critical question, then, is the extent to which a formal planning process by the multicampus university will enhance political acceptability. There is little evidence that it makes any difference. Neither governors nor legislatures seem disposed to treat the "master plan" as more than a vague prophecy which will assume reality only when forced into the political maelstrom.

As if divided authority and responsibility at the state level are not enough to confuse planning, federal funding is emerging as another dominant force. Even the most rigorous long-range plans are vulnerable to the shifting patterns of federal financing. For example, enrollment forecasts based on anticipated federal student loans assume—with little basis for confidence—federal financing of construction to house these students. In addition, the relative power of students, faculty, the campus, the multicampus university, the coordinating agency, the governor, and the legislature to shape academic plans is highly dependent on the impact of alternative patterns of federal financing.

Despite the increasing pervasiveness of the federal dollar in long-range academic planning, there are few instances of effective interstate planning by neighboring universities. Instead, an isolationist mentality is a feature of most plans. For example, discussions of the need for a new campus in a remote area of one state ignored the existence of a public campus a few miles away across the state border; one suspects that the plans of the neighboring campus as well were being pursued with little consideration of the impact of the proposed institution. Interstate coordination is highly desirable, and the multicampus university is a potentially effective instrument for such activity. But the dynamics of politics and fiscal controls handicap cooperation across state boundaries. It is probable, however, that the federal government, with its own interests in specialization and cooperation, will press increasingly for regional interstate plans.

While formal long-range academic planning is subject to all the above limitations, within each university decisions are being made with long-range implications. Architects, engineers, and others on the physical planning staff are the most visible of the "invisible" academic planners. Typically, they are required to operate with five- to seven-year lead times, a dynamic which proceeds whether or not the educational need for the facility has been evaluated relative to other alternatives. A frequent comment from the capital outlay staff at both campus and systemwide levels concerns the difficulty of getting adequate and timely advice from faculty and academic administrators. Physical planners are often poorly instructed on academic requirements in terms of program content for the building, or how the program may change by the time the facility is opened. A parallel complaint is that "they" (professors and deans) change their minds, but "they" also have complaints. Detailed academic plans are prepared for a physical facility, but there are insufficient funds to build the project as originally contemplated. In either case the burden falls upon the architect to make adjustments, many with important long-range academic implications.

A potential advantage of the multicampus university as a governing and not merely a coordinating agency is that academic planning can be more closely integrated with both physical planning and the operating budget. Examples of fruitful interrelationships were found, but none of the systems claim successful meshing of the three activities. While this undoubtedly reflects parallel diffusion of authority at state and federal levels, there is also an internal reason: academic planning in the multicampus university is characterized by inadequate staffing.

While a paradox, perhaps, that a knowledge-oriented institution should give such little attention to its own research and development, this is unquestionably the case. Only in isolated instances are staff assigned primarily to taking the long look, freed from day-to-day operating responsibilities. Persons with formal planning duties frequently spend most of their time putting out fires. Long-range planning tends to be deferred.

At times, this appeared to evidence a lack of belief in planning as a useful enterprise, but the more frequent impression was that it is a symptom of a general understaffing of academic administration. Typically, long-range planning is the duty of an administrative officer who holds several other portfolios. As a result, planning is often delegated to faculty committees, who are expected to carry out this assignment in addition to their normal activities, and with little staff assistance or professional help. The concern that the multicampus will foster a bureaucracy of professional planners seems far from the truth. More typically, they are hard to find at all.

Regardless of the many qualifications on systemwide activity, the multicampus university often plays an important role by upgrading campus planning. Better campus plans result from system specification of requirements, the establishment of procedures, and the provision of technical assistance. Campuses have improved their planning and program review responsibilities because of the existence of a higher level of review, although some examples were given in which difficult decisions had been passed up to the system rather than resolved locally.

We suggest, from the vantage point of the study, that long-range "master" planning has been oversold, both within and without the university. Under pressure from governors, legislatures, and co-ordinating agencies, multicampus systems are, at one and the same time, attempting too much and accomplishing too little. First, too much time and attention are being devoted to attempts at comprehensiveness at the expense of emphasis upon the critical points of decision; to a bland cataloging of all the possible goals of the university rather than concentration on a few critical issues — high-cost programs, major capital facilities, and significant changes in direction or orientation. The system's unique responsibility to foster and enforce diversity, specialization, and cooperation among its campuses has often been lost in a sea of detail.

Secondly, many academic planners appear reluctant to recognize that their work is not a substitute for the political process but a critical part of it, that the academic plan is not an end result but a step in a continuing, fluid stream of decisions. The university cannot itself resolve all the conflicts inherent in an institution with competing goals, but it can greatly improve the quality of the evidence upon which the state's political arms will make their decision. Because of its broader planning base, there are opportunities for cross-campus comparisons, for program experimentation and evaluation, for pilot projects, and for assessing the relative validity of certain goals of the university rather than attempting to accommodate all of them. With its responsibilities for implementation and governance, the multicampus system has unique opportunities to test and refine the assumptions of academic planning in a way that no coordinating agency can achieve.

The potential is there, but it requires an assertion of university-wide academic leadership vis-à-vis the campuses that has not yet been accepted at either campus or system levels. If the system is to be more than a collection of autonomous campuses, new and different approaches to long-range academic planning will be required. And if the university does not provide these innovations, there are others in the wings — in coordinating agencies and state capitals — eager to take over.

PROGRAM REVIEW: QUALITY CONTROL Academic program review has two distinct but interrelated aspects. The first concerns the *appropriateness* of a specific program proposal within the mission of the campus; this mission is sometimes expressed in a formal academic plan but often found in a more general and informal understanding of campus goals. In one university, a classics major for only five undergraduates had been proposed by a campus. This proposal was denied by the system administration on the basis that the major was not a specialization central to the urban mission of the campus and would prejudice consideration of more essential programs by the coordinating agency. The campus accepted the judgment and shelved the proposal for the foreseeable future.

The second element of program review involves the *readiness* of the campus to mount a program in terms of such matters as numbers and quality of faculty, library, and laboratory resources. The system serves as an internal accrediting agency. A specific example of such review was the denial by a systemwide faculty committee of a campus proposal to initiate a new doctoral program. The committee determined that the departmental faculty was not yet large enough to provide the several specialties required in the field. The campus was invited to resubmit the proposal in two years after it had more experience with its relatively new master's program.

Patterns of Authority

There are several elements of academic programs, including individual courses, curricula, majors, degrees, and new schools and colleges. Similarly, there are numerous potential participants in the process of review and approval, including the department, college, campus, university system, coordinating agency, and state government.

Within the nine universities, the review process weaves these elements and participants in highly varied patterns. In theory, once a long-range academic plan is approved, for example by a coordinating agency, specific program approval is a matter for the multicampus university to determine internally. But this seldom occurs in practice. The academic plan in most systems is either nonexistent or too general for operational purposes. Both governing boards and coordinating agencies tend to approve long-range plans "in principle" and require that each specific program be submitted individually, with no assurance that approval will be forthcoming. In effect, specific program review by the coordinating agency substitutes for the academic plan, much as individual zoning decisions come to dominate the physical plan for a city. And just as in the city, this "real" academic plan often represents a series of individual ad hoc decisions rather than a carefully integrated resolution of questions about the future.

While coordinating agencies typically retain authority to approve individual programs for consistency with the mission of a campus or university, only rarely do they assert authority over readiness to undertake a program. Whether explicitly set forth or not, there appears to be a clearly understood division of labor between the role of the coordinating agencies and that of the systems, with the former asserting final authority over program allocation (i.e., planning), the latter over program quality.

The modal distribution of authority is somewhat as follows. Establishment of a new school or college, which almost always carries with it the establishment of a new degree, requires coordinating agency approval, whether specified by statute or under procedures agreed to by the agency and the university. Occasionally, new schools and colleges also require explicit legislative authorization.

Similarly, whether or not a new school is involved, a proposal to award a new degree also requires coordinating agency review — for example, the authorization to a campus to award a Ph.D. or a new professional degree. However, the pattern is quite uneven for the extension of a degree already existing on a campus, such as the doctorate or master of arts, from one field to another. In some states, this requires coordinating agency approval, while in others the question is internal to the university.

While there is no uniformity and occasional uncertainty over the relative role of the university and the coordinating agency in program review, there is no question over the appropriateness of universitywide review of campus proposals. With a rare exception, decisions involving new degrees, extension of existing degrees to new fields, creation of academic departments, and related matters require system approval. Almost by definition, membership in the multicampus university involves systemwide review of major program changes. It is also generally accepted that, at the other end of the program continuum, the approval of individual courses is a matter internal to the campuses, although one coordinating agency had legislative authority to monitor all courses in the entire state!

New or Changing Campuses The useful role of the system in program review is most evident in the nurture of new campuses and, secondly, in the change in role and orientation accompanying the transition of an existing two- or four-year college into a university campus. These roles have been played in two quite different environments. Most typically, growth has been outward from an established flagship campus, which has served as a source of expertise and, often, as a model. Here, transitional development is characterized by combined departments and academic committees, dominated by the flagship campus faculty; administrative ties to the flagship campus; a single universitywide graduate school; and campus advisory committees composed of flagship faculty.

A second pattern occurs in the absence of a dominant flagship campus. Here, the system itself must provide the program review resources, and quite different styles of assistance, support, and quality control are required. For example, nonflagship systems more frequently turn to outside consultants for guidance, whereas the older flagship universities rely on resources internal to the university.

With respect to new campuses, the fear that the multicampus university always turns out carbon copies of its flagship campus or replicates existing campuses in nonflagship systems is not supported by the facts. Although basically within a traditional framework, there are examples of important experiments in higher education inspired, supported, and facilitated by the larger university. Santa Cruz, Green Bay, Chicago Circle, Old Westbury, and other campuses like them represent some of the most significant developments in higher education. There is no doubt that the university system has provided these campuses with the protection, technical assistance, and confidence that has made the experiments possible. Furthermore, at critical times the systems have been able to provide seed money not often available to a new campus fending for itself before state fiscal authorities.

The development of a new campus can be credited as a major achievement of the multicampus university, but perhaps a more difficult and demanding task is the transformation of an existing two- or four-year collegiate campus into a major university center. In one way or another, this has taken place in seven of the nine universities. Problems of transition, of blending new and old faculty, of phasing out established programs and initiating new ones were often described as involving a high level of trauma and tension, both personal and institutional. Universally, the system is credited with facilitating the changeover in a manner that would have been difficult for a single-campus institution alone.

Less dramatically and less noticeably, the multicampus university also provides effective quality control for established campuses. While criteria are difficult to formulate and apply, the distinct impression at both campus and system levels is that academic program decisions are the better because of universitywide review. In part, poor decisions, which might otherwise emerge from local campus pressures, are simply not forwarded for system review. No campus executive or faculty group wishes to be turned down, at least not very often.

In addition, for all campuses, the multicampus university symbolizes in most instances a standard of performance which is usually accepted by its members and which transcends that of any particular campus. The very existence of a review external to the campus is felt to promote a decision based on the merits of the program, and not on extraneous campus pressures. The university can bring to bear specialized talents and experience greater even than that at an established flagship campus. Technical assistance is available from both faculty and administration in more abundance than any single campus can provide. Particularly for the smaller campuses, the system is better able to identify and recruit outside consultants and otherwise assist in program development and review.

The Case of Graduate Programs

The review activities of the multicampus university are most visible for graduate programs. Relative to other university functions, graduate programs are generally high in cost. The need to avoid unnecessary duplication is far more pressing than it is in most undergraduate curricula. For a campus to obtain the critical mass requisite to a broadly based graduate offering, resources must be concentrated. Finally, for good or ill, the prestige of the modern university is tied to graduate work. "Creation of new knowledge" distinguishes the university from the college, and institutional reputations among the major universities are tied to this dimension of quality. None of the multicampus universities is unaware of this fact: all give special attention to the review and approval of graduate programs.

Almost without exception, governing boards reserve to themselves the authority to approve all major graduate program changes, specifically the creation of new schools and colleges and the establishment of new degrees. Sometimes, graduate program changes are treated in a rather *pro forma* fashion by the boards. But frequent examples indicate that this responsibility is usually taken seriously and that the boards do not consider themselves merely a rubber stamp. Programs have been modified and deferred as a result of board action. For example, simultaneous proposals from two campuses to initiate similar graduate programs led the board in one university to request a review of all such programs within the entire system. Outside consultants were appointed to conduct the study, and the end result was a sharp modification of the original proposals. The experience alerted the central administration to undertake intercampus studies in other subject areas before taking proposals to the governing board.

Most often, governing board review of a graduate program is concerned with the need for the new program, the extent to which it duplicates other offerings in the university or in the state, and its consistency with the mission of the campus. However, the board itself is sometimes interested in quality control, the reputation of the faculty or the proposed dean, particularly in professional fields in which board members have experience and competence, such as law, business, and architecture.

At the systemwide level, procedures for graduate program review can be divided according to whether the greater role is played by the administration or by faculty agencies. The former is the predominant mode. In most multicampus systems the central administration, not the faculty, bears the major responsibility for the systemwide review of new graduate degree proposals, both as to appropriateness and as to quality.

Typically, this administrative review is the individual responsibility of a senior system officer, but there is no modal pattern for the review process itself. For example, a panel of outside consultants is employed by the State University of New York to consider every proposal for a new doctoral degree. In Missouri, an administrative committee dominated by graduate deans from the several campuses is the primary advisory arm. In Wisconsin, however, no formal advisory agency has been established, the system administration believing that campus review procedures are rigorous enough to provide adequate advice on program quality. A strategy followed by the University of North Carolina system administration is to refer a new degree proposal to the several campuses, asking each campus executive for comment. The routing is designed primarily to prevent unnecessary duplication but is also credited as serving a quality control function. At the University of California, a graduate affairs committee of the universitywide faculty government is charged with the primary responsibility of approving new programs for existing degrees and of recommending the establishment of entirely new degrees.

In all systems, whether universitywide program review is dominated by the administration or faculty, both have an essential part, and the problem of coordination between them remains. The administration has to fit specific programs or degree proposals into long-range plans and short-term budgets. A strong academic voice adds an essential dimension to ensure adequacy of faculty, libraries, and other education resources. Not all systems have achieved a satisfactory balance between these two critical participants in program review, and a continuing task of the system executive is to promote effective communication at both system and campus levels among the diverse parties.

As expected, use of outside consultants in a program review capacity is greater in smaller systems, in which the necessary experience and specialized talents are not contained within the university. Campuses view the universitywide requirement for independent review as advantageous to them. In fact, the general approval of the practice in the systems employing it suggests the desirability of external review in large university systems as well. Academic program decisions, for example a graduate degree proposal, are enduring, costly, and difficult to reverse or modify. The system executive's recommendation of such proposals and the governing board's approval of them are among the most important decisions made by the university; they should be based on the best information and advice available. None of the multicampus universities are so well staffed and equipped that independent commentary upon program proposals, both as to need and as to quality, would not be of benefit.

But to whom should the outside advice be rendered? The prevailing practice is for review—whether by the outside consultants or by the responsible systemwide administrative or faculty agency —to take place *after* the proposal has been recommended by the campus executive to universitywide authorities. Our analysis suggests that it might be more appropriate for the program review to be primarily advisory to the campus executive, *before* a recommendation is made to universitywide authorities.

Such an approach would overcome several shortcomings reported as problems under present practice. The campus review would be enriched by the comments of the panel. The position of the campus executive would also be enhanced, for he would have a broader range of evidence and opinion upon which to base his recommendation. Potential conflict between campus and system might be eliminated, since both would be considering identical assessments. And, finally, the system executive's judgment would be founded not only on the recommendations of the independent panel, but the additional comments of the campus executive upon that recommendation.

Under this approach, the system administration might appropriately shift its emphasis from substantive review to assurance that the process of campus decision making is of the highest quality; it would do so by establishing procedures to be followed, by providing the necessary technical and staff assistance, and by facilitating employment of outside consultants when desirable. The ultimate responsibilities of the system executive and the governing board would remain, but in a more constructive and effective relationship to the campus than the existing pattern appears to provide.

The single graduate school

In five of the nine universities, including all but one with strong flagship campuses, a single, universitywide graduate school continued as a transitional device long after the establishment of separate campuses. In these cases, quality control for the initial years of the new or transitional campuses was in the hands of the flagship campus. The graduate dean of the campus assumed, in effect, universitywide responsibilities, generally with an executive committee dominated by flagship faculty.[3] We found almost universal agreement among the newer campuses that the single graduate school served a useful purpose. New programs and degree proposals were forced to pass muster in a nationally recognized review procedure, and the flagship campus's stamp of approval on the quality of the degree was considered a significant contribution of the multicampus university.

There was equal agreement on the next step. A symbol of "coming of age" was campus freedom from this tie and establishment of

[3] The organization of graduate affairs within the University of California took a different historical turn. Rather than the original single graduate division splitting up into campus divisions, there was an intermediate phase of some 20 years in which a northern section was dominated by Berkeley and a southern one by UCLA. In 1962, separate campus divisions were established under the general supervision of a universitywide faculty council.

its own graduate school, its own dean, and its own review procedures. The symbol was no less important when, as was usually the case, many elements of authority remained at a universitywide administrative level. It is one thing to be reviewed by central administration, quite another to be reviewed by a flagship-dominated faculty committee.

The creation of a campus graduate school also enhances the authority of the campus executive and marks his coming of age as well as the maturity of the campus. No longer is the campus executive required to gain the approval of a graduate dean nominally responsible to another campus executive, albeit the flagship head. No longer is the flagship campus dean in the ambiguous role of being an adviser to both the campus and system executives.

In one admittedly unique case—the City University of New York—the intention is to continue the single, universitywide graduate school permanently. Made possible by the relative proximity of the campuses and the "subway tradition" of intercampus travel, the decision has imposed a universitywide, discipline-oriented structure of governance upon a campus-based organization. The graduate executive officer (first titled provost, then president) is responsible directly to the system executive, in marked contrast to campus counterparts in the other systems. A separate graduate center has been established, physically removed from any existing campus and staffed by a carefully screened "graduate faculty," most of whom hold joint appointments at the center and one of the campuses.

This distinctive organizational pattern is critical in the context of academic plans and programs. In the City University, the system is the leading force in the development of graduate programs. Although the subject is an issue of contention, the controlling policy is that only by combining faculty and staff from the several basically collegiate campuses can the critical mass necessary to a successful graduate program be obtained.

Given the special circumstances of the New York City scene, there is much to commend the approach. Nevertheless, it raises serious problems of system-campus relationships. Although the policy of a separately designated graduate faculty already existed, the establishment of a separate physical locale dramatizes the issue of "first-class" and "second-class" faculty status, particularly given the more handsome physical amenities of the Graduate Center. There is concern that graduate faculty will concentrate their activities at the Center, appearing on the campuses only to give their undergraduate lectures, and that, inevitably, undergraduate education at the campuses will suffer. Graduate science instruction requiring laboratory facilities continues at the campus, while social science and humanities instruction are at the Center, and many feel this separation will further fragment the campuses.

When the campuses themselves reach sufficient size and sophistication to propose their own separate doctoral programs, pressure for the abandonment of the center concept will surely increase. Whether the Center will remain a part of the university scene is a matter of dispute, but there is general agreement that it is a necessary transitional step.

Other Approaches

System review and approval of graduate programs is the most prominent aspect of multicampus quality control activity, but other strategies have been employed. In three of the five universities with flagship campuses, different approaches have been used to bring to new and transitional campuses the strengths and experience of the old.

In two systems, new campuses were established near enough to the flagship campuses to permit combined academic departments. A single chairman, almost always from the older and larger department at the flagship campus, served as administrative head of the programs on both campuses. Courses, curricular changes, and degree proposals were reviewed by committees of the combined department, in which flagship faculty members were dominant. This transition period continued several years, until the university determined that the faculty at the new campus could adequately shape its own programs. Although this close flagship control created frictions and frustrations, most participants agreed that it had effectively transmitted the values of the flagship throughout the entire university.

A somewhat different method of quality control permitted separate departments, but maintained a combined faculty government for the flagship and the new campus. Here, the values of the flagship were maintained by their domination of the committees which reviewed academic courses and programs. Once again, a marked maturity for the new campus was the establishment of its own independent faculty government. Again, there is an important symbolic distinction between being subject to universitywide review machinery which applies equally to all campuses and review by a faculty government which is merely an extension of the flagship campus.

A principal element of quality control in one university was the appointment of a systemwide faculty committee, representative of the older campuses, to advise the chief executive of the new campus during its early years of operation. Although the primary responsibility of the committee was to screen potential faculty, it also played an active and important role in initial and critical academic planning and program decisions.

In some instances in the transitional era, a campus has been treated as a school or college, reporting to a dean or provost with responsibilities for parallel programs at the flagship campus. This tended to be the pattern during the pre-multicampus period of university history, when the system executive also doubled as head of the flagship campus. Until a separate executive—with both title and authority—was appointed to head it, the new campus was subject to all the administrative controls of the flagship.

With respect to all these approaches, the existence of satisfactory transitional relationships between the flagship and the new campuses rests on agreement as to the definitions of quality. In each of the above cases, the new campuses set out to achieve the standards of the flagship, and the requirements and procedures of review involving the flagship proved effective. The situation is quite different when the flagship is not considered a model to be emulated or, in another case, when the flagship has little sense of common identity with the campuses brought into the system. In both instances, as with the multicampus universities not possessed of a flagship campus at all, the burden has fallen upon the systemwide administration to exercise quality control, whatever the definition of that term might be.

UNIVERSITY-WIDE ACADEMIC PROGRAMS

An additional field of system effort is the conduct of university-wide programs, drawing upon and serving the campuses, but multicampus in scope. We exclude here the administration of continuing education and agricultural extension, previously discussed.

Several universities have marshaled specialized resources from several campuses to reach the critical faculty mass necessary to mount a research project beyond the capabilities of any one campus. This takes many operational forms: the development of a coordinated research program, often related to external funding, with a division of labor among campus-based specialists; the organization of a universitywide committee to plan, administer, and dispense funds to individual faculty members with respect to a common problem or universitywide grant; or the conduct of periodic symposia or scholarly conferences attended by persons in the same academic field. The forms vary from system to system and within each. Universitywide centers, institutes, and coordinating committees are the most common structures.

These cooperative efforts are not peculiar to the multicampus university. Many examples of similar programs exist involving campuses and colleagues from outside the university. Nevertheless, the system is seen by most administrators and faculty as an effective structural focus for such programs, and there are examples of significant systemwide administrative support.

A second, more visible, universitywide academic activity is the specialized physical facility established to serve faculty and students from several campuses. Examples include observatories, marine biological laboratories, centralized computer facilities, a high-altitude research station, and educational television networks. Again, such intercampus consortia can exist independent of the multicampus university, and the facilities named are not necessarily limited to faculty or students of the particular system. It is clear, however, that the multicampus university provides significant opportunities for effective planning and administration that otherwise might not be as readily available.

Other types of universitywide activity include the coordination and administration of cultural enrichment programs such as lecture and concert tours and rotating art exhibits. Here, the system facilitates the scheduling of outside performers who are often beyond the reach of a single campus. Some examples of similar programs are internal to the university: interlibrary loan privileges, interchange of student drama and music groups, and other quasi-curricular programs. Of somewhat larger impact, several universitywide "campus-abroad" programs provide opportunities for an overseas educational experience to students from all the campuses.

Finally, there are isolated examples of joint instructional and degree programs involving faculty and facilities from more than one campus of the university. A future for such activities seems particularly promising for programs combining the specialized resources of a medical center with the basic science programs of a general campus, but other examples exist.

In virtually all systems, the issue has been raised, with respect to one program or another, whether a universitywide activity should be administered directly from the system offices or be assigned to one or more of the campuses for direction and support. There is no one pattern, and both approaches have their advantages and disadvantages. If the universitywide program involves a facility housed on a particular campus, there are advantages in assigning it to that campus, but with an advisory or coordinating committee appointed by the system executive. Although the campus executive has explicit systemwide responsibilities, there is always the danger that the campus will "capture" the program, at least in the eyes of the faculty and administrators from another campus. Allocating responsibility is less obvious in the case of an off-campus facility. Here, it is possible to make the unit directly responsible to a universitywide executive. The risks are that the facility will not receive adequate housekeeping support and that the system will become involved in administrative details rather than in the policy-planning activities for which it is uniquely equipped. Universitywide administration of a facility such as a statewide television network has much to commend it, but fixing responsibility for a single isolated laboratory remains an open question.

In only two of the nine universities studied are systemwide academic programs the *prime* responsibility of a major administrator. Instead, concern for universitywide activities is generally only one of several items in the portfolio of the principal system officer for academic affairs. Typically confronted with problems of academic personnel, long-range planning, and review of specific program proposals—the care and feeding of the campuses—the system administrator has had little time to consider ways in which the university, as a system, might itself contribute directly to academic programs.

The impression remains, however, that there should be more concern for systemwide programs in all the universities. Although each system is doing something, in each there is much more that might be done. What we find lacking—and what might but does not distinguish the multicampus system from voluntary cooperative efforts among autonomous institutions—is the provision of adequate staff at the system level to plan, promote, and administer universitywide programs. There simply is no one who has the time and responsibility to tap the rich potential for educational activity beyond that represented by the programs of the separate campuses.

Admittedly, the problems are many. Universitywide programs run counter to the basic campus-oriented organizational pattern and departmental control over discrete disciplines. There is evidence that the system is not always an effective agency to administer programs directly. Furthermore, there are obvious problems of obtaining state financial support in budgets dominated by formulas strictly related to enrollments and campus-based activities. In addition, a potential exists for much gimmickry in all-university activities. In more than one system, the complaint was heard that these had become an end in themselves, with few substantive results.

But the risks run the other way. Although there may be resistance from the campuses and reluctance from state financial authorities, an expanded program of universitywide activities seems essential if the multicampus university is to be more than the sum of its parts.

9. Budget Preparation and Administration

"The operating budget," said one system executive, "is the single most important educational document in the university." Here, the academic goals of faculty, administrators, and students confront the societal values of governors, legislators, and taxpayers. In the budgetary process, academic governance receives its most severe challenge.

At the *campus,* tentative and ambiguous long-range plans become concrete. The relative values of teaching and research or undergraduate and graduate education cease to be weighed in generalities and are forced into the reality of concrete expenditure estimates.

For the *multicampus university,* the budget forces another level of decision. Questions of optimum campus size, relative rates of campus growth, and duplication of academic programs can no longer be couched in the open-ended language of academic plans, with something for everyone. Even more pointedly, the multicampus budget requires a choice between sustaining "excellence" on one campus or achieving "balance" among all campuses, however these terms may be defined. Diversity, specialization, and cooperation are publicly and quantitatively defined. Qualifying the rhetoric of annual reports and commencement addresses, the budget may well be the truest indication of the ruling philosophy of the institution.[1]

---

[1] One system administrator, with experience in two of the multicampus universities, wrote as follows qualifying this point:

"We suggest that annual reports, commencement addresses, introductions to college and university catalogues, master plans *and budgets,* collectively be charged with failure to indicate institutional philosophy.

"We speculate that the failure to convey the philosophies of colleges, universities and systems *as institutions* lies in the fact that no such philosophies exist. We know of no institutional philosophy which transcends the variety of scholarly purposes within. We delude ourselves if we regard the concepts of

For the *state,* yet a broader set of values is involved. What should be the size and role of the public sector? Within this sector, to what extent should higher education be supported from taxes or tuition? And within higher education, should state policy emphasize a broad collegiate education for all high school graduates or the education of an elite meritocracy? How shall these contrasting values be accommodated?[2]

Most budgets do not explicitly ask or answer these questions, whether at the campus and multicampus levels or in the state capital. The issues are often deliberately kept ambiguous by all participants, for few institutions—academic or political—are capable of attacking such fundamental questions head on. Nevertheless, the budget represents the only *policy* answers to these crucial and controversial questions, however vaguely they may be phrased. The answers of the budget are policy declarations, explicit in the figures regardless of the words.

One important area of budgeting—federal funding—is virtually ignored altogether in this study. Although federal expenditures have a special significance for the multicampus university, the pattern of federal grants is sufficiently complicated and uncertain as to escape our analysis. We are not alone! After detailed study, the coordinating council in one state concluded that there was a

lack of dependable knowledge concerning the annual volume of federal funds spent in the state [for higher education], and the nature of the individual projects on which they are being expended. We are unable to determine if there is cooperation or duplication on projects, if the projects are being completed on a timely basis, or if the funds have a major impact on the need for more research facilities.

We found no state which reported a markedly different situation and regretfully leave this important subject to other, more hardy investigators. This chapter is concerned with state funds.

'community of scholars' or 'multipurpose institution' as expressions of philosophy. In Selznick's terms, these are evasions of '. . . the more basic and difficult problem of defining and safeguarding the ends of an enterprise.'"

We agree that the budget is not a "philosophy" in the sense of a deliberately planned and articulated statement of values. Nevertheless, it represents the operational values of the institution as they exist in fact.

[2] The issues at the state (and federal) governmental level are enormously complex. For a short analysis, see Hansen and Weisbrod (1969).

The possible advantages and disadvantages of the multicampus university may be highlighted in the budgetary process. Indeed, the raison d'être for a coordinated system of campuses is often stated to be the development and presentation of an integrated operating budget, a budget which permits academic administrators some flexibility in allocations among the campuses.

In theory, the fiscal needs of higher education are more effectively presented to the state if integrated by a multicampus budget. The multicampus university is in a better position to develop staff specialists in specific problem areas, such as libraries, medical education, and programmed learning, than are individual campuses.

For this reason, it can be argued, the multicampus system does a more effective job of *internal* allocation of resources among its campuses. Furthermore, in both its external presentations to the state and its internal allocations among the campuses, the budgetary decisions are, it is said, more effectively insulated from immediate political influences than would otherwise be the case. The longer organizational life span of the system affords a perspective on higher education that is impossible in a typical state administration, tied to two- or four-year political terms. Educational values that might not be politically popular with state finance authorities—for example, support for libraries or the humanities—should be better protected under the multicampus umbrella.

In addition to mediating external political influences, the multicampus university, many assert, effectively offsets internal academic politics. The system executive can maintain a harder, more tough-minded approach to resource allocation than a campus executive who is subject to immediate pressures from faculty, department chairmen, and deans. Without a systemwide administration, critical budgeting decisions for diversity or specialization among campuses might be forced upward to the desks of state budget officials who are not well equipped to coordinate financial *and* educational planning.

Finally, the multicampus system can improve budgeting at the campus level. State authorities may have neither the time, inclination, nor expertise to assist the campuses in upgrading their budget practices. The multicampus system can draw upon the experience of one campus to improve the entire system.

These potential advantages of the multicampus university may be offset by contradictory possibilities. The virtues of a coordinated budget may hide the danger of leveling, of tending to treat all campuses alike. In the interest of harmony, the budget may stress balanced development rather than maintenance of diversity. Such emphasis may be particularly troublesome for the comprehensive universities which govern both collegiate and university campuses with their specialized yet overlapping missions. It is difficult to reward and sustain excellence at one campus without slighting another within the same university family. The flagship campus may lose its preeminent position among national universities as resources are diverted to newer campuses.

There are fewer budgetary advantages to the multicampus structure if state officials negotiate with the individual campuses and develop the budget on a campus-by-campus basis. Any theoretical advantages are meaningless if the state government does not accept the authority of the system as a basic operating principle. If the state does not, the role of the universitywide officials becomes merely one of paper shuffling, an artificial intrusion into the realities of the budgetary process.

Finally, even when they are empowered to do so, the multicampus systems may be slow in recognizing decentralized practices of modern budgetary preparation and administration. Detailed system review of line items or central clearance of minor fund transfers may be continued long after they are necessary—out of habit, usually, but sometimes at the insistence of the governing board. The flagship campus may unduly impose its budgetary approaches upon the system as a whole, discouraging experimentation on the part of new campuses with different staffing and support patterns. The multicampus structure can be an obstacle to efficient financial management rather than an agent of progressive change.

We cannot evaluate all these arguments, pro and con. We can, however, look to the nine systems for evidence that, if flexibility is allowed, the campuses benefit.

EXTERNAL CONSTRAINTS No one ever answered our seemingly simple question, "Who really prepares the university budget?" It is not one which can be easily answered, for as one senior budget officer stated, "Participation at all levels is essential if the budget is to be accepted as an operational plan." Within the nine universities and seven states encompassed in this study, the cast of characters is everywhere the same, but roles vary among the states and, within each state, over time.

Both professional and political contacts of the university are shaped by the dominant forces in state government. In one state, the principal external group with which university budget officials negotiate is the legislative budget committee, while in another, they work with the governor's budget staff. A third pattern exists where legislative and executive branches of state government are relatively equal in power and influence and the university is required to deal with both. In still a fourth state, the coordinating agency is dominant in the budget process.

The budgetary problems of state versus system are not confined to only one or two of the nine universities but, in varying degrees, are common to all. In each state, we found uncertainty and frequent controversy over the respective budgetary roles of the multicampus university and state government. The range of budgetary practice extends from detailed, campus-by-campus, line-item control by the state to a lump-sum appropriation for the entire system. Yet a common thread runs clearly through the entire range: the dominance of the budget process by state fiscal requirements. While one university strives to obtain even a minimum degree of budgetary flexibility, another fights equally hard to retain the flexibility it has achieved over the years. These are *public* institutions.

State Government Dominance by state fiscal agencies takes two forms. First, *political* influence over the university budget is rising. Almost all system administrators agree that the increasing importance and cost of higher education have made the budgets of universities and colleges major issues of policy and politics. In the words of one system administrator, "Whenever money becomes scarce, those who allocate it question the past practices and are more discerning in their judgment to give or withhold." Although we heard frequent grumbling about state meddling in financial details, there was no agreement among the systems on just which issues of budgeting should be outside state scrutiny.

The second form of state control, related but having its own dynamic, is the reported rise in *administrative* influence by state executive and legislative staff. Allocations among campuses and programs are being questioned with increasing frequency and, often, with increasing sophistication, providing an almost entirely new dimension to governmental interest. Universities are being challenged to justify "quality" with quantitative data by staff analysts who know a generality when they see one. Present concepts of teaching loads and student-faculty ratios are no longer accepted at face value.

The universities are being asked to demonstrate their effectiveness in the new langauge of program budgeting and cost-benefit analysis. Neither the necessity nor desirability of much of this pressure can be discounted. In none of the systems is program budgeting so far advanced that its virtues or faults are clearly evident. Our impression, however, is that few administrators would quarrel with the opinion of the system budget officer who said, "Program budgeting is elevating more and more educational decisions up the bureaucratic ladder, sometimes to this office, but increasingly to the power centers in state government." Many important values of higher education, however, are not easily measured, if at all, by these new fiscal instruments which emphasize quantification. Much may be lost in learning just how difficult, if not impossible, such measurement can be.

For the multicampus university, the implications of increased state political and administrative influence on the budgetary process are contradictory. Such increased influence can reduce the authority and discretion of the systemwide administration, with the state moving into internal budget allocation among programs and campuses. As state officials at coordinating agency, executive, or legislative levels find their professional competence increasing, they may substitute their own judgments for those of the university, and specific examples were found during the study.[3]

On the other hand, increased state interest can also be a basis for increased authority at the system level vis-à-vis the campuses. Most systems are under pressure to demonstrate to state govern-

[3] For example, the Illinois Board of Higher Education in reviewing the university's budget request for 1969–1971 delved directly and deeply into academic policy questions in commenting that ". . . most of the requests for these units [centers and institutes] are an expedient means of overcoming weaknesses in the traditional departmental structure of the university. Organization along lines of disciplinary areas does not prove viable in an age when interdisciplinary approaches must be undertaken both in research and in instruction. . . . Institutions should be encouraged to correct organizational deficiencies in offering instruction rather than creating more machinery to overcome them."

ment that they can do a better job of resource allocation than the governors, the coordinating agencies, or other state agencies. One state budget director contended that the multicampus system would only improve its analytic capabilities if forced to do so. He saw it as his task to apply such force and described his efforts at requiring the university to examine critically the premises underlying its budgetary decisions rather than merely to project past practices. "Only if we require specific program information," he went on, "will the system demand this of the campuses."

We cannot generalize about the impact of increased state involvement across the nine university systems. In one state, the role of the systemwide administration in university budgeting has been greatly diminished, and there seems little likelihood of an immediate change. In most, however, requirements of external control —whether more sophisticated traditional practices or new program budgeting techniques—are forcing the system executive to strengthen his own internal budgetary capabilities. Everywhere, the budgetary processes linking the campuses to the system are formed and dominated by the constraints and expectations imposed upon the system by the state government.

The philosophy of state-university relationships, as well as practice, are graphically illustrated by the form of budget request required by each state and by the nature of the ensuing appropriation. At one end of a continuum, a detailed line-item budget request from each campus serves as the basis for a detailed appropriation schedule. Adjustments to this line-item budget require approval of state officials, generating a constant paper flow throughout the year between the university and the state capital. At the other end of the continuum, a single lump-sum appropriation provides operating expenses for all campuses in the university system. Most adjustments to such a budget can be made within the university itself, without approval by state authorities. The modal pattern

---

One system administrator saw an additional reason for increased state involvement: "Is it possible that all the recent talk by educators and students about the need for curricular reform, relevance, new purposes, new standards for admission, and so on, which amount to a confession of the need for change, have somehow made state budget analysts a little bolder in 'substituting their own judgments for those of the university?' Given such boldness, are such state analysts above using student unrest or the taxpayers' revolt as causes to compel the university to accept the educational judgments of the state?"

among all nine universities resembles the latter rather than the former procedure. Universitywide appropriations, with some major control points set by either program or expenditure categories, are the rule.

Regardless of whether the budget format and appropriation stress line-item detail, separate campus budgets, or a single universitywide approach, each system develops its own budget request on a campus-by-campus basis. Even if control accounts are not established by the state, each system is clearly limited in its ability to move funds from one campus to another. Budget requests justified by the peculiar needs of one campus cannot lightly be altered to support the programs of another, regardless of the form of state appropriation. There is far less difference in actual budgetary flexibility among the several systems than is implied by formal procedures and control accounts.

However small it might be, the added flexibility *is* critical. The system executive and the governing board can view the system budget as a whole. Although exercised infrequently and with discretion, their power to make adjustments among campuses and programs without approval of governor or legislative committee is an essential instrument of university governance.

The Coordinating Agency In five of the seven states, statewide coordinating agencies on higher education have budgetary responsibilities, and state-system relationships are even more complicated. We did not find a clear understanding or stable agreement in any state among the university system, the coordinating agency, and state fiscal authorities on the relative authority of each. Each group seeks the last word in the budgetary process.

The power of the coordinating agencies covers a wide spectrum. In one state, the agency is described as weak. Although it has the power to recommend, no one takes the recommendations seriously. The agency has, in fact, become a political agent of the governor, with the apparent mission of providing him with ammunition in his campaign to reduce the higher education budget. The coordinating agency of another state, on the other hand, is described as the "principal state agency for the review of university budgets." For several years, its recommendations have been accepted by both the legislature and the governor, and the multicampus university has virtually ceased appealing budget changes. At times, this agency's reputation for independence from both state government and the educational institutions has been unsettling to all parties. The considerable effort which the system has devoted to its relationships with the coordinating agency would be directed at state fiscal authorities in other states. Even here, however, continued dominance by the agency is problematic. Both state executive and legislative budget staffs are developing their own expertise, and increased contact between the university and these officials is predicted.

BUDGET FORMULAS: GAMES PEOPLE PLAY A university budget attempts to bring some semblance of order to literally thousands of separate variables, ranging from the number of pencils required per typist-clerk to the number of professors required per 1,000 students. In a simpler age, most such judgments were made individually. A wise executive could weigh the merits of specific requests and, by hunch, intuition, and experience, develop a defensible financial program. Today, such a personal approach is neither administratively practical nor politically feasible. Budgetary complexity requires formal rules to reduce the task to manageable proportions, and the size of the budget requires the development of funding principles acceptable to political authorities.

Both administrative practicality and political acceptability have given rise to *budget formulas.* These attempts to reduce myriad subjective elements of budgetary decision making into a few objective measures of academic financial management go under many names: student-faculty ratio, support costs per faculty member, library books per student, maintenance costs per square foot, and teaching load, to name but a few. Some measure of success is attested by the use of formulas in every one of the nine systems. But this apparent agreement on a formula approach disguises two underlying disagreements which suggest inadequacy. Among the nine systems there is little agreement on what the formulas should be, and between each system and state officials there is disagreement over their validity.

To varying degrees, almost everyone uses formulas at three stages of the budgetary process to influence: (1) higher education's share of the total state budget; (2) the multicampus university's share of the higher education budget; and (3) the campus's share of the total university budget. Often, different formulas are employed by the state in developing the universitywide budget compared to those used by system authorities in distributing the budget among the campuses. In other instances, state formulas determine the campus allocation as well, particularly where the state appropriates funds on a campus-by-campus basis. In all states, the formulas are mainly aimed at the *work-load* or *enrollment* budget, as opposed to *new programs* or *program enrichment.* Formulas determine the amounts necessary to continue present patterns of support and meet projected costs such as enrollment increases and salary and cost rises. New programs, in contrast, are reviewed at both system and state government levels on an individual basis, although formulas may be utilized in determining specific costs. Running battles are fought in several states between system and state officials to determine whether programs are in fact new and subject to close scrutiny. As merely a continuation of an ongoing budgeted item, on the other hand, they are entitled to inclusion in the work-load budget.

Every state attempts to bring "rationality" into the budget process by quantification, and even a single-campus institution must become adept in manipulating formulas. A multicampus university, however, has a more compelling need for objective criteria in the process of budget development: the system administration must justify its *internal* decision making. This is true within the central staff simply to make the budget task practical, but it is critical in system-campus relationships. Even the strongest system executive must have objective bases for his campus budgetary decisions. His relationships with the campus executives and their authority on the campuses depend heavily on mutual acceptance of the validity of the budgetary process. Total agreement cannot be expected, but each campus must feel it is being treated "fairly" vis-à-vis other campuses in the system. Internal pressures for equity among campuses would impel the creation of formulas, even if they were not required by state government or by the need for simplification.

The variety of formulas used in the nine universities defies generalization or easy analysis. In more than one state, it was suggested that only one man—at the most two—truly understood the basis for the formulas. We never met this person, and it was easy to doubt his existence. (We were reminded of the monks of Chartreuse, who pass on the secrets of that liqueur by word of mouth.) Moreover, some formulas appear to be rationalizations for decisions already made on quite independent grounds, rather than logical constructs. For example, the decision to maintain nationally competitivc faculty salaiies in one system was implemented by a formula which produced the necessary dollar amount but which was built around quantitative factors unrelated to the national marketplace.

Formulas vary in their range of applicability: some cover all public campuses in the state, some the multicampus university as a whole, and others individual campuses. In Texas, for example, identical formulas for each budget category are applied uniformly to every campus in the state, both in and out of the multicampus university. Distinctions between undergraduate and graduate programs are maintained, however, so that the overall support varies according to enrollment mix. In other states, formulas make explicit distinctions in terms of academic support costs among campuses as such, within as well as outside the system. In a few instances, universitywide formulas apply uniformly to each campus in the system. More typically, however, certain formula items apply to each campus without exception (e.g., uniform maintenance costs), while others vary from campus to campus (e.g., instructional costs). [4]

[4] We do not detail the various formula approaches, but the following patterns are illustrative. In one instance, an all-inclusive ratio of instructional costs per student credit hour encompasses faculty salaries, libraries, and other support categories. In other cases, each of these components is represented by a separate formula. Yet a third pattern employs a student-faculty ratio, weighted to give additional credit for graduate enrollment; still another university reaches much the same result by developing its academic budget on the basis of a ratio of faculty salaries per student credit hour. Funds for faculty salary adjustments — whether cost of living or merit — are included within the overall ratio of faculty support per student in one instance, while separately budgeted in others (typically as an overall percentage of total salaries). And as a final example, one state provides *one* system administrative support as a percentage of its total budget, whereas for another system in the same state, administrative support is based on a detailed formula relating particular classes of administrative positions to campus enrollment.

These confusing patterns may be further illustrated by three specific examples. First, in one system, the overall faculty salary budget for each campus is based on the number of student credit hours in the previous year apportioned both by program and by level of student. In 1969, an undergraduate student credit hour in liberal arts had a rate of $15.24, whereas the rate for engineering was $27.21. Correspondingly, the doctoral rate was $153.95 per student credit hour in liberal arts and $220.97 in engineering. Parallel formulas exist for departmental operating expenses. Organized research support is based on an *Institutional Complexity Factor (ICF)* which gives greater support to campuses with higher proportions of science and engineering graduate students, adding a "bonus" based on the previous year's sponsored research activity.

Second, in another university, the budget is developed and subsequently

The implications of budget formulas are almost as varied as the formulas themselves. Is the budget formula a device to avoid hard decisions, a pretense at objectivity when, in reality, qualitative questions require sophisticated, subjective judgments? Or, are the formulas an empirical instrument for improving the quality of such decisions? Are formulas a straitjacket on the multicampus university, restraining desirable internal adjustments among campuses and programs? Or do the formulas provide a broad framework within which the state permits the university to operate flexibly? Finally, do formulas inhibit managerial innovation by discouraging new approaches to academic budgeting, both within the system and at the state level? Or do they hold the promise of becoming a creative instrument of budget planning?

Affirmative answers to each of these quite contradictory sets of questions exist among the nine universities, and even within the same state and system. Formulas are accepted, even thought necessary, where the university is free to utilize them flexibly and with discretion. There is deep-seated concern over formulas, however, where they hamper the exercise of executive judgment, or preclude discretionary action without prior state approval.

Even in systems with relative freedom, however, administrators are concerned that the formulas may become a Frankenstein monster. The more the university is forced to defend its budget to the state by use of objective criteria, the greater is the risk that the state will begin to accept these criteria as "truth" for all purposes.

---

apportioned among the campuses in accordance with a "faculty staffing formula." The formula details assumptions about class size in various subject matter fields, and the budget process requires precise estimates of the numbers of classes per subject. These are translated in turn into teaching loads, which are adjusted to reflect the different patterns involved in lecture, seminar, laboratory, and studio instruction. The final product of this detailed analysis is a projection of the number of new faculty required by the campus in the budget year.

Finally, using a completely different approach, a third university budget is based on "instructional costs per student credit hour," which vary from campus to campus and by level of instruction. In a recent year lower division costs ranged from $26.47 to $27.37, upper division costs from $41.93 to $48.73, and doctoral costs from $108.89 to $132.43. A single formula for academic salary increases for all institutions in the state provided a 4 percent budget increase plus institutional adjustments for merit increases based on the enrollment pattern of the university. Thus, an additional $200 was provided for each 484 lower-division student credit hours, while $600 was allocated for each 152 doctoral student credit hours. Although not an explicit policy, the purpose of the formula is to provide additional salary support for the major university campuses as compared with the undergraduate colleges.

In one state, for example, state fiscal officers have adopted administrative staffing patterns based on numbers of positions per 1,000 students. A large campus can have one vice-president and eight senior academic administrators (deans, associate deans, etc.); a small campus, one vice-president and four or five senior academic administrators. While these ratios make some sense as general budgetary guidelines for the system as a whole, they are being applied by the state, without exception, to every campus, frustrating organizational experimentation and innovation.

An administrator in another system expressed concern that "the formulas tend to become 'real' to some of the analysts who employ them and, eventually, become goals and ends in themselves." He went on to pose these problems:

Assume a formula for the budgeting of student services as we know them. Assume, also, that a majority of students reject parietal rules and residence on campus. What is real? The formula or the protest? Assume a computer-based simulation model of the future of a university which assumes that classes, classrooms, buildings, campuses, fees and books, and the formulas which govern them, will be features of a university forever. Will such a model of the future simulate reality?

The dilemma of university budgeting is apparent. To the extent the university is successful in empirically documenting the need for support of specific programs through tools of cost-effectiveness, program budgeting, and formulas, the state may insist that the university automatically follow these same criteria in detailed internal allocations. Flexibility often seems to be the first victim of more detailed quantification. There is no reason why this should be, however, and every reason why it should not.

A second danger arises at the campus level, where a tendency exists to regard the campus or even departmental share of the formula budget as "theirs" as a matter of right and to resist efforts of the system executive to reallocate on other than formula criteria. In both instances, formulas can inhibit diversity. The statement of an administrator from a remote campus is in point:

. . . through the years, the flagship campus has had a very strong chemistry department and has justified strong budgetary allocations which have worked their way into the formula. Consequently when we adopt their formula allocations, we tend to provide a strong base for a chemistry department here which in turn develops strength more rapidly than other departments. The result is that we replicate, rather than complement, the flagship campus.

In short, general recognition of the necessity of some sorts of formulas is coupled with uncertainty concerning their long-range implications.

This dilemma results, too, from growing disenchantment at the state level over university budgeting. With few exceptions, the various formulas are based on straight-line projections from previous experience, rather than on an evaluation or modification of that experience. Despite their elaborate nature, many of the ratios and cost indices are the result of arithmetic rather than analysis. As one budget officer described it, "The formulas have been developed after the fact to justify the status quo." But rising costs and taxpayer resistance are threatening the status quo, and state fiscal officials no longer accept the formulas at face value. There is a growing doubt both in and out of the university over present methods for evaluating the costs and effectiveness of higher education. At an earlier date, when goals were less complicated, and the number of students limited, such problems were far less serious. But several "explosions"—social, scientific, and population—have now compounded and reinforced the complexity and cost of higher education. Programmed learning and computer networks, nuclear accelerators and electron microscopes, urban extension and action-oriented research are a long way from Mark Hopkins and his famous log. It is small wonder that a growing army of budget officers and analysts stretching from campus to capital can do little more than magnify the uncertainty over just what a formula should contain.[5]

In many systems, staff are pursuing definition and measurement of educational outputs, quantitative assessment of the impact and

[5] An experienced university administrator commented in this vein:

"In spite of all the talk about the new era of program budgeting, the nation's public colleges and universities have never really graduated from 'performance budgeting,' which was the prevailing fashion of administration a few years ago. University and state authorities alike are still engrossed in unit costs and cost accounting. Formulas for 'work load' have not really been agreed upon hardly anywhere, awaiting more and more intensive studies of the elements of cost, including time and motion studies. A 'leveling' phenomenon arises in the practice of making unit costs of campuses, schools, and departments, unilluminated by educational research concerning the difference in costs. Inevitably, the desired unit cost then becomes 'cause' rather than 'effect,' and the campuses then tailor programs to become more and more alike. Like Pavlov's dogs, they learn to salivate to the tune of a single bell.

"We could start from the premise that much of the difference in costs from one institution to another is legitimate. Formulas may aid in providing a pattern for allocation of resources. They should not provide a pattern for expenditure."

quality of academic programs. Some efforts are merely responsive to the pressures of fiscal stringencies. We were told, however (and believe), that most such activities have been undertaken at system initiative, primarily in search of more rational tools for budgetary decisions. Some programs are related to the cost-effectiveness concepts required by program budgeting. Others are refinements of more traditional budgetary procedures. The multi-campus structure not only gives rise to the need for cross-campus comparisons but also provides the specialized staff to undertake them. Diversity and specialization can be encouraged by proper mixes of dollar and faculty inputs; but enrollments and the number and type of degrees awarded are, at best, a first approximation to adequate output measurements.

There is much to be done, and none of the systems can assert that, from a budgetary standpoint, they have taken full advantage of their multicampus status. Many opportunities for cross-campus analysis remain untapped. More significantly, there are few examples of universitywide study of such critical elements of the budget as student-faculty ratios and teaching loads or methods in terms of their educational effectiveness, rather than simply on the basis of their comparability with "competing" institutions.

The alternatives are for the multicampus university to develop more effective bases for its budgetary requests to withstand increasingly sophisticated state staff review or, alternatively, for state agencies to develop their own budget rationale.

A combination of both approaches seems likely. The implications for the multicampus university are paradoxical. On the one hand, the development of more effective bases for budgetary allocations may well strengthen the importance of the system executive and the validity of an all-university budget. The unavoidable danger is that the system can be captured by the formulas and that campus and program allocations will become automatic, seriously undercutting the academic role or even the need for a universitywide budget. The crucial question is the extent to which state government will permit the multicampus university to exercise independent judgment over internal resource allocation. The answer rests far more on political than on fiscal considerations.

THE PREPARA-TION OF THE BUDGET   All public universities have budgets which undergo a detailed review by state authorities. The unique characteristic of the multi-campus system is the introduction of a level of budgetary review between the campus and the state. What does this additional level mean in fact? As suggested in the discussion of formulas, the authority of the system executive and his staff can be substantially reduced if the university lacks the authority to make internal adjustments. This is the case in several states, where the state budget specifies each campus allocation, reserving to state officials authority to alter the distribution. In these states, the primary role of the system is outward, to convince state officials that the university is a single entity entitled to fix campus priorities. In other states, in contrast, system attention is directed inward, to develop internally—prior to state review—the needs and priorities of the entire university. The difference is one of emphasis, but it is evident in the specific policies and practices of the system staff in budget preparation.

Enrollment Major budgetary questions in each system are based on the relationships between enrollment and financial support. Two distinct policies exist. The first assumes agreement between the university and the state concerning the number of applicants considered "qualified" to attend the university. The budget is then adjusted to the number of students. The second policy assumes agreement as to the number of students who can be accommodated within the university given a particular level of budgetary support. The enrollment is adjusted to meet the state appropriation. The prevailing policy in most states blends these contrasting approaches, with the politics of the budgetary process centering around a series of negotiations (and occasional bluffing) over the ultimate relationship between enrollment and the budget.

Whether the dominant budget strategy is one of limiting enrollments to the budget or increasing the budget to match the number of prospective students, the multicampus system frequently projects enrollment estimates for each campus and assesses their implications for the overall budget. Problems of differential admissions standards among the campuses, as well as such pervasive factors as national selective service, make this assessment far from routine. State and universitywide officials sometimes disagree over the budgetary implications of particular enrollment policies. Texas has eliminated problems of estimation by basing all campus budgets on the previous year's *actual* enrollments, a policy free from argument but highly disadvantageous for growing campuses. In another state, finance officials have assumed responsibility for enrollment projections, deriving these from common admissions standards for the university as a whole. In this state, the system administration negotiates with each campus its share of overall enrollment. In a third state, the relationship between enrollment and budget impinges on specific academic programs. The system has instructed the campuses not to plan new undergraduate majors as long as existing curricula are underenrolled.

The problem of meshing enrollments and dollars is both aggravated and eased in states with biennial budgets. In each of these states, budget adjustment in the second year of the biennium depends on the enrollment experience of the first year. In one state, however, this "adjustment" is solely a budget-cutting device. Campuses are subject to a reduction in their original budget request because of unrealized enrollment, but there is no provision for an increase if enrollments exceed estimates; neither is there any possibility for adjustments within the system. But in a second state, funds available for unexpected enrollment increases during the second year of the biennium provide the system executive with added flexibility in making internal allocations to the campuses.

Almost automatically, most systems urge curtailment of enrollment in response to reduction of budgetary support. Quality, as measured by student-faculty ratios and teaching load, is a prime consideration. The reaction of at least one governor was to suggest that each professor teach an additional course and to direct the system to accept "every qualified applicant" despite a reduction in budgetary support. In all states, the argument over the proper relationships between enrollment and budgets will not soon be terminated. The continuing uncertainty will be a further unsettling factor in the governance of the multicampus university.

Work Load and New Programs

The development of the work-load or enrollment budget is fairly automatic in most states, depending on the extent to which the formula approach is followed. In the process of budget preparation, there is an increasing tendency for this work-load component of the budget to be handled on a universitywide basis, with allocations to the campuses coming after the state budget has been introduced by the governor. Alternatively, the work-load budget is treated in terms of campuswide totals, without a detailed breakdown among specific programs. However, with budget formulas under increasing challenge, a new era of system-campus relationships may be imminent. The increasing uncertainty of state and multicampus university officials over the continuing validity of some work-load formulas occasionally reflects a parallel disagreement among the campuses or between them and systemwide budget staff. As long as the work-load budget means only a projection of the status quo, such internal differences can be contained. But when the state requires that the basic premises of university budgeting be examined *de novo,* it is certain to upset the equilibrium within the multicampus structure.

For new programs, the states generally agree that the system administration has the major responsibility for meshing campus priorities. Integration of new programs is almost everywhere considered by system executives to be a fundamental aspect of system leadership, even when state officials ultimately consider each campus separately and sometimes substitute their own priorities. In two systems, for example, the system executives reduced the most recent campus budget requests for new programs by some 40 percent. Campus executives accepted the principle of shifting local priorities in the interests of overall university coordination, though often grudgingly. One campus executive summed up the process: "We gripe a little bit, but we're all happy someone makes the allocations for us rather than our having to bargain among ourselves or before the legislature."

A somewhat different approach is found in a system where new program items are vigorously reviewed at the state level. With respect to a recent budget, the system executive forwarded his tentative recommendations to the campus executive with the following observation drawn from his discussions with state budget officials:

We will support whatever decision you make about allocation of the $1.5 million for new and improved programs. However, in view of the stringent conditions that will strongly influence the final disposition of your request by the state, we offer the following comment and opinion which may be helpful to you as you work toward your final judgment.

This admonition was followed by a series of specific suggestions, such as one that "requests for improved library support will be highly vulnerable." The system executive was telling the campus, "Here is where you will get in trouble at the state capital. Don't blame us if you choose not to follow this advice."

In only one state does the system expend little effort in reviewing proposed new programs. The pattern of state appropriations is such that few new programs are funded, and when they are, it is because of specific legislative interest. The universitywide budget officer questioned the desirability of devoting staff effort to an essentially meaningless process. He described his role as one of "keeping the campuses from looking silly" by preventing them from asking for the impossible.

Just *what* is a new program and just *when* one is really established are not always obvious. In several states, an important element of budgetary strategy is deciding when to ask for official approval. Most administrators believe that it is better not to ask than to be denied. "If we're turned down," so goes the logic, "then we can't do it. But if we don't ask and simply go ahead, then we can come back in the future with an ongoing program." This fact of budgetary life is found at all levels, from the academic department to the state budget office. Regardless of the legal autonomy of the university and its theoretical flexibility in budget adjustments, specific disapproval of a budget item by state officials is not to be overridden in any but the most unusual circumstances. Universitywide budget officials face a twofold problem: monitoring the campuses to be sure that new programs are clearly identified in the budget for internal review purposes and deciding just how and when such programs should be presented to state officials for inclusion in the budget. These dual responsibilities are not always mutually consistent.

The Budget Process: Some Selected Aspects

The basic elements of budget preparation are similar in each of the systems and do not appear to differ markedly from normal educational budgeting. In general, differences among the universities are direct reflections of the formal requirements of the state budget process. One universitywide administration reviews specific departmental requests in some detail, while another concerns itself mainly with broad categories of the budget (e.g., instruction) for the campus as a whole. The modal pattern is toward the latter approach, with the system review concentrating on broad indicators such as the student-faculty ratio or overall support costs. In every university, the system executive or a chief aide meets individually with each campus executive on one or more occasions to discuss the budget, and these are said to be one of the most important official contacts between the two levels. Campus executives generally believe that the multicampus university makes a difference in the budget process, that without system review and aid the task of the campuses would be more difficult, and that the universitywide budget is a better resolution of the combined needs of the campuses than would take place in a free-for-all competition at the state level. It is not clear that all state officials necessarily share this view.

The governing board and the budget

If the multicampus university makes a positive contribution to the budgetary process, it is not because of the governing board. With few exceptions, the board's role is described as one of *pro forma* approval of the budget presented by the system executive. In fact, most persons interviewed about university budgeting failed to mention the governing board at all. This phenomenon is not peculiar to the multicampus context. The task of the lay board in reviewing complex university budgets is a difficult one at best, whether involving one campus or twenty. One system executive suggested that the absence of formal, prolonged review of the budget does not mean that board approval is only *pro forma*. The board, he stated, had itself made the policy decisions during the year which the budget implemented; unlike coordinating agencies or legislative committees, the governing board "lives with the business of the budget all through the year." Nevertheless, the virtual abdication of the board from discussion of the many policy implications of the budget at the time of its approval appears to upset traditional models of governance.

There are some recent exceptions. In at least two states, factions on the governing board representing the governor and apparently taking their cues from him have actively sought reductions in the university's budget request. The significance of these pressures is that the boards did not raise educational policy questions about the budget—which was presumably their responsibility—but were exercising political judgments as to the appropriate level of state support—which was presumably outside their charge. The multicampus system, because of its size and importance in the state, is particularly vulnerable to these kinds of cross-pressures on the governing board.

The faculty and the budget

Faculty participation in the *systemwide* review of the budget is more the exception than the rule. In one multicampus university the system executive appoints a universitywide budget committee composed of campus and system executives and the heads of the campus faculty budget committees. The committee reviews new program proposals from the several campuses and integrates them into a single priority listing.

A second university follows much the same course. Here, an existing universitywide faculty committee advises the system executive on general policy concerning numerous matters including the budget. In recent years, two members of this committee have met regularly with system officers during budgetary review. They provide an additional opinion on the priority of proposals and review the distribution of the university's budget among the campuses. Faculty members who have served in this capacity are concerned that at least a two-year term and substantial time and effort are necessary for them to advise effectively. However, both faculty and administration agree that the effort is worthwhile and that the faculty have made a valuable contribution.

It is problematical whether these examples of faculty participation will be followed elsewhere. Both systems have a tradition of strong faculty participation in the budget process at the campuses. On the other hand, in another system, a relatively new systemwide faculty organization has been useful in ordering budget priorities, even though faculty participation at campus level is weak. In all but these three systems, there is either little faculty voice in the budget process, or it is heard primarily at the departmental, school, or college level. In New York, the introduction of formal collective bargaining among the faculty of the two university systems is certain to complicate their advisory role regarding budget priorities. In all states, moreover, the questioning by state authorities of basic premises of academic budgeting—primarily the teaching load with its implications for the teaching-research mix—seems certain to attract the attention of faculty at campus and systemwide levels.

THE ADMIN-ISTRATION OF THE BUDGET Most observations on the relative role of the state, the system administration, and the campuses in the preparation of the operating budget apply also to its administration. In general, those systems required to submit detailed line-item budgets to the state have the least flexibility to adjust the budget, while those which receive a single systemwide appropriation have relatively greater authority. There is no one-to-one relationship, however, nor is there necessarily any correlation between the freedom of the system from state control and the extent of its delegation of that same freedom to its campuses.

One system contends with state control over a detailed budget already so cumbersome and time-consuming that transfers of funds are not even attempted. Instead, items of expense are simply charged against another account, whether related to the program in question or not. Any similarity between the budget and the pattern of actual expenditures is coincidental, and the budget is neither a planning nor a control device.

For another system, the situation is not quite so burdensome. Control accounts specify four categories of salaried personnel and ten objects of expense. Transfers from one to another within a single program or across major program lines (e.g., instruction or libraries) require state approval, as do intercampus adjustments. This latter provision for state review of transfers among major programs and campuses is also followed in two other systems. Several systems are prohibited from utilizing funds budgeted for personal services for any other purpose, while funds granted for salary increases are similarly restricted in others.

Universities with internal flexibility to adjust and amend the operating budget generally retain controls at the multicampus level, even though not legally required to do so. One, for example, requires that all transfers of more than $1,000 be approved by the universitywide budget office; another specifies that transfers can be approved at the campus so long as they do not exceed 10 percent of the original budget item being augmented. Yet another approach permits transfers of any amount to be approved at the campus level if they do not involve academic salaries and are within major program categories, such as libraries, instruction, and plant operation.

In general, however, obstacles to effective budget administration in a multicampus context are those created by state fiscal practices rather than by the multicampus system. Campus administrators generally agree that major shifts in funding should receive universitywide approval. Sometimes, criticism was leveled at system officials for not actively seeking greater fiscal authority for the university as a whole. However, the few states imposing serious restrictions seem unlikely to terminate legislative and executive control in the immediate future. These states have simply not accepted the multicampus university as a responsible agency for effective fiscal management.

Discretionary Funds   None of the multicampus systems have a contingency fund as such, although one system executive looked back fondly on years when the university received a fixed percentage of the budget as an unallocated account for disposition during the year. This fund was first changed to a fixed amount and finally eliminated. Four relatively common sources of funding flexibility are found, however: universitywide reserves, lapsed salary funds, contract and grant overhead, and endowment and foundation income. These discretionary funds are critical instruments of multicampus governance.

Universitywide reserves

In three universities, the system executive greatly enhances his budgetary role by holding in a universitywide reserve a portion of the entire system's work-load or enrollment increase budget. Instead of automatically allocating all the university's budget to the campuses in accordance with the original budget request, the system executive retains part of these funds for disposition during the year. Two such universities operate under a biennial budget, which provides a second-year fund for enrollment adjustments. In a recent year, graduate student enrollments at one campus fell far below estimate; rather than drastically reduce the campus budget to fit the formula, the system executive transferred to it funds allocated by the state on the basis of excess enrollments at other campuses. In the second system, the enrollment increase reserve is allocated by the system executive to the campuses over a six-month period following the beginning of the second year. Budget adjustments are based on a universitywide assessment of actual need, rather than made automatically on the basis of enrollments.

These patterns of multicampus fiscal management achieve needed flexibility and are accepted at the campus level. Other multicampus universities might consider similar programs, although budget and finance officers in several states would doubtless resist a grant of such authority to the system executive.

Lapsed salary funds

A degree of budgetary flexibility is found in a few states where the university is permitted to use "surplus" budget monies resulting from unfilled positions. These *budgetary savings* or *lapsed salaries* result from the inability of the university to fill all vacancies at the level budgeted or at all. Such savings cannot easily be allocated in advance to specific programs but tend to average out for the university as a whole.

In one instance, the system executive is authorized by state budget officials to use such funds "prudently" to fill needs for approved programs which cannot be supported in the original budget. Such expenditures are subject to a postaudit by the state. In a second system, the savings are an indirect method of budgeting nonrecurring expenditures such as minor remodeling and major equipment. Here, the explicit state appropriation is inadequate for these purposes, a position at least partially recognized by the state itself. System administrators believe that any attempt by the state to recapture the salary savings would necessitate an offsetting augmentation of the budget for these nonrecurring expenditures. In each case, the system executive has achieved a measure of control over the budget by not automatically returning the savings to the campus of origin but by instituting central review over their use.

In two other universities, the total budget from the state is reduced by an amount estimated to equal the savings. An important element of universitywide budget policy is the manner of allocating this reduction among the campuses. In one system, the identical percentage reduction is applied to each campus. In the second, differential targets are applied, depending on such factors as campus size and maturity and the number of newly budgeted faculty positions. In the second also, the state permits funds saved in excess of the state's original estimate to be used by the university for unbudgeted expenditures. As in those systems which retain all such savings, the allocation of this surplus is carefully controlled by the system executive to provide a valuable measure of budgetary discretion.

In the five remaining systems, the use of lapsed salary funds is not an issue. In one, the reason is clear: there are no savings! The state controls disbursements on a line-item basis and pays salary monies only after the fact.

Overhead reimbursement

The use of overhead reimbursements from federal contract and grant activity is a third potential source of system budgetary flexibility. The magnitude of these funds among the universities varies immensely, depending on the extent of faculty and graduate research. One system generates overhead approximating $400,000, while another approaches $20 million. In all states, a fiscal policy of major concern is the extent to which the university is permitted to retain overhead reimbursement for internal use.

The range of practice across the nine universities is complete. In one state, overhead reimbursements are deducted from the state appropriation in their entirety, consistent with the theory that these reimbursements are simply for services which have already been supported from state funds. In contrast, four systems are allowed to retain 100 percent of overhead receipts. In one of these, a "gentlemen's agreement" with the state recognizes that the state budget does not adequately support graduate education and research. State, coordinating agency, and university officials tacitly understand that the university will not press for substantial increases to support these activities if the state will not press for a recapture of overhead. In the three other systems, however, the issue has not yet clearly been resolved. In each of these, the amount of overhead reimbursements has only recently reached a level to attract state attention. University officials are not optimistic over their ability to retain unrestricted use of the income.

In the remaining four universities, agreements—both informal and official—have been reached with state officials concerning the use of overhead reimbursements. In one instance, the state claims all *estimated* overhead receipts, but permits the university to retain any excess over the estimate. Although this provided the university with additional funds during a period of rising research support, the university has also been required to make up any deficiency should its estimate not be met. Moreover, the state is paying increasing attention to the reality of the university's estimate. In the three other universities, formulas have been developed under which the state receives approximately 20, 40, and 50 percent of overhead reimbursements. Here, too, administrators are uncertain as to how long the present distribution will be accepted by state fiscal authorities. The negotiated nature of the percentages, as well as the more or less "accidental" excess in the prior case, make all extremely vulnerable to budget stringency.

Allocation of overhead reimbursements between the state and a university is not unique to multicampus universities, although representation of the interests of all campuses to state and federal authorities has become a significant responsibility of the system's central administration. The *internal* distribution of overhead income, however, is of special import. Excluding the one university in which all overhead receipts revert to the state, policies in this area are both complex and controversial.

Once again, the universities represent a complete spectrum. In two, virtually all overhead reimbursements are automatically returned to the campus of origin for use largely in support of campus research administration. In two others, in direct contrast, the bulk of such funds is allocated by the system executive and governing board without reference to campus research activity. In large measure, the income permits these two systems — in Robin Hood fashion — to support projects which are attractive neither to the state nor to federal granting agencies. Thus, library development, aid to disadvantaged students, and programs in the humanities and creative arts have all received substantial support from overhead reimbursement funds in recent years.

The remaining systems fall between these two extremes of automatic distribution to the campuses and virtually complete centralization at the universitywide level. Typically, the central administration retains a fixed percentage of overhead reimbursements to pay its own research management costs, including support of a Washington office in some cases. Remaining funds are distributed to the campuses and to the research departments of origin, largely in proportion to their contract and grant activity. Unlike the two systems discussed above, however, the recovery of overhead is used primarily to support the same kinds of projects as those which have generated it, rather than to "equalize the wealth" across disciplinary and campus lines. Both system and campus executives indicate a desire for more discretion in the employment of overhead reimbursements, but believe that their hands are tied by internal pressures from their scientific and technical faculty. The latter regard the income as "theirs" and resist any marked shift in the pattern of distribution. Despite these limitations, there is universal agreement that overhead reimbursements provide a critical margin of budgetary flexibility, as well as universal concern that state government may reduce this flexibility.

Endowment and foundation income

A final category of discretionary funds, free from customary state fiscal controls, is that of endowment and foundation income. As used here, endowment refers to gifts made to and administered by the university as a corporate entity. The foundation, in contrast, is a corporate entity related to but usually legally independent of the university. A very significant distinction between the two, in several states, is the independence of the foundation from at least some state fiscal controls.

In only one of the nine universities, surprisingly, is the university's own endowment a significant instrument of *universitywide* policy. A substantial pool of unrestricted money has been accumulated, and the ability of the system executive and the governing board to assist new campuses, themselves without independent resources, is regarded as a substantial advantage of the multicampus structure. Even in this system, however, most gifts are raised by and for a specific campus, a characteristic of all the multicampus universities.

A very similar pattern is found in the large independent foundations which exist in two systems. Both were originally established for their flagship campuses, both continue largely as fund-raising agencies for them, and both have provided valuable seed money for newer campuses in each system. It is not clear, however, that the pattern will continue. Whether or not there is only a single endowment fund or foundation at the multicampus level, the dominant impetus for fund raising is clearly at the campuses. University systems, as systems, are not magnets for fund raising. Although the specialized central staff of the multicampus university can provide useful administrative and investment services, it seems unlikely that system executives can count on a substantial increase in universitywide discretionary funds from personal or corporate gifts. System executives can, however, expect to be asked to continue their fund-raising activities for the campuses.

10. Academic and Administrative Personnel

The success of the multicampus university may be measured in many ways. A prime test would be the record of a system in recruiting and retaining a faculty and top-level administrators of high quality. Coordination of academic programs, efficiency and economy in business operations, an improved and unified admissions procedure, all these and many other factors of governance depend on skilled administrative personnel—whether deans or business managers. But such programs have no meaning without a qualified faculty. Here, we discuss both groups. In this critical area of academic life, does the multicampus university make a difference?

THE ROLE OF THE MULTI-CAMPUS UNIVERSITY The rationale for the multicampus university—with its emphasis upon diversity within unity, specialization, and cooperation—cuts across many aspects of academic and administrative personnel. For example, the prestige of a flagship campus may rub off on newer campuses in a system and enhance their recruitment efforts. Even if there is no flagship campus, a system may strengthen the young or transitional campus (for example, a campus changing from college to university status) in attracting new faculty. Older campuses in the system may "colonize" a new campus to provide a small, experienced base of faculty and administrators for effective external recruiting efforts.

In theory, the multicampus university increases the feasibility of joint appointments. A highly specialized professor can share his time on two campuses, neither of which, alone, could justify his full-time appointment. The system can also give the individual faculty member more mobility, because he can transfer from one campus to another without loss of benefits or rank.

Further justification for the multicampus university is found in its encouragement of quality control by its insistence on high standards of scholarship in the recruitment and promotion of faculty. This is especially true on new or transitional campuses. The system administration can insist on rigorous faculty review procedures and, in the absence of an adequate faculty base, on external review of appointments and promotions, utilizing faculty from other campuses. Even on established campuses, systemwide administrative review of appointments and promotions may provide a desirable double check on campus executives, who may be unduly subject to local campus pressures.

With respect to academic salaries, the multicampus university should promote more rationality and equity among the several campuses than occurs among autonomous institutions. Professors and citizens alike can know that faculty members in similar state-supported institutions are subject to the same policies and procedures. Insofar as these matters are tied to collective bargaining, systemwide negotiations and agreements may avoid whipsawing among the several campuses and promote both uniformity and stability.

There are offsetting disadvantages. The multicampus approach may lead to undesirable uniformity and inflexibility. Salaries, ranks, and evaluation policies and procedures may be forced into a common mold that is unfavorable to an individual campus. This may be particularly the case where a strong flagship campus uncritically imposes its practices upon newer campuses. Experimentation is frustrated and myths of academe perpetuated.

Such uniformity may be particularly troublesome in the comprehensive system. Here, there is an added concern over a tendency to treat all faculty alike, regardless of whether they work at a community college, undergraduate college, or university. Such leveling would be better contained, so goes the argument, in competing segmental systems.

The multicampus university may be criticized because it unnecessarily complicates academic personnel decisions. Except at new or transitional campuses, delays and paper work are increased, with no appreciable improvement in the quality of decisions. More broadly, and possibly more important, systemwide review and the involvement of the system executive in the appointment and promotion processes may obscure the focus on the campus as the immediate object of institutional loyalty and undercut the campus executive. Without clear-cut appointment power, he loses influence and leverage.

Finally, with respect to collective bargaining, the reverse of the positive argument favoring multicampus approaches can be posed: the campus should be the basic unit, and the particular needs, conditions, and desires of the faculty should be dealt with at the local level. The multicampus system, with its tendencies toward uniformity, may render a desired campus-by-campus approach impossible.

Every campus and system in the study provides examples of these advantages and disadvantages. The evidence to follow may suggest where the balance rests.

ACADEMIC PERSONNEL
In the nine multicampus systems, one thing can be asserted with certainty about "academic personnel": the positions covered by the term are uncertain. There is little ambiguity over the traditional teaching titles, from instructor to professor. Neither is there much confusion over the bulk of nonfaculty positions, clerical and maintenance, for example. But classification of the nonteaching, para-academics—librarians, professional researchers, technical specialists—is a problem in all systems.

The issue is both clarified and accentuated where the bulk of nonteaching employees belong to the state civil service (the case in four of the nine universities) or to a state university and college civil service system (as is the case in a fifth). In these instances, classification of a position as academic or nonacademic frequently determines whether the incumbent is a member of the state civil service system or subject to university personnel policies and procedures.

The numbers of the para-academics in American higher education are increasing, a development not peculiar to multicampus systems, of course, but to the multiversity—whether one campus or several. But in the multicampus system, a special problem exists as to whether campuses can independently designate a staff member as academic or faculty.

Universally, the answer is no. Typically, campuses desire to classify certain positions as academic to avoid some civil service restriction.[1] The system administration must permit the campus sufficient flexibility to meet special needs, while avoiding serious internal inequities among similar employees or more serious con-

---

[1] In one university that deals with an unduly restrictive civil service system, unfilled "lecturer" positions in the budget have frequently been used to obtain higher pay for deserving secretaries, who would otherwise seek private employment.

frontation with state civil service authorities and employee organizations intent on uniform treatment. Even in the states where the issue of civil service is not present, all-university consensus on the status of the para-academic, particularly in systems with campuses which vary widely in character and mission, is absent. The problem is nowhere serious, but neither does it appear resolvable. Minor but continuing irritation between system and campus in this area can be predicted.

Appointments and Promotions

Knowledge of formal academic personnel policies and procedures is never adequate to an understanding of reality and in some instances is actually misleading. We cannot presume here to have done more than scratch the surface of the myriad traditions, practices, and personal relationships that define the appointment and promotion of faculty.

Policies and standards

Few of the multicampus universities have published systemwide criteria for appointment and promotion. Published policies that do exist are often very brief, or too general to be of operational use to campus or system committees or administrators charged with academic personnel review authority. Only rarely is a written policy regarded as an important element of de facto university policy.

This reflects awareness that the faculty have won the right to choose their own colleagues and set the values of the institution. The multicampus university has not only accepted these values, but has become a major instrument in their perpetuation. As we suggest in discussing quality control, one feature of these systems has been the transmission of the values of the dominant campus faculty to the new or transitional campuses, a trend which both governing boards and system administrations have encouraged or even required. Even in the comprehensive systems, with a responsibility for two-year and undergraduate colleges, the values of the research-oriented university campus tend to dominate faculty selection processes. The multicampus university is both a victim and an active agent of the recently evident academic revolution, with its emphasis upon research and graduate training.

The flagship or dominant campus also shapes the procedures for faculty review of appointments and promotions. Faculty review is not generally required by the governing boards or the system administrations but represents the influence of the faculty of the flagship campus. Thus, in Wisconsin, the basic review of appointment and promotions by the faculty at Madison occurs at the divisional level (groupings of faculty in related subjects, such as physical sciences, social studies, humanities, and biological sciences, independent of the schools and colleges on the campus). Review committees of these divisions make their recommendations to the dean of the school or college of the candidate. The same pattern is being followed or proposed on each of the newer campuses of the university, the only difference being the number or designation of divisions. At the University of California at Berkeley, a campuswide review committee makes a recommendation on each appointment and promotion case to the campus executive. This practice, too, has been adopted by each campus within the university.

While this influence of flagship campuses is not unexpected, the acceptance of their procedures is noteworthy. Rarely have newer campuses raised the issue of whether the flagship practice is, in fact, superior to other alternatives. Adoption by the newer campuses of the procedures of the old has been regarded as a sign of membership in the multicampus university. One senses that failure of a new campus to follow the traditions of the flagship would be seen as heresy, an abandonment of "quality," regardless of the fact that there is no one best way to obtain faculty advice.

Neither the systemwide administrations nor the governing boards have attempted to introduce alternative review procedures as new campuses were established. "What is good enough for the flagship is good enough for the system" appears to be the watchword. According to one system administrator, however, use of the watchword means that "the sins of the father are being visited on other campuses."

In systems with no flagship campus, or where the flagship is not considered a model to be emulated, we found little fixed policy or uniformity among the campuses. In one university, for example, the basic faculty review of appointments and promotions at one campus is by a campuswide committee. At a second campus in the same system, there is no faculty participation in the review process beyond the initial departmental consideration. In another multicampus university, the all-university faculty senate has stimulated the development of effective review procedures at the campus level, but has favored no one model. Most typically, however, the pattern of faculty participation is left entirely to the individual campuses. Even in universities with highly centralized systemwide administrative review of appointments and promotions, faculty involvement is usually a matter for local determination, and there appears to be little systemwide consultation or discussion on this subject.

Authority to appoint and promote

In the nine universities, there is a wide gap between the formal authority over academic appointments and promotions and the reality of practice. Generalization is further complicated by the range of practices of the universities from one with a highly centralized administration of academic personnel to another that is equally decentralized.

At the one extreme are two large systems in which all academic appointments, without exception, are the responsibility of the campus executive — in one case as a matter of formal delegation and in both instances as a matter of practice. Both systems are, in our terms, consolidated, resulting from the merger of previously autonomous campuses and the recent introduction of a systemwide executive. Both had a prior tradition of campus authority to appoint and promote, a practice which was continued after the system was created. There is literally no systemwide participation in the recruitment, appointment, or promotion process, although in one case board ratification is required for appointments (but not promotions) to full professor.[2] Detailed systemwide budgetary control in both systems over numbers of positions and total salary dollars for each campus do not limit personnel decisions as such. The totally decentralized administration is possible, in part, because of a state-mandated ceiling on salaries. With no possibility of extraordinary or over-scale payments to "distinguished" faculty, there are no exceptions to normal rules which might require a systemwide review. Relatively automatic advancement also lessens the need for a discretionary system overview.

At the other extreme is a multicampus system in which the system administration reviews all academic appointments involving annual salaries of $4,000 or more, thus effectively including all

---

[2] In one of these systems, the system executive reserves the right to intervene in faculty personnel decisions (for example, to deny a tenure promotion approved by the campus executive). This right has been exercised twice in the past eight years.

faculty of the rank of instructor and above (the ceiling has recently been substantially increased). Review is not *pro forma,* as might have been expected, although the responsible system administrator indicated that he obviously spent more time with recommendations for appointment and promotion to the higher ranks. His review is made more important by the absence of a systemwide salary schedule. Because each faculty member is treated on an individual basis, regardless of rank or length of service, system review involves salary as much as appointment or promotion per se. Somewhat paradoxically, the governing board of this same university has made a greater formal delegation to the system executive than is the case in many of the other systems. He can appoint and promote faculty with annual salaries up to $18,000, regardless of tenure. There is no necessary relationship between the extent to which the governing board formally delegates its power to the system executive and his delegation, in turn, to the campus level.

The other universities fall between these extremes. The modal practice consists of systemwide administrative review of tenure appointments, regardless of salary, with an effective delegation of authority to the campus executive to appoint nontenured faculty (instructors and assistant professors). The system review varies in intensity from university to university and, within each system, from campus to campus. Most often, the responsible system administrator reviews appointments and promotions from the new or transitional campuses with greater care than those from the older ones. Differential attention was expressed in one university by a formal written delegation to the executive of the major campus to appoint and promote up to a salary level of $25,000, regardless of tenure. This delegation was not immediately extended to other campuses, but it was anticipated that this would take place in relatively short order.

Quite generally, appointments and promotions to tenure (and in some instances lesser appointments as well) require board ratification, but this is usually *pro forma.* In one university, board approval is required only for certain named professorships. None of the five universities requiring systemwide review of tenure appointments regard the practice as an issue between campus and system executives. Although there is campus grumbling over delays and paper shuffling, campus and system executives rarely fail to agree on an appointment or promotion proposed by the campus.

System executives exercise their authority very lightly, and campus executives accept it as a requirement of membership in a multi-campus university.

Rarely does review of appointments and promotions seriously interfere with the almost universal control which faculty have over the selection of their colleagues. Administrative monitoring of appointments to assure that campus diversity or specialization is being maintained usually takes the form of prior consultation rather than outright denial.

Individual appointments can be controversial despite consensus in most instances. One system executive was accused of "union busting" when he denied reappointment to a professor over the recommendations of both the campus executive and the faculty. In another system, the board rather than the system executive shows unaccustomed interest in its reviewing authority.

In this latter system, formal delegation of tenure appointments to the campus executives was a major issue, and several campus executives lobbied for a number of years to obtain it. They were not assuaged by the system executive's personal review of each case or the board's *pro forma* ratification. Faced with growing evidence that the systemwide review was mainly postponing promotions rather than weeding out the unqualified, the system executive successfully proposed that the governing board delegate its authority to appoint and promote to tenure positions. The delegation was to the system executive with the understanding that he would redelegate it to the campus executives. In 1969, however, the governing board, motivated by concern over the activities of politically militant faculty, amended its delegation to require that the tenure appointments and promotions made by the campus executive not go into effect until the board had the opportunity to review them. It is unclear whether and how the board will exercise its reclaimed authority. A collision between the board and one or more campus executives, with the system executive in the middle, is not unlikely.

Quality control

Systemwide review is justified by its advocates as an instrument of quality control, to be exercised by the system administration, by supracampus agencies of faculty government, or by both.

The administrative role is most pronounced in those universities where the chief academic affairs officer of the flagship campus assumes similar systemwide responsibilities. In these instances, he continues to exercise the same authority that he exercised previously at the campus level. He reviews the recommendations of the campus executives in terms of the candidates' qualifications and the proposed ranks and salary levels. Typically, the systemwide officer and the campus executive discuss any disagreements. The benefit of the doubt appears to go to the campus executive, if he wishes to press a case, but we were advised that mutual agreements are almost always reached.

Systemwide academic affairs officers spoke of their review role as advisory, but their influence, in fact, seems to be controlling. In one system, for example, even after the formal authority to appoint and promote had been delegated to the campus executive, the wisdom and experience of the system officer was so highly regarded that his advice was sought voluntarily, much as it had been obtained previously on a mandatory basis.

In two universities without flagship traditions, faculty personnel actions are centrally reviewed by a senior universitywide officer. In one, in fact, all candidates for initial appointment as full professor are personally interviewed at the system level, a practice regarded as helpful by the newer campuses but unnecessary by the older. These views were shared by the reviewing officer himself. He was removing himself from detailed review of recommendations from the older and larger campuses and realized that he would have to change his habits toward newer campuses drastically if the university added more of these.

Systemwide review poses a dilemma. In one university, for example, the campus academic affairs officer said he reviewed and recommended appointments and promotions more carefully because they were going to be thoroughly reviewed at the system level. Administrators at a large campus in another university conceded, however, that they might forward "close" cases, knowing that someone else would have to make the final decision. There is no consensus among the nine universities. Does the campus executive need a "helping hand" from the systemwide level in order to strengthen him against the immediate campus pressures surrounding academic personnel decisions? Or does the requirement of system review permit the campus executive to get off the hook and avoid difficult decisions which are properly his? Whatever the answer, the trend is clearly in the direction of increasing the de facto authority of the campus executive.

Universitywide *administrative* review of faculty personnel cases is regarded as a fairly permanent part of the scene. The use of *faculty* in systemwide review, on the other hand, is a transitional device, with primary application to new campuses. In three multi-campus universities with prestigious flagship campuses, administrators and faculty implicitly assumed that the faculty on the new campuses should meet the same "standards of productive scholarship" as those at the flagship and that it was the responsibility of the flagship faculty to see that this goal was achieved. In one university, this goal had been met in an earlier day by the establishment of single departments, combining faculty from the flagship and a nearby campus. This had been supplemented by an intercampus personnel committee, comprising members of both campuses but dominated by the flagship faculty. A similar policy had been implemented in another system where, for some years following the establishment of a new campus, all tenure appointments and promotions for the entire university were processed by an all-university faculty committee. This practice has been recently terminated on the grounds that the newer campuses now have a sufficient faculty base to conduct their own academic review. A third university used the joint department approach, with the additional requirement that all tenure cases be reviewed by universitywide subject-matter committees controlled by the flagship faculty. The dual review was to continue until the system administration regarded the newer campuses as self-sufficient in terms of their academic review capability.

A variation in one of the three universities was the appointment of a transitional academic advisory committee for each of the new campuses, composed of faculty from older campuses within the system. Although the committees were helpful to the newly appointed campus executives in advising on general educational policy, their principal mission was to assist in the review of all academic personnel cases in the initial and critical years of the campus.

A final device for universitywide review was superimposed on more general review in several institutions in which separate status is accorded to the *graduate faculty,* those formally eligible to teach graduate courses and to supervise doctoral dissertations. Typically, a single universitywide graduate school continued after the establishment of new campuses, and the all-university graduate dean was responsible for reviewing recommendations for graduate faculty status. This practice ceased almost entirely, however, as newer campuses established their own graduate programs under the direction of a local dean. One exception is the City University of New York, with its single multicampus graduate school with status parallel to that of a campus. In this instance, universitywide committees composed of graduate faculty members in broad disciplinary groups have the responsibility of reviewing all requests for membership in the graduate faculty.

Separate graduate faculty status is neither peculiar to the multicampus university nor universal, but the introduction of a universitywide review procedure into a multicampus context poses special problems. This is particularly evident in the City University, and system administrators expect conflict between the campus executives and the universitywide graduate dean (also entitled president) over appointments to the graduate faculty.

We are not able to evaluate the extent to which the academic personnel quality-control devices of the multicampus university have been successful. There are single-campus universities, new and old, in which the absence of a system review has not impaired recruitment of a distinguished faculty, by whatever measure. Nor can we correlate the quality of the faculty in each of the systems with the extent to which each has agencies of universitywide review. We can report, however, that where system review exists, there is agreement that it has served an effective, indeed essential, role in the growth and development of new campuses by assuring recruitment of qualified faculty. Quality-control devices of universitywide faculty and administrative review have been credited with providing solitary campus executives with information and advice, as well as making their work load more manageable in the hectic days of building a new campus. Systemwide quality control continues to be useful to established campuses where the universitywide reviewing officer has a reputation for giving wise advice.

Regardless of the extent to which universitywide review adds to the quality of academic personnel decisions, it gives the faculty at a new campus credibility in the eyes of the larger university community. This was particularly the case in the three systems where system faculty review had been established and dominated by the flagship campus. Here, it is widely believed that review of faculty appointments and promotions at the new campus by senior faculty from the flagship, by whatever structural device, established a sense of common university membership. This common membership was said to promote greater willingness to engage in cooperative intercampus enterprises, to transfer to other campuses without loss of status, and to strengthen faculty bonds to the multicampus university vis-à-vis the continuing desires of the campuses for greater autonomy. The validity of these assertions could not be objectively assessed, for other programs designed to engender a sense of universitywide faculty membership were found, both in these three systems and in the others included in the study. Moreover, the success of the universitywide faculty review depends on a common acceptance of the definition of quality. As suggested above, a feature of the multicampus university is the transmission of the values of the dominant campus to the newer campuses. If one accepts this goal, the multicampus university has been successful, and the universitywide review devices described here have been a key instrument in that success.

Recruitment

Whether at a newly established campus, a previously autonomous state college brought into the system, or a formerly private campus merged into the multicampus framework, administrators and faculty alike credit membership in the system as assisting in the recruitment of able faculty. This was frequently explained in terms of the name of the institution. "No one even knew we existed as Centerville State College, but now that we're the University of Transylvania at Centerville, we can get our foot in the door." The name associated with a prestigious flagship campus is particularly helpful. To many faculty, the opportunity to share indirectly in the heritage of the flagship while also participating directly in the development of a new university campus is to have the best of both worlds. "What's in a name?" is not an academic question in the multicampus university.

The implications of membership in the university go beyond sharing a name. Affiliation is also seen as a guarantee of increased and more stable financial support. Salaries, fringe benefits, and working conditions can be discussed with prospective applicants with more assurance. And other benefits of the multicampus structure exist: increased opportunities for research and the chance to participate in joint programs—instructional and research—with colleagues from another campus in the system. Importantly, membership in the larger university framework may offer new and expanded opportunities for faculty participation in governance.

The University of California is the only system with a distinct pattern—almost a tradition—of movement of older faculty from the flagship campus to a newer campus as "colonizers." Appointments to major administrative and faculty positions have been frequently made from among those with long experience at Berkeley and UCLA, providing the new campus with an obvious edge in recruitment from outside the state. Executives and the governing board have thus been assured that the new campuses would be full-fledged and first-class members of the system. Generally, the move of personnel from the older campuses has also provided assurance that older and proven values would be those of the entire university—for good or ill. Administrators at other systems explain their own practices in various ways. In one instance, it was stated, the new campus did not want faculty from the flagship but wished to chart its own course without influence, which many did not regard as desirable. The more typical explanation is that the system will not or cannot assure faculty that the new campuses will be as fully supported as the flagship; a move from the flagship is regarded as a step down, not a challenge.

Faculty are by no means unanimous in acclaiming membership in the multicampus university as a virtue. On the flagship campuses, particularly, there are frequent expressions of discontent: "Our prestige erodes as we extend the university's name to these other campuses." Or, more practically, "The new campuses inevitably take away some of our support and even some of our faculty." All these are seen as possible impediments to recruitment of able faculty at the flagship.

In truth, the multicampus system does not appear to help faculty recruitment or retention at major campuses, whose promotion and compensation policies are shaped by the national marketplace. Madison has little to offer as part of a system that Ann Arbor cannot offer as a single-campus university. One must look beyond the flagship to the entire system to see the advantages of the multicampus university, and some people feel the cost of the advantages excessive.

Salary Administration Governing boards and system administrations frequently delegate authority for making salary adjustments below specific dollar limits to campus executives. Wide variation in practice was observed. It ranged from one systemwide administration which reviewed all adjustments to salaries of $4,000 and above to another which reviewed only those at the top of the "regular" nine-month salary scale, $25,700.

In one system, there is literally no published salary scale. While there is some pattern among salaries and rank, each member of the faculty has an individually negotiated rate. This universitywide flexibility is accompanied by a lack of campus authority, a partial result of the absence of formal system guidelines. All annual salary transactions of more than $4,000 require system approval. A system at the other extreme publishes a detailed schedule listing eight salary steps for each professorial rank. Advancement through the schedule, within rank, is virtually automatic, with little administrative review even at the campus level. Automatic salary advances are sharply interrupted, however, by promotions to a higher rank. State fiscal authorities have established quotas for each rank, which have been distributed, in turn, to each campus. In consequence, large numbers of faculty are sometimes stalled at the top of the salary ranges for assistant and associate professors, waiting for openings to be created by retirement or resignation from the higher ranks. A campus executive in this system said his hardest task was to choose the one or two who would be permitted to advance from among several qualified candidates. He has total flexibility to increase salaries within the salary range for the rank, and the ranges are broad and overlapping, but neither he nor the system executive has any flexibility at all with respect to the quotas.

In another university with detailed, systemwide salary scales and decentralized administration, the situation is just the reverse. The campus executive has complete authority to promote from rank to rank but is prevented by state fiscal regulations from granting more than a one-step increase on the schedule. He can promote a man to associate or full professor with a substantial improvement in pay but cannot give a special—but lesser—salary increase within rank!

The six other universities range between these extremes of no salary schedule and highly centralized administration on the one hand, and rigid salary scales and highly decentralized administration on the other. Uniform salary ceilings for each rank are found in one system, while in another there are uniform floors. Neither salary ranges nor fixed steps within the ranks are set by the system, and campus administrators have authority over salaries subject to these guidelines and budgetary limitations. In two other universities, ranges with intermediate steps have been established for each rank, and campus administrators can set salaries within the ranges. In other systems, there are no fixed salary schedules, but the system administration maintains some control and intercampus balance by its authority over appointments and promotions to tenure.

In at least three multicampus systems, special procedures allow salary increases above the top of the approved or official salary range for the full professor. In one, these over-scale decisions are the only faculty personnel actions which the governing board reserves for itself, all other matters being delegated to the administration. In the other two, however, approval of state finance officials is required, and there is considerable ambiguity over whether the state review extends to the qualifications of the incumbent as well as the nature of the position. Although there have been no recent examples of state refusal to approve such requests, the requirement is viewed by university administrators as an unnecessary intrusion into internal university matters.

The decentralization of authority to approve over-scale salaries to the campus level has been proposed in two of the three universities. However, implementing the proposals would necessitate agreement between campus and system administrators (and state officials in one case) on the numbers of such positions at each campus, the extent of permissible increases, and the total amount of salary money which could be used for this purpose. Formal structuring of extraordinary salaries is not necessarily worth the benefits of campus autonomy. In this instance, at least, centralization is the price of administrative flexibility, and the campus administrators are not pressing the issue.

Within most systems, the relative authority over salaries on the part of the department chairman, the college dean, and the campus executive varies from campus to campus, as does the extent of faculty involvement. Absence of uniformity is not surprising, but we found the lack of universitywide knowledge about salary practices among the campuses to be unwarranted and perhaps unwise. Most multicampus universities have established fairly uniform procedures to ensure that appointments and promotions are carried out with wisdom and equity, but the same cannot be said with respect to salary administration. The establishment of universitywide criteria and procedural standards is worthy of far more attention.

Tenure and Dismissal

Tenure, the right of a faculty member to continuing employment and to review by his peers prior to any action by administrator or governing board leading to his dismissal, is well understood. The efforts of the American Association of University Professors

(AAUP) have not only been responsible for this understanding, but have made the substance of tenure relatively uniform at major campuses throughout the country. In the multicampus context, however, the procedures for faculty discipline are complicated by the existence of an additional level of authority between the campus and the governing board.[3]

In some systems, this question has been faced directly, and careful procedures outline the respective roles of the system and the campuses. In others, however, the question has not been resolved, and practices of an earlier and simpler day, when only one campus existed, have been carried forward without apparent consideration of the new environment. Given the infrequency with which questions of dismissal of tenured faculty arise, it is not surprising that this matter has escaped explicit consideration in all nine systems. Each university has treated the issue on the basis of local traditions and circumstances, and no consensus exists among administrators at either system or campus levels as to what constitutes proper practice in the multicampus context.

In every system, a general board statement describes the conditions for tenure in terms of length of service or rank, and then sets out the conditions for its termination: "incompetence," "neglect of duty," "misconduct," "gross inefficiency," "illegal advocacy of the overthrow of the government by force or violence," "gross immorality," or "only for good cause" being among the reasons listed. In every system, too, there is a specific statement of procedures approved by the governing board, but these vary widely in scope and content.

In all but one system, the board reserves the power to make the final decision in any dismissal case. In the case of the exception, authority has been delegated to the central administration, although the system executive is authorized to refer cases to the board for decision when either the faculty member or the campus executive wishes to appeal. Otherwise, a joint decision of the campus and system executives is final.

In most cases, dismissal policies provide that the governing board

[3] The AAUP (1968, p. 35) is cognizant of the problems in multicampus systems, and does not limit its investigation—or criticism—to a single campus when it believes that a violation of academic freedom has occurred. For example: ". . . it is our opinion that there are several conditions at the administrative level on the Whitewater campus and in the administration of the state university system through the Board of Regents and the Director of Wisconsin State Universities which are seriously detrimental to academic freedom at Whitewater and throughout the entire system."

act upon the recommendations of the administration, a faculty review committee, or both. In three systems, however, the board itself must hold a hearing, with the faculty member authorized to appear in his own defense, virtually repeating the procedure of the faculty committee.

The most important features of disciplinary procedure relevant to this study are the respective roles of the campus and system executives. Procedures to bring these roles into balance were developed in one system only through months of effort by senior administrators, a committee of campus executives, the systemwide faculty organization, and the governing board. However, this effort was the exception. In only three of the nine universities do written policies clearly define relative authority. In these three, the campus executive makes recommendations to the system executive for final action or recommendations to the governing board. In some of the other systems, there is no mention of the system executive, and it is implied that the campus recommendation will go directly to the board for action. In others, the campus executive is not included in the formal rules, and the role of bringing charges and making recommendations to the board is assigned to the system executive. Under either pattern, campus and system levels of administration would probably work cooperatively, but this assumption seems a poor substitute for explicit policy.

In every university, the need for prior review by a faculty hearing committee in any dismissal case is well recognized, although considerable variation exists in the procedures established to guide the committees. In two instances, committees are universitywide, composed of faculty from several campuses. In most of the remaining cases, however, hearing committees are campus agencies, appointed by the faculty itself. One exception is a university in which campus executives appoint committees. As might be expected, the universitywide committees exist in the systems where the role of the system executive is most clearly set forth.

COLLECTIVE BARGAINING FOR ACADEMIC PERSONNEL

Collective bargaining by faculty poses special problems for the multicampus university, problems which may well alter its future course and even threaten its existence. Within the bounds of relevant legislation, the issue revolves around the question of what the appropriate bargaining unit is for a multicampus university. The answer not only shapes the selection of the bargaining agent, but influences the character and organization of academic personnel as a whole.

It is no surprise, therefore, that in New York the hearings before the state agency empowered to determine the appropriate bargaining unit for each of the two systems resulted in literally thousands of pages of testimony. The different proposals in the two systems—each was treated separately—included almost every conceivable alternative. It was variously urged that there be one universitywide bargaining unit or that the basic unit be the campus. Similarly, it was argued that all academic personnel be combined in a single unit, or that they be divided among separate units for faculty and nonteaching personnel or for full-time and part-time staff. Both the City University and State University system administrations advocated a single, all-university academic bargaining unit, a viewpoint seemingly shared by campus executives. But among the affected academic personnel, there was little consensus. Support for a particular bargaining unit rested on the tactical advantage one approach or another would give to the organizations competing for faculty votes in the eventual election for bargaining agent.

The complexity of collective bargaining issues is evident in the City University, the only system in which both the bargaining unit and agent had been determined in 1970. The governing board and the two competing employee groups agreed that the university should be treated as a single bargaining unit for all permanent faculty. But each of the three parties presented a separate proposal for the temporary and part-time faculty, combining them with the permanent faculty and establishing separate units in different combinations. The two employee organizations knew where their own strength rested, and each sought a decision which would give its members the greatest leverage when voting took place. In a decision worthy of Solomon, the state agency discarded all three proposals and came up with a fourth which grouped the part-time and temporary faculty together in separate bargaining units in a manner different from any proposed by the three parties.

The election to determine if the faculty wanted collective bargaining and to select the bargaining agent demonstrated the consequences of the state's action. One employee organization won the right to be designated the representative of the permanent faculty, while the other organization was selected by the part-time and temporary faculty. The system administration and governing board must bargain collectively with two organizations, despite general identity of academic interests between the two faculty groups and the need to keep their salary and working conditions in balance.

The state determined the "proper" unit, and the election selected the agent, but the permanence of the arrangements is far from secure.

The State University presents a different pattern of relationships. Here, the widely dispersed locations of the campuses explain, at least in part, the position of the State University Federation of Teachers that campuses be treated as separate bargaining units. Finding it difficult to obtain support for this position, the organization then agreed to a single bargaining unit but proposed "dual-unit" negotiation; bargaining was to be divided into statewide and local categories, to be handled at the system and campus levels, respectively. Speaking to these points, the trustees of the State University replied in their brief:

The issues in this proceeding involve nothing less than the question of whether the State University of New York is to continue to proceed in its daily activities as a unified University rather than as a loose confederation of competing educational enterprises and therefore not a University at all.

Persuaded by such statements and the urging of the faculty senate and the universitywide council of AAUP chapters, the state decided on a single universitywide bargaining unit for the faculty and related personnel, and held that negotiable issues should not be divided as proposed by the federation. The state agency said, "The concomitant differences among the campuses do not establish such conflicts of interest between their respective professionals as to warrant geographic fragmentation."

Nevertheless, the intrusion of formal collective bargaining into the State University is a potentially divisive force. The faculty election in 1971 to select a bargaining agent will be but the beginning of a continuing struggle for influence among competing faculty organizations. The challenge to SUNY as a multicampus university is whether the differences in faculty working conditions among campuses ranging from two-year technical schools to graduate-dominated university centers can be contained within a single system of collective bargaining.[4]

[4] The potential impact upon the State University was evidenced late in 1969 by the announcement of the salary schedule for the City University of New York, resulting from negotiations between the faculty legislative conference and the city. Common salaries—"parity"—for both the four-year and community college campuses were established. The maximum of $31,275 for the professorial range is to be reached by the end of the three-year contract period. For community college faculty, this new ceiling compares with a previous high of $21,950.

The issue is much broader, of course, and goes to the heart of the strengths and weaknesses of the comprehensive multicampus university. To what extent will the inclusion of all the 8,600 faculty and 3,800 nonfaculty professionals of the State University in a single bargaining unit encourage or frustrate the essential diversity of employment conditions dictated by a complex institution? Will there be, as some fear, a leveling downward of salaries, teaching loads, and sabbaticals which will prevent the university centers from competing effectively for able faculty in the national arena? Alternatively, will pressures for leveling salary and faculty benefits upward curtail other parts of the educational budget, such as libraries and research support.

Faculty within the various segments of the State University share common interests which may not necessarily be those of the system as a whole. The faculty of the university centers are most distinct in this respect. Part of a national educational establishment, drawn from other universities, highly discipline-oriented, and least involved in collective-bargaining activities, they might well try to opt out of a single universitywide bargaining structure at a future date.

These two multicampus universities will never look the same, and the ramifications of their changes will have a national impact. Whether others follow their course or seek to avoid their difficulties, their example cannot be ignored.

ADMINISTRA-TIVE PER-SONNEL Much of the discussion of faculty appointment and compensation applies to top-level administrative personnel as well. A large number of these staff officers often hold professorial titles. But because of their small number, public visibility, and generally higher salaries, vice-presidents, vice-chancellors, and other senior staff officials at both campus and system levels present the executives and governing boards with special problems of appointment and compensation.[5] As with faculty personnel matters, formal regulations and actual practice sometimes differ.

Administrative Appointments The gap between formal authority and practice is most evident at the level of the governing board. One board formally approves virtually all administrative appointments, but another has formally

[5] See Chapter 5 for a discussion of the appointment of campus and system executives.

delegated such authority to the system and campus executives. In practice, however, regardless of formal delegation, all boards restrict their attention to senior system and campus administrators. In a few instances, they concern themselves with the appointment of deans of prestigious schools, but in general even the board's interest in system and campus "cabinet" positions is that of an interested onlooker rather than that of an active participant in the selection. Boards properly see the appointment of the system and campus executives as their prime responsibility. They rely upon these executives to select their own staff.

The interplay between the system executive and his campus executives in the selection of campus administrators is not always easy to follow, but a modal pattern can be described. Without question, system executives select the members of their own administrations, and with very little interference the campus executives select the members of theirs. The pattern is often difficult to discern because it is overlaid by authority formally centralized in the board or system executive, by state or system fiscal controls, and by extensive informal advice and consultation.

In only one instance is the freedom of campus executives to select their staffs made formal by an explicit delegation of authority. But these campus executives do not have any greater effective authority than those in another system where board approval is required. In both systems, however, state fiscal controls over salaries by position leave the campuses with little room for discretion.

The formal control which the systems maintain over campus administrative appointments varies. In one instance, campus executives are required to consult with the central administration before making an appointment. More commonly, the system requires its approval of appointments over reasonable limits set by salary or title to reflect system interest in only the more senior and highly paid campus administrators. These typical limits by title (e.g., associate campus executive) or salary (e.g., $15,000 a year) are counterparts to similar ones on delegated authority over faculty appointments.

System review is rarely *pro forma,* but neither does it infringe on the prerogatives of the campus executives. The review is for *system* purposes, and not for second-guessing the campuses. The responsible system officer, usually a very senior one, generally accepts the campus executive's judgment that a particular individual is qualified for the staff position. What he may question is the effect that the appointment may have on the rough but delicate balance among the campuses. Budgetary controls, whether system or state, are also of concern. The reviewing officer has a special interest in changes of title or in proposals for new staff positions, and he monitors campus attempts to recruit administrative staff from other campuses in and out of the system and from state agencies as well. Only one instance came to our attention of a system imposing its own choice of a staff officer on a campus, although faculty at a campus in another system believed that this had been done. In the first case, the officer was isolated and ineffective because of general knowledge that he was "the system executive's man at the campus." In the other, faculty and other campus administrators, as well, examined every act of the particular staff officer with the suspicion that it had been directed by the system offices. Clearly, the authority of the multicampus systems does not extend to appoint specific persons to campus staff positions.

On the whole, campus executives in all systems consult with appropriate central administrative officers before making major administrative appointments, whether such consultation is required or not. Some complaints were heard if a requirement existed. "I hate to go up there, hat in hand, to get permission to hire my own assistant." More often, however, formal limits on appointing authority simply recognize that campus executives usually seek, obtain, and follow advice from the system executive or the members of his staff in whom they have confidence.

Administrative Salaries
Because of the numbers of faculty and the broad ranges of salary schedules in all systems, intercampus comparison of individual faculty salaries has rarely raised serious questions. Comparison of average faculty salaries across campuses is always complicated by the wide variations between departments at any one campus. For administrative salaries, however, comparison is the rule rather than the exception. Having fewer administrators makes the task easier, and their titles generally imply specific and comparable responsibilities. Each system is presented with the problems of just how much *non*uniformity it can withstand and what procedures will best contain it.

The needs of the campuses in terms of the qualifications and salaries of top-level administrators vary immensely. The same titles in the same system can mask great differences in the actual job responsibilities. Surface distinctions between like positions, such as the size of the campus and the number of employees in the department, may be highly misleading, if not actually damaging. An administrator with responsibility for physical planning and development at a new and growing campus may hold a much more demanding position than that held by one with the same title at the oldest and largest campus. And yet, it is difficult to measure the difference and even harder to convince state fiscal authorities that there is one. Nor can a system executive avoid the pressure for equality and the need to maintain internal equity, not only among campuses, but between campus and system administrators, particularly those in the same functional area. His problems are aggravated by the public nature of executive salaries. Undue nonuniformity, however deserved, can produce serious morale problems for the university as a whole.

In general, the systems handle these difficult problems of administrative compensation well. They avoid uniform imposition of exact salaries on exact titles or positions but do keep a general balance among campuses and between the campuses and the system. Usually balance is accomplished through the same procedures that bring appointments up for review—that is, through specific dollar or rank limits on delegated authority or through consultation. The system executive or his chief deputy will usually handle each case individually, and some systems maintain more or less formal salary schedules to guide system decisions as well as to inform the campus executives of their authority.

Although in two systems formal administrative salary schedules are detailed and were long in the making, we had the impression that they would achieve balance and reasonable uniformity by their flexibility. One system has an administrative tradition that seeks to define campus freedom in formal documents, and the other appears to be developing one. Campuses in other systems are more inclined to see autonomy in the *absence* of such detailed rules, but all systems appear to be successfully managing administrative salaries to the extent that they have control over them. Several systems, however, lack essential elements of control.

In two of these universities, critical authority over executive salaries resides with state finance officials. In one state, a statute requires that the governor set all salaries other than civil service and faculty. Administrators are neither, and a state executive agency reviews all top-level salaries within the university on an individual basis. There is constant risk that the agency will upset internal equities among campus and system staff. The problem is aggravated by the low salary of the governor, for all other salaries from the system executive on down are ranked in relation to it. In another system, state and university officials have agreed to a formal plan which establishes broad and generous administrative salary ranges. However, the specific approval of the state's senior finance officer is required before a position can be assigned to a range or before an individual can be paid at a level above its third quartile.

Delegation to the campus executive of the final decision over compensation of his staff is an appropriate theoretical solution, but in fact this path is fraught with difficulty. Attempts to decentralize authority require agreement on job classification, on assignment to salary ranges, and on detailed, formal statement of these and related issues. Yet filling any staff position of importance demands a highly personal and subjective approach. For administrative appointments and salaries, at least, as with over-scale faculty salaries, flexible central control may be preferable to the more formal and circumscribed campus autonomy. That there can be both maximum flexibility *and* decentralization in this sensitive area is highly doubtful.

THE COMPRE-HENSIVE UNIVERSITY Any university, single- or multicampus, with a variety of faculty talents and levels is confronted with a conflict between the desire to treat fairly all faculty with similar titles and responsibilities and the need to recruit them from a highly complex and nonuniform market. The discrepancy between medical and all other faculty salaries is well known. The chairman of the surgery department may well earn more than the campus executive. Similarly, separate salary schedules, formal and informal, exist for law professors, engineering faculty, and other groups whose career lines take them in and out of the university.

Within the comprehensive system, such problems are aggravated. While he may not like it, a humanities professor can accept the reality of his status in the marketplace vis-à-vis a doctor or lawyer. It is quite different, however, for a humanities professor at an undergraduate campus to concede that he should not be paid as well as a colleague at a university campus. Here, the distinctions are not between two professions but between two persons ostensibly laboring in the same—or at least neighboring—vineyard.

The problem goes to the heart of the academic revolution and points up the different values which society places, or allows to be placed, on various aspects of the educational enterprise. Is graduate teaching "worth more" than undergraduate instruction? Is research "worth more" than teaching? Is teaching degree students "worth more" than teaching postgraduates in extension? Almost without question, universities answer each of these questions affirmatively. Indeed an affirmative answer is often seen as a defining characteristic of the university. The answers are evident not only in differences in individual salaries but in other support: offices, secretaries, travel budgets, sabbaticals. Perhaps most importantly, the distinctions are recognized in terms of the distribution of the work load. A higher teaching load is assigned to the professor charged only with undergraduate responsibilities. Supervision of five doctoral dissertations relieves a faculty member of the obligation to teach an undergraduate course. Relief from regular teaching duties is not given for direction of extension courses—*even* for doctors or engineers. All these policies state clearly and unequivocally the values of the contemporary American university which are being questioned by critics both inside its walls and out.

The issues posed here are universal, but in a single-campus institution they tend not to be addressed explicitly. The values of academe result from hundreds of separate and tenuously related judgments made over a long period of time. Within the multicampus university, however—particularly a comprehensive system— the issues have to be faced more clearly and the values addressed more explicitly.

The question may be simply posed: Can the multicampus university develop and sustain other dimensions of quality in addition to those implicit in the values of the graduate-research orientation of its major university campuses? From the evidence of this study, the answer is unclear and uncertain. In one system, partially because of pressures of collective bargaining, the issue is whether the formal distinctions in teaching load and salary between the two-year and university campuses can be maintained. *Parity* is the watchword of many community college faculty.[6]

However, more positive lessons can be learned from the experience of two systems with multiple segments of higher education. One, the State University of New York, includes two-year, collegiate, and university campuses. The other, the University of Wisconsin, has all of these, plus a large extension program treated organizationally as a campus. In both, all permanent faculty are

---

[6] We have noted above that the first result of collective bargaining in the City University of New York was to create a common salary scale for all faculty, including both community college and university campuses.

eligible for the traditional university title of professor. In both, faculty from all campuses are represented on universitywide faculty governing councils in proportion to their membership. In both, the *formal* salary schedule covers all faculty, although it is extremely flexible in application. Most significantly, however, both universities have adapted conditions for promotion and tenure to the mission of the particular type of campus; the standard of the major campus with its emphasis upon "productive scholarship" is not exclusive. These multicampus universities recognize multiple dimensions of quality by extending the prerequisites of membership in the academic community to all faculty. More full professors are found on the university campuses, and average salaries tend to be higher there, but *explicit* policy does not discriminate between faculty from the several segments within the system.

The lesson appears clear, although experience is limited. A multicampus university can define and sustain segmental differences among individual faculty as long as it does not make these the basis for explicit distinctions among campuses. However, if a comprehensive system maintains formal differences in faculty salaries and working conditions, the multicampus structure may well exacerbate these distinctions to the detriment of both the faculty and the institution. In the first instance, the university can be an agency to maintain and encourage essential distinctions in a creative and positive fashion. In the second, the university may become a forum for angry and destructive contention, perhaps better handled by separate segmental systems.

All multicampus systems can benefit from the special experience of those comprising more than one segment. In a broad sense, two-year, collegiate, and university campuses represent special cases of the internal diversity and specialization which are the concern of each multicampus system. Not all campuses can be or want to be carbon copies of the flagship. But varying aspirations and missions can be nurtured and sustained only if they do not involve invidious comparisons in salaries and status. In short, a desired amount of inequality can be contained administratively as long as it is not a matter of policy and as long as it is administered on an individual and not a campus basis.

THE TRANSI-
TIONAL
CAMPUS

Many of the nine systems have managed the transformation of a two-year or collegiate campus to one with university status. In some cases, this has been part of a merger into the university system of a previously independent campus or one that was part of another system. In one instance, it meant a change in character of a campus already part of the system. In all cases, the change was accompanied by difficult problems affecting the faculty, both old and new.

In at least two instances, entrance into the university system required a change in the length of service for acquiring tenure. Typically, the universities have a longer probationary period than many state colleges—seven years as opposed to three or five. Movement into the university system involved a continuance of tenure for those who had already achieved it within the college context, but for those who had not, an extension of the probationary period to the longer university standard.

More broadly, university status typically changes a fairly automatic pattern of salary advances and promotion to a more individualistic one based on appraisal of merit. This, in turn, is accompanied by the introduction of different criteria for promotion as the campus shifts from an exclusively undergraduate teaching mission to one emphasizing graduate instruction and research. Here, the transition can be most difficult, with frequent clashes of judgment between old faculty and new and between old faculty and new administrators charged with changing the traditional directions of the campus. The problem is not easily resolved. A cycle of as long as 20 years may be required before faculty recruited and oriented to the college pattern of academic life are completely phased out.

Despite the complexity and duration of the problem, the multicampus universities are credited by both old and new faculty and administrators with doing a laudable job during the transition period. As in the case of new campuses, the larger system has provided assistance and judgment to the transitional campus not otherwise readily available. With few exceptions, the systems have handled the personnel problems of the old faculty with sensitivity and skill, solving the human problems of transition without detriment to the educational process.

UNIVERSITY-WIDE PER-SONNEL PROGRAMS In every multicampus university, systemwide employee benefit programs—for example, retirement, insurance, medical, and other similar programs—include every faculty member but do not directly involve the campuses as such. (In some instances, the administration of such programs is a direct responsibility of state government.) On the face of it, a multicampus university seems particularly suited to develop and maintain such programs. Compared to a single-campus institution, it possesses such advantages as efficiency of scale and superior bargaining power with insurance companies. Whether this is the case or not, we found no pressure at the campus level to decentralize either the policy or administrative aspects of such systemwide personnel programs.

Despite the link of common status in terms of salary, retirement, and other benefit plans, faculty rarely move among campuses on either a temporary or a permanent basis. A pattern of faculty transfer from the older campuses to new campuses is apparent in only one instance. While this is undoubtedly facilitated by a university-wide retirement program, the absence of a similar pattern in other systems indicates clearly that continuity of benefits is not a decisive factor.

Nor is it clear that the multicampus university really provides a better opportunity for joint appointments among campuses than might take place on an ad hoc basis among separately controlled campuses. More than one system has a distinguished all-university professor who brings his talents to several of the campuses. But the examples are few and far between, and there are, in some instances, equally effective relationships with institutions outside the system.

11. *Admissions and Transfers*

During a regular administrative meeting at one multicampus university, a campus executive proposed that the surest route to "quality" was to cut back admissions. His solution is not generally available to a public campus, nor was it available to him. In discussions after the meeting, however, the ambiguity and fuller import of his suggestion rose rapidly to the surface. Did he believe that better education would take place on a smaller campus? Or did he simply want the same budget but fewer students? Or would selecting only the "better" students do the job regardless of size or money? All three possibilities were doubtless blended together, but the possibility of three such distinct inferences illustrates the complexity of admissions policy and administration.

This chapter is not concerned with admissions policies as such, despite their importance to the educational process. The relative importance of high school grades and test scores and the relationship between them and subsequent academic success are critical questions, to say the least, but they are common to all colleges and universities. Here, we ask who in the multicampus system determines admissions policy, and whether the policy is uniform throughout the system. We are interested in the roles of the system and the campus, respectively, in the administration of admissions and transfers to and within the multicampus university, including the question of articulation of programs with those of the two-year colleges.

We direct attention here to undergraduate admissions, the movement of students into the university from high schools and two-year colleges. The equally important question of graduate admissions policies and procedures is left untouched, for it is not critical *at this time* to our study. Within the multicampus university and out of it, graduate admissions policies and procedures are highly decentralized, and the critical point of decision is the department. Insofar as we observed controversy over authority, it was almost always between the department and the graduate dean at the campus.

Systemwide concern with graduate admissions is currently limited to such questions as the proportion of graduate students at a campus and, occasionally, their distribution among the various programs at the campus. Only rarely do systems review and evaluate graduate admissions policies, as such, but that they will continue to be relatively inactive is doubtful. Faced with increasingly tight budgets and confronted by evidence that, as in one university system, only 40 percent of entering graduate students complete work for a degree, a universitywide review of graduate admissions policies and practices is predictable. But in 1970 this had only infrequently taken place.

For undergraduate admissions, however, the story is quite different. Campuses in the university systems are all pursuing the elusive goal of academic excellence as actively as campuses anywhere, and the objective is always related—in one way or another—to admissions policy. But in a multicampus system, a campus usually encounters a sibling on a similar quest. Not all campuses in the same university can unilaterally adopt more selective admissions policies, nor—alternatively—can a campus go it alone on open admissions. Universally, the system administration is charged with the task of maintaining equity among the campuses. If equity is interpreted as equality in the sense of *uniform* admissions policies for all campuses, then the system administration must carefully consider the impact such uniformity might have on its additional responsibilities of maintaining diversity and specialization.

Competition is not limited to admissions, of course. Larger buildings, more distinguished faculty, a greater share of the operating budget—all are milestones on the road to excellence. Traditionally, however, a major criterion is the quality of students a campus can attract. Admissions policy and procedures involve far more than mere numbers: they determine prestige, the coin of the academic realm for institutions as well as individuals.

THE ROLE OF THE MULTI-CAMPUS UNIVERSITY In theory, the multicampus university seems particularly well equipped to develop and evaluate admissions policy from a broader vantage point than any available to a single-campus institution. The needs of a larger population of students can be considered and balanced against greater resources. Furthermore, the multicampus system should facilitate experimentation with different campus admissions policies and their evaluation against alternative approaches.

Another advantage is said to be surveillance or policing of campus admissions practices. With the ability to obtain comparative information on both original admission and subsequent performance of students across its several campuses, the multicampus system can assess the implications of differing admissions standards or, if standards are uniform, can determine whether the campuses are in fact administering them uniformly.

Two possible advantages of a multicampus university relate to student transfers. First, students should be able to transfer more easily from one campus to another within the same system. Study at more than one campus can be encouraged by the multicampus organization, or at least formal administrative impediments can be reduced. Second, two-year campuses should find it to their advantage to negotiate problems—courses, credits, and the like—with a single representative.

Moreover, a central multicampus agency can advise applicants at all levels about options available at its several campuses, counseling and directing or redirecting individual applicants according to suitability of programs or availability of space. In theory, quotas and ceilings for campuses and programs can be more flexibly administered within a system in the interests of both the students and the institutions.

Finally, a multicampus university has advantages of economy of scale in admissions administration and data collection and analysis. From the standpoint of both the student and the campus, efficiencies should result from a centralized administration—a single applications procedure for several campuses, for example. Academic planning can profit from analysis of consolidated information collected during admissions processes. Not only will the multicampus structure command a broader range of data, but it can have specialized personnel for its utilization.

The most obvious disadvantage of a multicampus university is the danger of rigidity and inflexibility of admissions in the name of universitywide uniformity. Unnecessary restrictions on the freedom of choice of both students and campuses can result from an insistence on a single all-university standard. Experimentation, or at least a variety of approaches, may be discouraged rather than enhanced by membership in the university system.

Many alleged advantages of the multicampus university may not, in fact, depend on the system. Articulation with two-year colleges, mobility among campuses, and the redirection of students to available campuses and programs might be just as effectively handled on a voluntary basis. Moreover, the ultimate source of admissions policy is really the individual student, whose ability to self-select campuses and programs transcends the most sophisticated campus machinery.

ADMISSIONS POLICY In one state, a legislator had long been told that the several campuses of the university adhered to uniform admissions standards. However, when a constituent's son applied to two campuses of the system, he was accepted by one but turned down by the other—his first choice—because his high school record was not adequate. The legislator asked questions which are also central to this study: What are "uniform" admissions standards? Who decides how these standards shall be applied?

The answers the legislator received were reportedly not entirely to his satisfaction. We shared his lack of understanding as we attempted without full success to bring order to the admissions policies of the nine multicampus universities and their several score campuses. Nevertheless, a general pattern does emerge, albeit one subject to a host of qualifications.

In brief, the nine systems can be divided into three groups.

1 In two universities there are, in reality, no universitywide admissions policies whatsoever and no desire to establish them. Admissions are entirely a campus matter, and there is substantial variety among the campuses.

2 At the other extreme, in three systems, admissions policies are uniform for all campuses, or, as in one instance, campus variations from the uniform standards are determined at the system level.

3 The four remaining university systems fall between these extremes. In each, there is a "uniform" standard which, upon closer examination, is better described as a *minimum* admissions standard. The campuses, either by written policy or unwritten practice, are free to establish higher standards than the minimum, and many have chosen to exercise the option. In several instances, this local option means de facto delegation of student selection to departments, schools, or colleges within the campus.

These three categories are not precise. Specifically, the uniform minimum standards are generally so low that the campuses have almost total flexibility in establishing their own standards. Alternatively, the prevailing practice on many campuses is to accept all applicants who meet the minimum standard. Thus, there are university systems which have uniform admissions among all campuses as a matter of systemwide policy, and those which have achieved the same result because of the independent choice of the campuses. In parallel fashion, there are systems which have *non*-uniform policies as a result of campus choice, and one system in which nonuniformity is a matter of deliberate universitywide policy.

Local authority over admissions is exemplified by one university in which each campus separately determines both the character and number of acceptable high school course units which determine eligibility for admission. Similarly, each campus sets its own minimum Scholastic Aptitude Test (SAT) scores which students are required to achieve. Although individually of respectable age, the campuses have only recently become part of a system; their independent histories are largely responsible for the varying qualification standards. But the campuses are widely separated within the state, and there is little indication that local admissions policies will be disturbed by the system administration. In the other multicampus university with local authority, the only system requirement is that applicants have a high school diploma or "qualifications which the admitting authorities may deem equivalent." The "admitting authorities" are the campuses, and each shapes its own policies, subject only to universitywide procedural requirements.

Minimum eligibility requirements with permission for campuses to establish higher selection standards — the pattern in four universities — have virtually no implications for multicampus governance within the systems themselves. The requirements are a floor below which campus selection standards cannot fall, but the campuses demonstrate little wish to set lower ones. In no case does campus authority over admissions pose a serious problem for the university as a system. This is at least a partial result of the relative nonselectivity of the admissions policies. In general, a student among the top half of high school graduates is assured of admission to one, if not all, campuses of these four universities, and the campuses within the particular system do not vary substantially among themselves.

An advantage of local selection is seen in one of the comprehensive systems. Containing both university and collegiate campuses, it could have adopted the policies of many states which have lower admissions standards for collegiate than for university campuses. It did not do so, but left the matter up to each campus, regardless of its character. Thus, implications of "second-class citizenship" which are creating problems elsewhere have been avoided. Local standards, aided by student self-selection, have approximated the same distribution of students, in terms of scholastic ability, between types of campuses as have more rigid differential admissions standards in other states.

Uniform and selective universitywide admissions policies are the pattern in the three remaining systems. Two of these three are in California, and admissions standards are part of a statewide master plan which allocates not only functions but students between the two systems. In the University of California, only the top eighth of high school graduates are eligible for admission, and in the California State Colleges, the top third. In neither system are the campuses permitted to adopt higher standards. Students meeting the standards are guaranteed admission to the respective systems, although not necessarily to the campus of their first choice.

The method of selection in the third system with uniform policies—the City University of New York—was substantially different in 1969. (We do not discuss here the open-admissions policy which was adopted in 1970.) A single universitywide procedure was used for evaluating scholastic criteria for selection. Students were assigned to the campus of their choice in rank order of high school scholastic performance, up to the agreed-upon capacity of the campus. An applicant might be admitted to one campus and not to another, based strictly on academic criteria.

These three systems, in which admissions were both selective and a subject of universitywide policy, are the only ones in which the expression *uniform admissions standards* has reality, but uniformity carries a price. These multicampus universities *as systems* have the same problems of many highly selective individual campuses in defending their selectivity, particularly as they are large public institutions. The defense of high selectivity is increasingly complicated by growing concern that admissions criteria are not entirely free of discriminatory characteristics. The interest of these systems in uniform standards of selection is, in part, the result of the historical need for a common and selective response by all campuses. By contrast, in the six systems where the campuses have local autonomy over admissions standards, selectivity has not yet been faced as a matter of *universitywide* policy.

The experience of the nine universities permits a generalization: Most of the six multicampus systems in which admissions policy is not yet a systemwide issue will soon find themselves in the same position as the other three. The dynamics of rising enrollments, budgetary stringency, and social conflict over admissions criteria guarantee that campus authority will be brought under increasing universitywide review, if not control. The lesson of the six systems, however, is that uniform admissions standards are not, and perhaps should not be, an essential characteristic of the multicampus university. Whatever solution there may be to the issue of equal access to higher education, there is no reason to suppose that the solution must be identical for all campuses of a multicampus system. Moreover, there is every reason to believe that diversity among the campuses is desirable and should be encouraged.

Admissions Policy: Allocation of Authority

In many areas of university governance, the relative weight of campus as opposed to system influence on specific decisions is fairly clear. This is not true for admissions. In each multicampus university, the governing board is the ultimate formal authority, but it is influenced by the coordinating agency from the outside and by campus and system faculty and administration on the inside. Generally, where admissions criteria are uniform within a system, the influence of the coordinating agency or of other statewide considerations predominates. In one system, indeed, general qualification criteria are statutory. On the other hand, in all but the three systems which enforce uniform selection policies, campus faculty set or strongly influence selection criteria, often at the department or school level. The distinction between eligibility and actual acceptance complicates analysis. In most instances, further complexity results from the combination of broad inclusiveness for qualification and the rather narrow range within which the standards for selection vary across both campuses and systems.

Two examples illustrate the difficulty of allocating authority with respect to admission. In one system, standards for selection are described as being set locally "by the campuses." However, by "mutual agreement" of the campus executives, all standards are identical! In another system, such standards are described both in writing and in an interview as attributable to a faculty decision sometime in the remote past. In neither situation does the ultimate authority of the governing board have explicit recognition. Yet in 1970, both governing boards became very active indeed in making quite specific changes in existing policies. It is no surprise that these specific policies concerned disadvantaged students in one instance and student disorder in the other. Whoever else had set preexisting policy, the governing boards clearly wanted a voice in current and controversial questions.

In California, the locus of decisions concerning admissions policy is relatively clear. As noted, the "top" one-eighth of high school graduates (measured on an index of scholastic performance) are eligible to attend the University and the "top" one-third, the State Colleges, resulting from action by the respective boards pursuant to a statewide statutory master plan. The two systems exhaust the field of public four-year higher education. The two systems treat standards concerning selection differently. In one, the policy is operational in terms of specific courses and credits, and the weighting of them has been expressly delegated to the faculty; in the other system, the implementation of the policy is an administrative matter.

Of the other seven systems, only one has centrally and administratively established uniform admissions standards. In the other six, campus faculty are the predominant influence. And in all systems, faculty establish criteria at the department and school level for prospective majors that cut across (and sometimes undercut) system and campus policies. Faculty participation in admissions policy at a systemwide level is the exception, a natural result of the relative absence of multicampus involvement with admissions policy. In only two cases are there universitywide faculty groups concerned solely with admissions policies. Admissions officers are formally part of one group but not the other.

The very real part which the faculty universally plays in decisions concerning admissions—particularly decisions on the scholastic requirements for acceptance at a particular campus—is subject to two qualifications. First, the range of variation in the decisions is relatively narrow: the continuity of secondary and higher education, the public status of the systems, and traditional academic conservatism are barriers to broad variations. Secondly, broader questions of educational policy—for example, the admission of non-resident students—overlap those of admissions policy, and such questions are more often determined by the governing boards, the central administration, and the coordinating agencies.

ENROLLMENT LIMITATIONS Private campuses can and do limit overall enrollment to preserve institutional character. Such limitation is not generally available for a public campus, which is usually obligated to accept as many qualified applicants as possible.

Nevertheless, in every multicampus university, problems with quotas, ceilings, or other forms of enrollment limitation independent of student scholastic qualifications are either real or in prospect. The actual and projected numbers of students in the system at each campus, and their level, discipline, residence, and marital status are essential data for producing academic plans, operating budgets, and 10-year land-use projections.

Vocabulary varies considerably, but here we distinguish between three overlapping concepts of enrollment limitation. *Capacity* generally means a limitation based solely or primarily on fiscal or physical bases rather than on educational policy. In contrast, an enrollment *ceiling* is an ultimate and permanent limitation on campus growth, usually based on educational criteria. A *quota* is either an interim or a permanent limitation resulting from planned growth or specific policies—for example, the ratio of upper- to lower-division students at a campus. All three limitations impose broad constraints on admissions policies of the multicampus universities.

Capacity Capacity seems the least influential, because it is usually a projection from existing admissions practices. The complex interrelationship of admissions criteria and capacity is illustrated, however, by the two sides of an argument in one state. In grossly simplified form, the coordinating agency accused the multicampus university of moving away from a more or less "populist" orientation to an "elitist" stance. The university replied that it wanted to accept all qualified students, but that it was becoming highly selective as a necessary result of the budgetary actions and selection policies of the coordinating agency itself. The agency had previously refused approval of sufficient student housing for all qualified applicants and had suggested scholastic criteria for selection among those qualified.

Quotas and Ceilings

Quotas and ceilings are narrower constraints, as a rule, and their implications for admissions policies are relatively direct. The infrequency with which they were encountered reflects the generally open admissions stance of most systems. This infrequency has implications beyond the admissions area, however. In the absence of quotas or ceilings, hard questions of educational policy can remain dormant—for example, the division of limited space and other resources between the social and the physical sciences. Major issues of academic planning, of admissions standards, and of size and type of enrollment are not easy to separate.

External Limitations

Although the budgetary authority of governors and legislatures is always the ultimate determinant of the capacity of a campus to accept qualified applicants, it is difficult to trace the exercise of this authority to specific numerical limitations and to admissions policies. The chapter on budgeting has outlined the complexity of budget formulas and the distinction in the use of these between acquisition of funds and allocation among the campuses. Percentage quotas such as those on nonresident students or graduate students are found in a number of states and are often the result of action of coordinating agencies. The extent to which coordinating agencies act unilaterally, however, is not clear.

No multicampus university is subject to an overall ceiling on its *total* enrollment, but in one state the coordinating agency set limitations for *campuses,* both as ultimate ceilings and as quotas for interim growth. The multicampus central staff learned of the agency's proposed limitations only after its campuses had been directly contacted for their plans. The university immediately sought legislation allowing it to set its own limitations. This attempt was unsuccessful in 1969, but the issue lacked urgency because the coordinating agency's limitations were not immediately applicable. Legislative confirmation or rejection of the agency's action awaited the time when the limitations were nearer at hand. This was the only example of enrollment ceilings being set for campuses by an agency other than the multicampus university itself. The protest that accompanied the initiation of the proposal and the subsequent attempt to overthrow the limitations in the legislature would undoubtedly accompany similar attempts in other states. The implications of enrollment ceilings for the budget, for admissions policies, and for academic planning are so great that no multicampus university can easily abdicate authority over them.

Internal Limitations Enrollment limitations are more likely to be set for campuses by the multicampus universities themselves than by outside agencies. However, such limitations have been set for all or some campuses by only three systems, although limits for a specific school or department may be set or monitored by the central administration. Medical education is an obvious example, but architecture, astronomy, and engineering are others. With the possible exception of issues surrounding admission of students who are "unqualified" by traditional scholastic standards, this type of limitation *by discipline within campuses* seems the most portentous of future controversy.

For example, a 1969 policy statement by one system executive spoke of a future with little resemblance to the past:

Each campus will establish enrollment quotas for new freshmen and for new advanced standing students, where necessary by category or discipline appropriate to the campus. The enrollment quotas will be subject to review and approval by the . . . [system executive]. Based upon the enrollment quotas a determination will be made of the number of applications by level and by category which will be required to fulfill the enrollment quotas.

In addition, the policy statement proposed uniform application forms, uniform dates for receipt of them, and redirection of applicants when quotas were exceeded. It was well understood that quotas or ceilings for one campus had implications for the others in the system, as well as for the internal affairs of the campus itself. Coordinating the academic programs of the several campuses required that the central administration be concerned with the *internal* distribution of students on each.

The possibility that systems might tell each campus how many prospective English majors it could enroll should not be our parting speculation. Numerical enrollment limitations by campus or within campuses, whether set by the coordinating agency or by the system, are clearly an exception rather than the rule. The example above probably does not evidence a trend for the immediate future. Rather, such precise quotas seem to confirm broader trends of overall state and federal fiscal policy, of possible pressures of program budgeting, and of a slowdown in the number of campuses awarding doctorates. Something will have to give as these forces converge. The most likely candidate for change is the traditional freedom of a campus to enroll any number of students in any number of disciplines.

Specific Internal Quotas
Numerical enrollment limitations for campuses are blunt instruments for governance, but ones which can be sharpened if necessary to reach into the campuses. They had been so sharpened in one instance, as evidenced by the policy statement quoted above in aid of a universitywide limit on overall enrollment. More often, however, quotas and ratios have purposes other than simple numerical limitations, and the types and nature of these are virtually unlimited.

Lower-division/upper-division ratios
In three multicampus universities, a policy to encourage the growth of two-year campuses has taken the form of setting ratios for lower- and upper-division students at the four-year campuses—for example, campuses are to plan for 40 percent lower-division and 60 percent upper-division students. Controlling and increasing the ratio of upper- to lower-division students seems a reasonable and workable method of encouraging and accommodating two-year campuses. In one system, the experience is too recent to assess. In the other two, however, success has been differentially related to the views of prospective transfer students as to the academic difficulty of the systems. The reputedly "harder" system has found it difficult to attract enough transfer students to raise its proportion of upper-division enrollment.

Two points may be made with respect to such ratios. First, the specific percentages are designed primarily to encourage two-year campus growth without much thought to their implications for the system's campuses. Does it make any difference that there are half again as many upper-division students on a campus? Will the answer be the same for a university campus as for a college campus? Second, and more pertinent to this study, a state with a multicampus university seems in a better position to implement such ratios than one in which all campuses have separate governing boards. A multicampus system has the advantage of options to meet an overall ratio, operating a particular campus near two-year campuses being an obvious example. In one system, however, a campus was unilaterally setting quotas for transfer students from specific two-year campuses in its area, quotas which had implications for the other campuses of the system but of which the system itself was unaware.

Undergraduate/graduate ratios

Although three systems use enrollment ratios to attain a desired mix of students at the undergraduate level, only two were, in 1970, beginning to consider similar control over a perhaps more important ratio: that of graduate to undergraduate enrollment. One system is concerned that if graduate enrollment exceeds 40 percent at the major campus, it will lose its traditional character as an undergraduate center. In the other system, the proposed limitation is a response to dilution of previously accepted budget formulas which have allowed—even encouraged—growth of graduate education. For this system, the state's fiscal retrenchment has meant a hard choice between limiting graduate students or denying admission to qualified freshman applicants.

Limitation of graduate admissions has greater implications for the multicampus university than restrictions on undergraduate enrollment. In theory, at least, most undergraduates can find a satisfactory place at other campuses within the system, but graduate programs—particularly the better ones—are likely to be one of a kind. Indeed, the best programs are often unique within the state itself, and the impact of a limitation on admission to them will reach well beyond multicampus boundaries.

Nonresident students

A third and currently controversial quota concerns out-of-state students. Of the seven states in the study, two "export" a substantial number of students and five are substantial "importers."[1] Three systems enforce quotas restricting enrollment of out-of-state students.

The City University of New York applies such a restriction uniformly across its campuses, denying admission to all out-of-city undergraduates. The desirability of admitting *some* nonresident undergraduates to *some* campuses is evidenced by the system's long-range plan. The blanket restriction is an example of the cost of keeping peace within the multicampus family.

[1] Fall 1963 data from U.S. Office of Education (1968, table 85, p. 71).

In a second system, quotas on out-of-state enrollment were lowered on each campus, separately but uniformly, in three steps: initially by the multicampus university itself, then by the coordinating agency, and finally by the university again. Each step found primary and explicit justification in the alleged cost to the state of educating another state's youth. The alternative of a quota on the *system* as a whole instead of one on each *campus* had not been considered. If out-of-state students were all alike and would reshuffle themselves within a state, uniform campus quotas would promote a desirable cosmopolitanism—a conceded secondary goal. But these students were not all alike; they were of at least two distinct kinds: those from distant states interested only in the major campus of the multicampus university; those from just across the state line interested only in the nearest campus. We were told that the limitation as imposed by the coordinating agency was definitely intended as a restriction on the major campus of the system. The impact reached much farther than the intent, however, emptying dormitories on those campuses in and out of the system located along the state boundaries.

The difficulty of locating influence in the multicampus context is well illustrated by the reduction of the nonresident quota in this system. The governing board's minutes fail to indicate whether the reduction was taken to forestall more drastic limitations by the legislature, to anticipate similar although perhaps less drastic measures by the coordinating agency, or simply on the initiative of the board itself. Although financial considerations were offered as a reason for the quota, it was also seen as a possible remedy for student disorder. The issue provides a surprising footnote to the study. Several local but disorderly students were suspended from the major campus of this system. Thereafter they were admitted to another multicampus university in another state. They remained disorderly, and their new campus was subjected to criticism for admission of out-of-state students!

STUDENT
MOBILITY AND
TRANSFER

If students admitted as freshmen would remain on the same campus until they graduated, admissions officers would have fewer problems, and the following comments would be unnecessary. However, students do move about. Many transfer from a two-year to a college or university campus to continue their education. Others shift among all types of campuses to seek particular academic programs. Some just move. A multicampus system differs from other academic organizations because the student not only has a choice among campuses at the time he first becomes a student, but his options may remain open even after he has made his choice.

Articulation with Two-year Campuses Of the various problems of institutional identity in higher education, none seem as pervasive as that of the two-year colleges. Our interest here is in that part of the problem relating to articulation of students from two-year colleges to the campuses of the multi-campus universities. Five of the nine systems in the study are without governing authority over any kind of two-year college. The campus of a sixth administers a two-year technical program, but the system itself does not claim authority over it. For these six multi-campus universities, transfers from two-year colleges are entirely from outside the system.

The University of Wisconsin governs several campuses which offer lower-division work closely resembling the offerings of the system's major campus at Madison, and designed to permit entry to it. These lower-division centers offer only academic as opposed to terminal vocational-technical programs. For Wisconsin, transfer students come from within the system as well as from campuses outside of it. The two systems in New York have substantial supervisory authority over two-year community college campuses with both a transfer and terminal orientation. In these two multi-campus universities, the transfer of students is primarily an internal matter.

However, little difference is apparent in the problems of articulation at the multicampus universities for which transfer is always an external matter and those for which it is essentially an internal one. In the latter, despite substantial agreement on the theoretical advantages of a single central administration over both two-year and four-year campuses, the results are not impressive. An almost universal problem is seen in *both* types of systems: The establishment of upper-division requirements by faculty at department or school level often prevents a transfer student from acceptance in a major even though eligible for transfer under general system guidelines. The problem exists in equal measure, whether or not the two-year campuses are part of a university system.[2]

[2] The University of Wisconsin utilizes the same standards of eligibility for transfer from its own lower-division campuses as for transfer from outside two-year campuses. However, courses, credits, and grades from the campuses within the system—designed to be identical to those of the main campus—are not subject to reevaluation at the time of transfer, unlike those obtained elsewhere.

In all nine systems, the primary vehicle for articulation is the close relationship between specific campuses of the system and those two-year campuses located near them. In all, such campuses have locally agreed upon useful lists of requirements for transfer, and such campus-to-campus agreements appear to be the only working basis for articulation in at least two states. Articulation does not appear to be a major problem anywhere, but this seems less attributable to the multicampus structure than to local campus activity.

Despite predominantly local solutions to articulation, some difficulties continue. In one instance, for example, long-standing universitywide policy prohibited the transfer of students who had completed two-year vocational-technical programs into a campus upper-division program. One campus proposed to breach this policy by offering, in substance, general education in the upper division to students who had missed it in their two-year program. The proposal met resistance from the other campuses. In another multicampus system, on the other hand, where such universitywide policy did not exist, an almost identical proposal was meeting with praise.

Although one statewide association of all public campuses has constructed a schedule of courses "readily transferable," the remaining states and multicampus universities are just establishing similar articulation standards. It is not clear how or whether these will work; there is general agreement only that the problems will not be easily solved outside the context of specific neighboring campuses.

Redirection Redirection describes a formal process for shifting an applicant from one campus to another within a multicampus university because of enrollment quotas or ceilings. Institution of formal procedures for redirection has not been given serious consideration in the past for at least two reasons, in addition to a general absence of enrollment restrictions.

First, redirection assumes that campuses within the multicampus university are reasonably alike. This is not generally the case. In most multicampus universities, the campuses are so distinct that students seeking admission at one are not generally interested in another. An extreme example is the University of Illinois with only three campuses: one rural and almost entirely residential; another urban without any residential facilities; the third a medical school.

In the other systems, campus differences arc almost as substantial, even though often not deliberately planned.

Second, redirection assumes that students are willing and able to be redirected. However, regardless of similarity of campuses, a student with a part-time job and family in St. Louis is not likely to move with alacrity to Kansas City. And the distance between Los Angeles and Berkeley is measured in more than miles for most Californians.

While redirection has not been of pressing importance in the past, it may well become so in the future. Campuses will remain academically distinctive, perhaps becoming more so at the graduate and even the upper-division levels. However, for an entering freshman, as new and developing campuses come of age, all campuses in a system may look more alike in 1975 than they did in 1965. Finally, the growth of higher education will level off—if not in overall enrollment, then surely in the number of campuses—and ceilings on campus enrollment will be imposed. As these events occur, if they do, the need for more formal arrangements for redirection will grow.

But in 1970 only the University of California had experience with undergraduate redirection procedures which did not involve selection by scholastic qualifications: if a student met universitywide requirements, a campus could not require higher standards for selection. Initially, redirection procedures were on a strictly voluntary basis. Applicants to campuses nearing an enrollment limitation were offered an opportunity to reconsider the hierarchy of campus choices which they had set forth on their applications. The most prestigious campuses doubted that *their* applicants would voluntarily go elsewhere, but many did. The voluntary redirection procedure was more successful than had been anticipated, but as enrollment grew it did not suffice. Redirection by the administrative process then was invoked. This meant that a qualified applicant, although assured of admission to the university, might have his application transferred to a campus of alternate preference.

At present, each campus of the University of California is given a quota of the number of applications which it must accept and retain, utilizing the universitywide standards as to high school grades and the like. If a campus receives more than the stipulated number of applications, it gives attention to special hardship cases and reviews applications in the light of majors which are already overcrowded. The student's relative academic ranking among all persons qualified is not reviewed. Excess applications are transferred to campuses of alternate preference.

The central administration considers the redirection program to be successful in that no qualified undergraduate applicant has been refused admission to the university as a whole. A faculty committee on the other hand noted that redirection is "nearly equivalent to rejection" because the majority of applicants do not register on the campuses to which they are redirected. In any event, the plan relies on a single application for admission and assures all qualified students that they will in fact be admitted to some campus of the university.

In the two New York systems at the time of the study, admissions *procedures* structured a form of redirection. In both universities, identical freshman application forms for all campuses were centrally processed. In City University, in which selection standards were uniform, the applicant's preferences for campuses, his scholastic qualifications, and the capacity of the campus were matched by computer in rank order. In the State University, in which the campuses set their own standards for selection, the individual campuses selected among applicants, but the central administration maintained a referral service for those rejected. In each instance, the procedure was substantially a referral of applicants rejected because of selective admissions requirements rather than because of capacity only.

Permanent Transfer within the System Attitudes about transfer of students between campuses of a multicampus university vary with the institution with which the particular speaker identifies. Identification with the larger multicampus university, as in the words of a dean of a professional school, means a favorable attitude toward such transfers:

> . . . Here is an area, of course, where there must be strong universitywide rules; otherwise, the university could be balkanized. . . . I think we too readily forget the interests of the students and their families and of the larger community as a whole. A workable multicampus . . . [university] . . . must make transfers between campus[es] as fluid as possible. . . . If it is a true system, there must be the ability for adjustment and movement between its parts, especially on the part of students.

An administrator more closely identified with a campus was of a contrary view:

. . . I don't think that the concept of many transfers for particular students is a good one. There is a continuity in academic work, and the interests of students are not promoted by multiple transfers. For almost all instructional and research purposes each campus needs to be an independent unit. . . .

Unlike some opposing views in academe, those above do not rise to the level of battle cries for rallying major faculty or administrative forces. Within the multicampus universities, transfers between campuses are too infrequent to create a serious problem; most faculty and administrators simply have not given the problem much, if any, thought as an issue of *educational* policy.

As with redirection, however, and for the same reasons, questions about intercampus transfers will probably be asked more often in the future. Growth in overall enrollment will continue, but growth in the number of campuses will not. Disciplines will continue to subdivide, and fewer specific professional and graduate courses will be available on more than one campus. In order to achieve their academic objectives, enrollment quotas may require more and more students to transfer from the campus to which they were originally admitted. Despite the current infrequency of intra-system transfers, those practices which do exist may be precedents for the future.

Policies or procedures concerning permanent transfer of a student from one campus to another are found in at least three of the nine multicampus universities. Such transfers undoubtedly exist in all, but they are not encouraged. Hope was universally expressed that a student's work at one campus would be given "full faith and credit" at another, but this is not always the case. That such credit should be given and the reasons for it were well stated by President Frank P. Graham (1964, p. 87) of the University of North Carolina, who first faced problems of a multicampus university in 1931:

Students at Chapel Hill, who, after taking the courses in the general college, find that they wish to concentrate on agriculture, forestry, textiles, engineering or architecture, could, with full credit, transfer from Chapel Hill to Raleigh. Likewise, students who, after two years in the two-year basic division or the general college at State College, wished to concentrate on the liberal arts, business administration, pharmacy, journalism, social work, etc., could transfer to the University at Chapel Hill with full credit.

The critical words in the excerpt are "after two years." Graham described what many multicampus administrators consider desirable: A student moves from the general education of the lower division of one campus to the specialized upper division of another. A change of campus is not just an artifact of organization, but part of the student's educational development. If this type of transfer takes place with any frequency in the multicampus universities, it was not brought to our attention. Indeed, a more common attitude is that campuses would rather admit transfer students from other institutions than from a sibling campus of their own university. If a particular campus is not selected by the student initially, then his education is considered his own problem, despite the fact that initial selection is probably made on the basis of geographic or economic criteria, rather than for academic reasons.

In theory, multicampus universities are well designed to encourage educational experimentation, and our informants almost universally repeated or confirmed this suggestion. Yet as a matter of operating admissions and transfer procedures, very little thought has been given to the belief of one campus executive that "the campuses within the system ought to be particularly hospitable to innovations and experimentation in such matters as organization of courses and grades. Thus, for example, we should not in our admissions policy inhibit the efforts of . . . [a new campus] . . . to innovate."

Temporary Transfer within the System

Study at a sibling campus by a student who remains formally enrolled at his own campus in the multicampus university is another aspect of student mobility. If the major difficulties of permanent transfer are lacking, opinions are still divided. In the words of one faculty leader, "Perhaps the least utilized advantage of our multicampus system is the student's temporary transfer to a second campus, a practice which would involve no major academic policy matter." The advantage is perhaps not utilized because it has been presented to only a few students. It would not be encouraged by one administrator: "I think also that the . . . [belief] . . . that a student can be instructed simultaneously at two campuses is impractical with rare exceptions. Too much time is wasted in transit to make the system work. . . ."

Although nowhere articulated, part of the apparent disagreement might disappear if a clear distinction were made between temporary transfer for a term or two and the simultaneous enrollment in courses on two campuses. The latter, for example, would not be seriously inhibited by distance in the City University of New York. Its organizationally and geographically separate graduate center is another campus, in effect, and education at more than one campus is certainly facilitated by the unique location of all campuses within one city with a subway system.

Temporary transfer of students is a subject of more interest and activity than permanent transfer. Several examples exist. In one multicampus university, a rural campus has been able to take advantage of the location and resources of the system's urban campus to develop joint programs in both social welfare and education. In another, and solely for the purpose of several specific courses, students are cross-registered under a complex scheme worked out by the administrators at the participating campuses, within the same system and the same city. The universitywide administration had not been involved in implementing this arangement, but compatibility of procedures within a single system was of material help.

Similarly, a medical campus and a general campus of still a third system are cooperating in specialized biomedical courses, and have found that common university membership facilitated discussion, planning, and operation. General and medical campuses also have cooperated in an innovative program designed for the early identification of prospective medical students. Financed by the medical campuses, the program is leading to integration of curricular offerings and illustrates a benefit of the multicampus structure: administrative unity can lead to substantial curricular innovation at geographically isolated campuses.

The multicampus structure is hardly a necessary condition for transfers between campuses, and examples of such transfers between independent campuses, public and private, were repeatedly described. On the other hand, multicampus status assuredly facilitates temporary transfers. A single governing structure, a common fiscal context, and relatively common admissions policies eliminate many substantive and procedural barriers to student mobility.

Geography as an almost insuperable obstacle to simultaneous enrollment in courses on more than one campus disappears when courses are available by television or telephone. These are utilized for credit work in at least two multicampus universities. In one, a closed circuit television network brings uniquely qualified science faculty at one campus to the others. In the other, telephone lines permit courses given at a four-year campus to be taken on a two-year one. Technology substitutes faculty mobility for student mobility.

Mobility of students to take particular courses will continue to be closely related to geography. On the other hand, mobility to permit a term or two at another campus is a concept often suggested but not, to our knowledge, widely implemented. If a student can spend a "junior year abroad," arrangements should assuredly be readily available to permit his attendance for a single term on another campus in the same system. The latter type of arrangement deserves careful attention. It may well suggest solutions that will allow all students to make maximum use of the unique but scattered resources of a multicampus university, solutions that are not presently apparent.

ADMINIS-TRATION

Admissions *procedures,* like admissions *policies,* can be uniform on all campuses or substantially different. Centralized admissions policies and centralized procedures are related, but not on a one-to-one basis. The continuum of procedures includes two quite centralized systems at one extreme, three in which the campuses do much as they please at the other, with the remaining four systems located somewhere in the middle.

The two most centralized multicampus universities not only require the use of identical application forms for all campuses but also centrally process them. In one, substantive admissions decisions are made centrally, but in the other, by the campuses.

The three universities at the other extreme exercise very little central control over the practices and procedures of the campuses. In none of the three is it clear just how or whether the central administration obtains a flow of uniform admissions data. As a matter of fact, doubt about the compatibility of such information was explicitly raised in one system.

The remaining four universities in the middle of the continuum all require certain types of information to be gathered by the campuses on application forms. In two, identical application forms are used, but the forms are processed at each campus. In the other two, the campuses are free to develop their own application forms, but the central administration specifies particular questions. In one instance, the required questions are incorporated into the locally developed application form in a fashion to facilitate machine processing.

Excepting the implications for redirection of applicants referred to earlier, organization of admissions procedures does not appear to have any notable implications for the governance of a multicampus university. This is a logical outgrowth of separation of policy and administration in the admissions field, but it is also related to characteristics of the administrators of admissions and their technical tools.

Admissions and Automatic Data Processing

There is only occasional systemwide use of advanced technology in the admissions area. Automatic data processing is costly, and its absence seems attributable to the low priority of admissions matters within the internal budgets. Federal funds for data processing equipment for research activities are far easier to obtain than state funds for administrative purposes, and admissions often has low priority on the administrative scale. In one or two instances, a small campus has automated its admissions and registration procedures, while the large major campus is still engaged in old-fashioned hand processing. It costs less at the smaller campus, but this cost factor means that available technology is being put to use where it is needed least.

Economy of scale in data collection and processing would seem an obvious basis for establishing a centralized admissions procedure. In one multicampus system, in addition, highly centralized procedures have been established less because of cost considerations than because of the value of timely information to the central administration. As noted earlier, admissions data have implications for many areas of academic administration. Centralization and the automatic data processing which seem concomitant could provide this information on a current basis to permit comparisons among campuses.

If centralized processing made greater information available at the multicampus level, it meant an information loss at the campus in one instance. Two multicampus universities which required identical application forms took opposite positions on the gathering of supplemental information by the campuses. In one, because of centralization, a campus had been required to abandon collection of information of particular interest to it. In the other, however, the gathering of such supplemental data was encouraged.

The Administrators

With perhaps one exception, in no system does admissions have the *full-time* attention of a *senior* staff officer. If any member of the central staff has admissions as a full-time concern, he is an administrator well below "cabinet" rank. In direct contrast, therefore, to other campus administrators concerned with physical or academic planning, the budget, or other management areas, campus admissions officers, in common with other campus administrators of student affairs, rarely have a system counterpart who is *both* prestigious within the central staff and primarily interested in their particular problems.

In 1970, an aide to the chief executive in one system handled most admissions problems in addition to his other duties. He had assumed the admissions tasks when an all-university dean of students retired and the vacancy was left unfilled. On at least one campus, the campus administrators were interested in seeing the former all-university position restored. In another system, campus student affairs and admissions officers were seriously concerned with the lack of prestige or status on the part of their central administrative counterparts. A long-time central administrator diagnosed this type of campus complaint as an "autonomy-dependence" syndrome—a desire on the part of the campus administrators for complete independence, but also for the multicampus administration to be actively concerned with how this independence was being used. This syndrome was not found in two multicampus universities in which the campus admissions officers had formed strong, active universitywide councils or committees. The peer group support was sufficient to cure the syndrome for the campus admissions officers. It is, however, aggravated by the lack of *formal*, high-level concern or responsibility for the overall administration of student affairs, of which admissions is an important part.

Except for these two systems, periodic meetings of admissions officers held in most of the other universities have few implications for governance either at the campus or the multicampus level. In one of the two excepted systems, the admissions officers had, on their own initiative, negotiated and were proposing policies for articulation with two-year campuses. In the other, a statement by the system executive at a universitywide admissions meeting had been interpreted as a trial balloon hinting at central allocation of students to the campuses. The admissions officers as a group and individually through their campus executives brought pressure to see that the balloon was punctured.

12. External Relations

This chapter concerns the efforts of the multicampus university to relate to three important publics. The public relations officer represents it to the world at large. The lobbyist represents it to a more limited but far more critical audience. Alumni officers have their own public.[1] In defending the good name of the multicampus system or placing it before their particular publics, these three specialists overlap, sometimes to the point of confusion. The interest here is less in their external activities, however, than in their internal organization.

The word external might suggest that these administrators are the only ones engaged in reaching the public. Nothing, of course, is further from the truth. Much activity of the central and campus administrations, the faculty, and the students falls under the label of external relations. More than one of the nine multicampus universities has characterized its boundaries as those of the state. Although these statements long preceded current interest in the boundaries between organizational systems, the earlier rhetoric is quite appropriate in modern usage.

More or less stable interrelationships among the most obvious components of a multicampus system—its campuses and central administration—define a structure which has "a kind of 'whole' with some degree of continuity and boundary" (Buckley, 1967,

---

[1] One long-time observer of national alumni activities commented as follows on this phraseology: "I hope you realize you are walking into a philosophical catfight between alumni officers and public information directors. Alumni officers don't regard alumni as 'external publics' but rather as much a part of the internal universities as students and faculties; public information directors and most development officers regard them as 'the institution's predominantly supportive converts in the ranks of the external masses.' In any case, alumni officers usually prefer *not* to talk about alumni as *their* public, though a few will acknowledge them to be a part of the public of the institution."

p. 41). For example, *within* a multicampus university, numerous interactions relate to academic degree programs, and with few exceptions, major decisions regarding these are made *within* the organization. However, the university must go beyond its organization chart and outside any student-faculty-administrative interaction to effect an interchange with someone or something "outside" the system, for example, when honorary degrees are considered. Whether granted to a politician for statesmanship or a rich benefactor for philanthropy, an honorary degree generates considerable publicity. Such boundary situations become exceedingly complex for the multicampus university. The authority to award honorary degrees is in the governing board, but each of the campuses has its own alumni and undoubtedly a local statesman it would like to honor. Only a central authority can resolve the issue, and the board or system executive does so.

The more open the system (the more interchanges with the environment), the more likely that the distinction between the organization and its environment is arbitrary and dependent on the purpose of the observer. Every modern university is clearly an "open system"; a multicampus university is even more so because of the scattered location of interrelated components. Organizational boundaries are not easy to locate. Most officers in the central administration deal regularly and frequently with some portion of the system's public. Those staff members of concern here, however, all share broad, direct, and explicit concern for the *general* representation of the system. Each attempts to control or regulate a portion of the flow of information across the organizational boundary.

The general external relations activities of the university are marked by another common element. The public relations and governmental relations officers always (but the alumni officers less often) have as their primary functions those which are also the actual (if not ideal) primary and personal functions of the system executive.

The system executive may delegate, formally and officially, specific shares of his authority to other system administrators. The officer responsible for physical construction, business management, or academic affairs can operate relatively free from concern that his decisions personally involve the system executive. They frequently speak for themselves. Their advice to the system executive is based on recognized technical qualifications and accepted on that basis. The system executive may be similarly well qualified in a particular field and act as his own "secretary of state" with respect to it. Internally, campus administrators and faculty can accept the legitimacy of delegated operating authority while recognizing the system executive's ultimate personal responsibility. But the situation is quite different with respect to external relations. Here, the system executive is not free to delegate in any comparable manner. While he may seek staff assistance of the highest quality, he must—almost by definition—be *the* expert on governmental and public relations.

THE ROLE OF THE MULTI-CAMPUS UNIVERSITY Functions of public relations officers, governmental relations staff, and alumni representatives overlap within both system and campus administrations. They also overlap between these levels, and at each are very much the personal concern of the system and campus executives. In this context, discussion of possible advantages and disadvantages of the multicampus university cannot be separated easily from discussion of the campus and system executive themselves. For example, a university system can—in theory—present a more comprehensive, coordinated account of the programs and problems of its campuses to both political and public audiences than would result from the independent pronouncements of a number of autonomous universities. In its ability to respond to requests for information or service from news media or the state, the system can provide a single point of inquiry and one that reaches greater resources. Uncertainty and confusion as to an "official" position of the university can be relieved, with a resulting gain in public understanding. As a single voice, the system can quell internal disputes and order priorities before it speaks, or so it should be.

But, more than in other areas of system administration, the realization of these potential advantages of the multicampus structure is within the province of the system executive himself. Whether the system can speak with a single voice depends significantly on his personal relationships with the campus executives. The "educational action" is at the campuses, and centralizing the flow of information to any extent at all runs a serious risk: for both media representatives and state legislators, the system can mean an undesirable filtering and delay of news and can create uncertainty —unknown in a single-campus context—over who *really* "speaks for the university." Attempts to coordinate or control campus informational activity can—potentially—undermine the campus executive's confidence in his local public relations staff. Far more critically, if carried to an extreme, such attempts can undercut the authority of the campus executive for whom *external* relations are a critical element of *internal* leadership. The physical and organizational distances between system and campus complicate most administrative areas, but none as much as external relations. Routine administrative solutions—such as explicit, formal allocations of authority—are only a partial answer.

There is more to it than this, of course. The multicampus university should have superior technical and professional resources, and these are not directly tied to personal leadership styles. On the face of it, the system should be able to mount television or radio programs of greater scope and variety than a single campus, to respond to legislative inquiries on policy issues with a range of expertise not otherwise available, and to mobilize the expanded alumni of a multicampus system. These are not insignificant benefits, and a measure of success of the multicampus university is the extent to which it realizes this potential.

PUBLIC RELATIONS Public relations in the context of higher education can be defined in several ways. Here, the term is used primarily to describe the functions of administrators responsible for contacts with the news media. The concentration is admittedly narrow, for this is not all that either campus or systemwide officers do in this area. But it is a central concern in every instance, and the one on which attention is focused here.

Two general aspects of public relations provide a backdrop. First, formal public relations of a system are inhibited by its public character. Compared to either industry or private higher education, obvious differences are present—the lack of quantifiable exchange features, for one. For example, several hundred dollars spent for publicity at the opening of a new building may buy good will, but they do not—in any measurable quantity—produce more students, better students, or more money from the legislature. Moreover, dollars spent for publicity are at the expense of library acquisitions, support of needy students, or whatever a potential critic's favorite educational cause might be. A university has no tax deductions, and money spent on publicity is real money. A less tangible inhibition related to public status attaches to the publicity function itself. Internally or externally, some tools and methods, stock in trade of Madison Avenue, are out of the question for a public university, and probably for private ones as well.

Secondly, in contrast to private businesses and most public organizations, a university has such a multiplicity of goals that their interpretation is very difficult. The difficulty is not just theoretical: diverse, indeed conflicting, goals are reflected in wide ranges of activity and in the contrasting and often competitive views of governing boards, system and campus executives, and—increasingly—organized faculty and student groups. Furthermore, there is little agreement on the priorities of the diverse goals and activity. Public relations officers are at the outpost line when inevitable disputes arise. They are asked to clarify the intangible, and with a straight face.

Public relations does not generally occupy a particularly lofty position in the hierarchy of the universitywide administration. In only one system does a "cabinet officer" have public relations as an exclusive responsibility. No pattern exists in the variations found in other systems. In one, the task is handled by an aide to the system executive; in another, by a cabinet-level officer with a variety of additional responsibilities, including some relating to the governing board and to students. As previously noted, he described himself as the "crisis vice-president." Generally, however, the public relations officer is titled a director, and in at least two systems seems to be explicitly excluded from meeting with the regular "high policy" committees of the central staff.

At the campus level, with one exception, administrators responsible for public relations are in a direct-line relationship to their campus executives rather than to the systemwide director, an arrangement deemed essential because of the campus executive's personal interest. (The exception is a public relations officer at the main campus who also acts as such for the system.) The line relationship between one campus executive we visited and his public relations office was only a few months old; even within the public relations staff, the implications of the new arrangement were not clear. At a campus in another system, the director had been reportedly recruited at the system rather than the campus level. At these campuses, in both systems, public relations activity—or lack of it—was suspect as "system-inspired."

Multicampus Public Relations: The Major Problem

Unquestionably, the overriding "governance" problem of the multicampus university in the public relations area is the impossibility of making explicit delegations or allocations of authority between system and campus levels. In faculty personnel matters, the campuses appoint assistant professors without approval of the central administration, but not associate professors. In this relatively simple case, at least three objective elements are present: the title itself, the probable salary range, and possible tenure implications. None of these obvious criteria, however, is of much help in assigning to the campus or the system responsibility for announcing the appointment if the particular appointee is a winner of a Nobel Prize or under indictment for leading a campus demonstration. The example is hypothetical, but the issue is not. A solution must reflect complex relationships between the governing boards and the system and campus executives and their staffs. Responsibility for public relations problems involves crucial questions of allocation of authority across all areas of governance.

Attempts have been made in most administrative areas to clarify these relationships in written policy statements. But only one multicampus university has done this for public relations activities, and the ambiguity of this formal allocation suggests, perhaps, why the practice has not been more widely adopted. Continuing with faculty appointment as an example, the procedural manual in this system provides that public announcement of the appointment of campus administrators and faculty will be made by the campus if the campus has authority to appoint, but by the system when *it* has such authority.

The problem of the indicted professor continues, however. While not much can be done about it, credit must be given for trying: "It is imperative the [system executive] be promptly advised of any significant local public or community relations problems, or of untoward events or occurrences." Thus, the campus executive and his own public relations officer must decide whether the appointment and indictment is an "untoward event." This written allocation is probably the best that can be done.

Whether formalized in writing or not, each of the nine systems has attempted to distinguish between "matters of strictly campus concern" and "subjects having policy implications for the entire system." But the softness and ambiguity of the distinction remains, with far more serious implications than the difficulty of writing administrative manuals. Recurring problems are presented for the chief executives at both system and campus levels. Each must function despite the lack of clear lines of authority, and do it publicly and on short notice. Each is involved in the need for maintenance of prestige. Who is to announce the name of a new building? Or a gift that might build one?

Public relations officers are continually confronted with this absence of firm, objective lines of authority. Not only is their problem full time, but as individuals they lack the authority and flexibility to cope with it. Policies and practices in a multicampus university can bend and stretch with the personalities of the system and the campus executives, but their respective staffs must adjust to the structure.

The problems of the public relations officers at both system and campus levels center around their ability to communicate frequently and regularly. The issue is one of size. Monthly meetings of three, four, perhaps six campus public relations officers are sensible arrangements for conveying and sharing information, and the product and activity of public relations is such that meetings of this sort seem the only effective means of coordination. Management of information is difficult; management of the managers of information borders on the impossible when their number is increased to 15 or 20. In few other areas of academic administration is it as apparent that the sheer number of campuses creates substantive problems. The implications of size were brought home quite vividly by one system public relations officer who confessed that because of size and turnover he might never individually meet all the campus public relations officers!

Universitywide coordination of campus public relations might be handled by controlling specific items of information, but such control does not reach the main issue. Nothing could or should prevent the campus executive from expressing an opinion in any situation if, in his view, one should be expressed. All that the system can do is be sure he has accurate and current information and is aware of the considered opinions of the governing board and system executive.

Although control and coordination of campus executives may very well begin and end with their appointment and dismissal, this is not true of the campus public relations officer. He is the person to whom the campus executive turns for professional advice, and despite the lack of a line relationship to the central administration, he is the usual and regular conduit for transmission of whatever universitywide rules there are governing public relations. "The rules," however, are not rules which can be writ once for all in a manual. They are shaped by a specific moment of time, a specific situation, and specific personalities. They can be conveyed, if at all, only by timely, personal conversations and discussion. Regardless of the number of campuses in the system, coordination in this area requires considerably more trust and confidence between the levels of organization than is true, for example, of accounting. Whether this trust and confidence can exist in a large multicampus system is an open question, but, we suggest, the somewhat ambiguous concept of "warm, interpersonal relationships" in administrative theory has substance as a necessary condition for effective coordination of public relations.

Other Problems and Solutions

The above difficulties aside, each of the nine multicampus universities is engaged in numerous systemwide public relations activities: universitywide programs conducted at the multicampus level, and universitywide coordination or assistance designed to spur on or rein in campus efforts.

Universitywide programs

Most, but not all, multicampus public relations administrators are responsible for general dissemination of news and information within the university itself. The many forms of such internal communication vary from a simple bulletin in one instance to a substantial, "real" newspaper with wide circulation both within and outside the campuses of the university, in another. We are not in a position to evaluate these different forms of internal communication. The impossibility of doing so is easily illustrated. During the study, we were sent several regular newsletters issued for internal use by the university systems in the study. We looked forward to receipt of one of these, the University of Illinois president's *Faculty Letter.* It was "better" or "more interesting" than the others, although we could not pinpoint the reasons for its particular distinction. Yet it was the public relations officer of this same system who was most emphatic when he stated that "some vehicle must be found to establish and maintain far better internal communications than have thus far been apparent in the experience of the university." His concern is shared by many others, most importantly, by the system executive himself. What communications device can span the gap between the central staff at system headquarters and the faculty and students at the campuses? Is there any universitywide substitute for the personal contact which is increasingly difficult to sustain without interfering with the status of the campus executive? Few, if any, of the systemwide executives are confident they know the answer. None can afford not to find a solution.

With respect to external relations, perhaps the primary responsibility of the multicampus public relations officer is an operational one—to provide services for the governing board, the system executive, and systemwide administrators. These activities distinguish him from others on the central staff who engage solely in planning or coordinating activities of the several campuses. Planning and coordination are additional and secondary duties for the public relations officer.

In virtually all systems, an additional duty of the public relations officer is the provision of news services supplementing those of the campuses. Items of "unusual significance" or "statewide importance" are reported in universitywide news releases, in addition to or in substitution for campus releases. In one university, the system pays particular attention to providing news items to the weekly newspapers throughout the state, a specialized function beyond the reach of several of the campuses. In another system, the universitywide office publishes a weekly "boiler plate" sheet of major stories which are distributed to a far wider audience than those of any single campus. However, there is little to distinguish these systemwide activities, other than their multicampus character, from those of any large university.

The production of systemwide television and radio programs varies widely in scope and attempted coverage. Extension and continuing education, public service, and some sponsored activities all blend together to obscure the specifically public relations function. Several multicampus universities own or lease operating facilities for television on a systemwide basis, but programming is typically handled by one or more of the campuses or by an all-university council or committee.

Universitywide coordination and assistance
The inherent ambiguity in defining the respective roles of the systemwide and campus public relations officers has been described. Nevertheless, every system has made an attempt—formal or informal—to maximize news coverage, on the one hand, and to avoid unnecessary duplication of activity, on the other, and in all cases to guarantee that system and campus executives will not unknowingly contradict each other. The most fruitful coordination arises

out of frequent personal contacts between responsible university-wide and campus public relations officers. This occasionally takes the more formal shape of periodic meetings of all campus public relations officers under the chairmanship of the systemwide officer.

Every system attempts to obtain (or impose) systemwide uniformity concerning certain critical "facts" about the university. These are not always without controversy. The different ways of counting enrollment and the different dates on which enrollment should be reported has created the need for firm systemwide control in more than one system.

An isolated but significant aspect of coordination and assistance occurred in one multicampus university in which senior administrative and public relations personnel from both system and campus, together with selected faculty, formed a council which met monthly to consider the university's relationships to the particular city in which a campus was located. The council was a clear recognition of a specific public relations problem greater than and different from those in a small town. It was clear that the council was an invaluable forum for bringing substantial talent together to bear on a known problem. It represented excellent use of the resources which generally only a multicampus university can muster. On the other hand, one council member suggested that it "proceed beyond generalities and suggestions to specific recommendations that could lead to action." This function of the council was less clear. It seemed to go beyond an advisory role to make a system-oriented group the operating public relations arm of one campus. It was probably satisfactory in the particular system because of the small number of campuses and extremely close-knit group of administrators. In other multicampus universities, however, campus executives balked at the "intrusion" of the system into "local" public relations.

One well-structured personnel classification scheme for public relations people at both campus and system levels evidenced the value of a multicampus administration. Other major activities with public relations overtones at the campuses had been able to pay higher salaries than the campus public relations offices. These fiefdoms, such as the medical school, the athletic department, and the school of agriculture, were ruled by deans able to quash any local complaints by the *campus* information heads. In the name of rationality and good personnel policy, however, the *system* information officer was able to tighten up his small corner of the system's somewhat loose personnel system for the benefit of "his" campus administrators, and perhaps, for the campus executives as well.

The need for expanded resources

We found little that is explicitly "multicampus" about the public relations activities of the nine systems. Our attention to the uniquely systemwide functions has left undescribed a wide range of activities at the campus level, activities typical of most large universities in the United States. It remains true, however, that — with one or two notable exceptions — public relations is not a major achievement of the multicampus university *as a system.* Some reasons for this, we have suggested, are inherent in public institutions. But much, too, is the result of the large gap between the system's public relations responsibilities and its resources. System executives and their staffs are well aware of the problem, but solutions are not in the offing. Public relations is a low priority item in fiscal plans. Legislatures do not easily accept that the multicampus universities are "selling" a vital commodity.

GOVERN-MENTAL RELATIONS: STATE AND LOCAL The chief executive of a multicampus university and the respective campus executives have a responsibility for relationships with state and local governments that belongs to them alone. To the extent that a full- or part-time staff person is assigned to work as a system "lobbyist," he acts as a personal agent of the system executive. Unlike other staff officers, he has virtually no *formally* delegated authority.

Although the authority of the system executive in this area cannot be delegated, it can be preempted, specifically by a strong board chairman. Although one former campus executive has suggested that a *permanent* board chairman might decrease the administrative burdens of the chief executive, we are not dealing with that situation here.[2] In two instances brought to our attention, strong board chairmen had taken over many functions normally belonging to the system executive. One was no longer in office in 1970, but the other remained most active. In the latter situation, the normally

[2] Inherent in this proposal is the idea, borrowing from the corporate model, that the chairman of the board be a full-time, paid official and that he be the chief executive officer of the institution. He would have primary responsibility for the financial, public relations, and legislative functions. Reporting to him would be the president, who would be the chief educational officer (Murphy, 1968).

direct line between system and campus executives had been interrupted because the board chairman, as the primary representative of the system to the state, had become involved in matters of internal university governance. The resolution of a campus faculty senate commending this chairman for expert lobbying of a salary increase was only a few months away from one from the same senate condemning his intervention in student disorder on the campus. Whether either action might have deserved a resolution or not, the system and campus administrations did not share in the credit or blame.

The Division of Labor between System and Campus

Repeatedly, campus executives reported that a major advantage of the multicampus university is the division of labor, allocating to the system executive major responsibility for governmental relationships and to the campus executives responsibility for governance at the campuses. With few exceptions, we were told that if the campus executive were to concern himself with lobbying the campus budget, it would be at the sacrifice of his academic responsibilities. Campus executives stated this viewpoint so strongly as to suggest that this essential division of labor is one of the prime assets of the multicampus university.

The division of labor is of *educational* significance for the campuses, but it is also of *administrative* significance in multicampus governance. The system executives jealously guard their access to the governors and legislatures as a measure of both prestige and status. A first act of one system executive upon assuming office was to forbid the campus executives to contact legislators directly. Administrative procedures governing political relationships by the campuses in other systems are shaped by similar, though usually less drastic, methods of maintaining multicampus leadership in the hands of the system executive.

The division of labor is not neat and orderly, however, and for quite good reasons. The difficulty of delegating the responsibilities of the system and campus executives has been noted. Governmental representation not only cannot be formally delegated by the system executive to a subordinate; neither can a campus executive surrender *his* responsibilities to the system executive. In this area, hierarchical standing between subordinate and superior simply does not exist. The campus executive's responsibility for his campus includes representation and interaction with political figures in the community in which the campus is located, and indeed throughout the state, for almost every campus is a statewide institution. Although true of any campus, it is especially crucial for a large institution of 20 or 30 thousand students, or one in a major metropolitan center. Several campus executives expressed doubts that the specific political interests of their campus were being adequately represented by the system administration.

How system and campus executives work out their overlapping areas of responsibility depends on the individuals involved. Campus executives are in a particularly difficult position: if they actively court legislators and other political figures, they are viewed with suspicion by the system executive and his staff. If their activity does not rise to the level of meriting such suspicion, however, they are accused of failing to pull their weight along with their colleagues.

A pervasive aspect of this ambiguity concerns what, for good or ill, still remains a key public and political event for many of the multicampus universities: the big football game of the year. Whose game is it, the campus's or the system's? Who is the host to legislators and other visiting dignitaries, the campus or the system executive? Who decides on the allocation of tickets and the protocol of the 40- versus the 50-yard line? The problem is confined to several of the universities with flagship campuses, with ancient and revered traditional rivalries and major athletic programs, and it abates during a losing season. But it *is* a problem, illustrative of the complex and subjective nature of external relations in a multicampus context.

Nevertheless, in the opinion of campus and system officials and from our own observations, the advantages of the multicampus system in the area of external relations clearly outweigh the disadvantages—both for the university and the society it serves. The conclusion is more obvious in governmental relations than in the broader area of public relations. There were few campuses among the nearly 20 contacted during the study which did not welcome centralization of university representation at the state political level. Although we heard several campus administrators state that "we could do better on our own," only one campus chief executive even hinted of testing the proposition. In fact, comments sometimes ran the other way, with complaints that the system had not been solid enough as a mediator between the capital and the campus.

In none of the multicampus universities did we find general satisfaction that an optimal strategy or organizational form for system-state relations had been discovered. The inherently ambiguous allocation of authority between campus and system has caused part of this lack of assurance. A second reason is the vulnerability of the university to charges that, as a public institution, it should not devote public funds to lobbying on its own behalf. As with all public institutions, perhaps, political representation must be disguised, adding another element of uncertainty to an already confused picture. Finally, and perhaps most importantly, there is an awareness that strategy and form are secondary to a network of fragile personal relationships.

The implications of this network are most evident in states with a long tradition of university-state contacts built around a flagship campus. Here, the old loyalties deriving from earlier and simpler days cannot easily be transferred to support for the larger, newer, less personal multicampus system. It is less obvious what substitute will prove as effective as older, personal relationships fade in the 1970s.

The System Executive and the Governor   In four multicampus systems in the study, the governor sits as an ex officio board member, and his formal relationship with the system executive undoubtedly influences the system's relationship with the state itself. The power of the governor to appoint board members in all but two systems also establishes patterns of university-state political contact. More subtle implications arise from the relationship of the governor and the system executive as individuals. Critical issues relating to higher education may be so deeply determined by interaction of the governor's and system executive's personalities that an exploration of the formal relationship is unproductive.

Nevertheless, frequent reference in every state to informal political relationships evidence their impact on governmental relations activities. Here again, the massive size of most systems and of their budgets give these informal relationships an importance they would not have for a single campus. Moreover, close personal relationships between a governor and, say, fourteen or fifteen individual campus executives simply are not likely to develop. For example, in one state it had been proposed that the system executive meet with the governor at luncheon once a month to discuss matters of current interest. The governor could not lunch separately with 15 individual campus executives, and a joint luncheon with all would be a formality. In a single-board state, such a meeting between the governor and the statewide board's executive officer would clearly be more than a formality. The breadth of concern — all higher education in the state — would seem so great, however, that personal relationships would be of less importance. In contrast, a multi-campus system narrows concern to a range of specific campuses or a specific segment of higher education.

The range of personal relationships between governors and system executives in the nine multicampus universities, as described to us, ran the gamut from friendship close enough to include family members and shared social life at one extreme to open animosity on the other. Such relationships obviously influence the multi-campus university's interactions with the state. It is clear that personal friendship between the two executives is beneficial to effective state-university relationships. The other side of the coin resulting from concentration of political representation in the system executive is the vulnerability of that representation to personal disagreements between the system executive and the governor.

Patterns of Governmental Relations

Here, as in public relations, there is no simple continuum from centralized to decentralized administration. Even in one state in which the budget of the system is considered by state fiscal authorities on a campus-by-campus basis, the system executive remains the primary conduit for state representation. As in public relations also, the activity at the multicampus level takes the form of system programs, on the one hand, or the coordination of campus programs, on the other.

Universitywide activity

The ability of a group of campuses to communicate with the governor and legislature through a single spokesman is close to the core of any working definition of a multicampus university. Indeed, the multicampus system has clear advantages for such communication not possessed by a single campus. Geographical diversity is an obvious political benefit. Another is the statewide arena of other interests, not only in the legislature itself but among the other pleaders and spokesmen. The concerns of modern agriculture, for example, extend beyond the school of agriculture at a single campus. Moreover, in support of his activity, the university lobbyist, whether the system executive or his deputy, can marshal campus executives, each of whom "gets along well" with several legislators.

Systems attempt to take advantage of their multicampus status in many ways. One multicampus system holds periodic informational meetings at different locations within the state. They are attended not only by legislators but also by members of the governing board. Several of these meetings are held annually, and although they are usually located at a campus, the agenda concerns the system as a whole.

Several system executives regularly entertain members of the legislature. Consistently, these are social occasions but hardly without political overtones.

In one state with a strong farm base, the officer of the central staff responsible for governmental relations holds weekly telephone conference calls with the county agricultural extension directors, advising them of matters of universitywide interest. In another system, annual conferences of the officers of the county boards advising on extension activity are held. In neither case is any explicit attempt made to obtain grassroots political help, nor is any either expected or given. On the other hand, the activity unquestionably strengthens the overall political and public image of the university.

The political implications of locally oriented, geographically dispersed two-year campuses have been discussed. Where these campuses are encompassed in a multicampus university, there has been little attempt to make use of them for purposes of governmental representation. As in the case of agricultural extension, however, the impression within the system is that two-year campuses are politically beneficial. We suggested that they may give legislators a relatively benign portion of higher education with which to identify in trying times.

Campus activity

The ways in which multicampus universities coordinate campus public relations activities are not paralleled in governmental representation. Even if there is a single universitywide officer whose subtitle includes "lobbyist," he rarely has a formal campus counterpart, although many campus executives have their local political consultants, both on and off campus. Coordination is also colored by the fact that, although the territorial responsibilities of the system executive include those of the campus executives, the functions of the latter are not subordinate. Coordination does not consist of a system executive directing the activities of his campus executives. Rather the total task requires that both have a keen perception of their interlocking responsibilities. At the University of North Carolina, this was described as "administration by fine feel rather than fiat."

Whether described as system activity or campus coordination, several universities encourage and facilitate meetings between campus executives and state legislators. These may be formal visits to the state capital, organized by the university's lobbyist, but they may also involve campus visits of local legislators and less formal social gatherings on and off campus. In one state, the executive of a campus near the capital has assumed responsibility for a large share of the university's social relations with legislators from throughout the state.

Campus location

The general statement that a campus has the primary responsibility for local political and governmental relationships fails to do justice to the variety of local constituencies with which campuses are faced.

Every multicampus university is directly concerned with the urban crisis because of a campus or campuses in a metropolitan area. The establishment of an all-university council to deal with public relations in one city has been noted. This council was equally involved with political issues in that city. Yet in another system, neither the system nor campus executives had ever met the mayor of the large city in which a campus was located.

Local representation in major cities varies, depending on the power of the mayor. In one instance, at least, where the mayor is a strong political force in both the community and the state, the system executive devotes considerable personal time and energy to his relationship with him. As a consequence, mayoral–campus executive communication is of more than passing systemwide concern. In another system, there was an aged rumor that a campus executive had been so well ensconced in local politics that efforts of the system executive to replace him had failed. State and local politics are not easily divisible, either within or without the university.

A campus in the state capital presents unusual problems for both system and campus executives and adds another dimension to the already complex pattern of governmental relationships. This is the case in five systems (excluding the case of the City University of

New York with its unique mayoral relationships). In three of these, systemwide offices are also located in the capital city. One campus executive in this situation stated that he dealt with the local problems and the system executive with those involving statewide matters. It was not easy, he confessed, to be sure where one left off and the other began.

A similar problem exists wherever a campus and the system offices are in the same community — occasional uncertainty as to who bears the responsibility to represent the university to the city, or alternatively, to whom city officials should talk in a serious dispute between the campus and the community.

GOVERN-MENTAL RELATIONS: FEDERAL Of the nine multicampus universities, only four maintain permanent offices in Washington, D.C. Each of these is funded out of overhead funds from federal grant and contract activity and exists primarily to facilitate the contract and grant activities of the several campuses. The Washington office schedules faculty and administrative visits with federal officials, attempts to coordinate the contacts of different campuses, and provides an administrative base of operations for visiting university personnel. In reverse fashion, the Washington representative is a focus of inquiry from federal officials as to which person or department should be contacted within the university with respect to a particular program or bill. Contact with national higher education associations is a parallel responsibility. The ability to support such activities is a clear by-product of the large scale of federal operations of the multicampus university.

In its organization for *general* governmental relationships at the national level, however, the multicampus systems are not similarly organized. In only two or three of the nine systems was it possible to identify a senior staff officer with responsibility for relations with the federal government — and this always in addition to other duties. In 1970, with limited exceptions, the multicampus university did not have any *special* role in the national Capital. The relationships between the federal government and any one university system simply have not yet developed to an extent requiring an explicit form of representation.

For example, the bulk of federal aid is in the form of research grants and contracts for which the individual faculty project director is far more able to "lobby" his interests than anyone else.

Broader policy issues at the federal level are on a scale that do not bring the multicampus structure *as such* into focus—for example, issues of federal aid to private higher education. System staff in Washington may assist in mobilizing support for an "institutional" position, but their activity in this regard does not differ from that of representatives from individual campuses or associations.

Nevertheless, a repeated theme of this study has been that the future pattern of federal funding relationships will be one of the major conditioning influences on the multicampus university. Present and proposed policies and strategies affect the distribution of authority of everyone with an interest in the system from the individual student to the governor. Federal funds for student aid, research support, or physical construction can potentially be allocated directly to a state finance office, a statewide coordinating agency, a universitywide system, a campus, or an individual professor or student. The multicampus university has a great stake in the choice made among these alternatives, but so does each of the other contenders. One thing can be predicted: Both the organizational presence of the universities in Washington and the federal impact upon the organization of the system will become more evident in direct proportion to the increase in federal support. The multicampus university has a unique potential in this regard, midway between the fragmented funding of individual research projects and the generality of a bloc grant for an entire state. Whether this potential will ever be tested depends on national decisions yet to be made.

MULTICAMPUS ALUMNI: CAMPUS LOYALTIES All campuses, whether public or private and whatever their organizational structure, have alumni. But it is the *campuses* of a multicampus university that have alumni, not the larger system. Alumni loyalties run to ivy-covered academic halls, not to the systemwide administration building.

The paucity of alumni activity at the system level parallels that of universitywide student organization. Although the "role of the student in governance" is on the agenda of virtually every educational meeting, little has been written about the role of the alumni. However, what may be the first major university (not a multicampus university) to revise its governing board in the wake of student dissent did so, not by putting current students on the board, but by having them elect members from among the most recent classes.

Board members so elected are no more representative of alumni in the traditional sense than are any number of new assistant professors representative of the traditional faculty.

We have no impressions or predictions of the future role of alumni in multicampus affairs. There will be more of them, however, and they have long had a respectable place in university governance. Although the alumni role may have decreased in recent years, the students who are now clamoring for participation in governance are going to be these alumni. These factors imply possible changes in structure, although we cannot guess at the form such changes might take.

Three organizational aspects of alumni activity—or lack of activity—are apparent at the multicampus level. Only one multicampus system has a senior officer of the central staff primarily concerned with alumni activity. In 1970, another had an unfilled vacancy at a high level, and a third was considering such a position. That the responsibilities in all three cases included not only alumni affairs but development and fund raising as well points to a second aspect: In none of the multicampus universities considering the issue is there any question whether the multicampus alumni group will be autonomous or part of the official university structure. It is assumed without question that alumni administration will be another part of the central administrative structure and integrated with it.

The third aspect is the absence of multicampus alumni organizations. Only in Illinois has a strong multicampus alumni organization emerged. The reasons why this happened are various, but certainly among them is the activity of the alumni association in the selection of trustees. Although this governing board is popularly elected on a partisan ballot, the reality of this procedure is that the universitywide alumni organization itself appoints nominating committees for each party. These nominees are, with rare exceptions, accepted at the political party conventions for the general election ballot. In Illinois, therefore, there is interest, not present elsewhere, in the continuance of a unified alumni organization. Also, the universitywide association is organized as a confederation of disciplinary or professional alumni groups, which may alleviate some of the concern of alumni from smaller campuses about dominance from the flagship. Nevertheless, increasing attention is being given to the need to distinguish, if not separate, alumni from each campus.

In the other systems with a flagship campus, separate alumni associations have developed on the new campuses, occasionally facilitated by the older organization. Of the multicampus universities which are a consolidation of existing independent campuses, only the State University of New York has made any substantial effort to build an alumni organization at the system level. Significantly, it is also a system which has done much to build similar student organizations. The future of this alumni effort is uncertain, but it is interesting to speculate that it may have a chance of success because of the absence of any strong campus alumni groups, a characteristic of many of the former teacher's colleges which have become part of this system.

A "paper" multicampus alumni structure in the University of California consists of the heads of the otherwise autonomous campus alumni organizations. The structure exists almost entirely as a vehicle to elect an ex officio member of the governing board.

In another system, thought has been given to a proposal for a universitywide council of past presidents of the several campus alumni organizations. It is hoped that this might be a high-level social, advisory, and honorary body, providing the system executive with his own alumni forum. Priorities for implementation were not high, although the idea is imaginative.

The legislator alumnus

Many alumni of the systems which grew from a single flagship campus are prominent citizens of their states. Some are governors; many are found in the legislature. Do these favor the system? Not at all, according to one system executive. "They smile, but go their own way." Legislators are and probably should be more concerned with issues immediately pertinent to their political careers (if not the public interest) than with abstract loyalty to their alma mater. Whether this is the case or not, the alma mater of any particular legislator is not the multicampus university but one of its campuses. However, despite opinions of most administrators at the multicampus level that alumni in the legislature are of little real help, two seemingly contradictory opinions are held at the newer or smaller campuses. First, campus administrators are of the clear and explicit opinion that alumni from the flagship campus in the legislature are of benefit to the new campus as well as the system. At the same time, we sensed an undercurrent of concern that the flagship campus is getting the best of whatever political heft the system itself can wield.

System executives and campus alumni

Despite the general absence of universitywide alumni organizations, most system executives both desire and are expected to maintain contact with campus alumni groups. Within the state, this requires regular visits to alumni gatherings. Occasionally, more than one campus has an organization in a large metropolitan community, and separate meetings are held. On other occasions, and usually at the instigation of the system executive, these organizations may hold a combined gathering at which he will appear to make a universitywide presentation. Such combined meetings are most often those held outside the state. For example, the New York City alumni of the several campuses of the University of Missouri have held joint meetings to hear the system executive. Such meetings tend to be dominated by alumni from the flagship campus, but there is a reality to the concept of a universitywide alumni which grows stronger with distance.

The extent of the interest of the central administration with alumni affairs is related to the system executive's relationships with the flagship campus. In at least four instances in recent years, the system executive had previously served as head of the flagship campus. In the latter capacity, he had all the traditional alumni contacts of any single-campus executive. These ties are not easily broken by either the executive or the alumni with this move to the system headquarters, and a sensitive aspect of system-campus relationships depends on the skill with which executives at both levels accommodate to the new organizational pattern.

13. Business Affairs

It is a phenomenon of contemporary higher education that the university has become an economic enterprise of substantial significance, coincident to its role as an educational institution. Directly or through agencies of state government, the nine multicampus universities are all major employers, purchasers of goods and services, and contractors for architectural and construction activity in their respective states. We deal here with these three activities in the context of the multicampus university, adding a fourth—the administration of research contracts and grants.

Together, these activities are generally classed as "business affairs." Individually or collectively, the effectiveness of their administration, although not explicitly central to the educational programs of the university, does much to affect their quality. In each of the nine universities, furthermore, their administration has a significant impact upon both the style and the substance of multicampus governance, reaching far beyond the specifics of the particular activity.

The four activities are not all that is encompassed under the business affairs rubric. Time prevented an exploration in this study of fiscal administration—accounting, auditing, and treasury management—despite its obvious significance to university administration.

Business affairs activities, though differing widely from one another and among the nine systems, have one feature in common: Administrators in these areas are not part of a career ladder that leads from instructor to professor and then up (or perhaps down, in faculty opinion) to a position as a dean, provost, chancellor, or president. The functions treated here are nonacademic, *not* because they lack implications for instruction and research, but because the responsible administrators are generally not faculty members.

A second common factor also distinguishes three of the four functions here discussed from other activities of university governance. To varying degrees, as outlined in Table 10, physical planning and construction (five universities), nonacademic personnel (five universities), and purchasing (six universities) are primarily administered by departments of state government or separate building authorities, rather than by the multicampus university itself. Here, more than anywhere else, the state's interests in the internal administration of the university are both explicit and formal.

THE ROLE OF THE MULTI-CAMPUS UNIVERSITY In most areas of academic governance, the purported advantages of the multicampus structure depend on the variety of resources that it can command, its ability to direct the efforts of particular campuses along specialized lines of educational endeavor, its wide array and variety of faculty talent, and its greater potential for encouraging intercampus cooperation. The ability to marshal great academic resources is derivative of size, and the nine multicampus universities are among the largest in the United States. The advantage of these diverse academic resources, however, is often hampered by inherent problems of large numbers of campuses, students, and faculty. Size alone is rarely considered an academic asset.

Nevertheless, the large size of the nine universities is the foundation of nearly all the potential advantages in the area of business affairs. Economies and advantages of scale take several forms, depending on the specific subject area. In physical planning and construction, the volume of activity is generally such that the central administration can not only retain competent generalists but can also utilize the continuing services of specialists. In this respect, a single campus with an individual board that builds a main library resembles a homeowner who has just constructed his residence: neither is likely to undertake the same type of construction again in the near future. The multicampus university, on the other hand, builds the same type of building more than once and should profit from its experience.

With this advantage, a possible disadvantage is always present: overstandardization. Like the service stations of a major oil company, the buildings may or may not be aesthetically or functionally suitable for the location. If physical planning is centralized, away from a campus, the central staff may not be aware of the defects.

	Physical planning and construction			
Multicampus universities	*Selection of architect*	*Supervision of construction*	*Purchasing*	*Personnel*
University of California	Board—some delegation to campus	Campus	System—some delegation to campus	System
California State Colleges	Board	State and system	State—deals with system	System
University of Illinois	Board	System	System	Statewide university personnel system
University of Missouri	Board	System	System	System
State University of New York	State university building authority	State university building authority	State—deals with system	State
City University of New York	Board and campus committee of board	City university building authority	City—deals with campus	City
University of North Carolina	Board and campus committee of board	State	State—deals with campus	State
University of Texas	Board	System	State—deals with campus	System
University of Wisconsin	State	State	State—deals with system	State

TABLE 10 *Primary responsibility for business affairs in nine multicampus universities, 1969*

In personnel, the size of the multicampus system potentially opens avenues for mobility, training, and promotion not possible at a single campus: the system should permit mobility with the possibility of accompanying promotion. The additional level of administration within the same university system provides similar opportunities. In addition, centralization at the multicampus level should provide personnel administration with the same benefit enjoyed by other areas: specialists whose services cannot be justified for a single campus, at least for the smaller ones. The system itself should be able to use its campuses as a pool of trained people to maintain system staffing in all administrative areas. Two possible disadvantages are related: physical dispersion and size can carry with them difficulties of communication and the possibility of formal and complex rules and regulations that may frustrate campus personnel activity. Extending beyond personnel administration itself, the physical and psychological distance of the central personnel staff can render it unresponsive to unique problems at particular campuses. Paul Goodman's *People or Personnel* (1968, pp. 3–4) affords a more than adequate text for these possible deficiencies.[1]

Purchasing would seem to present the most evident management advantages for a multicampus university. The economies possible through volume purchasing, for example, are obvious, as is the accompanying disadvantage: uncritical extension of volume purchasing procedures as an end unto themselves. Saving simply because procedures permit it may be costly to the more relevant economies of educational effectiveness.

Procedural aspects of grant and contract administration parallel the business functions in purchasing and personnel. The source of funds may be the only distinction, and the multicampus university should offer the same potential advantages of economy of scale. In addition to these purely business aspects, however, a multicampus system can collect and disseminate information on research funding sources and procedures as well as on current research activities and capabilities of the whole system. Procedural activity under these circumstances may lead to unique system-wide substantive programs.

These isolated examples of potential uses and abuses of the

[1] ". . . In a centralized enterprise, the function to be performed is the goal of the organization rather than of persons (except as they identify with the organization). The persons are personnel. Authority is top-down. Information is gathered from below in the field and is processed to be usable by those above; decisions are made in headquarters; and policy, schedule, and standard procedure are transmitted downward by chain of command. The enterprise as a whole is divided into departments of operation to which are assigned personnel with distinct roles, to give standard performance. This is the system in . . . the New York public schools and in many universities. . . ."

multicampus university in the business affairs area are but illustrative. While we found evidence of their validity, as suggested below, final assessment must be set amidst the complex nature of the enterprises—particularly the network of relationships with state government.

PHYSICAL PLANNING AND CONSTRUCTION A professor sharing an office with two colleagues and laboratory space with four or five others has immediate facilities problems that a reshuffle of the governing structure—multicampus or otherwise—cannot relieve. If the multicampus structure makes any difference in planning, construction, and use of facilities, it is over a longer term. There are, of course, *current* problems with physical facilities attributable to *current* governing patterns—construction in progress and capital budgeting are obvious examples. But the results of *prior* physical planning and the implications of planning for the *future* present more critical issues: How well do existing campus buildings serve ongoing education? How are campus academic plans for the future related to current construction? In either case, does it make any difference that the campus is part of a multicampus university?

The multicampus structure does, we conclude, make a substantial difference. Except, however, for the planning and construction of a new campus from the ground up, in which case the existence of the system is crucial, the differences resulting from the form of governing structure are obscured and overlaid by far stronger fiscal considerations.

Major issues are those common to public higher education generally, perhaps exacerbated by the multicampus structure, but hardly caused by it. Three are outstanding, and the first two are discussed at greater length later in this section.

First, long-range *state fiscal planning* is nonexistent, so that the best-laid facilities plans must project state funding by educated guesses.

Second, *federal funding* is complex, uncertain, and fragmented. Meshing state and federal support approaches an art form, knowledge of which is limited to the system's facilities staff.

Third, substantial uncertainty prevails across the nine systems as to just what *kind of facilities* will be required for the future. Problems associated with urban campuses predominate, but the shape and organization of any campus are puzzles everywhere. To predict the kinds of facilities that will be needed by faculties and students 5, 10, or 15 years in the future involves a steadily increasing order of speculation.

The lack of rationalization in state and federal funding and the increasing hazards of predicting educational needs are common to higher education, but they come to a focus in the multicampus structure. Here, usually large and sophisticated planning staffs recognize both the problems and the difficulties of solving them. On one hand, they have more and better information than in the past. On the other, they are in doubt about how to use it.

Physical planning is a continuous process from the initial recognition of the need for a new campus through design and construction to completion and occupancy. The continuity breaks down, however, into three connected but fairly discrete activities: (1) Campus and longer-range planning set the context for future building and land use. (2) In the building design phase, the user's particular requirements, current and long-range, are combined with the services of architects and engineers to produce definite plans and specifications. (3) The building is constructed.

The earlier in the planning process, the more difficult it is to pinpoint the level at which critical decisions are made. As one progresses from the beginning to the end of the process, however, the areas of discretion become narrower. A system executive and the chairman of his governing board have their own particular dream of a new campus on 500 vacant acres. The appointment of a campus executive for the new campus and then an architect adds two more dreamers. Credit (or blame) for the eventual campus plan can begin almost anywhere.

When buildings give reality to the plan, the design depends on specific enrollment projections and academic programs—as is true for a new building on an existing campus. Fixing the requirements of construction and selecting an architect are events in which the actors are usually highly visible and the activity well documented. Only in the building phase, however, is authority definite: someone has signed the construction contract, and whether acting for the state, the system, or the campus, he must follow the plans and specifications.

Physical and Academic Planning   In a perfect world, physical and academic planning would mesh. Universally, the expressed ideal is that physical plans follow and serve academic ones; academic planners carefully and accurately set forth their needs and enrollment projections: undergraduate,

graduate, and—now—postdoctoral. The campus mix in terms of disciplines is ascertained, with a careful appraisal of library, laboratory, and other needs. Consensus is reached on anticipated methods of instruction and on class-size distribution. Student attitudes about housing result in projections as to needed residence halls. These and numerous other judgments are carefully refined and the major ones brought to the governing board for its endorsement. Then, and only then, does the planning of a new or expanded campus move into the physical construction stage, with attention to general layout and individual building design. Fiscal constraints may modify priorities, but not the substance of those plans.

Such idealized planning is far from realization at any system. Long-range academic planning is often inadequate for facilities plans to follow, and funding often determines the substance of both. Although for unique reasons each system falls short—sometimes extremely short—of meeting the ideal, generalizations are possible because of several contrasting characteristics of physical and academic planning: physical planning is centralized, continuous, specialized, and administrative. Academic planning is decentralized, sporadic, generalized, and in the hands of the faculty. Furthermore, in planning new, "instant" campuses, there is often no faculty (or students) to draw up academic plans in advance. Within the multicampus university, the coincidence of all these characteristics gives the physical planners, located mainly at the system level, a muted dominance over the academic planners, mainly at the campuses.

The expression "muted dominance" is used advisedly, for dominance is generally denied by facilities planners and is usually acquired by default. It is, moreover, exercised in such broad terms that its bounds are little noticed. The central facilities planning staff reaches down to the campuses and out to the future with far greater certitude than do system academic planners. Facilities planners are professionals or, at least, technical specialists in their field. As architects and engineers, they have legitimacy in the eyes of their campus counterparts that system academic planners never have with campus faculty. Architecture is a profession; teaching is a profession; research is a profession; but academic planning is what teachers and researchers do if they have time for it. Academic planning is what architects and engineers do because no one else does it.

Planning on Old and New Campuses

When a new campus is being planned, building plans clearly reflect long-range academic goals and tend to include the building design phase. Conversely, planning for an older campus is absorbed by the building design phase. Existing buildings and innumerable vested interests converge to make the design of a new building merely an incremental change in the overall campus plan. Only rarely is the campus reevaluated as a whole.

New campuses, almost by definition, are planned by someone other than campus administrators or faculty. Three examples came to our attention, and in only one had the campus executive been appointed early enough to influence campus plans and building designs. In addition to his early appointment, his role was made possible by the system's unusually decentralized planning and construction procedures, by the academic plan that called for sequential construction of separate colleges and, quite materially, by access to external funding.

At the other extreme, the senior facilities planner on the central staff of another university explained that "we [he and his staff] designed the campus for a certain kind of education and then hired a campus executive to fit it." Even in this instance, however, the campus executive, appointed before construction started, was able to work out minor changes with the architects to fit his own goals for the campus. Before the campus opened, however, he had resigned!

Probably the more typical example is in the middle group. Here, although the campus executive had his own goals in mind—in this case, heavy emphasis on programmed instruction—limited funds and local need for a broad range of conventional programs left him with little actual influence over the final plan.

One generalization relating to new campus physical planning emerges from the three examples: concern in all instances with explicit educational goals and with academic plans.

Planning for *existing campuses,* on the other hand, while nominally dependent on academic plans, is severely limited by existing buildings and ongoing programs. The not unpleasing heterogeneity of architecture on most old and large public campuses so testifies. No fault rests with anyone for the absence of strict campus planning. Existing buildings cannot be demolished nor tenured faculty sent elsewhere solely to obtain symmetry of architectural style and consistency of academic programs.

Plans for existing campuses are usually in the hands of the faculty and the campus administration. In contrast, one system had centralized planning with the express intent of avoiding changes "every time new deans" were appointed. Faculty control, however, exercised by a substantial voice in the planning of each new building, meant that "new deans" would continue to have influence regardless of overall plans.

Even for existing campuses, plans for specific buildings may raise questions about the overall educational mission of the campuses. The interaction of building plans and campus diversity or specialization was the subject of a perceptive comment by a system administrator:

. . . The establishment of planning criteria for libraries is still an unresolved issue. Although it had been discussed in the past, the major impetus for attempting to define guidelines came after several of the colleges had submitted plans for new libraries of such a size that they implied that the mission of the college would change. The question of size, then, provoked an examination of institutional mission. One important aspect of facilities planning, then is that it *forces* (in most cases, albeit, for the first and last time) a consideration of program in much the same way that a budget is supposed to.

Governing boards take substantial interest in plans for both new and existing campuses. Because of the fluidity of these plans prior to their reaching print, we are unable to form any impression of the relative influence of the board as opposed to that of the central staff, the campuses, or state agencies. Nor are we able to distinguish among the systems with any accuracy. At one extreme, a special committee of the board was concerned with land use and campus facilities plans for an urban campus. Problems of physical growth in a highly populated area appeared the reason for interest not accorded to other campuses. In contrast, and in one of the larger systems, the plan for an "instant" campus of 14,000 students was approved at a half-hour meeting of the board.

In summary, land-use and physical planning for new campuses are very much related to both immediate and longer-term academic goals, but planning for existing campuses is not. "The only plan around here that lasts beyond the current budget year is a plaster model of the new campus." We saw more substance to such plans than this, but less than formal documents would imply.

**Building
Programs
and Design**

The generality of campus plans becomes specific when construction is in the offing. Translation of needs to working drawings is always in two steps. In the first, insofar as existing campuses are concerned, the faculty, with technical assistance from the campus and central administrations, prepares a building program for the specific building. In the second, an architect uses the program to prepare the plans and specifications. In all systems, the building programs are largely determined by the faculty at the campus, and in all systems the second step involves the governing board, the state, an outside agency, or any combination of these.

Each system has its own procedures for review and approval of both building programs and plans. But we agree with a campus administrator who had worked in two systems: "It's a matter of touching bases with the same people. Just different forms and in different sequence." There are differences, of course, but these are mainly in the degree of interest shown by the governing boards and the state agencies. Review procedures are complex, lengthy, and characterized by terminology that is not consistent across the nine systems. "Architectural concept" may mean schematic drawings in one system and a plan that includes the location of each electrical outlet in another.

Building programs

Campus faculty committees are found in every system, and there is little doubt about their real influence. Those who will use a building are generally recognized as good judges of its shape, size, and content. Criticism of the delay inherent in committee decisions and of their lack of technical competence is commonplace: "I expected them to design a horse that looked like a camel, but not that they'd take a year to do it." Physical planners also feel that the existing faculty, particularly prestigious senior members, are not always the best judges of possible future trends. Faculty members in the multicampus system are no less expert as facilities planners than those elsewhere. Nevertheless, the multicampus structure exacerbates delay and lack of technical skill simply because of the faculty's physical distance from the central staff and governing board. A faculty committee at a distant campus in one system changed the prospective use of a proposed building without consulting the central facilities staff. Since the use had implications for both the capital and operating budgets, the staff found itself in a dilemma. To the funding authorities, they could appear to lack control; to the campus faculty, they could appear to be interfering with an educational decision.

The complaint of the central staff was not, it should be noted, that the particular decision was improper, but rather that the system administration had not been advised of it. Similar administrative respect for faculty advice is characteristic.[2] One exception involved a senior central facilities planner who clearly wanted little to do with the opinions of anyone at the campuses other than the campus executive. In fact, some major design changes were made without advising even the concerned campus executives. Overall planning and construction in this particular system, as centralized as any in the study, was nevertheless being reorganized somewhat to bring the local faculty into the picture.

The general agreement that *campus* faculty have a real part to play in building design is usually limited to the preparation of specific building programs before architects are retained. In one system, however, two faculty members sit with senior administrative staff on a universitywide committee to review campus capital outlay requests. This unique systemwide academic role seems more attributable to traditionally strong and highly structured systemwide faculty participation in areas of normal faculty interest— e.g., courses and curriculum—than to any specific rationale in facilities planning or design.

Building design

Faculty building committees are similar in composition and function across the nine systems, but architects are selected in a variety of ways. Their appointment appears more nearly a "governmental" decision than an academic one and reflects the great variety of

[2] The philosophical adjustment of an experienced physical planner to faculty— and administrative—whim is best explained in his own words: "Some years ago, as a young architect with the University, I thought that life was simple. All I had to do was to get the chancellor, dean, department chairman, or faculty representative to tell me what he wanted or needed, and I could solve his problem: I could plan a campus or plan a building to satisfy their needs completely and finally. I must confess it took me many years, frustrations, upset plans, and changes of program (and minds!) before the insatiable appetite of the professor, and the empire-building proclivities of the dean, and often the lack of real understanding of the planning process on the part of the chancellor, led me to the conclusion that I was really coping with a can of worms. I came to realize that a university or college is not a static thing which one can plan once for all time. It is a growing organism which is always moving, always changing. Although the major goals of an institution may be constant, fundamental changes—academic, social, economic, and political—are inevitable."

political and governmental procedures in the seven states. Selection of architects is almost always made by the governing board, the state, or an independent construction authority.

The distribution of *formal* authority, indicated in Table 10, is relatively simple:

- In seven systems, the governing board names the architect. In two of these, the decision has been delegated to campus committees made up of members of the board. In one, limited authority has been delegated to the campus executives.

- In one system, the architect is selected by a state governmental agency.

- In one system, selection is made by a separate authority legally autonomous from both the state and the university.

Although the governing boards have formal authority in many other areas which they exercise in a *pro forma* manner, their authority to appoint architects is taken seriously. One board, in fact, has devised an elaborate procedure to assure objectivity in selecting from among qualified architects in the state, although in other systems we heard only one suggestion that selection might be politically motivated. In one system, architects from the particular community are selected for all campuses except the flagship campus, which is situated at the state capital. For it, care is taken to see that architects throughout the state are represented.

Although *formal* authority in this selection process can be discerned with reasonable ease, overall patterns of *informal* authority—the degree of influence exerted by the differing levels of governance—cannot be readily determined. Two factors, however, shape the relative roles of the campuses.

First, campuses have either no influence over selection of architects or very little in the two systems in which the governing board itself lacks formal authority. Where the state agency selects the architect, we were told that it does not even welcome suggestions from the board or the system staff, to say nothing of the campuses. In the other, in which a separate agency makes the selection, the system administration has an informal veto, but the campuses have no part at all.

Second, the three instances of substantial campus influence are attributable to formal governing board delegation or campus-board interaction. In two of these, a committee of the board is the vehicle for campus influence, and, in the third, the board delegates limited authority to the campus executives. In all three, however, the board retains its ultimate authority.

In no case has the state or the governing board delegated authority over selection of architects to the system executive or his staff. The latter, however, exercise substantial influence in four of the seven systems where the board has formal authority. Central staff influence exists in the form of either an administratively determined panel from which the board makes its selection or in specific recommendations. In three of these systems in which the central administration is influential, it also directly administers the construction —as well as the physical planning—program.

In sum, all systems look to the campus faculty for building programs. In selecting architects, however, the central staff or the campuses have influence only where the governing board itself is the appointing authority. Central staff influence can be quite informal, but campus participation is found only where formal procedures give it structure.

Construction   In every system, the preparation, review, approval, and modification of building plans, the checks and controls during construction, and the eventual acceptance of the building form a detailed procedural web. In general, the administration and supervision of capital projects is highly "centralized" in either the central staff, the state, or a separate authority. The listing here of the varieties of centralization disguises, of course, an even greater variety of detailed procedures. As suggested in Table 10:

- One system relies primarily on its campuses for the administration and supervision of construction.

- Four systems handle construction supervision directly through their own central staff, although in one of these some construction is in the hands of state agencies.

- Two systems have all construction performed by the state, while in a third system (see above), some work is done by the state.

- Two systems rely on specially established and separate "authorities" for the administration of building construction.

Campuses complained least about administration of the building program in the one system in which they had the most responsibility for it. The very great delegation of authority in that system, however, is highly dependent on the system's broad freedom from detailed state controls—greater freedom than found in the other systems. The independence of the campuses within checkpoints set up by the system provides them substantial flexibility. Such flexibility, however, has also created cost variations between campuses that have attracted the attention of state fiscal officials. Suggesting that increased costs are caused by construction "frills," they are seeking a greater role for the state in the administration of the construction program.

One such "frill" was also mentioned in other systems: Should partitions in lavatories be hung from the wall or set on the floor? Trivial? Probably, but illustrative of state involvement in detail. And illustrative also of the relationships between the capital budget (the partition) and the operating budget (the annual cost of mopping under or around it). The implications of building design for maintenance costs are of interest because reduction of building cost concerns the central building authority, whether state or system, but eventual and continuing maintenance costs concern the campus. The discontinuity between capital and operating expenses is emphasized by the separation of these into two levels of governance.

In one of the nine systems, there is virtually no formal system-wide activity in the entire capital outlay program. Physical planning and construction is almost entirely worked out directly between the campuses and the state building agency. A universitywide influence exists, however, in separate campus building committees of the governing board and in the activities of the system executive at the state capital.

In two systems, there are separate authorities for construction—authorities set up to permit more flexible funding and to avoid "excessive" state controls over physical construction, as well as over purchasing and nonacademic personnel. But although the building authorities successfully handle internal funding of physical construction, their much-prized autonomy carries a price. These authorities are not simply alter egos of the governing board or the central staff; they are formally quite independent of these, as well as of the state building agencies. For example, administrators at one campus believed that the space allocation of new buildings would allow only extremely small classes, with potential implications for the operating budget. But the campus felt it had little ability to influence the autonomous authority.

In general, we found little serious pressure by the campuses for greater decentralization or delegation of construction management. Campus complaints are generally addressed to better system administration rather than delegation of it. This lack of pressure seems specific to the area of physical planning and construction. Explicitly in one instance and implicitly in most, campus executives suggest that the specialized staff required for effective physical planning and construction cannot be locally maintained.

Even the most centralized systems cannot and do not want to handle all construction problems. Maintenance is universally a campus function and part of the operating budget. Sometimes the campuses have authority for new construction up to a very limited dollar value and for remodeling and repairs up to a generally higher amount. Although architects are sometimes members of campus administrations, they are rarely served by a substantial staff. Even in the system that has decentralized substantial authority over planning and construction, campus architects and engineers are supported by the capital budget rather than the administrative portion of the ongoing operating budget.

The problem of relating a specialized, central facilities staff to activity at the campuses is subject to an interesting experiment in one system. The campus director of physical planning and construction reports directly to the central staff administrator rather than to the campus executive. This pattern, involving geographic decentralization but organizational centralization, is also used in the same university for fiscal control and legal services and is new to the system and unique in the study. It is far too early to judge its effectiveness, but two potential drawbacks are evident. First, the system's representative at the campus is in the awkward position of serving two masters, in fact if not in theory, and must maintain close personal relationships with both. Moreover, and perhaps more important, the campus executive does not have a staff officer with ultimate responsibility; the senior staff officer of the central administration is always there to second-guess his campus representative. Lack of final authority on the campus clearly qualifies the staff specialist's usefulness to the campus executive.

Both the potential advantages of a large-scale, universitywide approach to capital construction and the distance which remains before the potential can be widely realized are illustrated by the University Residential Building System (URBS) Project of the

University of California. The university and private industry are cooperating in a venture to plan and construct student housing economically through the development of building components. The project depends on the ability of the university to commit itself to the construction of 2,000 student spaces over a five-year period, and on the availability of federal funding. A parallel program involves academic buildings. While a large single-campus university could have undertaken the project, the multicampus system provides advantages in contractual dealings with both private industry and the federal government that would be difficult for an independent university to duplicate.

Both the residential and academic building projects demonstrate possibilities of imaginative and innovative approaches to capital outlay planning and construction for which the multicampus university is uniquely qualified. But both depend heavily on commitments of long-range state and federal funding, which are increasingly difficult to project. In short, the success of the multicampus university in the capital outlay field is almost totally dependent on the economic and political realities of massive external funding, to which we now turn.

Construction Financing

Existing academic programs are subject to past facilities planning, and current long-range academic planning is influenced by the facilities plans for the future. Unfortunately, existing buildings and current construction often have little relationship to the prior facilities plans. With equal probability, current facilities plans will be drastically revised before realization. To the extent that academic planning reflects physical planning, the unevenness of the latter compromises the former. The already inherent shortcomings of academic planning are reinforced by the uncertainties of physical planning.

What causes the uncertainty and unevenness of facilities plans? On their face they are far more explicit than academic plans: exact dates for occupancy match dollars per square foot, and gas and vacuum outlets per laboratory station. The *internal* ebb and flow of student preference and faculty mobility barely touches these detailed plans. Their dependence on external funding, however, belies the surface appearance of order and certainty. The influence of state and federal funding is not unique to the multicampus systems, but in at least two systems, campus unhappiness over physical-planning problems meant loss of credibility for the central administration, even though the latter was powerless to have prevented the changes dictated by fiscal considerations.

The absence of long-range capital outlay plans on the part of the state governments is at the heart of the problem, but the eccentricities of federal support assuredly compound it.

State funding

With major exceptions, capital outlay funds are dependent on actions of state legislatures taken in annual or biennial sessions, or of the electorate voting on bond issues, or both. University requests are placed in these political hoppers with due consideration for both long-range facilities plans and academic plans. They come out in the form of appropriations that sometimes bear little resemblance to the requests. Indeed, they do not always come out at all: on the day of one of our campus visits, the headlines of a local newspaper announced that the legislature had adjourned without passing *any* capital budget for the university.

Most systems in the study do not know with any precision what their capital budgets will be from one year to the next. General levels of capital support are unpredictable, arising out of the inability of one legislature or one governor to bind the next to a particular level of funding. Even the much-criticized formulas that are major determinants of the operating budget at least provide a fragile continuity that the capital outlay budget lacks.

System facilities planners in two universities spoke with envy of those who worked in a third state because of its reputedly workable capital outlay plan. There was, however, as little and perhaps less planning by the state government in this third state as in the two others. State officials there had reduced the capital outlay request of the multicampus system by some 60 percent below the policy level. Reduced budgets are a necessary evil in all higher education, but in the multicampus context they have the added impact of jolting loose carefully worked out priorities among the family of campuses.

Intercampus meshing of priorities poses a problem in all systems. In one state, the order of projects in the systemwide capital outlay request appeared to have been totally ignored by the legislature. In fact, however, the legislature had generally adhered to system priorities; the appearance of disorder arose from the legislature's having decided first upon an exact amount for the appropriation, selecting later enough specific requests to total that amount! In another state, priorities are subject to revision by the coordinating agency, the governor's budget staff, and finally the legislature itself; all three have exercised their prerogative on occasion.

Federal funding

The multicampus systems are not specific victims of malevolent capital budgeting; they suffer with other state agencies from lack of statewide, long-term fiscal plans. But the university systems are also enmeshed in federal capital outlay programs to a greater extent than most state agencies. Federal capital funding adds complexity to the state budgeting process and creates further uncertainty at the campuses; it serves also to either encourage or maintain a more centralized administrative structure in the facilities planning area than might otherwise be the case.

In some systems, the point and counterpoint between state capital outlay requests and federal grant proposals almost surpasses belief and, certainly, description. Two states, at least, require that capital budget requests project maximum possible federal funding. However, the timing of state budget requests and federal grant proposals is such that the state's appropriation based on maximum federal funding comes several months before the proposal has even been considered by the federal funding agency. Since federal funding is rarely at the maximum, facilities planners must return to their drawing boards to revise plans and specifications.

Complex federal funding, combined with the great interest of the states in capital budgeting, creates an extraordinary network of rules, regulations, and regulators. The number of bases to be touched and when to touch them and the names of the players are the esoteric stock-in-trade of systems facilities planners. What popularity the central staff loses with the campuses by keeping controls in their own hands is balanced, they believe, by having this complex interaction remain in working order. Their attitude meets with mixed reaction at the campuses. Within a single system, one campus executive accepted almost total system control as reasonable, while another considered it a major issue.

Exceptions and variations

Our generalizations about state and federal funding are subject to several qualifications. Three systems are far less dependent on their state legislature for capital funds than the other six in the study. Two of these finance construction programs indirectly through tuition, and the third relies on income from a substantial endowment.

The importance of this internal financing is twofold. The university is relieved of many arbitrary fiscal and administrative constraints imposed by annual budgeting. Projects can be planned from start to finish with assurance that total funding will be available. Secondly, internal control over funds makes it possible to coordinate the university's financing calendar with those of federal agencies. Maximum use can be made of federal funding possibilities without running head on into contrary state requirements. In short, internal funding permits the capital outlay program to proceed from initial planning through construction in an orderly fashion and without the artificial hurdles imposed elsewhere.

Three systems, including two of the above, have internal variations in capital funding among campuses because local communities supply all or part of the capital needs of two-year campuses. These variations complicate administration to a greater or lesser extent, but no special implications for multicampus governance were noted. Although we have suggested elsewhere that local two-year campuses may gain in political strength and academic respectability in the foreseeable future, there is little evidence on which to predict growth of community interest in facilities planning. Here, local efforts will probably be directed toward having the state assume greater responsibility for financing, rather than toward greater autonomy.

NONACADEMIC PERSONNEL

The separation of the present section on nonacademic personnel from the chapter on faculty and administrative personnel reflects the organizational pattern in almost all nine university systems. We do not defend the logic of the division. Thinking of professors, teaching assistants, and secretaries as a single group rather than as different categories of personnel might produce more reasonable answers to difficult questions, although it would assuredly raise others. While we found only a faint trend toward the administration of both academic and nonacademic personnel matters under a single multicampus staff officer, administrators in virtually all nine systems are clearly aware that definitions of *academic* and *nonacademic* are useful but by no means final. There is also universal recognition of a growing and complex group of employees between the faculty on one hand and clerical workers on the other.

Librarians, research specialists, and many others can easily find themselves outside the purview of both academic and nonacademic personnel administrators.

In nonacademic personnel administration within the multicampus universities, employees should be able to transfer among a wider range of opportunities, both occupational and geographic. In such an educational institution, unique training opportunities for the benefit of both system and employees should exist. In fact, these possibilities have not been realized to any extent in any of the nine universities. The failures, however, are only rarely attributable to the multicampus systems themselves, for where the state itself does not control personnel matters, an unusual cross-hatching of competitive interests inhibits innovation or experimentation.

In part, this arises from the active competition of business, industry, and other state agencies. Unlike the marketplace for faculty—national and quite restricted—that for nonacademic personnel is local and very broad. Moreover, the multicampus structure itself creates an overlay of additional competition both with and among its campuses. The combination of these internal and external areas of competition often leaves little room for the multicampus university to exercise an independent role. Compensation, working conditions, and fringe benefits are largely shaped by forces outside the control of the university and often formally determined by the state itself.

Patterns of Personnel Administration

As indicated in Table 10, in four of the nine systems nonacademic personnel matters are directly in the hands of state government. At the other extreme, four of the universities administer their own personnel programs, although each has a variety of relationships with the state personnel agency. The University of Illinois participates in a separate state civil service system restricted to nonacademic personnel of all public colleges and universities.

State civil service

In the four universities where state personnel agencies are primarily responsible for nonacademic personnel, the system itself has little part in the administration of policies and practices. The University of Illinois, which participates in a separate state-wide personnel program for public higher education, has somewhat greater control—at least influence—than do the universities where state civil service blankets them along with other state agencies.

The imprint of the civil service "mentality" was evident when we suggested in the course of an interview at one of the four systems that it must be difficult to hire the wives of graduate students as secretaries. It turned out to be not only difficult but quite impossible because it would be "clearly nepotism." This particular system is the strictest of the nine insofar as governmental control is concerned. Even in it, however, when it becomes necessary to pay a high-level secretary more than the going civil service rate, a way is found: the secretary becomes a "lecturer"!

This deliberate misclassification of an employee from nonacademic to academic—from civil service to university control—is unusual but symptomatic of a more pervasive problem. The "gray area" of the professional, nonteaching staff member is an issue in all nine universities. Typically ineligible for faculty status but often unique to educational institutions, these employees pose a special problem in the civil service states, which require that employees be designated as "civil service" or "university." Each system has its own complicated and controversial case in which both the state and the multicampus system have claimed jurisdiction over employees such as librarians, laboratory technicians, or computer programmers. More is at stake than the outcome of bureaucratic competition between two public agencies. In some instances, it is to the personal advantage of the employee to be classed as civil service, regardless of the wishes of the university, or vice versa. Questions of relative job security, promotional opportunities, fringe benefits, and the strength of unions and employee associations are all factors.

The issue is not limited to routine administrative positions. In two university systems, "specialists in higher education," as well as professionals in law and architecture, are covered by civil service. Here, there are examples of redesignation as "assistant" to system or campus executives or their key staff to avoid the restrictions of civil service recruitment and salary scales. At issue, too, is the alleged lower prestige of professional staff in being classified under civil service.

Classification as civil service can involve disagreement between the universitywide administration and the campuses. The latter tend to be more willing to skirt carefully worked-out agreements between the state and the university over their respective authority, while the state looks to the system to police violations. Failure to maintain a balance can threaten the status quo and lead to increased state or union pressures to blanket even more employees under civil service.

In this area of nonacademic personnel, *system* autonomy and *campus* autonomy are unrelated. The freedom of the system from civil service does not necessarily mean an increase in campus authority. Conversely, inclusion of nonacademic staff within the state civil service does not automatically mean that the campus lacks autonomy relative to one in a university system with its own personnel program. In the systems in which employees are subject to state personnel agencies, there were several instances of effective staff relationships between a campus personnel officer and his state counterpart. When the state maintains a local office on or near the campus, the relationship can be even closer, with flexible administration overcoming the more formal barriers of civil service rules and regulations.

University personnel programs

In four multicampus universities, personnel programs for nonacademic staff are administered independently of the state civil service. Among these four, the distribution of authority between the campuses and the systemwide administration is similar, although significant variations exist. Retirement and fringe benefits are universally centralized and uniform across campuses. The broad outlines of classification and pay schemes are also generally uniform, although one system allows salaries to be determined locally. A detailed state budget formula in this same system, however, applies to all campuses, so that flexibility is sharply curtailed: At one campus, because painters received twice the wages as did those at a distant and rural campus, fewer could be hired.

Authority to allocate specific positions to particular classifications varies from one system that requires central approval to another in which the responsibility rests with each campus. Similar variations mark the establishment of salary and wage scales. In one university, these are locally determined but require the approval of the governing board; in another, the board has delegated its authority, and the scales are determined and approved by the central administration. The responsibility for training is typically local, with varying degrees of systemwide leadership and support.

Such formal considerations appear less significant than the external constraints under which each of the four systems operates. In fact, the distinction between the civil service and non-civil service university systems is not as great in practice as in theory. Circumstances of indirect control by the state personnel agency over both classification and wages, the necessity for state budget officials to treat university and other public employees in a generally uniform fashion with respect to salaries and fringe benefits, and the constraints of the employment market are similar in all universities. In each university system, in addition, personnel administration is shaped by demands for intercampus equality. Variations in wages or working conditions from one campus to another are quickly noted by employee associations or unions, which create pressures for uniformity—upward.

The similarity between civil service and non-civil service systems is a result, too, of the general failure of the universities to take full advantage of the potential benefits of their multicampus structure. Intercampus transfers of employees and in-service training for systemwide mobility are frequent topics of discussion, but there are few examples of either. Inadequate staffing often prevents system personnel administrators from implementing their plans. One system had been forced to postpone the development of a personnel manual for several years and, in a recent report, stated that " . . . any efforts to develop a comprehensive training program have been severely handicapped because of the lack of funds. It is more than ironical that an agency devoted to a total educational process is unable to even provide a minimum of training to its own employees."

We did find several examples of economies of scale in which universities were able to employ specialists in training and fringe benefit programs. Smaller campuses would not be able to support such specialists. It remains true, however, that systemwide programs or effective system promotion of campus activities is not a significant achievement of the multicampus universities.

PURCHASING   Every multicampus university produced its quota of horror stories about purchasing. Delay, red tape, and incompatible equipment, however, are endemic to any large, scattered organization, and particularly a public one.

That it takes time and effort to overcome them was suggested by a framed purchase order on the wall of a campus administrative office bearing the caption, "First purchase order issued by this campus. . . ." The campus business officer was quite explicit about the "blood that had been shed" to obtain the necessary delegation of authority from the system.

In purchasing, authority can almost endlessly be divided and recombined for allocation to different levels. While this is indeed the case with the multicampus systems, they fall into two general categories. As detailed in Table 10, purchasing in six is explicitly and directly controlled by the state. In the other three, the multicampus system itself has control. Within each category the variations are legion.

State-administered Purchasing

The six systems in which the major aspects of purchasing practice are controlled by the state are themselves in two distinct categories: in three, campuses deal directly with the state; in three others, state control is funneled through the system, and the state agencies are a step removed from the campuses.

Where campuses and state agencies deal directly with each other, the central administration plays a very small role. Indeed, two systems do not have any universitywide purchasing office or officer. In all three systems, the campuses have very little independent authority. For example, one state requires that three bids be obtained on all purchases over $100, and another limits campus purchasing authority without state approval to $50. The states may achieve both accountability and economy of scale by performing all purchasing functions, but the administrative costs seem unnecessarily high.

There was surprisingly little complaint at the campuses in these three systems about state control over purchasing. As in physical planning and construction, external governmental constraints appear to be more readily accepted than those of a higher level of governance within the university.

In the other three state-administered purchasing systems, state procedures, specifications, and general purchasing practices are followed, but the multicampus universities act as a conduit to impose them in substantially unmodified form on the campuses. In two universities, campus authority is substantially greater than noted above—purchases up to $1,000 and $3,000, respectively, can be made without bids. In contrast, the third, even at the system level, has very little discretionary authority indeed—$25. A specific campus in each of the first two systems had successfully pressed for delegation of greater authority from the state to the system and through it to the campuses.

Here, as elsewhere, once responsibility for a particular decision is removed from a campus, its actual location becomes, for campus faculty and many campus administrators, an unknown quantity. This problem appeared in the purchasing area in these three systems. In one instance, for example, a campus business officer did not know whether the purchasing rules were the state's or the university's.

In all six of these universities, the emphasis of state controls is upon state funds rather than over all university funds. In three of these six, for example, separately organized "foundations" handle the bulk of purchasing from non-state funds—particularly expenditures financed from reimbursed indirect costs generated by federal grants. The foundations are systemwide in two of these, but at each campus in the third. In the latter, campus foundations have been monitored only to a very limited extent by the small central universitywide staff, and in one or two instances, at least, have been charged with making purchases which, if not illegal, are assuredly unwise. Here, the refusal of the state to delegate its authority over purchasing to the multicampus university itself, although assuring control over state funds, has resulted in less clear accountability over other funds.

University-administered Purchasing

While three multicampus systems have substantial control over their own purchasing, there are reasonable limitations to the manner in which this authority is exercised. Common sense requires bids for certain items, and the amount specified by state guidelines for its own departments can be as appropriate as any others. Moreover, there are some items—automobiles, for example—for which the state may well be the most appropriate unit to seek bids. These three systems, therefore, are distinguished from the six in which purchasing is state-administered less by the substance of their purchasing practice than by internal distribution of authority.

As a generalization, purchasing arrangements in all three systems are substantially centralized, although in none are the constraints imposed on the campuses as narrow as those generally found in the six state-administered systems. The forms of centralization vary. In one system there is no dollar limit to the purchases which a campus may make, but purchases are subject to systemwide specifications. If specifications do not exist, the system engages in bidding or negotiation to obtain the best price. In a second, purchasing activities at the campus are organizationally a part of the central purchasing office. In the third, each campus purchasing officer is responsible to the campus executive, but is also designated as a universitywide "commodity manager," responsible for obtaining information, preparing specifications, and developing vendor lists of specific items for the entire university system. Here, centralized purchasing has been achieved without a large central staff. It is expected that about half of the university's purchases will eventually be handled in this fashion, the other half being subject to local control.

In one of the university-administered systems, purchasing practices had moved from earlier, almost complete centralization to a high degree of decentralization. When an analysis of campus purchasing indicated that the system was not achieving price advantages commensurate with its large volume, a "recapture" of some purchasing functions was undertaken. The original and almost complete decentralization of purchasing was less attributable to a deliberate decision about purchasing itself than to spill-over from a far broader reorganization of administrative authority within the university. Its experience suggests that "decentralization" as such has little virtue apart from the specific function in question.

RESEARCH MANAGEMENT *Research management* is an appropriate shorthand way of describing such matters as the initiation, review, and approval of grant applications, fiscal control, equipment purchases, personnel, and the computation and utilization of reimbursed indirect costs. As such, the topic has implications for academic governance far beyond multicampus systems.

In the chapter on budgeting, we discussed the diverse ways in which the nine universities utilize reimbursed indirect costs or overhead. In fact, the most important multicampus aspects of externally funded academic research are the variations in the use of these funds. Here, however, we are concerned with three other aspects of grants and contract administration: (1) the distribution of authority within a system to solicit and accept grants and contracts; (2) research management of a primarily fiscal or informational nature; and (3) research management of a more substantive nature. The primary focus is on federally funded research.

The nine systems vary greatly in all three aspects of research administration. Such variations do not, however, disturb the accepted pattern of direct relationship between the individual faculty investigator and the funding agency, a relationship substantially bypassing not only the multicampus administration but often the campus administration as well. As distressing as faculty grantsmanship can sometimes be for academic administrators, this traditionally direct relationship is generally accepted. The assessment of research proposals by an outside peer group is seen as furnishing assurance that quality is high and direction proper. And quality and proper direction are first and last a matter for the research investigator involved.

Solicitation and Acceptance of Research Funds
Although the authority to solicit grants and contracts is distinct from the authority to accept them, these run together in practice. Governing boards usually retain authority over the acceptance of research funds. But if a board ever rejects a grant or contract after the faculty has successfully solicited funds, such rejections did not come to our attention. Review by the central staff for board presentation is concerned only with the fiscal and administrative aspects of the proposals—except in rare and quite special situations (for example, projects requiring a significant capital outlay component which may alter campus physical plans).

In all nine systems, grants and contracts are solicited and negotiated by interested faculty without significant substantive aid or control at the multicampus level. Faculty are generally far closer to officials in their particular funding agency than they are to the central staff, including the staff of the Washington offices maintained by four of the systems. The Washington offices are themselves funded by overhead reimbursements from grants and contracts obtained by sophisticated research faculty. Indeed, the value of the "man in Washington" is probably greatest for faculty members who contribute least to his support.

Authority for formal acceptance of grants and contracts falls into three categories ranging from highly centralized to highly decentralized.

1   In three systems, only the governing board has authority to accept research funds. In one of these, the central administration has broad discretion over which proposals will be presented to the board as policy matters and which will be handled *pro forma*. A grant or contract is a policy matter if the staff thinks it should be presented to the board orally as well as in written form as part of a routine agenda—an agenda so large and detailed that it is

a barrier rather than an aid to board action. In exercising its discretion, the central administration gives less attention to the size of the proposal than to the opportunities it affords to "educate" the board about campus activities.

2 In three other systems, the authority to accept research funds is largely decentralized, except to the extent that the proposed research requires university as well as external funding.

3 In the three remaining systems, the size of the grant or contract determines the campus authority, the threshold amounts varying from $100,000 to $1 million.

Authority to solicit or accept—it was often unclear which was being restricted—is generally subject to specific limitations, the most common being a requirement for system approval if the research project is inconsistent with the mission of the campus or in conflict with its academic plan. Other limitations involve sponsorship by foreign countries, real estate transactions, physical construction, or the continuation of research operations beyond the period of external funding. These specific limitations cause little difficulty either at the campuses or in the central administration and appear to have no specific implications for a multicampus system.

The extremely limited substantive interest in grants and contracts at the multicampus level is paralleled, with two exceptions, by almost complete absence of any authority at all outside of the systems. Legislation in one state requires that certain applications for federal support of research be filed for the record with a state agency, but the purpose of the filing is unclear. In another state, approval of the coordinating agency is required when external funding exceeds $250,000. The stated purpose of the requirement is to allow assessment of the impact of external funds on the budget. Up to 1970, the requirement had not yet presented a problem to the system, although the potential for controversy is present.

Although centralization of formal authority is most often justified on grounds of the board's legal responsibility, the board or central staff actually retains formal authority because no one is annoyed or inconvenienced enough to make an issue of it. For example, the policy of some federal agencies permitting congressmen to announce grants to campuses in their districts was certainly responsible for decentralization in one system. Earlier system procedures requiring the central university offices to submit all proposals to Washington indirectly resulted in the congressman from that district announcing substantial grants to a campus in another district. The campus was annoyed; its local congressman was annoyed; and, by the time of our study, the campus was submitting its own applications. In another system with almost totally decentralized procedures, on the other hand, covering letters personally signed by the system executive on his stationery are locally mailed by the campuses. Before mailing, a small but colorful mimeographed slip is affixed, advising the funding agency that further correspondence will receive prompter attention if addressed directly to the campus.

Research Management: Fiscal and Informational Research management for fiscal control and related recordkeeping includes examples of both centralization and decentralization. Six of the nine systems have highly centralized fiscal control. Four of these six have simply integrated external research funds into their operating budgets, while the other two have established organizationally separate "foundations" through which the major portion of external research funds are processed. In the remaining three systems, fiscal control is almost totally decentralized to the campuses; one of these, also, has adopted the foundation approach. Central administrative monitoring of local control in these three systems appears somewhat less than rigorous, and primary reliance is placed on the audit procedures of the funding agencies. The three foundations administer and account for all proposals to other than state funding agencies. However, the foundations do not exercise substantive authority over any part of the grant procedure.

The original impetus for separate foundations was the complex set of state regulations on purchasing, personnel, and other management functions. Avoidance of state controls is not a hidden motive by any means. The regulations of one system explicitly state that a foundation is necessary because ". . . some activities cannot be operated effectively and without undue difficulty under the usual governmental budgetary, purchasing, and other fiscal controls. . . ." These foundations appear to be satisfactorily providing the flexibility and responsiveness in research management that would be difficult under normal state procedures.

Fiscal control is not a major issue in any system. In the highly centralized ones, the campuses think they should have more influence; and in those that are highly decentralized, the central staff generally believes the opposite should be the case. On balance, serious questions have arisen only in the system with a separate foundation at each campus. These campus foundations sometimes have found it difficult to obtain adequate or experienced local staffing, a problem compounded by lack of sufficient staff at the multicampus level effectively to assist or to monitor the campus operations.

A valuable by-product of one system, which centrally processes research applications and exercises fiscal control, has been its development of an informational capability utilized by both the central administration and the campuses. For example, the question of the number and nature of the university's contracts with the National Institute of Health can be answered in a matter of minutes. Few other systems had such information available centrally; even fewer had it so ordered that an answer would be forthcoming in less than a week, if at all. The availability of current data in this one instance appears possible because at the time the system was established it had a relatively small research capacity. The practicality of imposing centralized procedures in systems where campuses have substantial ongoing research—e.g., Urbana, Madison, or Berkeley—is open to question.

Although systems do not as a rule collect information concerning current research, aside from that needed for budgetary purposes, several campuses have these data available and ordered for retrieval. In at least two instances, information from existing campuses on funding sources and procedures was said to help the system's newer campuses.

In general, universitywide coordination of fiscal and other information concerning research is minimal. Complexity—even confusion—is probably an unavoidable concomitant of the similar condition that besets the funding sources themselves. This complexity and the variety of funding sources probably prevent any really useful dissemination of general research information. On the other hand, criticism can be leveled at the general failure of the systems to collect, store, and distribute data on current research projects in a manner that will aid both the system and its campuses. Although lack of adequate funding is generally offered as an explanation, a further reason may be the unwillingness of the central staff to "interfere" with the traditionally independent research activity of campuses and their faculty.

Research Management: Substance and Direction

In general, all multicampus universities leave the substance and direction of research to the individual faculty member, subject only to broad budgetary constraints. Little or no attempt is made to monitor conflicting or competing proposals. General exceptions to absence of central direction exist in specific academic areas with "respectable" applied research activities — e.g., agriculture and medicine — where a senior officer in the central administration may exercise some measure of control and offer explicit guidance.

Although a passive or permissive system role predominates throughout all nine systems, several senior staff officers are interested in a more positive approach, albeit in a most cautious fashion. If only three or four situations capture a "modal" approach, this has taken the form of a senior central staff officer finding that a particular problem could be solved more easily through intercampus cooperation. For example, interdisciplinary research might require academic resources from different campuses, or one campus might have an urban or coastal location from which the other campuses could profit. Campus resources by way of faculty interest and relevant current research could be inventoried. If sufficient interest and funding were available or in prospect, the program would be initiated and carried forward under faculty control, but with continuing encouragement by the central administration.

Although a central staff is not generally qualified to initiate or assess specific research projects, it does have an interest in the overall substance and direction of campus research that is not met by fiscal monitoring alone. With adequate information about both trends in funding and current campus research capabilities and interests, the central administration can play a valuable role in uniting these to produce a greater research potential than that of any single campus.

The most visible example of this potential during the study was the announcement in early 1970 by the University of California of a large-scale, multicampus "Project Clean Air," to promote applied research in air quality control. The analogies to the mission-oriented activities of the agricultural experiment stations of the land-grant universities are obvious, although it is not clear how far this "Manhattan Project" approach might be extended to non-crisis and nonapplied situations.

The project design called for "strong centralized direction," with a universitywide director reporting to the office of the system executive and with substantial visible authority over fund allocation and other aspects of research management. The impact of this program on the normal system-campus executive chain of command was not spelled out, and before the project was fully implemented, it was, in effect, transferred to an agency of state government, which itself assumed responsibility for "coordinating" specific research projects. In early 1971, the role of the university as an institution toward the project was unclear, although individual university faculty and departments received the bulk of state funds for the program.

In this instance, as in the nine universities generally, the multi-campus potential for more effective research management remains a relatively untapped resource.

Part Four

Problems, Trends, and Issues

14. The Multicampus University: A Summary

We have glimpsed the life of the multicampus university at a moment in time, appreciating that even while we studied each university, it was changing before our eyes. One observer described our attempt to study his rapidly evolving institution as akin to "changing tires on a moving car," and the same could be said of the other eight systems.[1] Nevertheless, common elements can be found in them all. We end the investigation with more confidence than when we started in our conviction that the multicampus university is a highly significant way of organizing higher education.

In this chapter we describe and evaluate some of these major common elements from the vantage point of, first, the environment of governance; second, each of the governing structures and substantive areas of university activity comprising the subjects of the preceding chapters; and third, the overriding "dimensions" of the nine systems in terms of origins, organization, and size. Finally, we attempt to draw a "balance sheet" of the strengths, shortcomings, and uncertainties of the multicampus university.

THE ENVI-RONMENT OF GOVERNANCE Our evaluation of the strength and weaknesses of multicampus universities must be placed within a context of governors and legislatures, of political campaigns and public attitudes, each shaped by such problems as the rising expectations of the poor and the black, of war and student activism, of inflation and taxes. Within this broad context, these specific observations—each noted in preceding chapters—emerge as critical to an understanding of the multicampus system.

---

[1] In a somewhat analogous statement, President Edward J. Blaustein of Bennington College has stated: "Administering a college today is like playing chess on the open deck of the sinking *Titanic*. To make matters worse, the chess rules seem to be changing as the game proceeds" (*U.S. News & World Report,* 1970, p. 30).

1　The state government is inextricably involved in the governance of higher education. In some instances, this involvement is explicit, as when state agencies act as the purchasers of goods, the designers of buildings, or the employers—through civil service—of nonfaculty personnel. In most cases, however, the involvement is less direct, but even more significant, as, for example, in the preparation and administration of the state budget. Although we found substantial room for complaint in the detailed nature of much state involvement, most administrators recognize that the legislature is the "ultimate coordinator" of public higher education in every state— constitutions and statutes notwithstanding.

2　As part of this general involvement, but accentuated by the increasing size, importance, and visibility of higher education, the governor is everywhere a key element in the multicampus university. Whether he appoints members of the governing board or not, whether he serves on the board or not, the governor in each of the seven states is central to the process of governance.

3　In no state is there clear understanding of the respective roles of the multicampus university and the coordinating agency or special recognition of their unique relationships. The possibility of confusion is greatest in those states with both multicampus systems and independent campuses and in which practices appropriate for campuses have been applied to systems. In every state, furthermore, there is uncertainty over the division of labor among the agency, the legislature, and state fiscal officers, an uncertainty aggravated by alternative organizational strategies over the proper distribution of federal funds.[2]

　　Within higher education itself, the difficulty of defining a "true multicampus university" remains with us at the conclusion of the study as it did at the start. Our formal criteria—a single governing board and a separate system executive with the prestigious title of president or chancellor—mask a host of crucial differences. We have noted both the ambiguity and the variety shaping the location of power in such matters as the executive's appointing authority, the budgetary flexibility of the system, and the responsibilities of a universitywide faculty organization—all among the variables necessary to an understanding of multicampus governance.

　　Among all other differences, the granting of a doctoral degree

---

[2] The problem apparently goes far beyond the seven states included in this study. Writing from the vantage point of a national survey of coordinating agencies, Robert O. Berdahl concludes that ". . . few agencies had in fact obtained . . . a position of equilibrium between higher education and state government, and [that] *none* had been able to maintain it through any significant portion of time" (1971).

by *more* than one campus emerges as most critical. The attainment by a second campus of the authority to engage in advanced graduate work—to become a "university" campus in the fullest sense—creates pressure for an independent campus executive. This in turn leads to demands for similar autonomy by other campuses, including the older, main campus, and the eventual emergence of a system executive free from direct operating responsibilities. Despite the existence of exceptions to this pattern, it points to the multicampus university, as we have defined it, as a major organizational response to the graduate-research orientation of the "academic revolution."

THE STRUCTURES OF GOVERNANCE

Governing boards

The most striking characteristic of governing boards of the multi-campus systems is their similarity to their single-campus counter-parts. Originally, six of the nine boards were exclusively concerned with a major campus and have been reluctant to alter habits and practices with the addition of new campuses. Board agendas underscore a concern for the governance of each campus, not for the system as a whole. Few boards have consciously reviewed their new role as *multi*campus boards, and even fewer have changed their ways. "Managerial" rather than "policy" is the adjective most descriptive of their activities, and this term generally applies to the three boards that have not previously governed single-campus institutions, as well as to the six that have.

As governing boards begin to reevaluate their role, it is helpful to place their activities into four general categories.

First, a governing board can place primary emphasis on its role as a policy board rather than an administrative board. Substantial authority can be delegated at campus and multicampus levels to the administration, to the faculty, or to both. This model represents the dominant pattern and the existing consensus among administrators as to the proper course of development, a consensus not universally shared by trustees. In this structure, there may or may not be local advisory boards at the campus, but they appear to make little difference.

Second, the board can retain its authority but rationalize the exercise of it in some fashion. For example, a very large board operating through an executive committee and with individual campus visiting committees may have substantial authority but still be able to relate to local campus problems. This particular arrangement, found only in North Carolina, has much to recommend it, but it has few admirers outside of its own state—and a number of critics within.

Third, as found in the State University of New York, local campus boards can be allocated limited authority, or, as in the California State Colleges, be strictly advisory. This imposition of a third tier of lay governance below those of the governing board and statewide coordinating agency is viewed with mixed feelings in both states; the usefulness of a local board depends upon an effective rationalization of governing board–coordinating agency–state government relationships, and this has not yet been achieved in any state.

Fourth, and perhaps most interesting, are possibilities that entirely new instrumentalities of governance involving students, faculty, and administrators will arise, either at the multicampus level or at the campuses. These proposals raise at least as many questions as they purport to answer. However, in the design of a governing structure uniquely applicable to a multicampus university, they deserve close attention.

The system administration

The system executive and the universitywide administration of the multicampus university are its unique features, and we have been centrally concerned with both. This organizational uniqueness has not resulted in a type of executive distinctly different from the traditional college president. (In 1970, two multicampus executives were appointed—at the University of Texas and the State University of New York—whose previous experience had been largely in systemwide, rather than campus, administration. A third executive moved from the leadership of one multicampus university—Missouri—to another—Wisconsin.)

But while there may be a continuity in the characteristics of the multicampus executive, his authority and power are in flux. Notre Dame's Rev. Theodore Hesburgh estimates that he has only one-tenth the power over university affairs that he had in 1952 upon assuming the presidency (*U.S. News & World Report,* 1970, p. 32). Clark Kerr suggests that in the redistribution of power taking place within the modern university, "The president loses to everybody, partly because he has no firm base of support in the power struggle, no natural constituency of his own" (1970*b,* p. 114). This is especially true for the head of the multicampus system. All nine system executives felt this lack of a "constituency" of students, faculty, or alumni. This lack was most evident and troublesome to those who, having only recently relinquished their direct campus responsibilities, found that their new position carried little of the traditional and symbolic authority they enjoyed as a campus executive. At the same time, there was no corresponding decrease in external responsibilities to the governing board or state government to offset their loss of support "in the power struggle." Compared with his single-campus counterpart, the system executive finds himself faced with an increasingly complex external environment but with a decreasing ability to mobilize his internal resources.

His problem will not easily be resolved. Growing external pressures seem certain to increase demands upon the system executive to exercise "educational leadership." Yet any response he might make to these demands will run head on into the often tenuous and fragile exercise of that leadership by the campus executives, who themselves need every bit of substantive and symbolic authority they can muster. A division of labor is essential, but it requires a high degree of sensitivity and flexibility on the part of both executives, a tolerance for ambiguity as to their respective authority, and a considerable measure of personal trust. This is a high order, as the experience of more than one multicampus system is clear. That it is not impossible is also apparent. What cannot be demonstrated is a formula for success, good for all systems and all times.

Faculty government

By our definition, every multicampus university has a governing board and chief executive. Each also has a faculty. But in 1970 only four of the nine universities had extensive experience with a systemwide faculty organization. In two additional systems, multicampus faculty bodies were holding their initial meetings even as we visited the universities, while in the three remaining systems, discussion of formal institutions of universitywide faculty governance were either just beginning or noticeable by their absence.

Two main questions are raised by systemwide faculty participation: (1) Should representation be based on numbers of faculty or equality of campuses? (2) Should the faculty representative speak for himself or for the unit he represents? The first question has been pragmatically answered: patterns of representation are a compromise, with compensatory weight being given to smaller campuses. The answer to the second question, however, is far more elusive because of the highly individualistic nature of academic life. Both system and campus executives find themselves in a dilemma. They can consult with official faculty bodies at length, but faculty are particularly resistant to allowing any agency, even one of their own design, to bind them. And, as already noted, leadership of the faculty by the system executive must take account of the campus executives, themselves often in a tenuous position.

These delicate balancing acts are not taking place in a vacuum. A paradox of higher education is that just as faculty are seeking a more effective role in governance, important decisions are increasingly removed from the university altogether. In each of the seven states, the coordinating agency, the legislature, the governor — singly and in combination — are assuming a far more active interest in major educational policy than in the past. This trend poses new challenges to faculty government and casts doubt on the ability of existing structures to respond. Traditional patterns of faculty organization (we found none that were not traditional) have developed from the need for a faculty voice in matters of internal governance. But into many of these matters the external world is now intruding. How, if at all, a universitywide faculty organization will relate to a state building authority, a legislative budget committee, or a coordinating agency is unclear. Without doubt, however, the faculty will seek a voice at these increasingly critical points of decision.

One possible answer is the intrusion of union activity into areas historically the concern of faculty government. The experience of the City University of New York, though recent and tentative, shows that collective bargaining by the faculty profoundly shapes their relationships to other institutions of academic governance. Diversity, specialization, and cooperation — three hallmarks of the multicampus university — are all affected by the inherent centralizing and leveling qualities of faculty unions.

Student organization

Increased systemwide faculty activity is a feature of multicampus life, whether under the guise of traditional institutions of governance, collective bargaining, or less formal ad hoc arrangement. The pattern of student activity, however, is far less certain. In truth, despite the probable characterization of the 1960s as a decade of student militancy, that militancy has had little impact upon the student-related organization of the multicampus systems.

The reasons are several. The action is usually confined to the campus level, whether the issue is ethnic studies, ROTC, industrial recruitment, four-letter words, or Vietnam. Each of these questions had led the governing board into detailed examinations of the affairs of individual campuses, an involvement that is typical of board activities in general. Each crisis, too, has tended to blur lines of authority between the system and campus executives, although there is awareness on the part of both that responsibility must basically rest at the campus level. The transitory and short-term nature of student life is perhaps more evident at the system than at the campus level. Faculty representatives on universitywide councils have been around for years; in a decade of high mobility and interrupted academic schedules, students measure their experience in months. It is small wonder that they have neither time, expertise, nor inclination to take their affairs beyond the campus, even if a systemwide area of concern could be discovered.

This fact relates to another. While faculty may not always wish to be represented, at least their governing structures are representative. The same cannot be said of systemwide student groups. Student body presidents are notoriously unrepresentative of their campuses, and this is not changed by putting a half-dozen of them in the same room. Other alternatives seem no more promising.

The end result is that, unlike universitywide faculty government, which has resulted in large part from pressures of the faculty themselves, systemwide student organization has been largely the creature of the system executive. This may no longer continue to be the case, but for the moment systemwide student activity reflects the personal style, previous experience, and organizational concepts of the system executive.

THE PRO-CESSES OF GOVERNANCE Both environment and structure shape the character of the processes of governance, and it is to the last that we now turn. For each process, we pose the theoretical advantages and disadvantages which opened each preceding chapter and attempt to answer the questions: Does the multicampus university make a difference? If so, how?

Academic plans and programs

With respect to academic plans and programs, the answer to the first question is a qualified "yes." In each state, there is, in fact, ready verification that differential plans and programs have been nurtured and sustained in the multicampus framework. Diversity, specialization, and cooperation have been promoted. Experimental programs—particularly the innovative undergraduate colleges in several systems—are a prime example of the first; unique graduate offerings concentrated on a single campus illustrate the second; while the third, cooperation, can be seen in joint research facilities.

Diversity and specialization, however, are contained within a relatively narrow and traditional spectrum. Despite the exciting and important innovations of campuses such as Santa Cruz, Old Westbury, Chicago Circle, Green Bay, and others like them, the academic response of the multicampus systems to the demands of the 1960s has been essentially conservative and conventional. By and large, the programs have been confined to the individual campus. Excepting selected joint research and service facilities, few *multicampus* innovations exist. The orthodoxy of the four-year undergraduate program is universally in evidence, with only slight deviations. In several systems, every campus (excepting medical campuses) offers work from the freshman level through the doctorate, and proposed variations are not welcome. The dominance of the flagship campus inheritance—with its emphasis upon the graduate, research-oriented academic revolution—is everywhere apparent. With few exceptions, continuing education is low on the priority list, and tends toward a pale image of on-campus programs. Observed from a distance, the campuses of multicampus universities resemble each other far more than is immediately apparent or necessarily desirable.

An argument offered in favor of the multicampus systems is that, in terms of academic plans and programs, they provide a desired "buffer" between the campuses and external political pressures. In fact, there have been few examples of outright intervention by state officials or politicians in matters of courses, curricula, and degrees. Intervention does not, however, appear to be blocked by the "insulation" provided by the system. Purely academic matters infrequently become political issues. When they do—as in the case of black studies programs or controversial art exhibits—state political figures have not hesitated to move directly into the affairs of the particular campus, with only a passing nod to the system. Here, as in the case of student demonstrations, formal lines of communication are easily broken, and there is little to distinguish external pressures upon the campus from those which would exist if it were an autonomous institution.

We have noted above that authority between the multicampus

university and the coordinating agency with respect to academic planning is everywhere unclear. Some ambiguity is inevitable. The uncertainty reflects the indecision of political leaders, competing university officials, and the general public concerning the relative missions of the various state institutions. But as the oldest and predominant university, the multicampus university is frequently cast in a negative, defensive role that is not always to its credit. In the context of statewide higher education, the university appears to know what it does not want, but it is not always clear what it does want.

With respect to long-range academic planning, the record of the multicampus universities is uneven. The major factors that have prevented realization of an undoubted potential are beyond university control: the usual complexities of academic planning are accentuated in several instances by the inexperience of the multicampus system, and in all cases by jurisdictional problems vis-à-vis the coordinating agencies and state government. At best, planning is difficult in a rapidly changing, often hostile, social and political environment with shifting financial support. Since the multicampus universities, however, do control internal factors, inadequacies of planning can be traced in some instances to failures of leadership within the university and to inadequate staffs, many of which are far too small to meet system needs. Increased attention to the internal factors within system control could counterbalance the external factors.

If unevenness characterizes the systems with respect to academic planning, this is offset by their unquestioned effectiveness in the establishment and nurture of new campuses, in easing the path for campuses in transition from college to university status, and in the review of specific academic programs. Systemwide leadership and the assistance of established campuses have been a clear plus for more than 25 new and transitional campuses which dominated the history of the nine university systems in the 1960s. Financial support, administrative expertise, and experienced faculty guidance are in short supply, and the ability of the multicampus university to provide such resources to a newly appointed campus executive is an immeasurable aid.

Systems have been equally effective in establishing new graduate programs on existing campuses. The "quality control" agencies used by virtually every system to guarantee that new degrees are backed up by adequate faculty and resources constitute an internal "accreditation" that benefits both the university and the state. The risks of flagship domination seem clearly outweighed in those systems by the obvious advantages which affiliation with a major campus brings. And the nonflagship universities have adopted administrative strategies which accomplish much the same end.

On balance, if dramatic innovation in academic planning and programs is the measure, the full potential of the multicampus university has not yet been realized. But if the preservation and extension of existing and valued patterns of higher education is the test, their record is strong.

Budget preparation and administration

We have suggested that to many observers a coordinated universitywide budget represents the raison d'être of the multicampus university. Many reasons are advanced to support the organization of several campuses under one chief executive and board, and we have noted these: the greater ability to make academic plans for a large share of higher education in the state as a whole, the nurturing of new campuses, the articulation of the goals and values of the university to state government—to name but a few. All these find their focus in the university's budget. If the university, as a system, does not have a key—if not the dominant—role in ordering the fiscal needs of the several campuses, then a critical element is missing. A multicampus university must be more than a mere bookkeeping conduit through which funds flow from the capital to the campus.

The issue is not one of total university control versus total state control, but of the appropriate balance in shaping internal priorities, both among and within the campuses. There is general agreement at the extremes: for example, campuses should determine the detailed expenditures of a departmental budget; and the state has a legitimate interest in the relative financial support of graduate and undergraduate education within the university system. But consensus is frequently absent, both among university officials and between them and their state counterparts, as to the relative responsibility of each level for the great middle range of university fiscal affairs. There does appear to be agreement, however, that whether or not it has been delegated ultimate authority, the systemwide administration is a positive influence in ordering the state's higher education budget. Although sharp disagreement over details was often reported, both the campus and the capital attest to the value of multicampus review and coordination of competing campus priorities.

Our evidence does not permit us to compare the success of the multicampus university in producing an effective budget with that of a coordinating agency or a legislative committee confronted with separate campus budgets. But we can assert that in every system—even those in which systemwide influence is least effective —there are examples in which the competing needs of the campuses for always insufficient funds have been thoughtfully and rationally integrated into a coherent universitywide fiscal program. Campus executives do not always agree with the universitywide priorities, but we found none who preferred to see intercampus fiscal competition take place in state legislative halls. State officials were perhaps less restrained, but there is general acceptance that the bulk of budget priorities can more appropriately be handled at the system level than at the capital.

As expected, the highest-quality universitywide budgeting is among the university systems having substantial fiscal autonomy. In these, the system administration has clearly made positive contributions to the budgetary process: by analyzing programs at the several campuses, by comparing unit costs among campuses, and by evaluating reasons for any differences. The central staff has promoted strengthened budget analysis at the campus level, in addition to universitywide budgeting. The scale of several systems permits employment of budget specialists—medicine, plant maintenance, libraries—beyond the capabilities or needs of a single campus. Although it cannot be proven, there is good reason to believe that internal resource allocations of the university are being made on a sounder, more objective basis than would occur without the multicampus structure. Diversity, specialization, and cooperation are being facilitated.

Academic and administrative personnel

At the heart of the university—whatever the relative emphasis upon teaching, research, or public service—is the faculty. If the multicampus system makes a positive contribution to the quality of faculty found on each campus, it may be said to be a success, regardless of other shortcomings. If it makes little or no difference, then one of the main reasons for the system's existence can be questioned.

An assessment depends, of course, upon some common agreement as to "quality" in the appointment and promotion process. The current working definition is both precise and narrow. With few exceptions, it emphasizes "productive scholarship"—research published in specialized technical journals. Utilizing this criterion, a significant achievement of the multicampus university has been the transmission of this value to new campuses and to those in transition from collegiate to university status. This is particularly evident, of course, in the flagship systems. Here, the values of the established university center in academic recruitment and retention have been explicitly extended—with few exceptions—to the newer campuses.

To talk about the *imposition* of values would be misleading, however. The research orientation of the academic revolution is far more pervasive than flagship systems or multicampus universities. Virtually without exception, faculty and administrators of the newer campuses speak of the advantages in recruiting able colleagues because the campus is part of a larger university system, particularly one with a nationally distinguished campus. The key recruiting argument, of course, is that the new campuses share the values of the old campuses and that the old are monitoring the new.

Emphasis upon productive scholarship as a criterion for recruitment and promotion is also found in the consolidated systems, free from the dominance of a single campus. Indeed, the California State College faculty, without a doctoral mission, is scarcely less insistent upon released time to conduct research than their university colleagues. The same can be said of many of the collegiate campuses in other systems. Thus, while they are not responsible for setting research as the primary criterion for academic selection, the multicampus universities appear to be an instrument in its perpetuation.

Not all agree that this value of academic life should be so widely accepted. Paul Woodring, for example, in describing the tendency of American higher education to treat the undergraduate as a "forgotten man," suggests that a main reason for this neglect is a "status system that makes the teaching of broadly liberal undergraduate courses unattractive to academic men." He states that "the question of whether research and scholarly publication can legitimately be required of *every* American professor, whether he teaches graduates or undergraduates, remains controversial" (Woodring, 1968, pp. 186, 188).

This criticism, with which we generally agree, has been largely ignored by the multicampus universities. Indeed, the pressures for a standard of academic excellence stressing research have been a prime force in influencing the several systems we have described as segmental into offering doctoral work on every campus, thus— in circular reasoning—serving to justify the standard. In the comprehensive universities with explicitly collegiate campuses, there is general recognition that the academic personnel standards of the university centers should not be automatically perpetuated at the collegiate campuses. Even in these, however, the status pattern Woodring describes persists. As with academic planning, the multicampus universities have demonstrated greater ability to protect and preserve accepted values than to break new ground.

The relative similarity in personnel standards has not increased intercampus mobility among faculty. The joint appointment of a faculty member among two or more campuses, although often touted as a special advantage of the multicampus university, is rarely encountered. The transfer of a faculty member from one campus to another within the same system is slightly less rare. Only in the University of California is there a record of faculty from the older campuses "colonizing" the new, a practice made possible because each campus has a "general" (i.e., freshman through doctorate) mission and the university has a uniform salary structure.

Policies for academic appointment and promotion and the respective authority of campus and system in these areas are usually well understood in each of the nine universities. This is not the case, however, with respect to the serious question of tenure and dismissal, where the respective roles of the system and the campus executive are often unclear. Although there has been little experience from which to form a model policy or procedure, the seriousness of the problem suggests that the responsibility and authority of the system and campus executives be clarified. A multicampus university appears to offer a distinct advantage here, for it has within it the elements for very effective appellate machinery. This may not require three levels of review—campus, system and governing board—but it could include both a campus faculty hearing committee and a universitywide faculty body to hear appeals, the final decision resting with the system administration. In any event, this is one area where the multicampus university has not yet been seriously tested.

Admissions and transfers

An evaluation of the multicampus university in terms of the admission and transfer of undergraduate students is clearly premature. For many reasons, external and internal, few of the systems have been forced to act like systems. The nine universities vary widely in the way they set their admission standards, in the degree of uniformity of these standards, and in the way they administer admissions. (Graduate admissions was a *systemwide* problem in only one or two universities in 1970 and was not included in the study.)

In only three systems has admissions effectively been a universitywide matter. For the other six, it actually has made little difference whether the system or the campuses decide what admissions qualifications will be or whether these are uniform or not. The scholastic qualifications for admission, generally the prerogative of the system, are with few exceptions well below the threshold of selection criteria, generally the prerogative of the campus, school, or department. Only where such standards for qualification or eligibility actually discriminate among applicants do they have implications for governance, and such standards existed in only a few instances as of 1970.

The most obvious conclusion is to put to rest the allegation that the multicampus university frustrates differential practices among the campuses or imposes a deadening uniformity upon them. While of unquestioned importance, uniform undergraduate admissions policies are not regarded as critical to most of the multicampus institutions. Highly selective and uniform policies are imposed upon all campuses only in the two California systems, where it is made politically palatable and educationally defensible by the safety valve of the state's far-flung network of two-year colleges.

The flexibility of admissions policies in most of the other systems seems less attributable to a fixed universitywide policy decision in the past than to the absence of any policy at all. Relatively low admissions standards and the absence of enrollment limitations on the universities' main campuses combine to remove the issue of admissions as a critical or controversial matter. Student self-selection, rather than universitywide policy, appears determinative.

From the standpoint of the student, there are clear advantages and no apparent disadvantages to the multicampus approaches, as evidenced in several of the systems. One example, a single admissions application good for all campuses, is most fully developed in the University of California, where campus enrollment ceilings have reality. The internal "redirection" machinery, possible because of common admission standards, has been established in that university and permits it to promise a qualified student a place within the system, hopefully in keeping with his first or second choice of campus. The State University of New York provides a different kind of service through its referral of applicants rejected by one campus to another campus of their choice. Similar administrative programs are in evidence or in prospect in other systems. But, as of 1970, these universitywide approaches were the exception; in general, students apply to a campus, not to the multicampus system, and when denied at one campus, send a separate application to another.

Nor is there a pronounced multicampus "presence" with respect to the issue of transfers from two-year colleges. Three of the nine systems contain community colleges, while six deal with community colleges entirely outside the university system. But, in general, little distinguishes the former from the latter in terms of articulation, ease of transfer, or coordination between the junior and senior campuses. Nor are relationships between the two-year college and the multicampus universities much different from those between the junior colleges and other institutions—public and private —within the state. Departmental, school and college requirements —which pose a barrier to easy transfer—seem to resist coordination by the multicampus university; regional relationships based on individual negotiations between two-year colleges and the surrounding four-year campuses appear to be the primary source of effective coordination.

Granting a certain reality to the "market" approach suggested by these comments, it is also true that few of the systems have been monitoring or evaluating the variety of admissions practices with the degree of attention that the subject deserves. The potential of the multicampus university for research and experimentation in the admissions area is almost completely untapped. Rarely is admissions the full-time responsibility of a systemwide officer of cabinet rank, illustrating, perhaps, the general lack of universitywide interest in the subject.

External relations

Most areas of academic activity—such as academic plans, budgeting, admissions—are primarily internal to the university, although influenced, of course, by external forces and events. With each, it is possible to describe the relative authority of campus and universitywide agencies, and there are definable limits to each.

No similar pattern, however, emerges from our review of public and governmental relations. Almost by definition, the subject area is loose and open-ended. Authority is difficult to describe, rarely documented, and highly influenced by personalities and events. The success or failure of programs is measured not in numbers of students, degrees, or research awards, but by external criteria of public opinion and politics not amenable to objective measurement—at least in the context of this study. Moreover, to a significant degree, the programs are the personal and overlapping province of *both* the system and campus executives. What, then, may be said about the effectiveness of the multicampus university?

Although hard evidence is lacking, persons interviewed agree that the multicampus system is a positive benefit to the campuses, individually and collectively, in the area of public and governmental relations. The very existence of additional spokesmen for the university, represented by the system executive and his staff, results in an expansion and extension of informational activities beyond the means of the individual campus. In virtually every university, campus and system executives spoke approvingly of the division of labor between them which—they alleged—made each job more possible. Campus executives generally welcomed the freedom from responsibility for state lobbying that would be theirs in a single-campus institution. Few complaints were noted that this division of labor had been abused. By and large, system and campus executives have reached an effective working agreement as to the appropriate sphere of action for each.

Nevertheless, it is also apparent that none of the systems has been able to take full advantage of its multicampus status in either its public or its governmental relations. Systemwide budgets to support press, radio, and television activities are generally minimal, and universitywide alumni activity is virtually nonexistent. In no instance is the ability of the university to tell its story to its varied constituencies fully mobilized. Almost every system has a public relations program of note—a radio broadcast series or an extensive newspaper service—but these seem scarcely more than any large campus would offer. Shortcomings in these programs appear to be an inevitable result of general legislative antipathy. That this absence of support may well result in less public understanding of the university is also true.

Lobbying activities of the multicampus systems are similarly constrained. Attempts to mobilize the university's *full* strength—for example, a parade of campus executives in legislative halls—may incur legislative or gubernatorial wrath, with charges that the university is "engaging in pressure politics." Such activities might be more easily accepted in a state with separate single-campus universities, each lobbying separately for its own budget.

Representatives from larger, established campuses suggested on occasion that they might better "go it alone," while smaller campuses almost universally expressed the view that they are better off politically because of their inclusion within a system. Even here, however, resentment is expressed against having their political fate tied to some other campus that is the scene of student unrest and, thus, legislative concern. In short, it cannot be stated with certainty whether the *collective* political influence of higher education is facilitated or handicapped by its organization into one or more multicampus systems.

Business affairs

To varying degrees, the five preceding processes of university governance represent activities peculiar to academic institutions, and each is subject to a variety of external influences. Furthermore, these activities are found in each of the nine university systems. The business affairs process, however, is markedly different. With the exception of research management, it concerns activities found at every government level—and in the private sector as well. In addition, the activities are often administered, not by the university, but directly by the state government itself, or by a "foundation" or "authority" somewhat outside the formal university organization. Purchasing is administered primarily by the state for six of the nine universities. The same is largely true of nonacademic personnel administration in five systems. And with respect to physical construction, the state or a separate authority directly administers programs for four universities.

In all instances, the potential strengths and weaknesses of the multicampus structure are obscured by the overlay of state control. Attention focuses on university authority vis-à-vis the state, rather than on the distribution of authority within the multicampus system itself.

With respect to *physical planning and construction,* there are frequent examples of the benefits of specialization and economies of scale resulting from the multicampus structure. These two advantages appear to offset the inevitable complaints of red tape, inflexible rules, and the like, resulting from universitywide review or administration of the capital outlay program. In none of the multicampus systems are there complaints about overstandardization of campuses, and many new campuses are nationally distinguished in the quality of their architecture. Nevertheless, these advantages are often undercut by the uncertainties and inconsistencies of state and federal capital funding. Systemwide planning and scheduling, careful attempts to integrate physical and economic plans with campus priorities into a systemwide program, or efforts to relate capital and operating budgets are all frustrated by the inability to project university building programs with confidence. This problem is endemic to higher education, but within the multicampus university it so strains relationships between campus and system that it also affects other areas of university life. The centralized physical facilities staff absorbs campus complaints that might better be addressed to state and federal departments. Only where the university systems, as in New York, have established patterns of internal capital funding (indirectly through tuition payments) are these obstacles at least partially overcome.

Although the net effect of the multicampus university in *nonacademic personnel administration* is beneficial, programs are clearly dependent on the extent of state governmental control and on a number of nongovernmental forces, such as the labor market, the strength of unionism within the state, and the character of public employee associations. This dependence appears stronger than in other areas of university governance. The impact of the multicampus system, as such, is least evident in those states in which university staff are part of the state civil service. In these instances, state governmental control is sometimes extreme, making little allowance for the unique characteristics of higher education— e.g., the employment of students and student wives, or the need for specialized employees outside traditional civil service classifications. To offset these constraints, at least three university systems have established separate "authorities" or "foundations" to administer construction and extramurally supported research activity. These semi-autonomous agencies permit the employment of personnel outside state civil service.

Even where the multicampus university has complete authority over nonacademic personnel administration, there are obvious limits to full-blown decentralization of authority to the campuses.

For example, substantial campus authority over the classification of positions must be carefully monitored to avoid straining sensitive relationships with state personnel authorities. The parallel activities of university and state create pressures upon the system to centralize nonacademic personnel administration, making it, at times, out of phase and inconsistent with other areas of university governance.

Of these areas of nonacademic administration, *purchasing* is the most centralized. Although we did not assess the effectiveness of the various purchasing programs, examination of its own practices by one multicampus system confirms that substantial economies can indeed be gained by the volume purchasing made possible by an all-university approach. Nevertheless, purchasing is the target of criticism at the local level because of its daily impact on the campuses. Too often, efficiencies of centralized purchasing are handicapped by inefficient, archaic, and inflexible administrative procedures, generally the by-product of state-administered programs.

In marked contrast to these three business activities, *research management* is exclusively handled by institutions of higher education. Paradoxically, however, it is also an activity that seems least touched by the multicampus structure. Here, the pattern is not one of the system attempting to gain authority at the expense of the state government, but, rather, of trying to monitor the activities of hundreds of individual faculty members, if only to be able to serve them better. Here also, however, the pattern is shaped by federal funding policies as much as by anything the university may do internally. To the extent that federally sponsored research is dominated by individually developed and financed projects, each based on an intricate network of personal relationships within the academic, professional, and federal communities, the multicampus system, *as a system,* is only of secondary importance. To the extent that such a funding pattern involves block or institutional grants or mission-oriented projects based on university rather than individual applications, new forms of systemwide activity are being developed. But these may also lead to new forms of state government or coordinating agency activity, and this is also occurring.

DIMENSIONS OF THE MULTICAMPUS UNIVERSITY The specific structures and processes of academic governance are, we have suggested, peculiar to each of the nine multicampus universities. Each has its own institutional history; each is subject to a special set of conditions and events that influence its present patterns of administration. From these separate histories and patterns, however, three conditioning factors emerge that do much to explain the varying course each institution has taken:

1 The *origin* of the multicampus university, whether arising from the expansion of a major *flagship* campus or created by the *consolidation* of previously existing campuses.

2 The *organization* of the multicampus university, whether *segmental* (composed exclusively of "university" *or* "college" campuses) or *comprehensive* (including collegiate as well as university campuses).

3 The *size* of the multicampus university in terms of the *number of campuses.*

These three themes of origin, organization, and size have intruded into every chapter of the study. They emerge as underlying internal characteristics that shape the lives of the nine systems. Admittedly secondary to the external political, economic, and social environment that confronts all institutions, they nevertheless provide the structural foundations from which the universities are moving into the 1970s.

While multicampus universities can be empirically classified by size — according to number of students or campuses — neither origin nor organization is an exact category. We class the University of Texas as a flagship system, because it has so long been dominated by the Austin campus. But Chapel Hill has played scarcely a lesser role in the consolidated University of North Carolina. Furthermore, four of the five flagship systems have expanded by adding preexisting campuses, as well as by creating entirely new ones. Similarly, our classification of a system as segmental is based on the plans of each campus to offer doctoral work in the "near future." Thus, Missouri is segmental, although advanced graduate work is barely under way at the St. Louis campus. And the California State College system, classed as segmental because none of its campuses can independently offer a doctorate, was, in 1970, seeking legislative authorization to do just that.

Further analytic uncertainty arises from the close relationship of the three categories. Although there are significant exceptions, flagship systems have the fewest number of campuses and tend to be segmentally organized. Consolidated (nonflagship) systems have the largest number of campuses and tend to be comprehensive (both collegiate and university campuses). Nevertheless, while it is difficult to isolate the particular influence of only one of the three characteristics, the attempt to do so provides an excellent vantage point to observe and evaluate the multicampus systems.

The three categories are *internal,* excluding the obvious *external* issue of the overall organization of higher education in the state. In Chapter 2, we described in some detail the highly dissimilar patterns the seven states had employed in structuring their public institutions of higher education. But these dissimilar patterns of statewide organization provide little guidance in understanding the internal governance of the multicampus universities, the subject of this study. Instead, we must turn to the three internal characteristics of origin, organization, and size as a basis for generalization.

The Origins of the Multicampus University: Flagship or Consolidated

The five multicampus universities we have termed flagship systems (California, Illinois, Missouri, Texas, and Wisconsin), began their life as single-campus institutions. Geographically distant branches (engineering, medicine, agriculture, mining) were in many cases organizationally attached to the main campus. Subsequently, either new general campuses were created by each university system, or already existing campuses were added to it. A sixth system, the University of North Carolina, was established in 1931 by the merger of three existing institutions. We classify it with the three clearly consolidated systems, although Chapel Hill has much of the prestige and influence typical of the main campus in the five flagship universities. A parallel line of development marked the City University of New York, which had its system origins in the merger of two existing colleges in 1926, one of which (City College) dated from 1847 and had a pronounced impact upon the development of the larger multicampus system. In sharp contrast, the California State Colleges and the State University of New York were created by the consolidation of a large number of previously existing college campuses, no one of which had a noticeable influence on system development.

The distinction between flagship and consolidated systems is not a question of either/or; it involves, instead, placing each system along a somewhat unclear and shifting continuum. This continuum ranges from universities in which one campus long dominated the scene (and may continue to), to those in which this influence was early shared with other campuses, to those in which the university system was formed by the merger of campuses relatively equal in size and status.

The basic characteristic of the flagship systems is the dominance of the values, traditions, organizational forms, and practices of the main campus. This dominance, noted in almost every chapter, has colored relationships between the system administration and the flagship campus, between the system administration and other campuses, and between the flagship campus and other campuses. An important example: Flagship systems have tended to be those in which all campuses of the university offer a doctorate or advanced professional degree. These universities have been, in no small part through the influence of the main campus faculty, an instrument in the perpetuation of what Harold Hodgkinson has termed a "monolithic status system" in which all institutions seek "upward mobility" in terms of higher degrees offered (1970, p. 20). The departure from this model in both Texas and Wisconsin, in which strictly collegiate campuses have recently been established, marks a key step in the life of these multicampus universities.

Domination by the flagship campuses is a natural outcome of this pattern of system development. In all five, for example, the head of the main campus either served simultaneously for a period of several years as head of the multicampus system or became chief executive of the system when a separate campus executive was appointed. The values and experience of the flagship head, added to those of the faculty, have been a major influence on the system as a whole. This, we have noted, is reflected in the title of the system executive: in four of the five flagship systems, he retained the presidential title which had been his when heading the main campus.

Of course this influence extends beyond the personal values and interests of the system executive alone. Accompanying him into office in his new systemwide role have been a number of subordinates with a background of flagship campus experience. In three instances, for example, the academic affairs officer of the main campus assumed a parallel systemwide role, bringing to the process of review of faculty appointments and promotions the standards he had long employed on the campus. Other system staff, accustomed to detailed operational authority at the campus, have not always found it easy to adapt to the broader policy role which systemwide status has required. And in general, it has been easier to apply flagship campus procedures to the multicampus system than to establish a new style of administrative behavior. While many practices appropriate to the large campus may effectively serve the multicampus university as well, many examples exist of academic and business practices that have been uncritically adopted for an entirely new set of problems. Frequently there has been neither time nor manpower to consider the implications of the changed environment. New strategies and policies are being developed out of the growing experience of the systems to meet the special needs of the larger, multicampus context. But the heritage of the flagship, for good or ill—and there were examples of both—is an enduring one.

The transmission of desired flagship values and practices, including the difficulty of changing those less appropriate to a multicampus university, has been influenced in each of the flagship universities (and in North Carolina as well) by the location of system offices on the main campus. Personal relationships between system administrators and college deans are difficult to break when the persons involved occupy neighboring offices. Ambiguity in the minds of students, alumni, and legislators as to "who is in charge" is compounded when, as in two instances, flagship and system executives are for a time housed in the same building. The adjustment of system staff to their new multicampus role is inhibited by their proximity to problems on the main campus, and these have affected relationships—actual and perceived—on other campuses as well.

There are advantages to a close relationship with a main campus, but there is also a price. Both the advantages and the costs distinguish the flagship systems from the three consolidated universities in which universitywide administrative offices are distant from a campus. Our appraisal of these three systems leads us to conclude that, in general, the physical removal of systemwide offices from a campus is a net plus. We missed the flavor of the campus and the co-ed, but we never doubted we were in *university* offices.

The flagship campus has a continuing impact on the governing board. Both board members and their staff have memories of days when they were concerned primarily with the main campus, and board minutes reveal the influence of these memories on current behavior. Practices and procedures appropriate to a single campus continue without reference to the board's new systemwide responsibilities. But board involvement in management was found in at least two of the four consolidated universities, suggesting that it rests on more pervasive factors than origin.

With respect to faculty government, a sharp distinction must be drawn among the flagship campuses, based on both the prestige and practices of the faculty organization on the respective campuses. Where faculty government is strong, as at Madison and Berkeley, other campuses within the two universities have followed their model, and strong, universitywide organizations have been created. Where, in contrast, traditions of strong faculty organization are weak, the case at Columbia and Austin, other campuses of the universities of Missouri and Texas have developed their own patterns, and there is little pressure for universitywide faculty government. In contrast, systemwide faculty government in the consolidated universities tends to reflect the ideas and the initiative of the system executive.

A distinct advantage of the flagship heritage, not immediately obvious, relates to the university budget. In general, the multicampus budget in flagship systems is considered as a unified document, an outgrowth of the main campus budget to system proportions. In the consolidated systems, in contrast, state budget officials have traditionally dealt with separate campus budgets, and this practice continues even though the campuses have been brought within a single, multicampus framework. Paradoxically, despite the dominance of the main campus, system executives in flagship systems generally have more flexibility in making adjustments among campuses than do their colleagues in the consolidated systems.

This same pattern tends to mark other state-university relationships in the consolidated systems. The individual dealings of state officials with separate campuses does not cease when these institutions are placed within a multicampus framework. Campus executives with a past history of direct relationships with state government do not easily break these ties, even when a system executive is given primary responsibility for state government contacts. Here, the prior history of the consolidated universities contrasts sharply with the experience of the flagship systems, and the history influences contemporary relationships. One of the primary tasks of consolidated system executives is to alter past practices. Only by so doing can they effectively mobilize the resources of the entire university. This is not always pleasing to the state capital, and state officials have a tendency to deal directly with the campuses in both flagship and consolidated systems. Indeed, this difference in state relationships between the two kinds of systems is narrowing.

Consolidated multicampus universities are distinct from flagship systems in yet another way: their use of local advisory boards or committees of the main governing board. These have been discussed in detail. Here we note only that they have not markedly affected other elements of university governance. Local boards or committees may have a future in the multicampus university, but the model will undoubtedly differ from the examples existing in 1970.

Diversity, specialization, and cooperation are three criteria by which one can judge the success of the multicampus university. On its face, the consolidated university seems to provide a more fertile field for innovation because of the heterogenous background of its campuses. Flagship systems, in contrast, theoretically would seem to provide a better basis for effective cooperative relationships because of the shared values flowing from the main campus. In truth, there is little to choose, and we would be hard-pressed to suggest that one kind of system has been more effective than another in promoting these values. The new collegiate campuses of the University of Wisconsin seem no less (or more) innovative than those of the State University of New York. The cooperative programs of the University of North Carolina seem no more (or less) effective than those of the University of Missouri. Both kinds of systems seem to be equally effective (or face the same obstacles) in promoting specialization and avoiding unnecessary duplication among campuses.

To what extent can the unique qualities of the flagship campuses as nationally prestigious graduate-research centers be sustained within the overall system? Having done much to establish, often uncritically, a single definition of quality—specialization, graduate training, research—throughout the entire university, will they now be able to continue to set themselves off as something worthy of special support? And to reverse the coin, can the multicampus systems create truly "distinctive [collegiate] institutions with high standards and traditions of excellence . . . [which will] attract first-rate students and distinguished faculty members" (Woodring, 1968, p. 31)? The answers are to be found, in part, in the organization of the multicampus university, whether it continues as a segmental or a comprehensive system.

The Organization of the Multicampus University: Segmental or Comprehensive

A close relationship exists between the origins of the multicampus university—whether flagship or consolidated—and the organization of the university system—whether segmental or comprehensive. In the flagship systems, the definition of a multicampus *university* has generally carried with it the connotation that *each campus* be a university campus as well, offering work through the doctorate or advanced professional degrees. One looks primarily to the two consolidated systems of New York for examples of multicampus universities containing both collegiate and university campuses.

However, this pattern is shifting dramatically. In 1969, the Texas legislature authorized six new campuses for the university system, including two which will not, for the foreseeable future, offer doctoral work. In the same year, two existing collegiate institutions were added to the four campuses of the University of North Carolina. And it may be only a matter of time before one or more of the campuses of the California State Colleges will be granted authority to offer limited doctoral work. In the 1970s most multicampus universities will include both collegiate and university campuses. The organization of the multicampus university—segmental or comprehensive—will in the future increasingly surpass its origins—flagship or consolidated—as the dominant internal characteristic shaping its development.[3]

In Chapter 3, we posed theoretical arguments concerning segmental and comprehensive systems. Proponents of a segmental multicampus university composed exclusively of college *or* university campuses claim that important values peculiar to each segment are lost when both kinds of campuses are included in a multicampus system. Concern is expressed over the difficulty a collegiate campus faces in internal competition with its university siblings within the same system. Simultaneously, university campuses express concern that *their* special needs will not be adequately recognized in a system with a heavy responsibility for undergraduate campuses. Advocates of the comprehensive system counter that unfortunate segmental competition can best be avoided

[3] Our definition of a multicampus university as comprehensive is based on whether it includes campuses basically collegiate (no advanced graduate work) as well as university (offering the doctorate). In addition, both the City and State Universities of New York include several two-year colleges, and the University of Wisconsin has a number of lower-division "feeder" campuses. It is significant but not surprising that only the university systems with collegiate campuses have experimented with two-year campuses as well. While of unquestioned importance in the overall pattern of higher education, the existence of these two-year campuses appears to have had little effect upon the governance of the three universities as a whole, or in distinguishing them from the five segmental multicampus systems.

and important segmental differences effectively sustained within the family.

Evidence to support both claims has been advanced in the body of this study. Without question, the segmental university systems — largely because of the influence of their flagship campuses—have promoted and protected the academic values of research and graduate education. It is less clear that the one collegiate system included in the study, the California State Colleges, has been equally capable of preserving its unique values as primarily a teaching institution; both internal and external forces have pushed it to seek university status. The comprehensive systems have, by definition, the capacity to be more inclusive in their academic planning and to consider more options and alternatives in confronting issues of higher education than systems composed exclusively of university or college campuses. Particularly in New York, where the two comprehensive university systems comprise the totality of public four-year colleges and universities, and in different ways the two-year colleges as well, long-range planning has, in fact, exhibited a coverage that no segmental system could approach. Because of the larger number of variables, planning and program implementation are more complex in a comprehensive university system. But by the same token, they appear more manageable, because controversial issues of intersegmental coordination can be resolved internally by those also responsible for its governance. For example, in confronting the issue of open admissions in New York, both the City and State Universities offer a wider range of possible solutions than does a segmental system. In the latter instance, such questions are more quickly forced upward to the level of the coordinating agency or the state legislature, which alone can resolve intersegmental disputes. Indeed, we have suggested that the two New York systems are very similar to single-board systems of higher education, save for their existence within the same state, and the advantages alleged for the New York pattern are those advanced for this method of organization.

Compared with the segmental institutions, diversity and specialization (but not necessarily cooperation) are, in fact, enhanced *within* the comprehensive university system because of its broader range of options. It is clear, however, that a serious price may be exacted for this apparent gain. Internal pressures in a comprehensive system may bring about among all the campuses a leveling of budgetary support, standards of academic employment, and working conditions. This result may undercut the kind of desired distinctions between college and university campuses that are more easily maintained in a segmental system.[4]

And there *are* important differences among collegiate and university campuses. A system composed of one or the other is a quite different organization from one composed of both. This was evident, for example, in the meetings both of system executives and faculty in the State University of New York. Segmental differences were clearly leading toward the establishment of college and university subunits of both groups so they could more easily deal with their special problems. Such a development might prove beneficial, but it will impose additional pressures upon a system administration attempting to develop a comprehensive, universitywide approach. In part, these problems are compounded by the large number of campuses of the New York systems. It may well be that segmental differences within such smaller university systems as Wisconsin and North Carolina can be both sustained and contained because they can be reviewed more personally and subjectively by faculty, system administrators, and governing board members.

The warning is clear. Improved intersegmental coordination in a comprehensive system can lead to diminished intersegmental differentiation at a time when both coordination and differentiation are required. This dilemma can be avoided if the multicampus university is provided with enough flexibility and authority by state officials to discriminate, to be "unfair" as one system executive put it. It can be avoided if system administrators and governing boards exercise the leadership necessary to implement such flexibility wisely and effectively. It can be avoided if faculty among the segments of a comprehensive university system are willing to recognize differences in the character of their work that justify differential working conditions and compensation.

The drafters of "constitutions" for higher education—legislators,

[4] Thus, we note Paul Woodring's concern that the movement of New York college campuses into the State University system will be ". . . likely to cause them to lose their separate identity, their individuality, and their freedom to innovate" (1968, p. 164). But it may equally be the case that inclusion within the system may promote and sustain these very factors. This is certainly the guiding philosophy of the SUNY administration. Systemwide collective bargaining may well be a greater threat to campus individuality and freedom to innovate than inclusion in the multicampus university.

educators, consultants—will have to appraise the likelihood of such developments before the relative merits of segmental or comprehensive multicampus systems can be assessed.

The Size of the Multicampus University: Number of Campuses

The size of the multicampus university, in terms of number of campuses, is, we have noted, related to both its origins and its organization. Three of the four consolidated systems (the two New York universities and the California State Colleges) have the largest number of campuses. The New York universities are also comprehensive in their pattern of organization, comprising both university and college campuses. In contrast, the two smallest university systems in terms of number of campuses (Illinois and Missouri) originated from a flagship campus and are segmental in character. The interrelationships are, of course, logical. Flagship systems have generally expanded by creating or adding university campuses, the need for which is limited. Comprehensive systems have, by definition, included collegiate campuses, which have been established in far greater numbers.

The number of campuses is not the only dimension of size. Total enrollment of systems and relative size of campuses within them constitute other critical characteristics. These, too, are highly and logically related. The three systems with the largest number of campuses are those with the largest total enrollments, while the three with the fewest campuses have the smallest number of students. And, less obvious, the largest systems in terms of numbers of campuses are those in which enrollment is most equally distributed among the campuses, with no one large campus predominating. All three facets of size are important, of course, and we have noted their impact at various points in the study. Here, we draw particular attention to the consequences of the number of campuses upon the governance of the nine systems. While many of the relationships were anticipated, others were not.

For example, we expected that the larger the university system, the more explicit and overt would be its importance in state politics. A large university system would attract more attention from legislators and governors than a small one, if only because of the size of its budget relative to other state expenditures. To an extent, of course, this is true, but to a critical degree it is not. The smallest system, the University of Illinois, is no less involved in the political life of its state than is the largest, the State University of New York.

Moreover, a ranking of other systems by number of campuses simply does not shed much light on the complex political pattern of state-university relationships. The historical role of the university within the state, the existence of a major campus, and the movement of the university into major urban centers are far more central to the character of the university's political environment than its size.

The number and location of campuses are not politically irrelevant, of course. A legislator prizes the fact that his district contains a campus of the university; by the same token, however, his extraordinary concern for that campus is not always in the interest of the system as a whole. System executives keep careful tab on the number of state legislative districts in which the university has an interest. Concern was sometimes expressed that a "competing" system was gaining "too much influence" because of its growing number of campuses and direct ties to legislators. In more than one state, the establishment of new university campuses was based in part on the desire to expand the university's "presence" into some hitherto unsettled region.

The obvious political virtues of a large number of campuses cannot be overlooked. But there is another side of the coin. As the number of campuses within the system increases, the special role of the flagship campus may be reduced. Sharing the label of "the university" with organizational siblings may mean loss of special status and concern for the main campus. The proposition cannot be tested, but it was frequently posed in every flagship system. The issue had been explicitly raised in Illinois. University officials were clearly disappointed over the decision of the board of higher education to assign responsibility for the development of a new campus at Springfield, the state capital, to another multicampus system, limiting the University of Illinois to three campuses. Nevertheless, it is clear that the limitation will permit the university to concentrate upon its critical role as *the* prime center in the state for graduate education and research, its university mission. Each state offers its own distinct example of the relative importance of number and character of campuses in the context of the state's political system. There is a close relationship between educational and political considerations in determining the "proper" size of the multicampus university.

Consequences of the number of campuses within the system

upon its *internal* governance are more obvious. The governing boards of the largest systems clearly have greater difficulty in gaining a close understanding of a particular campus than do those confronted by the problems of only four or five campuses. In theory, the offsetting advantage would be for the boards of the larger systems to devote more time and attention to universitywide problems and less to details of management on the several campuses. In fact, however, we have noted that this is not the case. Board members often involve themselves in operational detail as though they were trustees of a single campus, without the requisite knowledge of the institution. In general, the size of the system has not altered this pattern, and the implications for governance are both obvious and serious.

For the system executive and his staff, there is less difference in working patterns between the large and small systems than we anticipated. We were assured by the executive of one of the smaller systems that his job was materially different from that of his colleague confronted by a large number of campuses. In fact, this is not the case. The duties and daily schedules of each are remarkably similar, and this extended to the entire systemwide administration. The critical distinction, we conclude, is between the executive directly responsible for the operations of a campus and one who is not. Once the decision is made to divide the responsibilities of administration between campus and system, once distinguished and experienced executives are appointed at both levels, a different pattern immediately emerges, regardless of the number of campuses. The system executive of the University of Illinois with only three campuses has, we suggest, more in common with his counterpart in the State University of New York, with 30 campuses, than with the executive of the Urbana campus.

Size undoubtedly affects the style and substance of executive leadership, but no clear pattern is evident among the nine multicampus universities. To only a limited extent, for example, is there a relationship between the existence of formal policies and administrative regulations and large size; or between an informal pattern of administration and a small number of campuses. Rather, as we have suggested, system administration is very much the projection of the personal style and background of the chief executive, often dominated by his previous experience as the head of the flagship campus, and heavily influenced by the constitutional or statutory framework of state relationships in which the university finds itself. These are only marginally, if at all, related to the size of the system.

One significant exception concerns the relationship between the system and campus executives and, perhaps equally important, the relationships among the campus executives themselves. Here, numbers are important because of the practical necessities of time and space. With only three or four campuses, contacts between the system and campus executives can be relatively informal. With 15 or more campuses, frequent personal contact is difficult. Collegial meetings of campus executives, chaired by the system head and without the participation of other system administrators, are most frequently held in the larger systems. These were reported to be less effective when the number of campuses exceeded a dozen or so. When these large systems also include both college and university campus executives, another barrier is raised to effective systemwide communication. These differences in the pattern of system-campus executive relationships quite clearly affect the style of administration and executive leadership, but we were unable to determine if they also affect policy and program.

Larger systems have a far higher incidence of *formal* systemwide faculty and student activity than the smaller, despite the obvious greater organizational difficulties associated with large size. System executives confronted with three or four campuses can meet regularly and separately with campus groups. In the larger systems, in contrast, this is clearly an impossibility. If there is to be regular contact between faculty and students and the system—at either the administrative or board level—formal organization is required. Significantly, the creation of such organizations has been just as often the result of stimulus by the system executive as by students or faculty acting on their own. He needs contact, even if the groups do not. Such organization is much farther advanced and stable with faculty than with students.

The impact of the number of campuses on the substance of governance is difficult to establish. For example, there is more evidence of formal, published academic planning in the larger systems, but we were conscious of a great deal of informal planning in the smaller. Admissions is clearly a more critical issue in the four larger systems of New York and California than elsewhere. But this is a reflection less of the number of campuses in these two states than of the inclusion within the systems of all public higher education beyond the two-year college.

In the field of budgeting, logic suggests that the larger systems should have greater flexibility under detailed state fiscal controls than the smaller, if only to avoid an undue flow of paper. This is not the case. Budgeting, and the whole field of business management, reflect a heritage of state controls from a presystem period. If a flagship campus has achieved relative autonomy, this is carried forward into state relationships with the entire system. If, in contrast, the pattern is one of detailed state involvement with previously separate campuses, this tends to continue. The respective needs of the universities and the state in the field of budget and finance administration have rarely been systematically reviewed in the light of the new demands placed upon both by the size of the systems.

In sum, there is no "ideal" size for a multicampus university. A large number of campuses introduces problems into the system which—for good or ill—would otherwise be resolved by coordinating agencies, legislatures, and governors. The introduction of new problems carries a price, but size also brings a unique capacity to deal with their solution, a potential available only to a multicampus university directly responsible for governance. But a large number of campuses does not—in and of itself—provide a university system with the capability to solve problems and, indeed, if not properly organized and led, can make their solution less likely. Size is not the critical variable.

THE MULTI-CAMPUS UNIVERSITY IN THE 1960s: A SUMMING UP The growth of multicampus universities has been a key development in American higher education. But growth has been the hallmark of all higher education in the United States, regardless of organizational form: single-board systems have expanded, autonomous campuses have been established. What may we conclude about the special impact of the multicampus university?

In this chapter we have reviewed the role of the nine systems from the vantage points of the *environment* of governance—social, economic, and political; the *structures* of governance—governing board, administration, and faculty and student organization; and the substantive *processes* of governance—including academic planning and the preparation and administration of the budget. It remains to prepare a balance sheet of the strengths and weaknesses of the multicampus university as suggested by the record of the 1960s. Only then can we indicate the changes which will have to be made if these nine systems are effectively to meet the new and even more demanding challenges of the 1970s.

Generalization, obviously, is both hazardous and highly subjective. Evidence is contradictory. Virtually every conclusion is marked by an exception. What appears important to us as a general principle may be of little significance to a particular state or university. Many concerns are beyond reach of the university but rest on relationships with state and federal governments. Nevertheless, judgments must be drawn and opinions rendered.

First, the strengths:

Strengths 1 Quite clearly, the major achievement of the multicampus university has been the establishment of new campuses and the transformation of old ones, and the recruitment of able faculty to both. The existence of a board, system administration, and faculty *with previous governing experience and current capability* has been of immeasurable importance in the rapid development of more than a score of new and transitional college and university campuses, including among them some of the most significant educational experiments of the decade.

2 Of scarcely less importance, the multicampus universities have promoted among existing campuses specialization, diversity, and cooperation in academic planning and in the preparation and implementation of the budget. Examples abound of difficult decisions to assign a particular high-cost program to one campus, to defer a program at another, to develop complementary programs among several. It is difficult to imagine these decisions being reached on a voluntary basis among autonomous institutions; it is also difficult to conceive of equally effective resource allocation being made by persons in coordinating agencies or state government, removed, as they are, from operating responsibilities.

3 Quality control, particularly the internal but independent "accreditation" of new graduate degree programs in terms of the adequacy of faculty and supporting resources, is a prime responsibility of virtually every multicampus university. Review procedures are impressive in their scope and in the quality of reviewing personnel, both faculty and administrative. Both procedures and personnel are strengthened by the existence of the multicampus system.

4 In university business management (where these activities are not directly performed by the state government), there are signifi-

cant examples of efficiencies arising from systemwide administration. Specialization and economy of scale are possible beyond the resources of a single campus.

5 Public and governmental relations for the several campuses are enhanced by their common membership in a university system. A division of labor between campus and system executives, with the latter assuming primary responsibility for state relationships, makes both their tasks more manageable. (As noted below, this does not necessarily create a more favorable and effective relationship with state government than would otherwise be the case.)

Second, the shortcomings:

Shortcomings 1 The clearest weakness of the multicampus university is a shared one: the absence of a stable agreement on the relative authority of the state government, the coordinating agency, and the university over various phases of the governance of higher education. Partly because of this uncertainty, the university systems are often unable to develop optimal internal organizational and procedural relationships with and among the campuses. External uncertainty leads to internal instability, seriously limiting the ability of the multicampus university to act as a *system.*

2 This uncertainty is matched by the state government's inadequate delegation of fiscal authority to the university. Detailed controls are often noteworthy primarily for their red tape rather than for their substantive contribution to effective educational administration. Reliance on arcane budgetary formulas rather than an assessment of means necessary to accomplish specified ends characterizes many state-university budgetary relationships.

3 In no small part, inadequate budgetary delegations result from the failure of multicampus universities to develop indices of budgetary support in which state finance offices have confidence. There is little research and development in university budgeting, despite the unique ability of the multicampus systems to engage in it. In truth, however, few states have provided any incentive to the universities to engage in more innovative budgeting. Faced with increasing tax pressures, state officials seem less concerned with increasing educational effectiveness than with reducing educational costs, and the two are not the same.

4 Arising in part from budgetary inflexibility, but more from the internal institutional conservatism of both faculty and administration, multicampus universities are not sufficiently innovative in

terms of academic plans and programs. Diversity and specialization are carried on within traditional lines. The Ph.D. orientation of the flagship campus has too often and too uncritically been the dominating value of the system as a whole. Possibilities for variety and experimentation, for which a multicampus system is uniquely qualified, are not being fulfilled, and the range of alternatives represented by the campuses among the systems is relatively narrow. In addition, there is little evidence of programs which are *multicampus* in nature and involve the resources of the entire system. Student and faculty mobility, where it exists, represents the choice of the individuals concerned, and is only rarely the result of systemwide planning. Among the nine universities, we discovered only one example (medical education in Texas) of a coordinated teaching program of any consequence *among several campuses of the university system.* There are undoubtedly other examples, and plans for such programs under discussion, but their lack of visibility is significant. With a few notable exceptions, and in the face of a growing need, continuing education is nowhere a high-priority item on the system agenda despite the obvious advantages that a multicampus university possesses for such programs. Briefly, in terms of academic programs, the multicampus university is not clearly enough greater than the sum of its parts.

5 Governing boards have failed to consider their unique *multicampus* role. They tend to act as a managerial board over a number of individual campuses, rather than as the board of a system. There is little to distinguish their agenda from that of a single-campus institution. The results are twofold. The boards often involve themselves in the operational details of an individual campus without the information necessary for effective exercise of their managerial role. More important, concentration on operational detail has led the board away from concern with many basic issues of educational policy for which it is qualified, for example, programs and experiments unique to the multicampus system.[5]

[5] Earl F. Cheit, former executive vice-chancellor of the University of California at Berkeley, speaks to this point: "It is always difficult to lead large organizations. Events often overtake procedures and in the case of universities there are no fixed criteria—such as a profit-and-loss statement—of successful performance. This difficulty is increased when the board of directors is centralizing the organization and getting into administration, because then the major board problems get buried by the administrative problems, which come in a rapid flow of questions for decision. These questions consume much of the regular agenda, and the board finds it impossible to devote enough time to thoughtful discussions about growth, direction, finance, and priorities" (Cheit, 1970).

6 The multicampus system is not always an effective buffer against undue political pressures from state government. On the contrary, by its very size and importance, it often attracts political attention, at times interference, which might be less likely were each campus a separate entity. We do not suggest that any major university should not be subject to political attention; that it should become involved in *partisan* politics with all the attendant pressures is quite a different thing. We found evidence of such pressures in every state. This is at least in part because the governor serves as chairman of the governing board (in four of the nine systems) and partly because he has the power to select trustees[6] (in seven of the universities). An appropriate division of labor between the political arms of the state and the governing board is difficult when the chief political figure of the state is himself *directly* involved in the governing machinery of the university, and the university is increasingly a major public policy issue in the life of the state. Both the involvement and the interest are in some measure derivative of the multicampus status of the university.[7]

These strengths and shortcomings of the multicampus university were all evident as of 1970. In addition, there are three matters, certain to be issues of the future, in which the system role is not yet evident and conclusions are premature.

1 The admission of undergraduate and graduate students has not yet become a *universitywide* problem in several multicampus universities. For the undergraduates, relatively low admissions standards and open-ended campus enrollment policies have postponed the necessity to review the issue of entrance into and mobility within

---

[6] This includes the mayor of New York City, who selects the trustees of CUNY.

[7] Martin Trow (1970*b*, pp. 52–53) states the case as follows: "The transformation of the constituencies of a university from a relatively small known set of relevant publics to a large undifferentiated mass public may be the inevitable consequence of the expansion of a state university system governed by a single board, and thus perceived as a single entity. Decentralization has been argued in universities on educational grounds. . . . I would argue decentralization on political grounds: that enormous universities and university systems which constantly extend their influences must engender mass audiences. . . . it seems inescapable that the university in the future will be involved much more frequently in highly controversial issues and actions for which mass support cannot always be gained. Such activities may have a better chance of not becoming the focus for a major crisis . . . if decisions about them are not taken at the statewide level in ways that require politicians and other politically ambitious people to take public stands on them."

the system as a whole. For graduate students in most of the universities, admissions is largely the prerogative of the departments. The need to consider coordinated graduate admissions policies for the multicampus system has not yet been faced.

2 The impact of faculty unions and collective bargaining upon the multicampus university is unclear, as is the question of whether the New York pattern will be extended to other states. Collective bargaining may inevitably lead to greater centralization of administrative authority to counter the centralized power of a multicampus union. On the other hand, the disparate needs and desires of different kinds of campuses may create both internal and external pressures to break up the university into separate institutions to counter the inherently leveling consequences of systemwide bargaining.

3 Finally, the role of students in *systemwide* governance is even more uncertain than at the campus level. Size and distance, coupled with basic issues of representation, pose practical problems that make other than *pro forma* participation difficult. At the same time, students appear increasingly interested in those policy decisions made at the systemwide level which affect them. The development of a structure equal to the interest is not in sight.

These considerations—strengths, shortcomings, and uncertainties—are, we conclude, the dominant characteristics of the multicampus university as it presently exists. But the conditions confronting the nine university systems are changing. New problems are on the horizon; new challenges are emerging. And new institutional strategies are required to deal with both. The strengths of the multicampus university must be continued, the shortcomings remedied, the uncertainties resolved. In Chapter 15, we suggest what must be done if the multicampus university is to remain an effective institution in an increasingly complex environment.

15. The Future of the Multicampus University

On balance, the record of the multicampus universities is impressive. In the face of social, economic, and cultural changes of massive proportions, the nine systems have administered teaching, research, and public service programs of high quality. New campuses have been brought into being and old campuses expanded; thousands of students have been educated, and scientific discoveries have been made and critical public policy decisions aided — all under the aegis of the nine multicampus universities we have studied.

But this record does not lead to the automatic conclusion that the same judgment of overall effectiveness will be rendered 10 years hence. The decade of the 1970s will mark a far greater break with the past than that of the 1960s with that of the 1950s. We suggest some of these changes below. Cumulatively, they underscore the warning of William J. McGill (1970b), newly appointed president of Columbia University: "We must begin soon to confront the need for major educational reform in America. Concentration on the symptoms of student unrest has largely diverted us from a rigid degree system that was conceived more than a hundred years ago, and from an undergraduate four-year program last reformed in the 1920s."

The *organization* of higher education will not determine the place or the future of the university in society. Whether a state has a single-board system or single-campus institutions; whether it has a strong coordinating agency or a multicampus system like those we have studied; or whether it has some combination of these — none of these factors will *in and of itself* solve the problems of higher education in the 1970s. Indeed, our inability to understand the political and social context of organizational form has beclouded our understanding of the dynamics of university governance. None of the alternative patterns of organization is better or worse in abstract. They take shape and can be evaluated only in terms of the environment within which they are set. Particular sets of political and social circumstances may dictate a pattern of organization which could not survive in a different context.

The organization of higher education, therefore, is critical *in combination* with its environment. Organizational form affects the access and power of the different participants in academic governance with respect to specific decisions. It influences the agenda of all institutions of higher education, the manner in which that agenda will be handled, and the very substance of educational plans and programs. Organizational form affects the goals and values that control the life of the universities and colleges—singly and collectively—and will determine to a significant degree the response of these institutions to the more fundamental forces shaping higher education in the 1970s.

What are some of these fundamental forces? Under what conditions can the multicampus university effectively respond to them, consistent with both its traditional and contemporary responsibilities to society?

HIGHER EDUCATION IN THE 1970S   The 1970s will be a period of change, indeed trauma, for colleges and universities across the nation.[1] It is not our purpose here to add to the many descriptions of the political, social, and economic environment of higher education in the coming decade. A brief listing of the factors with special, but not exclusive, significance for the large multicampus systems makes the point: The 1970s will be a testing ground. Conventional wisdom will not be a sufficient guide. Higher education in 1980 may not be "better." It will almost certainly be different.

1   The multiversity—of which every multicampus university is an example—will continue for the foreseeable future. The trend of

[1] Among recent studies of the contemporary scene, these may be cited: William M. Birenbaum, *Overlive: Power, Poverty, and the University,* Dell, New York, 1969, 206 pp.; Alvin C. Eurich (ed.), *Campus 1980: The Shape of the Future in American Higher Education,* Delacorte Press, New York, 1968, 327 pp.; Alvin C. Eurich, *Reforming American Education,* Harper & Row, New York, 1969, 269 pp.; Fred F. Harcleroad (ed.), *Issues of the Seventies,* Jossey-Bass, San Francisco, 1970, 192 pp.; Christopher Jencks and David Riesman, *The Academic Revolution,* Doubleday, New York, 1968; Paul Woodring, *The Higher Learning in America: A Reassessment,* McGraw-Hill, New York, 1968, 236 pp.; *Daedalus,* Winter 1970, and *Daedalus,* Summer 1970.

looking to the universities to serve society in a variety of ways
continues. These demands are often inconsistent, if not on collision
course. Whatever the case in an earlier age, the combination of
teaching, research, and public service missions in the context of the
1970s poses the threat of institutional overload.[2] The need for new
organizational responses to these substantive pressures will become critical.

2   Universities and colleges will be asked to educate increasing numbers of students, constituting an ever-rising proportion of the young.
Current enrollment projections indicate that opening fall enrollment will increase from 7.9 million in 1969 to about 13 million in
1980. These students will comprise 44 percent of college-age youth
(ages 18 to 24) in 1980, compared with 31 percent in 1969. A much
larger proportion of these students will be in public institutions and
—coupled with this fact—in two-year public institutions. Enrollments in public four-year institutions are expected to increase from
4 million students in 1969 to over 7 million in 1980, while graduate
enrollments (public and private) will more than double, exceeding
2 million by 1980.[3]

There is wide agreement that figures such as these are realistic.
Reform of the draft may soften some of the pressures leading to
what Kingman Brewster has termed "the involuntary student,"
but other social and economic factors urging college attendance
show no signs of weakening. Universal public education through
"the fourteenth grade" is being accepted as the pattern which will

[2] A highly critical and pessimistic view is that of Philip C. Ritterbush (1970,
p. 647): "The danger signals indicating malignant incompatibility among
objectives have become conspicuous in many universities. It becomes impossible
to settle policy differences and the sores of discord do not heal. Competing
claims for resources cannot be resolved. The principal officers of administration decline in effectiveness, unable to fulfill the agenda of necessary decisions. Central forums for collective judgment are disregarded by autonomous
operating units which do not bear the institution's imprint. External demands
gain in influence as the institution no longer operates a field of force to govern
its endeavors. If the objects of an institution are not stated so as to govern its
commitments, its internal regulating authorities will be overthrown by cancer-
ous growth and the institution will lose the ability to pursue objects of its own.
If the university presidency is the impossible office it is so often said to be, it
is because the institution has lost its identity and become unmanageable. And
so the fiercest trials of society come to be re-enacted in a university arena unable
to contain them."

[3] The data and projections in this paragraph were supplied by Dr. Gus Haggstrom of the staff of the Carnegie Commission on Higher Education. The
rationale behind his projections can be found in his unpublished paper (1969).

dominate public education. It will have significant implications for the senior colleges and universities.

These projected enrollment increases suggest five trends which may operate within and upon the multicampus universities during the coming decade. Not all these trends will be found in any given state, for some, in fact, are contradictory.

First, enrollment growth will not be matched by a proportionate increase in the number of institutions. For the states as a whole, new two-year campuses will appear regularly, but few new four-year campuses will be built. Many campuses are new and substantially below planned enrollment. Moreover, diversion of lower-division undergraduates to two-year campuses is in prospect in several states.

Second, within the multicampus universities, most campuses will tend to look more alike at the undergraduate level, but become somewhat more distinct at the graduate level. At the undergraduate level, the increasing maturity and size of the newer or smaller campuses will account for their increasing similarity both to each other and to older campuses, although a contrasting development — exclusively upper-division campuses — is also likely. At the graduate level, there is little evidence that the proliferation and regrouping of disciplines and subdisciplines will slow down. However, support for *each* such new area of knowledge at *each* public campus in a system (or in a state, for that matter) is becoming increasingly less feasible.

Third, the transfer of students from two-year to four-year campuses will become more common as the former increase in number and larger percentages of students are diverted to them for lower-division work. The two-year campuses will gain a larger measure of academic "respectability" and increased political strength, often at the expense of senior institutions. The relationship between curricula at the two-year and four-year campuses will become of greater concern to both segments. Upper-division, or upper-division–graduate campuses — as recently established in the University of Texas system — will be given more widespread consideration.

Fourth, the personal financial status of students will be of greater interest. Those who can afford to do so will be asked to pay directly an increasing share of the rising cost of their education. On the other side of the coin, most financial barriers against true equality of access to higher education will probably come down.

Finally, qualifications for admission to public campuses will change substantially from the almost universal reliance in the 1960s on high school averages and national test scores. There will be contrasting pressures for open admissions on the one hand, and increasingly sophisticated measures of selection on the other.

At the graduate level:

The graduate deans . . . will soon be sharing the woes of present undergraduate admissions officers in trying to bolster the dikes to keep out waves of students for whom they have insufficient facilities. This pressure will have serious consequences for admissions-policy and screening procedures. . . . This expansion in graduate education will raise (or further complicate) many problems concerning admissions, fellowship needs, faculty requirements, and imbalance in support of educational programs, not to mention the physical problems of providing university facilities, equipment, and housing for a graduate-student population three or four times larger two decades hence (Cartter, 1968, p. 259).

3 Increased numbers of students to educate, together with increased demands on the university to serve society in other ways, will inevitably lead to greater public involvement in the governance of higher education. The university will become more central to more people, more of a public issue, and more involved in politics. Part of this will result from rising costs, but more fundamentally it will spring from the stake which everyone has in higher education. Martin Trow (1970a, pp. 11–12) has described this change:

Many of the popular functions of the universities in the past—mass education and public service—have indeed been popular in the other sense of the word and have gained the support or indifference of the general public. But it seems inescapable that the university in the future will be involved much more frequently in highly controversial issues and actions for which mass support cannot always be gained. The expansion of the universities, both in size and function, means that we will be living in an environment increasingly sensitive to what the university does, and especially to what it does that has direct effects outside the university. It is not generally recognized how much the university's freedom and autonomy were a function of popular indifference and of the management of special interest groups outside the arena of popular politics. But for various reasons the society is less and less indifferent, at the same time as trustees and regents are less able to perform their traditional function of defending the university through the forms of elite politics.

4 As a consequence of rising public awareness and concern over higher education, state and national governments will play a greater role in many facets of academic governance.

Higher education has become too important to the welfare of the various states and regions and to the whole nation for its development to be left entirely in local or private hands. The pressures for expansion and improvements require huge sums of money. Many of the urgent issues and problems cannot be handled adequately in piecemeal ways. With the growing collectivism of modern life, more and more decisions and actions affecting the development of higher education are being transferred from the private to the public arena, and from the local to the state or national level (Wilson, 1968, pp. 25–26).

A recent Canadian report provides two examples of governmental involvement which are certain to become more important issues of public policy in the United States in the 1970s:

. . . the state already controls some aspects of admission in so far as they overlap governmental responsibility for social policy. It is also clear that because admissions policies form an inextricable part of general social policy on educational opportunities, governments ought to have a say in their determination.

. . . Salary levels and scales, staff structure and staffing ratios are all of obvious interest to government because they are closely related to the total cost of universities (Hurtubise & Rowat, 1970, p. 63).

And Allan Cartter (1968, p. 278) suggests that by 1980, all advanced graduate students will be federally supported and all universities will receive general aid for costly advanced degree programs.

The point is clear: In the decade of the 1970s, higher education will become even more inextricably connected to a host of state and national policies than ever before. Questions of access, financing, and staffing can all too easily lead to interference with fundamental freedoms of teaching and research. Developing effective university-government relationships in areas of legitimate public concern while retaining essential university autonomy in others will be a crucial issue.

5   Increasing state and national concern will lead to more demands for interinstitutional cooperation and coordination, but based on the experience of the seven states, to continued uncertainty over the role of state coordinating agencies. Many educational issues of the 1970s will require solutions beyond the capabilities of a single institution or even a single multicampus system. But it is into many of these same areas of educational policy that state budget offices and legislative committees are entering directly, bypassing coordi-

nating agencies. We see little evidence that either governors or state legislators will delegate important policy responsibilities. On the contrary, the trend appears to be the reverse. Many agencies are being bypassed, overridden, or ignored. Generally lower on the status totem than the system governing boards, coordinating agencies have, in several states, become more the virtual agents of the state administration than effective bridges (and buffers) between the universities and state governments.

Will coordinating agencies remain as active participants in the governance of higher education? If so, will their participation result from the delegation to them of present responsibilities of state agencies, or by increased authority in matters hitherto the province of the university systems? We do not know. The outcome of the present confused pattern is unclear, and will doubtless vary among the seven states. We can conclude only that the present pattern is unstable, that the 1970s will see changes, and that these changes will have a significant impact upon the multicampus universities. Logan Wilson's point (1968, p. 26) is equally true of either coordinating agencies or state governments:

. . . they are potent political mechanisms making for the *outer* direction of higher education, and they will inevitably tend to diminish the *inner* direction; that is, the control of the college and universities by professors, deans, presidents, and trustees.

6   To return to President McGill, the 1970s will be (perhaps "must be" is the more cautious term) a period of major educational reform if the universities are to maintain their central role.

The University must some day confront the fact that the requirements of an advanced technology are generating major educational problems. In order to achieve professional status and serious involvement with the affairs of society, education is now more and more difficult and takes longer. . . .

It seems to me that we need to move away from our present circumstances in which we work from educational concepts that were last modified in the twenties: two years of broad gauge education followed by two more years of major study, then a master's degree of dubious validity in any current educational structure, followed by a Ph.D. program which is notably insufficient in science and social science, followed by an indeterminate amount of post doctoral work.

If we do not begin soon to replace this creaky structure with some kind of career curriculum concept in which it becomes possible for students to exit from the University and enter society at a useful educational level for occupations they choose, to re-enter the University and study again, then move out again, so that education is considered to be a lifelong enterprise—we are in, I think, for continuing and basic trouble (McGill, 1970a).

William Birenbaum (1968, pp. 61–62) has suggested the massive dimensions of President McGill's challenge that education must be a "lifelong enterprise":

Except for the limited public to whom the principle of the second chance can legitimately be applied, it is doubtful that undergraduate programs designed for eighteen-year-olds can ever successfully be translated into adult education. [In addition] . . . the graduate model of higher education is inappropriate for most adult-education programs because it is too narrow or too special, too timid or too easy, too late or too irrelevant. . . .

The future university—reliant upon a wide variety of industrial, governmental and artistic resources and talents, but unable in view of the competition to *monopolize* the best of these talents available—will be compelled to redefine its concept of "campus." Necessity will lead to an extension of its day-to-day operations beyond the pieces of real estate upon which its special buildings stand. The functions of the university will inevitably reach into the theaters, museums, industrial laboratories, libraries, and centers of financial, social and political research housed in other urban institutions.

If even a few of the predictions and prescriptions of these two commentators come to pass, the 1970s will see major changes in higher education. These changes will have implications for governance, just as the pattern of governance will shape the character and pace of the changes.

7   In response to most of these developments, collective activity by faculty will increase in the 1970s, whether in autonomous unions or traditional senates. The reasons for this and the ways it will take shape will be various and will shift over time, but the issue may be put in the form of several propositions:

- If governing boards prove to be a conduit for political pressures rather than a buffer, faculty will organize to oppose such pressures.

- If collective bargaining in the public sector comes to be the dominant mode of determining employment conditions, faculty will organize to secure equal benefits for themselves.

- If proposals for educational change affect traditional prerogatives, working conditions, prestige, status, and budgetary allocations—as they will—faculty will organize to shape such changes more to their liking.

- If students—radical and otherwise—press demands which affect faculty in a manner they deem adverse, they will organize to counter such demands.

The primary implications of collective faculty action for university governance concern the faculty-administrative relationships. The present partnership approach to decision making, with its stress on "shared authority" and joint cooperative activity, may be replaced by separation of powers with an emphasis upon bargaining and negotiation. The university executive, at campus and at system levels, will confront new pressures and adopt new modes of administrative behavior in his relationships to both the faculty and the governing board.

A second issue, however, posed most clearly in the formal collective bargaining in New York, is whether the administration will have a role at all. Will the negotiated contract replace the executive budget as the primary instrument of fiscal management? The question is not farfetched, as a review of the City University agreement of 1969 clearly indicates. Scarcely a phase of university resource allocation is not touched upon in that document. The inevitable question follows: Will labor negotiators representing government replace university administrators in the development of this key fiscal instrument? Unable to bind the state to a particular level of financial support, will both the administration and the governing board find themselves mere onlookers as faculty deal directly with state officials in critical aspects of university governance?

8 As for the students, not only will they be around in greatly increased numbers in 1980, but Nevitt Sanford (1968, pp. 196–198) tells us there will still be plenty for them to protest against:

> . . . on the higher education scene student demands for better education and a larger role in determining their own affairs will have spread to virtually all institutions in the country. . . . as time goes on, more and more students of the activist persuasion will be in graduate schools, where, encouraged by the presence of people like themselves, they will lend support to the reformist efforts of undergraduates. Indeed, by 1980, it will be possible for people who were activists as undergraduates to retain their youthful orientation even as assistant professors. They will be joined by formerly "suppressed activists" among the older professors and together they will supply the leadership that activist students want and need.

This continued student activism will take place in a context of frequent interruptions in the academic schedule for work and travel,

and greatly expanded mobility between institutions. The anticipated increase in the proportion of undergraduates who take their
lower-division work in a community college before transferring may
well be matched by transfers among four-year colleges themselves.
The end result will be—it seems inevitable—a further erosion in
identification with a particular college or university and an increase in commitment to a free-floating student culture. In their
own way, students will parallel faculty in the latter's substitution
of a national, disciplinary orientation for institutional loyalty.

9 With respect to the multicampus universities in the 1970s, the flagship systems will come increasingly to resemble the consolidated
systems: both will be composed of a number of large campuses of
relatively equal size. Flagship dominance will diminish, and important second (and third) campuses will rival or even exceed the main
campus in size, budget, and influence. As the multicampus universities mature *as systems,* and new generations of administrators are
appointed, lines of authority will become more formal. Decentralization of administrative authority to the campuses will be more
clear-cut and uniform, but the scope of authority will not necessarily
be broader, because of greater constraints upon the system from the
state level.

10 The second campuses referred to above will often be located in
urban centers (Chicago, Milwaukee, St. Louis, Kansas City, Charlotte, Dallas), consistent with William Birenbaum's contention
(1968, p. 47) that ". . . it will become increasingly difficult for institutions of higher education to be great apart from the urban environment." Demands upon these urban campuses to serve their
immediate society will challenge both the campus and the system of
which it is a part. Demands for some form of "local board" to reflect
the needs of the community is a possible development, and these
would almost certainly be more broadly representative of the
citizenry than the existing multicampus governing boards. Conflicts over jurisdiction between such local boards and the system
board will be likely; executives at both levels will be affected.

11 Finally, campus and system executives begin the decade of the
1970s with the institution of the university presidency or chancellorship at a low ebb. If the university is faced with the threat of
institutional overload, so is its chief executive. He is unlike any
other public official in the nation.

Comparisons to appointed executives at the state or national levels are inappropriate, for these persons report directly to a single political leader, deriving their authority from him. Analogies to city managers and school superintendents in large cities come nearer the mark, but are inadequate when one confronts both the actual and symbolic responsibilities of the university presidency. He is, we conclude, a political leader denied the legitimacy of popular election, yet unable to abandon his leadership role to the governing board which appointed him.

Turnover figures chronicle this dilemma: according to figures maintained by the American Council on Education, the average presidential tenure in 1960 was 10 or 11 years. In 1970, it was less than six.

Presidents are reported to feel they are an unorganized group and without allies. On one side, they are squeezed by trustees, legislatures, alumni and the general public, all demanding educational economies and law and order on the campus. On the other side, they are faced with "liberal" faculties, militant students and the threat of more rioting . . . (*U.S. News and World Report* 1970, p. 30).

Educational leadership is and will remain a critical necessity. Yet, as John W. Gardner suggested at the inauguration of Stanford's President Pitzer in 1969, "We have yet to prove that we can provide the kind of atmosphere in which a good man can survive." (Pitzer resigned in 1970.)

The issue is greater, of course, than the survival of the university president; it involves the future of the university itself. What kind of institution can operate effectively in the face of the trends of the 1970s: trends of growth; of increased responsibility; of more intensive political and governmental involvement; of rising demands for interinstitutional coordination; of significant, perhaps drastic shifts in emphasis; of internal stresses brought about by collective faculty and student activity?

For some, the answer is to be found in the development of single statewide systems of higher education with their stress on coordination and control. For others, the disassembly of university systems to separately governed campuses is held necessary to promote diversity and to counter inappropriate political control. The multicampus university provides a third alternative.

THE CASE FOR THE MULTICAMPUS UNIVERSITY The universities of America face a tremendous challenge, a challenge not only to their institutional structure and processes, but, more fundamentally, to their rationale and objectives. Therefore, their viability as organizations depends, in large measure, on their ability so to arrange their governance that the requirements of the age can be met (Roth, 1970, p. 73).

There are forces at work that will change the function of the university, that will substantially expand the university, and that will establish new demands on the university. In coping with that change, some of the most venerated concepts, practices, and traditions of an old, old institution will be altered or abolished (Corson, 1970, p. 80).

Can the multicampus universities meet the challenge of change? Can they promote far-reaching innovation and preserve the best of the past; provide first-rate undergraduate collegiate programs and maintain graduate centers of excellence; expand to enroll several thousand more students and avoid the perils of uncontrolled growth; meet the needs of an increasingly complex society and remain free from crippling political involvement and interference?

The answer *can* be yes, for the multicampus university has by its very nature and special structure a unique ability to promote specialization, diversity, and cooperation. These characteristics can be a critical cutting edge of higher education in the 1970s.

The underlying organizational premise of the multicampus university is that planning, budgeting, and coordination can be most effective in an institution which has the power of governance. Not only should planning in such a context be better informed and more realistic, but there is added assurance that the plans will be implemented. By placing several campuses and programs under a common framework, the scope of planning and implementation is enlarged.[4] The logic of this position leads to a single system for an entire state, and the arguments in this direction are persuasive. Yet, the advocates of the multicampus university draw back. There are advantages to dividing the total higher education responsibility among separately governed systems and institutions. Segmental interests can be protected; pluralism of control—if not always of program—can be assured; dangers of over-bureaucratization can be avoided. We need not enter this argument here, much less resolve it. The answer is, we have suggested, inextricably bound up with the social and political climate of each state. To suggest but one

[4] An alternate view is that boards with governing responsibilities pay too much attention to day-to-day administration and not enough to planning and coordination. See Hurtubise and Rowat (1970, p. 110). This Canadian study provides an excellent account of reasons supporting alternative organizational patterns among the provinces. Almost all the discussion is directly applicable to the United States.

critical factor, decisions concerning the desirability of one governing board, or two, or twenty cannot be determined on educational grounds apart from the political grounds of who will select the board members and on what basis. All this aside, multicampus universities do provide a middle ground between the monolithic single state system and the unplanned confusion of separately governed campuses, a middle ground which has undoubted advantages. Among them are opportunities for specialization and innovation; the creation of a critical mass of educational resources not available to a single campus; economies of scale; quality control; the promotion of differential dimensions of quality; and an effective division of administrative labor between system and campus executives.

But these advantages will not be realized automatically. One underlying condition must first be met: The multicampus university can meet the challenges of the 1970s only if, in fact as in theory, it can develop as a *system*. More than in the past, the multicampus university must be greater than the sum of its parts. What will it take to achieve this?

We return to the three main dimensions of governance—environment, structures, and processes—which have guided our inquiry. Each must be adapted and changed if the multicampus university is to match its potential. Not every generalization to be offered is applicable to every system or to every state. Nor are all the generalizations equally important. But taken together, they indicate the broad directions in which we think the multicampus universities must move. To the extent these directions can be followed, a rich and promising future is in prospect for this pattern of organization of higher education. To the extent they cannot, Americans will—and should—seek other alternatives in the governance of their public universities and colleges.

The Environment of Governance

"The truly major changes in university life," suggests Clark Kerr (1963, p. 105), "have been initiated from the outside." In the United States, he notes that the federal government and the foundations have been agents of innovation in many areas of academic programs. Here we would add that these external institutions also have impact upon the organization, as well as the substance, of the universities. Such an impact is not always recognized and seldom becomes an issue of public debate. But in the decade of the 1970s, external funding strategies may dominate organizational form.

Bloc grants to states, subject to distribution and veto by legislatures and governors is one alternative; insistence that a single state agency administer certain federal programs will have a second impact; aid given directly to students another; while a continuing flow of research funds directly to individual faculty with little institutional scrutiny—at either campus or system level—suggests a fourth. We cannot settle here what the strategy should be, but the questions of organizational impact should be explicitly recognized. If, as we believe to be the case, the organizational form of higher education is laden with substantive implications, funding arrangements which affect the organization may quickly lead to unanticipated programmatic consequences. Persons concerned with both substance and form must pay increasing attention to these interrelationships.

More directly, neither foundations nor federal agencies have generally recognized the multicampus university *system* as the focus of institutional support. In the 1970s this should no longer be the case. External funding should more directly promote diversity, specialization, and cooperation within the university by making institutional *systemwide* grants. If, as John Corson (1970, p. 68) states, the university's chief executive requires greater authority "to achieve coordination within, to utilize effectively increasingly scarce resources, and to stimulate requisite change," funding strategies must support and not undercut his power. In the face of uniform state budget formulas and a steadily shrinking area of universitywide fiscal discretion and risk capital, the innovative role of the multicampus university must be more effectively articulated and adequately supported.

Greater use of the multicampus system possesses another virtue: the interposition of a third force between the sponsor and the scholar in order to guarantee the utmost freedom of research and teaching. Stephen K. Bailey (1969, p. 38) has raised the issue:

The real threat to academic integrity imposed by categorical funding is not that it induces administrators and scholars to rationalize their curiosity in the direction of publicly defined and funded priorities. The real danger is the lessening of their academic will to bite the hand that feeds them. This danger increases as categorical funding involves the behavioral and humanistic sciences and the professional schools . . . if one of the larger purposes of the state is to provide for its own criticism, philosophies, mechanisms, and practices must be found to insure that such criticism remains vital and uncompromised.

To the extent the university can itself shape priorities and allocate resources across categories, the values to which Bailey refers
will be more effectively protected.

At the state level, much of the current uncertain nature of relationships among state government, coordinating agencies, and the
multicampus universities will continue. But this does not make
the resulting ambiguity a virtue. The problem is not simply one of
a failure to define responsibility for long-range planning among
the several participants. Rather, it is the inability of the multicampus systems to put their internal affairs in order because of external
instability and uncertainty. Time and again, it was borne in on us
that campus officials simply did not know what happened to a
recommendation once it left the campus. Some of this can be assessed to bad communication, but much results from the shifting
ground rules among state government, coordinating agencies, and
multicampus universities as to their respective areas of responsibility.

Absolute clarity concerning ultimate authority in higher education is not possible, but the present degree of uncertainty is most
undesirable and unnecessary. Some agreement on an appropriate
division of labor is essential to free the multicampus systems so
that they can operate with greater confidence within whatever
guidelines are developed. But at present, the architects of coordinating agencies have simply not taken the existence of multicampus
systems into account. Concepts applicable to single-campus institutions have been applied uncritically to the multicampus university, with a predictable impact upon internal system-campus
relationships. Decisions more properly those of a multicampus
university have been assumed by a coordinating agency, divor-
cing—as one system executive stated it—responsibility and authority.

The multicampus universities will not readily acclaim *any* significant role for coordinating agencies. Competition for power and
influence will continue. But this competition should be contained
within the bounds of a general understanding of respective responsibility and jurisdiction.

Whatever the agreement, coordinating agency–university relationships will not be effective unless two conditions are satisfied.
Only if the agencies exist as an independent force in higher education—more than arms of the governor's office or a legislative committee—will their recommendations be accepted by the institutions

they hope to "coordinate." Only if their staffs are comparable in experience and wisdom to those of the institutions will their recommendations be deserving of acceptance. In most of the seven states, neither of these two conditions exist. They cannot be ignored.[5]

But clarification of relationships between multicampus systems and coordinating agencies alone will not suffice. These are but two of the three parties concerned. The third, state government, must also more effectively define its role in the governance of higher education. Just as there is uncertainty over jurisdiction between university systems and coordinating agencies, so there often is confusion over the respective authority of the agencies and state offices. In truth, a rational distribution of higher education governance among campuses, system, coordinating agency, and state government is not easy, particularly in a state with a tradition of able and aggressive executive and legislative staff. Such a division of labor is rendered even more difficult when governors and legislators themselves fail to take the long look, and this is all too often the case. Short-run considerations of tax policy and intense concern with student unrest have combined to distract attention from how state government will provide for the educational needs of some 2 to 3 million more students during the 1970s and promote the kinds of reforms to which we have referred. The issue appears only rarely to be met by attention, energy, and resources equal to the task. In the absence of these, state government's role in higher education will remain one of continual ad hoc interventions by often ill-informed state officials. In the process, they will neglect the more fundamental policy judgments which are their proper concern.

A related aspect of this overall problem of state-university relations is the university's need for adequate fiscal flexibility. Additional comment on academic budgeting is provided below. Here, we note only that in at least two of the seven states, the level of

[5] Robert O. Berdahl describes the situation in these terms: "Two of the major problems confronting [coordinating] agencies eager to hire and retain qualified directors and staff specialists are salaries and state personnel rules . . . it is difficult to see how a board or council can, at existing salary rates, attract staff members of sufficient professional competence to do the job that the state government needs and expects or that the institutions will have confidence in. Even if the challenge of coordination and planning attracts competent people, their visibility and their modest salaries are likely, before long, to make them willing candidates for high college and university positions that are better paid and, perhaps, less sensitive and grueling" (1971).

detailed financial controls appears unwarranted and unwise. Line-item budgeting, state approval of minor budgetary transactions, and inflexible staffing formulas are all devices which prevent the multicampus universities in these states from acting like systems— from making necessary adjustments among campuses and programs in the interest of the entire enterprise. Neither educational effectiveness nor true economy is served by such external controls. If permitted to continue, they will seriously offset the inherent advantages of the multicampus university to make essential internal adjustments with the wisdom which arises from operational responsibility.

In sum, we conclude that the multicampus university will fully prosper as a system only to the extent that state government and coordinating agency responsibilities toward each other and toward the university are more clearly defined. The design of a new model of statewide responsibility for higher education, developed in full recognition of the unique aspects of the multicampus university, must be a matter of high priority in the 1970s.

The Structures of Governance

The external environment will do much to shape the future of the multicampus universities. Although the latter can influence their environment, they cannot control it. Much of the external uncertainty and instability, however, can be offset if the structures of internal governance are strengthened.

The governing board

One of the most critical needs of the multicampus university in the 1970s is to rejuvenate and simultaneously to reshape the governing board to meet its unique multicampus responsibilities.

Martin Trow (1970*a*, pp. 8–11) has described the reduction in power and influence of trustees in recent decades: alternative sources of funds (federal and foundation) over which trustees have limited influence have increased; and faculty and administrators have asserted that powers originally delegated to them are theirs by right. While losing power over their own institutions, Trow suggests, the trustees' constituencies and their relation to these constituencies have also been changing:

Boards have traditionally dealt with very specific "relevant publics": legislative committees, wealthy donors, alumni organizations. In the leading universities, their job has been to get support from these publics while resisting inappropriate interference. And in this task trustees of public universities have not been so different from those of private universities: In most of their relationships, they have been dealing with people very much like themselves—in many cases graduates of the same state university, men of similar sentiments and values and prejudices. These relations could be, for the most part, cozy and private. . . .

Today, the constituencies, the relevant publics, of state universities are much wider, more heterogeneous, and less familiar. In part, the growth of relevant publics has accompanied the simultaneous expansion of the universities and of their functions. . . .

These two tendencies—the trustees' sense of a loss of control over "their" university and the emergence of a mass public of uncertain size and composition and temper with whom the trustees have no clear representative or communicating relationship—can undermine a board's conceptions of who they are and what their role is, and generate in them anger and anxiety. And out of that fear and anger, trustees appear to be more inclined to intervene directly in the academic life of the university: its curriculum, faculty appointments, and student discipline. . . .

. . . Instead of defending the university to its external publics, it begins to function as a conduit of popular sentiment and pressure on the university. And this, as I have suggested, places all the functions of the university in grave jeopardy.

One solution to Trow's problem is to abolish the citizen board as an anachronism from a bygone age, for the lay board is not an essential of university governance, as experience in other nations demonstrates. But our own traditions cannot so quickly be set aside, practically or substantively, and we do not so recommend here. Instead, we suggest that the governing boards of multicampus universities must reassert their policy-making role at a new and higher level. But, and the qualification is crucial, this reassertion will neither be effective nor accepted unless the composition of the governing boards is radically changed.

John Corson (1970, p. 78) has suggested the direction of our first theme: ". . . trustees have allowed the broad authority that they were endowed with by law and historical practice to atrophy by concentrating their attention on the financial, physical, and public relations problems of the university. . . . [They have ignored] the very guts of the university operations." Many concerned with the behavior of some boards would express a sigh of relief that this has indeed been the case. But such a response is inadequate:

The universities have moved to the public domain. . . . Not only costs, but content, organization, enrollment, kind and quality of service are public issues. . . . In the language of the lawyers, the universities are now revealed as an "industry affected by public interest" . . . (Corry, 1969, p. 105).

This is indeed the case, but we were repeatedly reminded during our inquiry that governing boards have concentrated on managerial detail and failed—as Corson suggests—to deal with many issues of major educational policy. We are not unmindful of the contribution in time, energy, and leadership exhibited by the trustees of the nine university systems. Nevertheless, much of this effort is misplaced in the face of the demands of the 1970s described above: the relationship between teaching and research, the efficacy of admissions standards, continuing education, the consequences of student mobility, new modes of faculty and student participation in governance. In part, the intrusion of coordinating agencies and state government into such areas of university life has resulted from the failure of governing boards to assert their proper role. This intrusion will continue apace unless major adjustments are made.

In the context of the multicampus universities, the most serious need is for the board to become concerned with systemwide matters—with promoting and evaluating the diversity, specialization, and cooperation in educational programs among campuses for which the multicampus university is uniquely qualified. They cannot do so if they continue, as most boards do at present, to devote their major time and attention to details of governance at each of the campuses.[6]

The demands of the 1970s require a reorientation of board activity. Internally, campus and system executives, who must provide

[6] Although we would not raise the point to a matter of principle, the regular presence of every campus executive at every meeting of the governing board—the practice in eight of the nine systems—illustrates the fact that the boards have not defined a new role for themselves, consistent with their multicampus status. At one and the same time—and at considerable expense—the practice invites the board to engage in administrative detail, discourages clear delegations of authority, clouds relationships between system and campus executives, and prevents all parties from devoting adequate attention to the major universitywide policy issues which should be the central concern of the system administration and the board.

leadership to their faculties and students, will confront serious obstacles in their efforts to bring the multicampus universities into tune with the challenge of the times. Externally, legislators and citizens will require education to understand and support the changes which are necessary. Both internal and external pressures suggest the necessity—contrary to the criticisms of many students and faculty—for a strong governing board: to prod and support the administration, to make difficult decisions of educational policy, to hear appeals from the faculty and students, to interpret the university to a questioning and demanding community and the community to the university—in short, to represent the public interest in the governance of the multicampus university.

But—the revitalization of the governing boards cannot be achieved as they are generally structured. Among nearly all the nine multicampus universities, present methods of board selection fail to aid the effectice discharge of the responsibilities we have described above.[7] The selection process falls short on at least three counts. The boards are highly unrepresentative of the society served by the university. They do not possess legitimacy in the minds of those most directly affected by their power. They are not sufficiently independent of partisan political currents. All three shortcomings impinge upon the board's ability to assume an expanded leadership role essential to effective governance. All three arise out of the method of board selection.

We refer specifically to exclusive gubernatorial appointment to the boards and to the ex officio presence of governors and other

[7] Rodney T. Hartnett (1970, pp. 43–44) concludes, on the basis of his review of governing board membership across the nation, that women, blacks, and people under 40 are traditionally underrepresented as trustees, and that this factor has a direct bearing on board attitudes and behavior. He goes on to assert: "Just as the nature of the collegiate experience today bears little resemblance to the collegiate days of yesteryear, so the role of the trustee has changed. Consider just a few of the 'problem areas' troubling many college campuses today—demands by many black student groups for a separate curriculum and segregated housing facilities, demands by student redicals to abolish ROTC units and 'classified' research, the move to coeducation at many institutions with a long tradition of cloistered campuses (and the resulting furor from alumni), and faculty strikes of one kind or another. Though in many instances the problem can be solved by representative groups of students, faculty or others, often a satisfactory resolution is not possible. In such instances the trustees, willingly or otherwise, are becoming the pivotal force. Selecting trustees with backgrounds and experience relevant to these problems would seem to be sensible and desirable."

political figures on the boards. While not confined to the multicampus universities, the issue is particularly applicable to them because of their relative size and importance. Trow's comments, quoted above, suggest the reason for the current dilemma. Governing boards were designed in a time when the university's relevant constituencies were very specific and its relationships to society relatively circumscribed. Today, the pattern is reversed: the relevant constituency has become the mass public, and the university's societal relationships have few bounds.

Higher education has become and will remain a critical and continuing political issue. In this new world, the exclusive selection of trustees by governors (whether or not ratified by state senates) and the kind of board we have described as essential for the 1970s are inherently contradictory. The question goes far beyond the program of any party, the political climate of any state, or the personality of any governor; it involves the realities of higher education in contemporary society. Traditional modes of board selection have relied (with mixed success) on such devices as long and overlapping terms to avoid the dominance of *partisanship* in the governance of the university. But the issue today is of a different order of magnitude—the dominance of *politics* in the governance of the university. In the context of the 1970s, a governor can no more ignore political considerations in the selection of trustees and in their subsequent activities than deny the reality of the next election. In consequence, representativeness of the external community, legitimacy within the university community, and political independence—three prerequisites of effective board performance—all suffer.

We do not want to be misunderstood. The university—at least the nine multicampus universities—will never return to some bygone age in which politicians take little interest in its affairs. Nor should it. It is inherent in the nature of the times that the university be a political issue. Governors and legislatures will be heavily and appropriately involved in many areas of governance under any circumstance, particularly in their review and adoption of the university's budget. But for the same reason, new structures are required to permit the university to function effectively in this changing environment. Robert O. Berdahl puts it in these terms: "The real issue regarding autonomy, then, is not whether there will be 'interference by the state' but rather whether the inevitable interference will be confined to the proper topics and expressed through a suitably sensitive mechanism" (1971).

A new approach to the selection of trustees is no academic frill— not in the context of the 1970s. It is, rather, an essential of governance. Trustees closely tied to a governor—or two succeeding governors—simply will not be able to perform the critical functions described above in a manner acceptable to the public, the politicians, and the internal constituencies of the university—all of whom must accept the legitimacy of board decisions if these are to be truly effective. And if the trustees cannot function, the governance of the multicampus universities will be in jeopardy.

The issue goes, of course, to the heart of the university and its relationship to society. The university requires the support of society for its existence. The reverse—for a free people—is equally true. It is to the university that society looks—often grudgingly— for that analysis and self-criticism essential to its survival. Academic freedom rests on the imperative that society maintain an institution of self-criticism. And university autonomy finds its main justification in the protection of genuine academic freedom. Two Canadian observers have written:

It would be possible for academic freedom to exist in the absence of institutional autonomy. But since institutions exist within a specific historical evolution and a given political culture, it is necessary to anchor the instruments for the protection of academic freedom to our existing institutions. For this reason we are convinced that, at present, and in the foreseeable future, substantial institutional autonomy is needed as an instrument for the preservation of academic freedom. For in its best form, it can shield the academic community from not only the actuality but even the fear of illegitimate outside pressures.

This acceptance of the need for autonomy does not invalidate the interests of the state. It merely acknowledges that traditions and present circumstances thus condition an acceptable and well-functioning system of government-university relations. . . .

. . . governments—as presently organized and working—are simply not prepared to assume direct responsibility for higher education. This does not mean that they could not take it over. But it does mean that if universities were to continue to perform their proper functions and to enjoy the protection of academic freedom, the governments would have to develop some new and different institutional structures and styles of work. This they are not at present capable of doing. We therefore advocate the retention of substantial autonomy both to protect academic freedom and to prevent the proliferation of inappropriate, monolithic bureaucracies (Hurtubise & Rowat, 1970, pp. 72–74).

These conclusions have special meaning for the multicampus universities. The aggregation of campuses under one governing board results in desirable internal coordination, but it also provides a potent and convenient vehicle for introducing external political control. Just as it is easier for state finance departments to develop a budget by dealing with a university system rather than with a dozen or more separate campuses, so is it easier for a governor to extend his influence downward, assuming a governing board of his own choosing and subject to his continuing influence. If society wishes the advantages of the former, without the risks of the latter, special care must be taken in the design of governing structures, particularly in the face of the university's emergence as a major public issue. To repeat, such a structure is required, not to divorce the university from politics, but to provide a context that will permit effective and appropriate public control in a highly politicized environment.

But does the general public, responsible in the last analysis for "their" state university, share these views? We think so. In a statewide survey of California citizens, conducted in February 1971 by the highly respected *California Poll,* questions were asked especially for this study. The responses of the public were surprisingly consistent with the viewpoints expressed here. Asked to select their preferred choice as to which of four alternatives should constitute "the main qualifications for the public members of the board of regents," only 3 percent of the sample favored the selection of regents "who will listen closely to the wishes of the governor." In contrast, 19 percent favored regents "who will decide things strictly on the basis of their own best judgment," 34 percent chose regents "who will listen closely to the wishes of the faculty and students," and 36 percent indicated a preference for regents "who will listen closely to the wishes of the people of the state." (Eight percent reported, "none of these" or "don't know.") And when asked how the public members of the board should be selected, only 2 percent favored the existing California pattern — exclusive choice by the governor.[8]

---

[8] The membership of governors and other state political figures as ex officio trustees is obviously related to this general issue. In California, where three partisan officeholders and the directly elected state superintendent of public

We complete these observations by brief reference to North Carolina and Illinois, in neither of which the governor selects the trustees. On its face, the election of the 100-man board by the North Carolina legislature would seem to lend itself to many of the ills we have described. The situation seems otherwise. Board activity is essentially carried on by an executive committee chosen by the trustees from among their own membership. While we do not suggest the absence of political involvement, the size of the board, plus the indirect selection of the executive committee, appears to have lessened the explicit partisan overtones noted in other states. The Illinois pattern is totally different. Although formally elected on a partisan ballot, the effective choice of trustees is traditionally made by select alumni committees, themselves independent of both the political parties and the governor. Adoption of either the North Carolina or Illinois pattern to other political environments would be hazardous, indeed.

Aside from popular or legislative election, what alternatives are there to exclusive gubernatorial selection? These suggest themselves: alternative avenues of selection, the establishment of screening panels to nominate candidates from whom selections are made, or both. Professional and civic groups; business, labor, and agricultural interests; educational associations; the political parties themselves; alumni; faculty; and students are among the groups which might be empowered either to name trustees or to nominate panels from which the governor, the legislature, or some other appointing authority might select.[9]

Alternatively, and perhaps more practically, a blue-ribbon

---

instruction serve as ex officio regents, the staff of the state's constitution revision commission commented in a background study: "The most important objection to the membership of elected State officials on the Board of Regents is the danger of political interference. Although Section 9 specifically forbids political interference in the affairs of the University, Regents' meetings offer a forum for political activity that is easily abused by candidates seeking public favor. Since the official members will sometimes represent opposing political parties, Regents' meetings can become the scene of divisive political clashes. Lay Regents may feel compelled to take sides, and University issues may be resolved in terms of political power rather than the best interests of the University" (California Constitution Revision Commission, 1969, p. 56).

[9] The general question of whether the students or faculty should be permitted to name persons from their own ranks goes far beyond this study; our feeling with respect to the multicampus universities is that they should not be.

commission could be established, composed of representatives of such groups, which would be empowered to nominate a panel of candidates (at least two for each vacancy) from which the governor or other appointing authority would be required to make his choice of trustees.[10] We do not minimize the practical or political problems of developing a satisfactory structure. Each university and state must be reviewed in the light of its specific needs and history. But we do assert that the approaches suggested here would effectively promote the three goals of representativeness, legitimacy, and independence which are essential to effective trustee performance.[11]

As important as is the rejuvenation and restructuring of the governing board, other changes may be needed if trustees are to fulfill their critical role. Proper exercise of the leadership responsibilities over universitywide matters will require that boards delegate a substantial degree of their present managerial responsibilities. Many of these can properly be assumed by system and campus executives. But other important areas of campus life would benefit by the kind of lay interest and evaluation in which systemwide governing boards now engage, generally with little effectiveness. Campus executives need an outside forum against which to test new proposals; faculty and students need regular contact with the public constituencies the university serves. For their part, the governing board requires an evaluation of the progress and prob-

---

[10] One of the rare discussions of alternate methods of board appointment is found in Morton Rauh's recent study (1969, p. 121): "One suggestion for providing some degree to control without altering the statutory procedures of selection is to follow a modified version of the practice used in certain judicial appointments where candidates are subjected to screening by the local bar association. The counterpart in trustee appointments would be to have an advisory council composed of educators and citizens of standing which would advise with the governor in the selection process."

[11] In the above-mentioned California poll, conducted in February 1971, a statewide sample of 984 adults was asked to indicate from a list of alternatives their preference as to how public members of the university's board of regents should be selected. Forty percent of the sample preferred popular election, 17 percent chose gubernatorial appointment with approval by the state senate, 10 percent favored appointment by the governor from a list provided by a panel of leading citizens, 9 percent indicated selection by an independent group of leading citizens, 8 percent preferred appointment by the legislature, and 2 percent favored exclusive appointment by the governor, the existing California pattern. (Thirteen percent responded "none of these" or "don't know.")

lems of the several campuses, which few boards can now successfully accomplish without sacrifice to their critical universitywide
responsibilities. And they may properly wish to delegate certain
jurisdiction to a campus subject to some independent lay approval.

The need for new mechanisms of citizen participation in the
governance of each campus, separate from the normal activities of
the governing board, is much more pressing for the larger systems, but even the smaller might profit from more formal lay activity at the campus level. Existing examples have not generally
proven effective and will not serve the expanded role we see as
necessary in the future. The possible models are various, and we
can suggest but a few here. The visiting committees of the 100-
man North Carolina board provide one alternative, which could
be expanded in that state and modified to fit other states. Boards
of visitors have a long and honored tradition in the United States,
but have been little utilized in the multicampus systems. A prestigious and representative board of visitors for each campus, which
might meet quarterly or semi-annually and render a report to the
trustees, is a realistic possibility. Another alternative might be
that of the State University of New York, with its local boards
with limited jurisdiction. But, as with the governing board itself,
it will be desirable to seek approaches other than selection exclusively by the governor. In fact, a different base of selection for a
local board might offset some of the pitfalls arising out of exclusive
gubernatorial selection of the system board.

Consideration of local boards will not be unanimously approved,
for reasons suggested in Chapter 4. And, indeed, there are risks
in their creation. Carefully developed relationships between campus
and system executives may be threatened as the former relates to
his local board or committee; and log-rolling by local boards may
be an ever-present prospect. Faculty and students may see the
local board as erosive of their hard-won jurisdiction. Universitywide trustees, long used to dealing with managerial details, will
not quickly adapt to the much more important but immensely more
difficult task of planning, coordination, and evaluation, which so
many have effectively ignored for so many years.

But higher education *is* a high-risk enterprise. More effective
citizen involvement at the campus level is a necessary counterpart
of more effective overall board concern for the affairs of the entire
multicampus university.

The administration

Restructuring the governing board of the multicampus university is necessary to create an environment within which both campus and system executives can operate effectively. The unwillingness of trustees to avoid involvement in details of campus management has made it difficult for system and campus executives themselves to divide their labors clearly and effectively. Lacking assurance that campus matters will not suddenly appear on the board agenda, system executives have been reluctant to make firm delegations of authority. In consequence, they have been drawn into operational details at the expense of their unique potential for universitywide leadership.

An important requirement of the 1970s, therefore, is for the multicampus universities to develop a clear and precise understanding of the respective authority of the governing board, system administration, and campus executives. In some important areas, appropriate delegations of administrative authority are impossible because of restrictions imposed by state fiscal authorities. Here, the role of the system must be to press for authority to set its own house in order. Without regard to the state, however, there is room in almost every system for a delegation of authority to campus executives that is both more realistic and commensurate with their leadership role.

An equally pressing need is to assure that, between a strong governing board and effective campus executives, the system executive himself retains adequate authority. The multicampus university will not be greater than the sum of its parts, will not effectively promote diversity, specialization, and cooperation among its campuses, unless its chief executive is encouraged to act as an educational leader and empowered to do so. We hold little brief for the notion that the system executive should be basically a manager, smoothing the way for the campuses to pursue discrete academic paths. The needs of the multicampus university require something more—educational statesmanship of the highest order that can only be provided by the university's chief executive.

Such statemanship rests on two bases: authority and staff. One of the unfortunate by-products of the formula budgeting observed in several states is the automatic distribution of funds to the campuses, as required either by law or practice. In consequence, the system executive retains little opportunity to make midyear adjustments, to seek targets of special opportunity, or to provide critical seed money. University foundations, endowments, or overhead distribution provide some leeway, but these are often heavily restricted, inadequate in amount, and subject to attachment by either the campuses or state government. The precedent set by two states, in which system executives retain some of the state budget appropriation for distribution to campuses during the budget year, has great merit. Regardless of budget totals, it would be highly desirable to permit all system executives to reserve perhaps 10 percent of the state budget for discretionary purposes, subject to postaudit and evaluation. This strategy may be particularly essential in times of budgetary stringency, when innovation cannot be expected to arise out of normal program expansion.

Other aspects of executive authority are implicit in the above recommendations for transforming the governing board from a body concerned with managerial problems to one concerned with policy. But expanded and clarified authority will be meaningless unless the system executive is provided adequate staff. While generally recognized in most of the nine multicampus universities, in an unfortunate few the universitywide table of organization is too thin to aid adequately the chief executive and the board. In most, both the quantity and quality of universitywide administrators is impressive, although not a few are—like the governing board—finding it difficult to adjust to a multicampus role. Moreover in only one or two are top-level staff free to engage in the speculative and innovative long-range planning necessary to permit the universities to realize their full potential.

Trustees and state governments alike must recognize that universitywide staff are essential—in numbers and experience—if the individual campuses are collectively to become a system. So must the universities themselves. Only rarely have they taken advantage of the unusual structure of the multicampus system, with its opportunities for executive interchange, for use of faculty as staff and consultants, and for a systemwide executive career program.

Finally, in several multicampus universities, opportunities for optimal system-campus relationships may continue to be undercut by uncertainties arising out of the location of administrative offices on the flagship campus. Physical and organizational distance are related. The problem is being minimized in Chapel Hill and Columbia by the movement of system headquarters away from the campus; in mid-1970, system offices of the University of Texas, previously housed in the same building as the campus administration, were moved to downtown Austin. But at Berkeley, Champaign-Urbana, and Madison, no such plans are in sight.

The faculty

In each of the nine university systems, to a greater or lesser extent, the universitywide organization of the faculty has received far less attention than the administrative structure. System administrators are generally reluctant to impose their views on the faculty as to its own organization, and the faculty themselves have often failed to give adequate attention to their role in a unique multicampus environment. As a result, the two structures—academic and administrative—are not always in phase. In two universities, as we noted in Chapter 6, there is no universitywide structure at all, while in two others an organization had just been formed as of 1970.

Past patterns will no longer suffice if the faculty voice is to be effectively heard in universitywide policy circles. And heard it must be, for the needs of the decade cannot be met without full and effective faculty participation. The implications of this are twofold. Faculty must accept the fact that many of their activities are legitimate objects of public inquiry. Questions of admissions, of teaching load, of major curricular changes are matters in which there is an essential public interest—and one quite independent of the fundamental protections of academic freedom, "the ability of professors and students to pursue their lines of inquiry without any political or social pressure."[12]

These questions will be discussed at universitywide levels, and decisions will be reached by system executives and trustees concerning them. The corollary to this is that the faculty must so shape its own governing structures as to have an appropriate impact. It will no longer do for faculty at major campuses to assert, as we heard in more than one system, that they will participate in a universitywide organization only so long as it is ineffective— that is, so long as it has no influence on the activities of the campus. There must be an appropriate division of labor between univer-

---

[12] Hurtubise and Rowat (1970, p. 67). See their discussion of the distinction between academic freedom and institutional autonomy.

sitywide and campus faculty bodies, just as between system and campus executives. Campus faculty bodies should be jealous of their local prerogatives and zealous in protecting them. But there must also be recognition of the necessity and the legitimacy of faculty activity at the system level.

During the 1970s faculties will also have to decide whether or not they will abandon their traditional methods of academic participation for collective bargaining. Their choice will be influenced as much by the external environment as by internal pressures. Legislatures and trustees may force the issue to produce an outcome desired by no one. We cannot predict the result, but all parties should be aware that the choice will go to the heart of university governance.

The students

Despite the certainty of continued student activism in the 1970s and the development of new modes of participation, we see little in the way of formal student organization of a peculiarly multicampus nature. The odds are too heavily stacked against effective student participation in universitywide governance. Transient and highly mobile student bodies of upwards of 200,000, shifting from institution to institution and periodically dropping out, hardly provide a stable constituency, even assuming adequate patterns of selection and representation can be developed. Nothing in prospect is likely to change this pattern. More formal academic programs involving intercampus transfers, or participation in a course on a neighboring campus within the system, might produce more of a sense of a student community with universitywide responsibilities and loyalties; and the establishment of student-nominated trustees, as suggested above, might create the basis for a formal universitywide student organization. But there are few straws in the wind which point to a substantially different role for students at a multicampus level than already exists.

Such universitywide participation, we have noted, generally involves periodic meetings between the system executive and campus student presidents or ad hoc groups, and occasional trustee-student contacts. These relatively informal relationships are, and will continue to be, highly desirable. But the primary system role should be the encouragement of effective machinery for student participation at the campus level, the provision of guidance and consultation as to alternative modes of such activity, the evaluation of campus experience, and the interpretation of it to uneasy trustees, alumni, and legislators.

The Processes of Governance

Structures of governance are not ends in themselves. Our proposals will have validity only to the extent that they facilitate the more effective performance of the processes of academic governance: academic planning, budgeting, admissions, academic personnel administration, public and governmental relations, and business affairs. These are not, of course, the ultimate ends of the university either, but they are central to their achievement — the creation of centers of learning, research, and related public service. Within the multicampus universities, how can these processes be altered to permit such centers to make their fullest contribution in the 1970s?

Academic plans and programs
As impressive as is their record in terms of the establishment of new campuses, the transformation and expansion of old ones, and the maintenance of quality control over academic programs, the multicampus universities must achieve even more. Their unique capacity to promote specialization, diversity, and cooperation must be fulfilled to a much greater extent than has heretofore been the case.[13]

To approach fulfillment, the nine universities will have to intensify long-range academic planning in new and different ways. Much planning in the 1960s appears, in retrospect, to have been based on the reactions of the universities to external pressures, rather than on academic imagination and initiative. Handicapped by inadequate staff, but also by tradition, the resulting statements and proposals often simply consolidate campus plans, rather than afford a fresh and comprehensive look at the needs of the entire university system and state. Respect for campus aims is desirable, but uncritical respect has understated the potential contribution

---

[13] Congresswoman Edith Green (1970, p. 1) has suggested one dimension of the problem in stating that educators must explain why they "seem not to care about producing a surplus of Ph.D.'s and quite honestly pay little heed to relevant manpower predictions. For too long, the educational system and the predictions of our real manpower needs have been passing each other arrogantly and blissfully by like foreign ships in the night."

of the multicampus university. Governing boards and state legislatures have a right to expect more and will undoubtedly demand it.

Two specific aspects of academic planning are suggestive of the direction in which the nine systems must move, appropriate to their own environment. First, far more attention should be given to systemwide programs that capitalize upon the strengths and needs of several campuses. Isolated examples of effective intercampus utilization of faculty and facilities suggest one direction which should be much more vigorously pursued. In the comprehensive systems, possibilities for faculty interchange between collegiate and university campuses might go far to lower artificial status barriers. For students, much can be said for the present unplanned and unstructured opportunities for intercampus transfer. But an equal case can be made, too, for the development of experimental multicampus programs, running from the freshman year through a professional degree, which would draw upon the resources of the entire system and provide new and exciting educational options. Such options need not universally be built upon present patterns in which the collegiate and university campuses offer virtually identical undergraduate programs. Upper-division and graduate campuses, separate or in combination, are one approach, mentioned earlier, that is currently being pursued in Texas. It should be carefully evaluated.

A systemwide approach to academic plans and programs can enrich offerings. But more is required if the multicampus universities are to address the challenge of President McGill that, instead of a curriculum based largely on the artificialities of a nineteenth century academic calendar, higher education turn to a "career curriculum" based on the reality of life-long education.

The opportunity for the multicampus university to meet this challenge is immense. Drawing upon resources denied to a single campus, able to implement programs in a manner beyond the ability of a coordinating agency, the institutional vehicle seems almost ready-made. Internal acceptability, given the conservatism of the academic toward his own affairs, and external support, given the demands of competing public expenditures, will not come easily. Nevertheless, the effort must be made.

Budget preparation and administration
Wherever we turned during our inquiry, the bases for university budgeting were under attack. In a complex and costly environment,

traditional formulas based on extrapolations from past experience are under scrutiny. Budget requests based on input (numbers of students per teacher, support costs per professor, books per student) are no longer accepted by state budget officers and legislative committees. The demand is for information on results and their relationship to expenditures. And in a society increasingly dependent on higher education but increasingly uneasy concerning its activities, who can fault the demand?

The challenge to the multicampus university is to demonstrate its willingness and capacity to develop new concepts of financial measurement, to take the lead in sophisticated and sensitive evaluation of its major cost factors, and to develop a basis for budgeting which will command the confidence of both professionals and politicians. Unless it can accomplish this, it will neither obtain nor effectively utilize the funds necessary for its programs.

The nine universities seem particularly well-equipped to respond positively. The scale and complexity of the systems and the relative detachment of system administrators—from the immediate pressures of the campus on one side and from the political pressures of the capital on the other—provide a vehicle for evaluation and analysis not easily duplicated in other state agencies.

The challenge to the multicampus university is matched by an equal challenge to the state. What incentive will it provide the university to develop more effective budgeting? Will state fiscal authorities—governors and legislators as well as professional staff—accept that much of the educational process cannot be reduced to formulas, that a high element of subjectivity is required in many budget decisions, and that these decisions can more properly be made by responsible university administrators than state officials? Will they permit a continuation, indeed an increase, in the use of discretionary funds, a flexible approach that has led to developments of distinction in several of the universities?

There is a dangerous paradox in these twin challenges to the university and to the state. If the university experiments with new, more objective approaches to budgeting, will the state prematurely seize upon these to make its own decisions, denying essential flexibility to the multicampus system? If the university develops more effective gross indices of need for universitywide purposes, will the state insist that these be applied automatically to each campus and program? A deadening uniformity can too easily replace the essential diversity among campuses that is the hallmark of an effective university system. The development of new techniques of resource allocation at both state and university levels requires both time and highly skilled personnel. It also requires that state and university officials develop mutual confidence and some sense of a division of labor. But neither time, competence, nor confidence are in oversupply in the seven states. Undoubtedly, increased tension between university and state will be the unfortunate but inevitable response to the increasing costs and complexity of higher education.

The real issue is whether this tension cannot only be contained but turned to creative ends. Pressure from state officials can be a positive force for more effective budgeting if accompanied by recognition of the university's fragile nature—that it cannot be measured absolutely and accurately by the tools of cost accounting. For its part, the university must be willing to take a hard look at itself and to reevaluate the conventional wisdom on which so much of academic budgeting has been based. The multicampus university has a unique contribution to make in meeting this challenge. Whether it will have the opportunity to do so remains in doubt.

Academic and administrative personnel
Diversity, specialization, and cooperation in academic programs and multiple dimensions of quality in admissions will impose new pressures upon both faculty and administration. Different kinds of faculty will be required to meet the widely differing needs of higher education in the 1970s. The single standard of productive scholarship will be too inflexible as a criterion of recruitment and advancement, as indeed there is evidence that it already is. Collegiate, university, and post-degree or continuing-education programs will require quite different talents, patterns of recruitment, and systems of compensation.

The creative containment of these differences may prove to be one of the most perplexing aspects of multicampus administration and one of the most important. The multicampus universities cannot develop their full potential if tied to a single systemwide reward structure, yet separate patterns within a common institution will create serious difficulties.

The issue may be posed as a question: Can a system executive and governing board within the same system effectively and constructively discriminate among faculty from different kinds of campuses? The highly tentative conclusion drawn from the experience of the State University of New York is "yes." Distinctions between the university centers and the colleges in that system have been effectively maintained. The pervasive tendency of college campuses to become universities, generally at the expense of their collegiate mission and often regardless of need or ability, has been brought under control. Although many reasons can be advanced for this circumstance, the inclusion of the college campuses within a comprehensive system, including university campuses, is clearly a factor. The reality and the symbolism of a common universitywide faculty organization and a single academic salary schedule (administered very flexibly) are elements which create a viable combination of university and college campuses.

But collective bargaining in New York may reverse this condition. While administrators and governing boards may be able to discriminate among campuses and segments, it is doubtful that a universitywide faculty union can. Indeed, perhaps the most significant aspect of the City University contract of 1969 is the creation of a single academic salary scale covering—in a virtually automatic pattern—all faculty from the community college to the graduate center. Semiautomatic promotion may replace the highly personalized practices that mark most universities today. Other aspects of academic employment—from sabbatical leaves to secretarial assistance—are similarly treated. Whatever benefits this egalitarianism may provide to the university and the city, segmental differentiation between college and university campuses is not one. Extension of this same monolithic approach to the State University of New York may make it difficult to maintain the differential dimensions of quality upon which that university is based.

Thus, the uniformity imposed by the research-oriented values of the academic revolution may take second place to that resulting from the emergence of collective bargaining in higher education. Here the role of the multicampus university is not yet clear. On the one hand, the system might contain a good deal of the whipsawing that marks union relationships with autonomous institutions in the same labor market. However, the existence of a common systemwide bargaining agreement may more easily lead to a general leveling of salaries, erasing essential differences that might be sustained in an autonomous campus. The ability to deal differentially with campuses and individuals in the face of system-wide bargaining may well be a critical test of the multicampus universities in the 1970s.

Admissions and transfers

In the 1970s, trends presently evident will be increasingly felt. With a slowdown in the construction of new campuses, more attention will be paid to the assignment of students to existing ones. The increasing proliferation of disciplines and subdisciplines will put campuses under increasing pressure to specialize, and machinery will have to be established to distribute students in accordance with their interest and abilities. The need to articulate the transfer of students from two-year campuses, whether part of the multicampus system or not, will greatly increase. Demands for new measures of scholastic ability and open-admissions policies will create new pressures relating to the assignment of students to a campus beyond the ability of a single campus to resolve. Finally, policies and practices now utilized to screen undergraduate applicants will have their graduate counterpart. Subject-matter and departmental quotas, now evident in one or two systems, will become common at both undergraduate and graduate levels.

To meet this changing environment, admissions policies and practices will require substantial change. Increased counseling and guidance at the campuses will be balanced by increased universitywide concern over admissions policy. Information concerning the admissions process and the relationship between admissions standards and student performance will be centrally gathered, analyzed, and distributed. Central staff will provide increasing services to campus counselors, and perhaps even have operating responsibility for structured and deliberate transfer of students between campuses.

In the organizational and educational middle ground between statewide coordinating agencies and single campuses with individual boards, the multicampus university is especially qualified to meet these needs for centralized admissions policy and practice. Several systems have already given signs of meeting this promise — not many signs, but perhaps all that the situation presently requires. These efforts will have to be expanded and extended.

This shift in relative responsibility between campus and system will lead to conflicts among administrators, faculty, and students.

Balancing the values of student choice, faculty preference, and universitywide needs will impose requirements upon the system administration and governing board of all nine universities that only two or three had felt as of 1970. Adequate staff and executive leadership will be in even greater demand, underscoring more vividly the need for the structural changes outlined above.

The overriding concern in this shifting environment will be to recognize and support the need for different dimensions of "quality" — in admissions as in other areas of higher education. The increase in centralized activity must not mean either a leveling of traditional academic qualifications, where these are relevant, or the deadening uniformity of standards, where they are not. In 1962, T. R. McConnell (1962, p. 190) considered it ". . . indefensible, even in a coordinated and differentiated system, to assign a student once and for all to a particular institution or a specific curriculum." He warned that higher education must be ". . . flexible enough to enable each student to reach the highest level for which his aptitude and performance qualify him." This essential flexibility for a student to choose and change his own "dimension of quality" will be realized only by giving greater attention to the interinstitutional multicampus context of admissions and transfers.[14]

---

[14] The open-admissions policy of the City University of New York, first implemented in the fall of 1970, represents a far-reaching example of systemwide activity. All city high school graduates, regardless of academic standing, are guaranteed admission into the university system, a marked departure from previous New York City practice.

Students in the top half of their individual high school class (regardless of relative academic rank in the city as a whole) and students in the top fifth of all high school graduates (based on academic rank in the city as a whole) are eligible for direct admission to senior campuses. Those falling below these cutoff points may enter a two-year college, and may subsequently transfer to a senior college, depending on their academic performance. In 1970, it was estimated that 9,000 students not previously eligible to enter the university system were admitted, many directly into senior colleges under the "top-half" provision.

The City University plan is somewhat analogous to the open-admissions policy of the California Master Plan, which involves three independent segments of higher education. The California pattern is more restrictive with respect to immediate entry of high school graduates into the senior colleges and universities, but does permit easy entry into the community colleges with the possibility of subsequent transfer to senior colleges. In theory, the problem of articulation of transfers between two-year and four-year campuses is presumably eased within the single New York system.

External relations

A changing external environment and internal adjustments in structure and program will be heavily influenced by public and governmental understanding. Opportunities for expanded external relations programs, however, will continue to be heavily circumscribed by constraints of budget and tradition. Every system will confront steadily increasing pressures to present its side of the story more effectively, but this demand will not be matched by resources equal to the task. Because of this, system and campus executives will have to reevaluate the total public and governmental relations commitment of the university. In every system untapped opportunities can be exploited. Specialization, diversity, and cooperation have their place in these areas, no less than in academic programs. Sophisticated and sensitive centralized leadership will be required if the full capability of the system is to be mobilized without ignoring the extraordinary and specific demands for each campus. The unique connection between these programs and the style and substance of executive leadership at both universitywide and campus levels will constitute another element of complexity, for in many ways the programs are those of the executives.

Business affairs

In many areas of business activity, the university resembles less an autonomous institution than a department of state government. For example, only three universities administer their own purchasing and four their own nonacademic personnel programs.

We see little that will change this picture in the 1970s, with one possible exception. Forces of both state politics and collective bargaining will continue to keep the question of an independent university personnel system unclear. Nonacademic employees may use the threat of legislation placing them within state civil service as a counter in their bargaining with university management.

The implications of state control over these activities are not, we conclude, central to the major concerns of multicampus universities. All state-dominated systems look with longing—but little hope—on the university systems that have jurisdiction over nonacademic personnel and purchasing. None of the latter express any wish to sacrifice their independence, nor are we aware of any pressure on the part of state government to move in this direction.

For the university-administered programs, continued emphasis on the advantages of scale resulting from systemwide activities should be coupled with the need for clear delegations of authority to the campuses, and there are opportunities for both in more than one university.

State-university relationships are far more critical in the area of physical planning and construction. Here the issue continues to be one not of actual state administration but of the massive uncertainties of state and federal funding, both in amount and in timing. The possibility of coordinating approaches to academic and physical planning, of integrating the priorities of several campuses, and of achieving economies of construction arising out of system-wide activity will remain unfulfilled to the extent that state and federal governments are themselves unable to determine their own priorities. In the absence of this, only the multicampus universities with relatively autonomous funding strategies—for example, the special building authority of the State University of New York—will be able to perform, in fact, as effective systems.

The multicampus universities have a special stake in the rationalization of fragmented state and federal funding programs. But system administrators and governing boards will have to make a far greater effort in state capitals and in Washington if the necessary changes are to be forthcoming.

Purchasing, personnel, and physical planning and construction are heavily dominated by state practices. In contrast, the administrative management of research is special to the university, and the implications of predicted changes in the 1970s for the multicampus systems are significant.

In 1970, Clark Kerr (1970a, p. 7) reported, "The group I think is in the greatest trouble of all [as a result of the financial squeeze on higher education] is the big research universities." These are ". . . the institutions hurt the most by cuts in federal research money and the ones that feel the greatest pressure to keep up with expanding educational technology."

These universities also include virtually all of the multicampus systems. Faced with declining support and rising costs, it is likely that both internal and external pressures will lead toward a stronger system hand in research management. Internally, the multicampus systems will have to give greater attention to the distribution of a shrinking research dollar if balance, however defined, is to be maintained within the university. The laissez faire approach of the individual faculty entrepreneur will have to be both stimulated and corralled, if the system as a whole is to progress.

Externally, federal and other granting agencies may well demand a greater degree of coordination when universities solicit research funds, particularly among campuses ostensibly within the same university system. In part, this will result from a growing attention to policy and mission-oriented research activities in an attempt to apply the approaches of the space program to domestic problems. In part, too, federal agencies will look to the universities themselves to develop new strategies for the distribution of funds as a way of relieving the pressure on Washington. However, it is likely that the federal government will also look to the coordinating agencies or to other departments of state government for this kind of assistance, rather than to the multicampus university.

In either case, research management will create added pressures upon the systemwide administration, underscoring even more vividly the need for the structural changes described above.

THE FUTURE OF THE MULTICAMPUS UNIVERSITY There is growing concern that the multiversity, the complex educational institution with responsibilities for teaching, research and public service, is faced with the threat of institutional overload. Hitherto complementary activities have become competing, if not conflicting, in a hostile external environment. The research orientation of the modern university is charged with driving it away from its responsibilities both for undergraduate teaching and continuing education. There is equal criticism that in its desire to be of service to society, the university has become its slave, that instead of following the truth wherever it may lead, the universities follow the federal and foundation dollar.

There are no signs that either the internal pressures or the external environment are changing. One alternative to the threat of overload is to disaggregate the multiversity—to divide the functions of teaching, research, and service among separate institutions, a pattern prevalent in much of Europe. Autonomous research academies, separately staffed and budgeted (RAND, the Urban Institute) would replace university-related institutes; service activities would be turned over to the host of constituencies which the university serves—public and private; continuing education would become the responsibility of some new kind of institution.

Farfetched? Robert Nisbet (1970) reminds us that the university as we know it is not preordained:

Great societies and periods of history have existed before in human history without universities; they certainly can again. Despite the well-sown myth of the university's indispensability to our technologically advanced society, there are other, existing sources of such knowledge needing only to be developed and multiplied. They will be cheaper and more efficient, being unhampered by the plethora of ranks, privileges and immunities that go with the essentially guild-like, quasi-aristocratic, Middle-Ages-sprung university.

The issues posed by the transformation of the multiversity, much less its demise, move far beyond our inquiry. We can note, however, that every gain from disaggregation of the multiversity has its price, and it is far from clear where the balance might rest. At its best, the multiversity is a marvelous amalgam of the strengths of American society and of higher education, with few parallels and many imitators in the modern world. But the concern over institutional overload remains. We cannot ignore it.

Can it be that the multicampus university offers one way out of this dilemma, that the opportunities for specialization and diversity among campuses and cooperation between them might produce a division of labor that would make the task of each possible?

The answer can be yes, but the directions described above suggest the kinds of changes that are prerequisite to an affirmative answer. There is little doubt that the multicampus universities will be asked to test the proposition. How they respond will influence not only the future of higher education in America, but the future of the nation.

Commentary

Anyone involved as an administrator, as I have been for a period of years, in the emergence of a multicampus university perhaps must acknowledge his less-than-objective point of view about this type of structural arrangement. To argue for this particular administrative form solely because it apparently affords clean and clear lines of institutional management obscures its real value. In my view, any administrative structure must, during the 1970s, contribute to an atmosphere of freedom for the faculty and the institution itself, offer a climate of creative exchange on major issues in its community, and provide the quality of leadership and financial support to accomplish the instructional, research, and public service missions of the university. It is my experience that the multicampus structure does provide a sound means of accomplishing these objectives.

I believe the real strength of multicampus university governance owes little either to formula-oriented plans or to theoretical systems of required uniformity. To be sure, it is easy to demonstrate that governance throughout higher education is becoming increasingly involved in restrictions and restraints in the name of coordination. For example, "allocation of function" is a principle which, positively interpreted, accepts the diversity of institutional origins and encourages the development of complementary strengths among correlative disciplines while recognizing the necessity for cooperative enterprise; yet, allocation of function is sometimes invoked as the guideline for limiting the activities of a single campus or school. The success of the multicampus university, as I have known it, is accounted for by the absence rather than the presence of a dictated uniformity. The present strength of the multicampus university results from the transformation into *actuality* of the *potential* for specialization, diversity, and cooperation (about which Lee and Bowen speak more than once). These goals of specialization, diversity, and cooperation have themselves become the means for undertaking and completing specific and complex tasks demanded of the multicampus university.

The shape and structure and careful planning of the multicampus university are important considerations, but most important of all are the men and women who are a part of it. It may be convenient to speak of specialization, diversity, and cooperation as university functions, but in fact they are human operations, necessarily individual and personal. The governance of the multicampus university can be successful only as long as human enterprise is valued above a formula or a control.

As state-supported higher education continues its growth and development, particularly in its public service functions, it will experience greater public scrutiny and involvement. As state-supported institutions have a greater opportunity to respond to this heightened public concern, they will have a superb opportunity to involve the supporting citizenry in the great mission of public higher education in America. The multicampus university, because it is not localized in one area of its state, has an obligation to provide interpretation and leadership which is related to the resources it requires, to the complexity of its mission, and to the distribution of its services for the development of the state.

In meeting this obligation of interpretation and leadership these difficulties sometimes arise: (1) The years of campus unrest and crisis have eroded public confidence in higher education. Even though the young people who were involved came from the homes, the churches, the schools, and the communities of America, where they developed their attitudes and moral standards, in the eyes of many the university has failed to meet its obligation as disciplinarian and residential guardian. (2) As the university objectively seeks to discover new knowledge with which to eradicate the pollution of the environment, improve public health and the delivery of health care, or remove urban blight, it sometimes disturbs entrenched interests and is charged with improper activity. (3) Within a community of state-supported institutions in some states the old and long-established university, called the "flagship campus" by Lee and Bowen, is sometimes charged with elitism by its younger and aggressive brother institutions outside the multicampus structure. (4) As services provided by the state to its citizens increase in number and cost, the competition for the tax dollar accelerates.

The answer often sought by some political and a few educational leaders is state control through a centralized agency far removed from the campus and dominated more by a limited concept of management than by commitment to the purposes of higher education.

State universities are fully accountable to their supporting citizens and should seize upon the opportunity of providing full and complete information on their activities. Unwarranted or wasteful duplication among campuses should be eliminated. Institutional bickering and political intrigue have no place among institutions of higher learning. Indeed, when universities engage in such activities, the hue and cry against legislative intrusion falls on deaf ears.

A workable balance must be struck between institutional accountability to the state on the one hand and the essential flexibility and freedom to function as a university on the other. The obvious need for public accountability for tax funds and for wise planning and efficient resource use through procedures mutually satisfactory to the state government and the state university must be reconciled with the equally obvious need for the freedom of the institution to perform responsibly the functions of teaching, research, and public service.

The multicampus university is, as Lee and Bowen conclude, one generally satisfactory answer to this major issue. Their study reveals the successes and the failures of existing multicampus universities in developing the internal procedures and policies that provide for allocation of academic, professional, research, and service functions among its constituent campuses and the freedom to develop institutional identity. More importantly, the study identifies some of the areas of future concern and growth.

One can contribute to the debate on state structure of higher education only the experience and knowledge gained from his years of personal involvement. Experience does have some value and should be shared. In my view, most states of our union do not possess tax resources to build more than one or two distinguished, research-oriented universities. Furthermore, the need does not presently exist for a multiplicity of these universities. But within each state there is a great need for a diversity of educational opportunities and, therefore, for a number of institutions with different purposes and missions. To argue for differences of need or opportunity is not to suggest inherent inferiority or second-class citizenship among a state's family of campuses; quite the contrary is true. Each institution should be encouraged to seek the highest level of performance of its assigned and always reviewable functions.

The multicampus university, being an enterprise involving component campus administrators, faculty representatives, students, and alumni, does afford to those campuses under its single board of trustees and system administrators a real means of achieving this kind of integrated, orderly, and productive university development.

So long as the number of its competent institutions is large enough to achieve a meaningful union of effort but small enough to be administered effectively and harmoniously, the multicampus university can be a highly successful instrumentality for achieving the important goals of higher education.

The future of the multicampus university will depend, in part, on the intelligence and wisdom of the political and educational leadership of a state which is struggling with the issue of coordination of its public system of higher education. We may hear such questions as these: Is it worthwhile or even desirable to protect the qualities of individuality and campus uniqueness which distinguish our several institutions? Are the experience and knowledge and substantive gains achieved over the decades by the multicampus universities of the country to be preserved. Can administrators be found who combine with their superior knowledge, skill, and good judgment a self-restraint adequate to encourage, and not suppress, initiative and responsible campus leadership? These questions may suggest the great danger of easy answers to such an intricate and difficult problem.

My experience with what one multicampus university has accomplished in and for the state which has generously supported it has convinced me that university governance which is predicated on ensuring excellence of education, research, and public services clearly surpasses a system of governance predicated on guaranteeing coordination of effort and uniformity.

Most citizens and political leaders care for the quality of the system of higher education they finance. They respect and indeed love the campuses they know. The labor of trustees and lay leaders in higher education reveals their loyalty, devotion, and the joy of personal involvement that produces success for the institution. Hard-won and recognized quality must be safeguarded and enhanced as we strive to achieve effective relationships between state-supported institutions and state government. Above all, the institutions must be secure in their freedom to function as responsible and creative centers for the betterment of society.

We possess a great opportunity for constructive leadership as we devise more effective means of governing the various elements of state-supported higher education. The obvious common interest we all hold should be recognized, and rational judgment should be brought to bear in meeting the present situation. After all, the 50 states have no enterprise more essential to their advancement than the schools, colleges, and universities they finance for the education of their youth and for the enrichment of the lives of all their citizens.

William Friday

References

American Association for Higher Education: *College and University Bulletin,* vol. 22, no. 4, Washington, D.C., November 15, 1969.

American Association for Higher Education: *Faculty Participation in Academic Governance,* Washington, D.C., 1967.

American Association of University Professors: "Academic Freedom and Tenure: Wisconsin State University–Whitewater," *AAUP Journal,* Spring 1968.

American Association of University Professors: "Statement on Government of Colleges and Universities," *AAUP Bulletin,* Winter 1966.

Association of Governing Boards of Universities and Colleges: *State Boards Responsible for Higher Education in 1970,* Washington, D.C., forthcoming.

Bailey, Stephen K.: "Public Money and the Integrity of the Higher Academy," *Compact,* June 1969.

Barzun, Jacques: *The American University,* Harper & Row Publishers, Incorporated, New York, 1968.

Beck, Hubert P.: *Men Who Control Our Universities,* King's Crown Press, New York, 1947.

Bennis, W. G.: *Changing Organizations,* McGraw-Hill Book Company, New York, 1966.

Berdahl, Robert O.: *Statewide Systems of Higher Education,* American Council on Education, Washington, D.C., 1971.

Birenbaum, William M.: "Cities and Universities: Collision of Crises," in Alvin C. Eurich (ed.), *Campus 1980: The Shape of the Future in American Higher Education,* Delacorte Press, New York, 1968.

Birenbaum, William M.: *Overlive: Power, Poverty and the University,* Dell Publishing Company, Inc., New York, 1969.

Bloland, Harland G.: *Higher Education Associations in a Decentralized Education System,* Center for Research and Development in Higher Education, University of California, Berkeley, 1969.

Brown, J. Douglas: *The Liberal University: An Institutional Analysis,* McGraw-Hill Book Company, New York, 1969.

Buckley, W.: *Sociology and Modern Systems Theory,* Prentice-Hall, Inc., Englewood Cliffs, N.J., 1967.

Byse, Clark: "Procedure in Student Dismissal Proceedings: Law and Policy," in L. E. Dennis and J. F. Kauffman (eds.), *The College and the Student,* American Council on Education, Washington, D.C., 1966.

California Constitution Revision Commission: *Background Study,* Art. IX, Education, sec. 9, January 1969.

California Joint Committee on Higher Education: *The Academic State,* Sacramento, 1968.

Campus Facilities Associates: *Old Shapes, New Forms,* Boulder, Colo., 1963. (Mimeographed.)

Caplow, Theodore.: *Principles of Organization,* Harcourt, Brace, & World, Inc., New York, 1964.

Carbone, Robert F.: *Resident or Nonresident,* Education Commission of the States, Denver, 1970.

Carter, J.: "University of Texas: On the Way Up—But Politics Still Intrude," *Science,* vol. 64, no. 3884, 1969.

Cartter, Allan M.: "Graduate Education and Research in the Decades Ahead," in Alvin C. Eurich (ed.), *Campus 1980: The Shape of the Future in American Higher Education,* Delacorte Press, New York, 1968.

Cheit, Earl F.: "Regent Watchdog," address before Town Hall, Los Angeles, September 24, 1970.

Clark, Burton R.: *Educating the Expert Society,* Chandler Publishing Company, San Francisco, 1962.

Congressional Quarterly Weekly Report, September 4, 1970.

Coons, Arthur G.: *Crisis in California Higher Education,* The Ward Ritchie Press, Los Angeles, 1968.

Corry, J. A.: "Canadian Universities—from Private Domain to Public Utility," *U.B.C. Reports,* February 27, 1969, in Rene Hurtubise and Donald C. Rowat, *The University, Society and Government,* Report of the Commission on the Relations between Universities and Governments, University of Ottawa Press, Ottawa, 1970.

Corson, John: *Governance of Colleges and Universities,* McGraw-Hill Book Company, New York, 1960.

Corson, John: "Social Change and the University," in "Who Runs the University?" *Saturday Review,* January 10, 1970.

Cox, L., and L. E. Harrell: *The Impact of Federal Programs on State Planning and Coordination of Higher Education,* Southern Regional Education Board, Atlanta, 1969.

Dunham, E. Alden: *Colleges of the Forgotten Americans: A Profile of State Colleges and Regional Universities,* McGraw-Hill Book Company, New York, 1969.

Dykes, A. R.: *Faculty Participation in Academic Decision Making,* American Council on Education, Washington, D.C., 1968.

Eulau, Heinz, and Harold Quinley: *State Officials and Higher Education,* McGraw-Hill Book Company, New York, 1970.

Eurich, Alvin C. (ed.): *Campus 1980: The Shape of the Future in American Higher Education,* Delacorte Press, New York, 1968.

Eurich, Alvin C.: *Reforming American Education,* Harper & Row Publishers, Incorporated, New York, 1969.

Gardner, John W.: "Universities as Designers of the Future," *Educational Record,* Fall 1967.

Glenny, Lyman A.: *Autonomy of Public Colleges: The Challenge of Coordination,* McGraw-Hill Book Company, 1959.

Goodman, Paul: *People or Personnel,* Vintage Books, Random House, Inc., New York, 1968.

Graham, Frank P.: Letter to William Friday, quoted in L. R. Wilson. *The University of North Carolina under Consolidation, 1931–1963,* University of North Carolina, Chapel Hill, 1964.

Green, Edith: in *The Chronicle of Higher Education,* vol. 4, no. 37, p. 1. August 3, 1970.

Greenberg, Daniel S.: *The Politics of Pure Science,* New American Library, Inc., New York, 1967.

Gross, Neal: "Organizational Lag in American Universities," *Harvard Educational Review,* vol. 33, no. 58, 1963.

Hacker, Andrew: *The End of the American Era,* Athenaeum Publishers, New York, 1970.

Haggstrom, Gus: "On Analyzing and Predicting Enrollments and Costs in Higher Education," University of California, Berkeley, 1969. (Unpublished.)

Hansen, W. L., and B. A. Weisbrod: *Benefits, Costs, and Finance of Public Higher Education,* Markham Publishing Company, Chicago, 1969.

Harcleroad, Fred F. (ed.): *Issues of the Seventies,* Jossey-Bass, Inc., Publishers, San Francisco, 1970.

Hartnett, R. T.: *College and University Trustees,* Educational Testing Service, Princeton, N.J., 1969.

Harnett, R. T.: *The New College Trustee: Some Predictions for the 1970's,* Educational Testing Service, Princeton, N.J., 1970.

Heineman, Ben W.: "Higher Education in Illinois—One View of the Future," address to Illinois Citizens School Committee, October 11, 1966. (Mimeographed.)

Hodgkinson, Harold L.: *Institutions in Transition: A Study of Change in Higher Education,* Carnegie Commission on Higher Education, Berkeley, 1970.

Holy, Thomas C.: *A Long-Range Plan for the City University of New York 1961–1975,* The Board of Higher Education, New York, 1962.

Hungate, Thad L.: *Management in Higher Education,* Teachers College, Columbia University, New York, 1964.

Hurtubise, René, and Donald C. Rowat: *The University, Society and Government,* Report of the Commission on the Relations between Universities and Governments, University of Ottawa Press, Ottawa, 1970.

Illinois Board of Higher Education: "Governing Structure," Report of Master Plan Committee N, Springfield, 1966.

Illinois Board of Higher Education: "Report of Special Committee on New Senior Institutions," Springfield, 1967. (Mimeographed.)

Jencks, Christopher, and David Riesman: *The Academic Revolution,* Doubleday & Company Inc., New York, 1968.

Kammerer, Gladys M.: "The State University as a Political System," *Journal of Politics,* vol. 31, May 1969.

Kauffman, J. F.: "The Student in Higher Education," In L. E. Dennis and J. F. Kauffman (eds.), *The College and the Student,* American Council on Education, Washington, D.C., 1966.

Kerr, Clark: in *The Chronicle of Higher Education,* March 16, 1970 (1970*a*).

Kerr, Clark: "Governance and Function," *Daedalus,* Winter 1970 (1970*b*).

Kerr, Clark: *The Uses of the University,* Harvard University Press, Cambridge, Mass., 1964.

Kintzer, Frederick C., Arthur M. Jensen, and John S. Hansen: *The Multi-Institution Junior College District,* American Association of Junior Colleges, Washington, D.C., undated.

Klotsche, J. Martin: *The Urban University,* Harper & Row Publishers, Incorporated, New York, 1966.

Kristol, Irving, and Paul Weaver: "Who Knows New York? and Oth Notes on a Mixed-up City," *The Public Interest,* no. 16, Summer 196$

Martorana, S. V., and E. V. Hollis: *State Boards Responsible for High Education,* U.S. Office of Education, Washington, D.C., 1960.

McConnell, T. R.: *A General Pattern for American Public Higher Edu tion,* McGraw-Hill Book Company, New York, 1962.

McGill, William J.: Remarks before the Regents of the University of Ca fornia, July 17, 1970, as reported in the *University Bulletin,* August 1 1970 (1970a).

McGill, William J.: Testimony before the President's Commission Student Unrest, August 4, 1970 (1970b).

Millett, John D., *The Academic Community,* McGraw-Hill Book Compan New York, 1962.

Moos, Malcolm, and Francis E. Rourke: *The Campus and the State,* T Johns Hopkins Press, Baltimore, 1959.

Murphy, Franklin: Address before the American Council on Educatic Denver, October 10, 1968.

Nisbet, Robert: "The Restoration of Academic Authority," *Wall Stre Journal,* August 19, 1970.

Office of the Vice-President for Planning and Analysis: *Attachment* November 11, 1969, to *Report to Regents, University of Californ* University of California, Berkeley, November 12, 1969. (Mimeographe

Orlans, Harold: *The Effects of Federal Programs on Higher Educatic* The Brookings Institution, Washington, D.C., 1962.

Palola, Ernest G.: "Changing Centers of Power in Higher Education: Challenge to Institutional Leadership," paper presented to the Juni College Presidents Seminar, sponsored by the Center for Research a Development in Higher Education, University of California, Berkele June 21, 1968.

Palola, Ernest G., Timothy Lehmann, and William R. Blischke: *High Education by Design: The Sociology of Planning,* Center for Resear and Development in Higher Education, University of California, Berk ley, 1970.

Palola, Ernest G., and Arthur R. Oswald: *The Urban Community Colle New Structures for New Functions,* (forthcoming 1971).

Paltridge, James Gilbert: "Organizational Forms Which Character Statewide Coordination of Public Higher Education," Berkeley, 196 (Unpublished.)

Peat, Marwick, Mitchell & Co.: *The Future of the Public Two-Year College in New York State,* report presented to New York State Department of Education, 1969.

Perkins, James A.: "The Campus—Forgotten Field of Study," *Public Administration Review,* vol. 20, no. 1, Winter 1960.

Pliner, Emogene: *Coordination and Planning,* Public Affairs Research Council of Louisiana, Inc., Baton Rouge, 1966.

Rauh, Morton: *The Trusteeship of Colleges and Universities,* McGraw-Hill Book Company, New York, 1969.

Ritterbush, Philip C.: "Adaptive Response Within the Institutional System of Higher Education and Research," in "Rights and Responsibilities: The University's Dilemma," *Daedalus,* Summer 1970.

Roose, Kenneth D., and Charles J. Anderson: *A Rating of Graduate Programs,* American Council on Education, Washington, D.C., 1970.

Roth, William M.: "The Dilemmas of Leadership," in "Who Runs the University?" *Saturday Review,* January 10, 1970.

Rourke, Francis E., and Glenn E. Brooks: *The Managerial Revolution in Higher Education,* The Johns Hopkins Press, Baltimore, 1966.

Salisbury, R. H.: "State Politics and Education," in Herbert Jacob and Kenneth N. Vines (eds.), *Politics in the American States,* Little, Brown and Company, Boston, 1965.

Sanford, Nevitt: "The College Student of 1980," in Alvin C. Eurich (ed.), *Campus 1980: The Shape of the Future in American Higher Education,* Delacorte Press, New York, 1968.

Select Committee on the Future of Private Higher Education: *New York State and Private Higher Education,* New York, 1968.

Sellitz, C., M. Jahoda, M. Deutsch, and S. W. Cook: *Research Methods in Social Relations,* Holt, Rinehart and Winston, Inc., New York, 1967.

Texas Board of Regents: *Rules and Regulations of the University of Texas System,* part 1, sec. 1.3, chap. 11, 1960.

Thompson, James: *Organizations in Action,* McGraw-Hill Book Company, New York, 1967.

Toffler, Alvin: *Future Shock,* Random House, Inc., New York, 1970.

Trow, Martin: "Reflections on the Transition from Mass to Universal Higher Education," *Daedalus,* Winter 1970 (1970*a*).

Trow, Martin: "Urban Problems and University Problems," *Experiment and Innovation,* vol. 3, no. 1, pp. 52–53, University of California, 1970 (1970*b*).

U.S. Department of Commerce: *County and City Data Books, 1956* and *1967,* Washington, D.C., 1956, 1967.

U.S. Department of Commerce: *Statistical Abstract of the United States, 1969,* Washington, D.C., 1969.

U.S. News and World Report, "Why College Presidents Are Quitting," August 3, 1970.

U.S. Office of Education: *Digest of Educational Statistics,* 1968 edition, Washington, D.C., 1968.

U.S. Office of Education: *Opening Fall Enrollment in Higher Education, Part B—Institutional Data 1968,* Washington, D.C., 1969.

Veblen, Thorstein: *The Higher Learning in America,* Sagamore Press, Inc., New York, 1957.

Weinberg, I., and K. N. Walker: "Student Politics and Political Systems: Toward a Typology," *American Journal of Sociology,* vol. 75, no. 77, July 1969.

Wilson, Logan: *The Academic Man,* Oxford University Press, New York, 1942.

Wilson, Logan: "The College or University in Its Environment: External Constraints," in T. F. Lunsford (ed.), *The Study of Academic Administration,* Western Interstate Commission for Higher Education, Boulder, Colo., 1963.

Wilson, Logan: "Higher Education and the National Interest," in Alvin C. Eurich (ed.), *Campus 1980: The Shape of the Future in American Higher Education,* Delacorte Press, New York, 1968.

Woodring, Paul: *The Higher Learning in America: A Reassessment,* McGraw-Hill Book Company, New York, 1968.

Index

This book was set in Vladimir by University Graphics,
Inc. It was printed and bound by The
Maple Press Company. The designers were Elliot Epstein
and Edward Butler. The editors were Herbert Waentig and
Cheryl Allen for McGraw-Hill Book Company and Verne A.
Stadtman for the Carnegie Commission on Higher Education.
Frank Matonti and Alice Cohen supervised the production.